PATHOLOGICAL GAMBLING

PATHOLOGICAL GAMBLING

ETIOLOGY, COMORBIDITY, AND TREATMENT

NANCY M. PETRY

American Psychological Association
Washington, DC

Published by
American Psychological Association
750 First Street, NE
Washington, DC 20002
www.apa.org

To order
APA Order Department
P.O. Box 92984
Washington, DC 20090-2984
Tel: (800) 374-2721
Direct: (202) 336-5510
Fax: (202) 336-5502
TDD/TTY: (202) 336-6123
Online: www.apa.org/books/
E-mail: order@apa.org

In the U.K., Europe, Africa, and the Middle East, copies may be ordered from
American Psychological Association
3 Henrietta Street
Covent Garden, London
WC2E 8LU England

Typeset in Goudy by World Composition Services, Inc., Sterling, VA

Printer: United Book Press, Inc., Baltimore, MD
Cover Designer: Cassandra Chu Design, San Francisco, CA
Technical/Production Editor: Tiffany L. Klaff

The opinions and statements published are the responsibility of the author, and such opinions and statements do not necessarily represent the policies of the American Psychological Association.

Library of Congress Cataloging-in-Publication Data

Petry, Nancy M.
    Pathological gambling : etiology, comorbidity, and treatments / Nancy M. Petry.
      p. cm.
    Includes bibliographical references and index.
    ISBN 1-59147-173-7
    1. Compulsive gambling. I. Title.

  RC569.5.G35P48   2004
  616.85'841—dc22
                         2004014279

British Library Cataloguing-in-Publication Data
A CIP record is available from the British Library.

Printed in the United States of America
First Edition

In memory of my mother,

Esther Marie Petry

CONTENTS

ACKNOWLEDGMENTS

I thank the American Psychological Association Books Department and Lansing Hays for suggesting that I write this book. When I was first approached about publishing a book on the treatment of pathological gambling, I did not think that I could write such a book, or that I wanted to. I felt that there was not enough research to conclude much, let alone anything definitive, about this field. A lot has changed in the 3 years since I first started this project. More and more research emerges every month.

Over the years, I have been fortunate to work with a number of people who have fostered my interests in gambling and pathological gambling. Chris Armentano and the staff at the State of Connecticut Problem Gambling Services and the Bettor Choice Programs guided my understanding of the disorder from a clinical perspective. The many individuals who have participated in my gambling treatment studies shared their stories and their problems, and I thank them for their willingness to partake in these projects.

I am grateful to the National Institute of Mental Health (Grants R01-MH60417 and R01-MH60417-Suppl), the National Institute on Drug Abuse (Grants R01-DA016855, R01-DA14618, R01-DA13444, R29-DA12056, and P50-DA09241), the National Institute on Aging (Grant P60-AG13631), the National Institute on Alcohol Abuse and Alcoholism (Grant P50-AA03510), the Donaghue Medical Research Foundation Investigator Program, and the University of Connecticut Health Center for funding some of the projects that are described in this book. Colleagues, clinicians, and research assistants have been instrumental in conducting these and related studies, including Yola Ammerman, Sheila Alessi, Mark Austin, William Blakey, Jaime Bohl, Ellen Ciesielski, Anne Dorsch, Heather Gay, Ron Kadden, George Ladd, David Ledgerwood,

Marilyn Lewis, Steve McKinnon, Bonnie Martin, Cheryl Molina, Robert Pietrzak, Susan Sampl, Sean Seirra, Karen Steinberg, Jackie Tedford, and Mary Weiners. In addition to my colleagues at University of Connecticut Health Center, I gratefully acknowledge friends and colleagues who have helped to shape my career: Warren Bickel, Kathleen Carroll, Steve Higgins, Bruce Rounsaville, and Maxine Stitzer.

I am also appreciative of many colleagues throughout the United States and Canada who have shared their interests in gambling with me, including Carlos Blanco, Renee Cunningham-Williams, David Hodgins, Eric Hollander, Robert Ladouceur, Mary Larimer, Loreen Rugle, Howard Shaffer, Ken Winters, and the women involved with the Women's Problem Gambling Research Group. Some provided preprints of their work, and others read sections of the text, offering excellent suggestions.

Edward Meidenbauer provided expert comments on and critiques of the manuscript that greatly improved it. I also thank two anonymous reviewers for their thoughtful input.

Most important, I am indebted to Susan Garthwaith for her endless and tireless typing and checking of references and for her sense of humor throughout the process. I could never have finished this book without her help.

Writing this book was a 3-year process, and during this time my life changed dramatically. I am appreciative of friendships I have maintained with John Roll and Maryann Chapman; Caroline Easton and Jay Creighton; Vania Modesto and Bruce Lowe and their children who were born during this time: Marshall, William, and Christian; and my family, including all my new nieces and nephews: Andrew, Anna, Abigail, Chloe, Collin, and Clara Petry. And, I met the man I was waiting all my life to meet while writing this book—thank you, Billy, for all your support.

I

FOUNDATIONS FOR UNDERSTANDING

1

INTRODUCTION

Gambling is a common activity in societies across the world. Although most people wager from time to time, the vast majority never experience adverse consequences from this behavior. Nevertheless, gambling can become a serious problem for many people. Almost 11 million Americans, or about 1 in 20 adults, experience some form of a gambling problem during the course of their lifetimes (Shaffer, Hall, & Vander Bilt, 1999).

Why some people develop gambling problems and others do not is an enigma. In this book I review the research that has examined the etiology and treatment of gambling disorders. Because gambling research is a nascent field, many questions remain unanswered, including how best to treat individuals with gambling problems. In the later chapters of the book, I detail a cognitive–behavioral model for treating pathological gamblers. This treatment approach is based on the one used in the first large-scale, federally funded study of interventions for pathological gambling in the United States.

This book is intended for clinicians and treatment providers—those with limited experience in treating gamblers and those with experience in the field. Throughout the book, vignettes illustrate personal situations of gamblers and how their gambling has affected them and their families. Clinicians unfamiliar with the field may gain a balanced understanding of the issues that gamblers face. Clinicians who are experienced in treating gambling problems may recognize similarities between these cases and those of their own patients and, I hope, gain new tools for assisting patients with gambling problems.

For researchers, this book provides a comprehensive source of information in this emerging field. I detail prevalence rates for epidemiological studies conducted worldwide, and I review and critique the different instruments used for assessing pathological gambling. I present data on comorbidity of pathological gambling with other psychiatric disorders and discuss treatment studies. I also include suggestions for areas of further study.

A BRIEF HISTORY OF GAMBLING

Gambling refers to betting on specific games, such as cards, dice, slot machines, lotteries and instant scratch tickets, bingo, roulette, races, and sporting events. In the past, gambling almost always involved a modicum of socialization. One needed to go to poker halls, bars, the neighborhood dice game, or casinos to place a bet. In recent years, Internet gambling has become available and grown in popularity. The Internet has increased people's access to all these forms of gambling to 24 hours a day, 7 days a week, from the comfort of one's own home.

Gambling can include wagering on all the above-mentioned games, as well as other activities. A formal definition of *gambling* is placing something of value on an event that has a possibility of resulting in a larger, more beneficial outcome. Inherent in gambling is risk. Another defining feature of gambling is that chance influences the results.

Chance is an intrinsic feature of life, and gambling has been part of human society since prerecorded times. Dice were found in an Egyptian tomb that dated from approximately 3000 BC, a gaming board is cut into a step of the Acropolis at Athens, and gambling was rampant in Roman times (France, 1902). In cultures as diverse as the Bushmen of South Africa, Australian Aborigines, American Indians, and the ancient Chinese, lotteries and guessing games have been long-standing traditions. The Hebrews divided the Promised Land through the drawing of lots. Often, gambling has been associated with a spiritual context; the will of the gods determined the winner. Accounts of dice, card, and horse racing wagering can be found in most written histories and literature of European countries (Wildman, 1997). Likewise, in the New World, the colony of Virginia was financed through lotteries, with some historical reports claiming that George Washington purchased the first ticket (S. S. Smith, 1948). Early universities, including Harvard, were founded on proceeds from lotteries. Although more recent forms of gambling, such as casino slot machines and Internet gambling, have become quite technical, the appeal of gambling crosses generations and cultures. The popularity of gambling may be related to a fundamental aspect of life: its unpredictability.

One can also consider gambling from a sociobiological perspective. For example, a squirrel might expend energy gathering nuts and storing them in a nest for the winter. These nuts may then become available for consumption during leaner times, when they are of much greater value to the squirrel. However, in expending the energy to gather the nuts and not eating them on the spot, the squirrel is, in essence, risking the possibility that another animal will find and confiscate the stored food or that a natural event, such as a flood or a storm, will sweep it away. Similarly, a coyote in the wild must make a decision when it encounters a group of rabbits. It can go after a young bunny, which will be easy to catch and almost ensure a small meal, or it can risk not getting any food at all and chase the larger rabbit, which offers the possibility of a larger, more satiating meal. Thus, all species must make choices that are guided by probabilistic outcomes. The concept of gambling appears to be a basic aspect of life.

Although gambling is a part of all cultures, and perhaps even all species, its popularity and acceptability have changed over time, perhaps in response to cultural or environmental variations. For example, casinos and cardhouses were ubiquitous in Italy throughout the 12th through the 15th centuries, but attempts to abolish gambling are noted from the early 16th century to the end of the 19th century (e.g., Wildman, 1997). The first wave of heavy gambling in the United States began with the settlers and continued throughout the 18th century, but then gambling activities waned in the early 19th century (Rose, 1980). Gambling resumed in popularity after the Civil War. The migration to the western territories seemed to attract adventurers and fortune seekers, and some accounts describe vivid tales of drinking and gambling in mining towns (Cahlan, 1964; Edwards, 1995). One story even recounts that the entire Territory of New Mexico was offered in a poker game (DeArment, 1982). During this time period, lotteries back East were being shown to be corrupt and dishonest. Over the years, they were gradually abolished, state by state, with even Nevada passing antigambling legislation in 1910 (Rose, 1980).

The third wave of resurgence of gambling activities in United States history is currently taking place. After approximately 50 years of strict governmental control, gambling has become a common and sanctioned aspect of day-to-day life. New, tightly regulated and state-managed lotteries were initiated in New Hampshire in 1968, and 38 states have since followed suit. In the late 1980s, more and more states began allowing casino-style gambling on Native American Indian reservations or on riverboats, and 32 states now have this form of gambling. At present, legalized gambling is available in every state but Utah and Hawaii (National Research Council, 1999).

Although gambling is ubiquitous, and many people partake in it as a relatively harmless pastime, some individuals appear to make poor decisions when chance influences outcomes. From a macroscopic perspective, repeated risky decisions likely will lead to the death of an organism. Natural selection would ultimately dictate the elimination of any lineage that was inclined to engage in behaviors that result in very unlikely but large benefits, especially if such behaviors require a substantive investment of resources.

Across recorded history, societies have recognized that gambling in excess leads to adverse effects. Gamblers have been known to lose resources and property, status and titles, families and friends, and even their freedom. Under Roman law, a debtor was brought to court and enslaved to his creditor (Glare, 1982). A 1713 column in the *Guardian*, cited in Wildman (1997), noted that "Hallow eyes, haggard looks, and pale complexions, these are the natural indications of the female gamester." Almost 200 years ago, Taylor (1838), a physician, described the guilt, shame, and secrecy of the excessive gambler, along with an associated pattern of neglecting one's spouse and family, engaging in illegal acts, and even committing suicide.

Some cultures have attempted to control gambling to protect individuals who are vulnerable to the adverse consequence of excessive wagering (e.g., Fleming, 1978). King Richard restricted dice playing during the crusades. Henry VIII, who himself reportedly lost the Bells of St. Paul in a dice game, made gambling illegal for commoners—except during Christmas. Some Native American tribes would not allow gamblers to borrow what they wagered. In other words, if one bet a home, food, tools, or a wife on a game, one could only bet what he had available up front. It is unfortunate that modern society has not had the foresight of some of our ancestors in limiting the amount of losses to what one has on hand. With the availability of ATMs and credit advances, amounts that one can lose while gambling in modern-day casinos can be astonishing and result in devastating consequences.

Why some individuals are inclined to go these extremes when gambling, and others are not, is a question of great importance. From time to time, all people have to make choices and decisions that are influenced by chance. Life without choice and uncertainty is incomprehensible, and seemingly impossible. However, why some people repeatedly risk losing things of significant value on outcomes of probabilistic events, and others do not, is unclear. Some people find gambling to be highly exciting, intriguing, and fun, whereas others consider it rather boring and not worth their time or money.

The behavioral and perplexing nature of pathological gambling has led to numerous interpretations and methods for managing individuals with gambling problems. Excessive gambling has been stigmatized as a moral failing, resulting in social isolation and even imprisonment of gamblers and debtors. However, the relatively recent movement toward the medicalization of psychiatric disorders led to the inclusion of pathological gambling in the third revision of the *Diagnostic and Statistical Manual of Mental Disorders* (American Psychiatric Association, 1980). Still, pathological gambling is a rarely diagnosed psychiatric condition even in very high-risk populations, such as substance abusers (see chaps. 2, 4, and 5). Very few clinicians are skilled in treating pathological gamblers, and estimates indicate that less than 8% of pathological gamblers seek treatment for the disorder (National Research Council, 1999). Scientific research on the etiology and treatment of disordered gambling is only just emerging.

OVERVIEW OF THIS BOOK

This book provides an overview of problem and pathological gambling from a psychological perspective. In it, I review theories and data regarding the causes, correlates, and treatments of disordered gambling. I describe clinical manifestations of problem and pathological gambling, and I detail methods for assessing and diagnosing the disorder. I also present prevalence rates from studies conducted worldwide. Disordered gambling often co-occurs with other psychiatric conditions, and I provide a detailed analysis of comorbidities.

I also investigate risk factors associated with the development of gambling disorders. One explanation is biological in nature, and thus I review the evidence for a genetic basis for pathological gambling. Other possibilities include developmental, cultural, psychological, and cognitive perspectives. Certain age groups, ethnicities, and genders develop gambling problems at higher rates than other groups. Individuals with some psychiatric conditions appear to be more drawn to gambling as well. I also review evidence regarding a cognitive component to gambling; I describe the relationship between understanding probabilities and belief in control over chance events and their association with gambling. Other explanations of disordered gambling are related to access. The percentages of people experiencing gambling problems seem to have increased with the spread of legalized gambling. A shift in demographic characteristics among individuals developing gambling problems has paralleled this increase in gambling opportunities. Specifically, I review evidence regarding changes in the proportions of older adults who gamble and women who present for treatment.

In the second half of the book, I focus on treatment strategies. Most problem and pathological gamblers do not seek formal treatment, and many appear to recover from gambling problems on their own. I review these data, along with the use of more formal interventions. Controlled clinical trials evaluating treatments are sparse, but I present both the rationale for and the outcomes of treatment studies. I review eight forms of treatment: (a) Gamblers Anonymous, (b) pharmacotherapies, (c) family–marital therapies, (d) psychoanalytic and psychodynamic approaches, (e) behavioral therapy, (f) cognitive therapy, (g) cognitive–behavioral therapy, and (h) brief and motivational approaches. Throughout the book, I present case descriptions of gamblers to depict the issues confronted by clinicians treating this disorder.

This book is designed to serve as a guide for both new and experienced clinicians who encounter individuals with gambling problems. It is also intended as a resource for researchers in the field. It synthesizes the available data across a range of domains associated with psychological aspects of disordered gambling. However, the scientific study of problem and pathological gambling is only just emerging. New research is being published every month. Some of it will dispute, other studies will clarify, and additional efforts will extend the issues raised in this book. One text cannot provide all the answers or conclusions; instead, I hope that the concepts and ideas reviewed herein will influence a new generation of research in this field as more researchers and clinicians begin developing interests in this area.

2

TERMINOLOGY, PREVALENCE RATES, AND TYPES OF GAMBLING

Policymakers, treatment professionals, and the public are interested in prevalence rates of disordered gambling and whether these rates have changed over time, especially in relation to the widespread increase in legalized gambling opportunities in recent years. Whether certain forms of gambling are more "addictive" than others is also of interest.

In this chapter, before describing studies of prevalence rates, I review nomenclature related to gambling and disordered gambling. In the next section, I describe lifetime and current prevalence rates of disordered gambling in general populations. I describe in detail studies from North America as well as those from other countries. In the third section, I explore prevalence rates in specific populations, including substance abusers, elderly individuals, employees, and patrons of gambling establishments.

I conclude this chapter with a two-part section on changing trends since the regrowth of legalized gambling in North America. In the first section, rates of participation in and problems with various types of gambling are presented. Internet gambling is included, although little scientific data are yet available regarding participation in or prevalence rates of disordered Internet gambling. In the last section of the chapter, I review evidence that addresses the proposition that rates of disordered gambling have increased with the spread of legalized gambling in North America.

NOSOLOGY

The degree to which individuals gamble or wager varies along several dimensions, and different terms have been used to classify individuals on the basis of their gambling patterns. The National Research Council (NRC, 1999) and Shaffer, Hall, and Vander Bilt (1997, 1999) have adapted one conceptualization. They described gambling as occurring along a continuum, with a number of levels indicative of the degree of gambling involvement and related problems. Although practitioners do not commonly use this nomenclature in the field, in this book I use the levels terminology when describing prevalence rates to improve clarity of descriptions.

Level 0 Gambling

The NRC used the term *Level 0* to refer to individuals who have never gambled. Thus, only people who have never purchased a lottery ticket or a raffle ticket and have never placed money on the outcome of a sporting event or in a slot machine would be classified as lifetime Level 0 gamblers. *Past-year Level 0 gamblers* is a term used to classify individuals who have not wagered at all in the prior year.

Level 1 Gambling

Level 1 gambling refers to "social" or "recreational" gambling; it is gambling to a degree that does not result in any significant problems. This is the categorization that describes the vast majority of the population. Because Level 1 gambling includes such a large number of people, the frequencies and types of gambling it encompasses also vary broadly. Some Level 1 gamblers wager only $1 per year, whereas others may wager daily, such as buying one lottery ticket a day. Other Level 1 gamblers spend more time and money gambling, such as going to the casino once or twice a month and spending $200 each time. As long as no gambling-related problems result, individuals who gamble in all these manners would be classified as Level 1 gamblers.

Level 2 Gambling

Level 2 gambling refers to wagering to such an extent that some gambling-related problems have developed. This type of gambling is also sometimes referred to as *at-risk gambling, in-transition gambling, problem gambling,* and *disordered gambling*. The last two terms have also been used to refer not only to Level 2 gambling but also to Level 3 gambling, the most severe form of gambling, which is described below. In some situations, *at-risk* gambling refers to a condition that lies between Level 1 and Level 2 gambling (Gerstein et al., 1999). Thus, much controversy exists regarding nomenclature for individuals who gamble frequently and who have encountered some, but not severe, gambling-related problems.

Because little consensus exists regarding Level 2 gambling, descriptions of its clinical manifestations also vary widely. The problems experienced by Level 2 gamblers may include being criticized by others for their gambling; feeling guilty about the way in which they gamble; spending more time or money than intended; and borrowing gambling money from household expenses, family members, or credit cards. Some Level 2 gamblers may have accumulated gambling-related debts. Level 2 gamblers may have gambled in a more problematic manner at other points in their lives, or they may have spent years or even decades gambling recreationally before developing problems. With the exception of prevalence rates that are detailed later in this chapter, very little is known about Level 2 gamblers. The only thing that is clear is that these gamblers rarely, if ever, present for treatment services (see chap. 8).

Unlike substance use disorders, for which a subthreshold syndrome of dependence known as *abuse* is listed as a diagnostic category, Level 2 gambling is not included in the *Diagnostic and Statistical Manual of Mental Disorders* (4th ed.; *DSM–IV*; American Psychiatric Association, 1994). The omission of a subthreshold condition has significant implications for diagnosis and treatment, as clinicians are unable to bill for services when treating individuals with this condition. Furthermore, the failure to include the subthreshold condition in the *DSM–IV* has likely stagnated research regarding the clinical presentation and symptoms associated with Level 2 gambling.

Level 3 Gambling

Level 3 describes gambling to a degree that it is associated with significant problems. This classification typically refers to individuals who meet *DSM–IV* criteria for pathological gambling (American Psychiatric Association, 1994). In layman's terms, Level 3 gambling is called *compulsive gambling*. Again, the terms *problem gambling* and *disordered gambling* may also be used to describe this population, although those terms sometimes describe individuals with any degree of gambling problems, including both those with nondiagnostic (Level 2) and those with diagnostic problems.

Level 3 gamblers demonstrate significant gambling-related problems that interfere with their daily functioning. In the most extreme cases, Level 3 gamblers may spend entire paychecks gambling, jeopardize their marriage or family relationships to gamble, lose their home or jobs because of gambling, and even resort to criminal activity to support their gambling. *DSM–IV* criteria for pathological gambling are outlined in Exhibit 2.1. To meet

EXHIBIT 2.1
Criteria for Pathological Gambling, Reworded From the
Diagnostic and Statistical Manual for Mental Disorders

1. Preoccupied with gambling.
2. Needs to gamble with larger amounts of money.
3. Repeated unsuccessful efforts to cut down or stop gambling.
4. Restless or irritable when attempting to reduce gambling.
5. Gambles to escape problems or relieve negative mood.
6. "Chases" lost money; returns to gambling to get even.
7. Lies to others to conceal extent of gambling.
8. Commits illegal acts to support gambling.
9. Jeopardizes or loses important relationships or jobs because of gambling.
10. Relies on others to relieve financial problems caused by gambling.

Note. From *Diagnostic and Statistical Manual of Mental Disorders* (4th ed., p. 615), 1994, Washington, DC: American Psychiatric Association. Copyright 1994 by the American Psychiatric Association. Adapted with permission.

lifetime criteria for pathological gambling, one would need to endorse five or more of the symptoms. In addition, the gambling cannot be subsequent to mania to be classified as pathological.

Although the most severe cases of Level 3 gamblers may be relatively easy to classify, the less severe cases may be difficult to identify and may be inappropriately categorized. Gambling-related difficulties can be attributed to other problems or hidden, often for many years. As evident by the above-mentioned *DSM–IV* criteria and in the following case example, many of the symptoms are based on self-report and subjective interpretation of the effects of gambling on one's life.

Case example. Mary is a 53-year-old woman with three grown children. She divorced about 2 years ago, and sold her home of 25 years, even though it was fully paid off and left to her in the settlement. Mary worked for over 20 years as a bookkeeper, but she recently lost her job because of layoffs at the company. Over the past few years, she accumulated more than $15,000 in credit card debt, but she rationalized it as a need to buy new furniture for her apartment and poor money management, because her ex-husband had always been responsible for managing the finances.

Mary's social activities consist of spending time with family members as well as going to the casino. Her children noticed that, since their parents' divorce, Mary was less available. She was rarely home when they phoned; failed to recognize one of her grandchildren's birthdays; and didn't attend several family functions, stating that she wasn't feeling well.

Comment. This example represents a typical case of an individual who can conceal, to both herself and others, the extent of her gambling problems. Mary may be beginning to notice work, family, and financial difficulties, but she may not be connecting them to her gambling. Although her family may recognize a change in Mary's behaviors, many of these changes may be attributed to other life events, including a divorce, a bad spell at work, and having to manage her own finances for the first time. Unless gambling is specifically queried, the relationship between many of Mary's problems and her frequent trips to a local casino may not be acknowledged.

Case example continued. One year later, Mary's children have become very concerned about their mother and her gambling. One night, the police telephoned them because their mother had passed out at the casino, hit her head, and was taken to the hospital. On further investigation, Mary admitted to having spent over 24 hours straight at the casino, without eating. While recovering in the hospital, her daughter found months of unpaid bills, messages from credit card companies and banks, and an eviction notice from the landlord.

When Mary's daughter questioned her about the extent of her gambling, Mary admitted that the monthly trips to the casino she used to take with friends, and even with her own children, had increased in frequency. She was now going once or twice a week, spending whatever money and credit she had available, and staying each time until all her money ran out. Mary said she was having a hard time sleeping and often went to the casino rather than lie awake all night worrying. She was grateful to finally admit to her daughter that she was having severe financial problems and did not know what she was going to do about all the creditors, or where she was going to live.

As illustrated in the above case, the severity of gambling problems exhibited is a dynamic process. Although Mary initially began as a recreational, or Level 1, gambler, her gambling escalated and began creating some problems (Level 2), and finally severe problems (Level 3). Even without escalating the frequency or intensity of gambling, other life changes can also affect the manner in which gambling is interpreted. For example, an individual who spends $20 a week on scratch tickets may be considered a Level 1 gambler, so long as that amount of money is not causing financial concerns. However, if that same Level 1 gambler loses his or her job or has a new baby such that the $20 per week becomes a financial hardship or leads to arguments between the gambler and his or her spouse, then Level 1 gambling may become classified as Level 2.

Level 2 gamblers can also become Level 3 gamblers, by either increasing the frequency or intensity of gambling activities or by a change in situations such that the gambling begins to interfere more with their family, friends, or work situations. Mary's change over the 1- to 2-year period illustrates this phenomenon. Little research exists characterizing the events that precipitate, or the amounts of time that elapse, between moving from Level 2 to Level 3 gambling. Data from a study of treatment-seeking Level 3 gamblers (Petry, 2002a) suggest that, on average, regular gambling persists for about

7 years before it becomes problematic, and problem gambling continues for an additional 3 to 7 years before initiation of treatment seeking.

Of course, Level 2 gambling can also remain constant, never increasing to Level 3 criteria. Level 2 gambling may also decrease to Level 1 or Level 0 rates. The reasons and predictors for escalations versus reductions in gambling are not well understood.

Level 3 gamblers also can reduce their gambling to such a degree that they become Level 2, Level 1, or even Level 0 gamblers. Participation in gambling activities is a dynamic process (Slutske, Jackson, & Sher, 2003). After a reduction in or cessation of gambling, it may again escalate to such a degree that problems again resurface. Some Level 3 gamblers describe a phenomenon whereby at certain times in their lives, or times in the year (e.g., sports seasons), gambling may become very problematic for them, but at other points it does not adversely affect them at all. To date, very little research has examined the progression from one level of gambling to another. Moreover, the measurement, conceptualization, and classification of individuals into one or another level of disordered gambling is associated with widespread debate. Difficulties in classification are not unique to gambling behaviors, but they are controversial in many psychiatric disorders.

In the next section, I describe estimates of the prevalence rates of Level 2 and Level 3 gambling from studies conducted in North America as well as throughout the rest of the world. The use of different instruments and methods for classifying individuals who engage in disordered gambling is at least partially responsible for the somewhat-discrepant results that occur across studies. I describe more specifically the instruments used to derive these estimates of prevalence rates, and their strengths and weaknesses, in chapter 3.

LIFETIME AND PAST-YEAR PREVALENCE RATES

North America

Many researchers have investigated rates of disordered gambling within discrete populations. These investigations typically evaluated prevalence rates within specific states, or small populations of interest (see Shaffer, Hall, & Vander Bilt, 1999). To date, only four studies have addressed the prevalence rate of disordered gambling in the general population of the United States.

The first of these was a national study undertaken by the University of Michigan Survey Research Center in 1975 (Kallick, Suits, Dielman, & Hybels, 1979). The study was commissioned in response to the prospect of increasing forms of legalized gambling in the United States, which at that time consisted mainly of lotteries and horse racing. Much of the survey focused on assessing gambling behaviors and attitudes toward gambling. Note that this survey was conducted before pathological gambling was introduced in the *DSM* (APA, 1980). A scale that measured "compulsive gambling" was only one small aspect of the survey. Of the more than 1,700 adults who responded, 68% reported gambling at least once in their lifetimes, and 61% reported having gambled in the past year. In terms of lifetime disordered gambling, 2.33% were identified as "potential compulsive gamblers," or Level 2 gamblers, and an additional 0.77% were classified as "probable compulsive gamblers" (Commission on the Review of the National Policy Toward Gambling, 1976).

The second attempt to evaluate rates of disordered gambling was made by Howard Shaffer and his colleagues (Shaffer et al., 1997; Shaffer, Hall, & Vander Bilt, 1999), who conducted a meta-analysis of all prevalence studies conducted in North America. This type of analysis combines prevalence rates from multiple independent studies by weighting the number of respondents in each survey. Using all studies that met minimum requirements for methodological rigor and reporting of necessary data (sample size and prevalence rates), Shaffer, Hall, and Vander Bilt (1999) identified 120 studies to include in the analysis. They found that 94.7% of the population had ever gambled (Level 1), 3.85% (with a confidence interval [CI] of 2.94%–4.76%) were lifetime Level 2 gamblers, and 1.60% (CI: 1.35%–1.85%) were lifetime Level 3 gamblers. Thus, with a combined rate of Level 2 and Level 3 gambling of 5.45%, slightly more than 1 of 20 individuals have some degree of a gambling problem in their lifetimes.

Past-year prevalence rates, by definition, are lower than lifetime rates, with the exception of chronic and nonremitting disorders, in which case the two rates are equivalent. For disorders that abate, past-year prevalence rates are substantially lower than lifetime rates. In the case of disordered gambling, about one third of the ever-afflicted seem to resolve their gambling problems (Shaffer, Hall, & Vander Bilt, 1999; see also chap. 8, this volume). Past-year prevalence rates were estimated to be 2.80% for Level 2 gambling and 1.14% for Level 3 gambling. These rates of disordered gambling translate to about 10.9 million Americans experiencing some form of gambling problems in their lives. More than 3 million suffer from the most severe form of gambling problems during their lives. Furthermore, almost 8 million Americans are currently experiencing some degree of gambling problems, with 2.3 million experiencing Level 3 gambling in the past year.

The National Gambling Impact Study Commission recommended another national study, which was conducted by the National Opinion Research Center at the University of Chicago in 1998 (Gerstein et al., 1999). The study found substantially lower rates of both lifetime and current prevalence rates of Level 2–3 gambling than those reported by Shaffer, Hall, and

Vander Bilt (1999). In part, the different populations sampled may have been partially associated with the discrepant rates; that is, Gerstein et al.'s (1999) survey classified respondents as disordered gamblers only if they admitted to wagering more than $100 in a given day, whereas other surveys administered the entire battery of questions to all respondents. Discrepancies in prevalence rates may also be related to the different instruments used to assess and classify individuals with regard to their gambling behaviors and problems, as I describe further in chapter 3.

Welte, Barnes, Wieczorek, Tidwell, and Parker (2001) conducted the most recent national telephone study. To better estimate rates of disordered gambling, they used two different instruments (see chap. 3). Although rates differed depending on the instrument used, even the more conservative estimates were within the range of the results presented in Shaffer, Hall, and Vander Bilt's (1999) meta-analysis, and they were higher than the rates found in Gerstein et al.'s (1999) survey. The results of these nationally based surveys are summarized in Table 2.1.

Several general population surveys have also been conducted in Canada. Bland, Newman, Orn, and Stebelsky (1993) conducted face-to-face interviews of adults in Edmonton. Using a brief, 4-item screen that has not undergone much psychometric testing, a low proportion of the sample (0.4%) was classified as lifetime Level 3 gamblers. In contrast, other Canadian researchers who used better developed instruments found rates similar to those reported in most of the U.S. surveys. Ladouceur (1996) summarized these studies; rates of Level 2 gambling ranged from 1.9% to 7.7%; for Level 3 gambling, the rates were 0.8% to 1.7%.

Other Countries

Prevalence rates of disordered gambling in other countries are generally less well established than in the United States and Canada. Nevertheless, data from studies conducted throughout the world tend to indicate that rates of disordered gambling are somewhat similar to those described in North American studies.

New Zealand and Australia have been some of the forerunners in gambling research. The first study of prevalence rates in New Zealand was undertaken in 1986. In that study, Wells, Bushnell, Hornblow, Joyce, and Oakley-Brown (1989) found that 3.6% of respondents were Level 2 gamblers and 0.4% were Level 3 gamblers. Volberg and Abbott (1994) and Abbott and Volberg (2000) conducted two nationally based studies. They found slightly different rates, ranging from 1.0% to 2.7% for lifetime Level 3 gambling, as shown in Table 2.2.

In Australia, a stratified random door-knock procedure was used to interview 2,744 adults in its four state capitals in 1991 (Dickerson, Baron,

TABLE 2.1
Prevalence Rates of Gambling and Gambling Disorders in Nationally Based General Population Surveys From the United States and Canada

Country and studies	N	Response rate (%)	Population source	Instrument(s) used	Past year (%) Ever gambled	Past year (%) Level 2	Past year (%) Level 3	Lifetime (%) Ever gambled	Lifetime (%) Level 2	Lifetime (%) Level 3
United States										
Commission on the Review of the National Policy Toward Gambling (1976)	1,749	65.3	National telephone survey	Attitude survey	61	n.s.	n.s.	68	2.3	0.8
Shaffer, Hall, & Vander Bilt's (1999) meta-analysis	79,037	Varied	Meta-analysis	Usually SOGS	n.s.	2.8	1.1	94.7	3.9	1.6
Gerstein et al. (1999)	2,417	55.5	National telephone survey	NODS	63.3	0.4	0.1	85.6	1.3	0.8
Welte et al. (2001)	2,638	65.4	National telephone survey	SOGS 13-item DIS	82.1	3.6 2.2	1.9 1.3	n.s.	7.5 2.8	4.0 2.0
Canada										
Bland et al. (1993)	7,214	71	Urban household survey	4-item DIS	n.s.	n.s.	0.2	70.3	n.s.	0.4
Ladouceur (1996)	Range of 801–1,200	34–68	7 provincial telephone surveys	SOGS	Median of 63	n.s.	n.s.	Range of 67–93	Range of 1.9–7.7	Range of 0.8–1.7

Note. SOGS = South Oaks Gambling Screen; NODS = National Opinion Research Center *DSM* Screen for Gambling Problems; DIS = Diagnostic Interview Schedule. n.s. = not stated.

TABLE 2.2
Prevalence Rates of Gambling and Gambling Disorders in Surveys From Countries Other Than the United States and Canada

Country and studies	N	Response rate (%)	Population source	Instrument used	Current (%)			Lifetime (%)		
					Ever gambled	Level 2	Level 3	Ever gambled	Level 2	Level 3
Australia										
Dickerson et al. (1996)	2,744	n.s.	Home survey	1-item[a]	n.s.	n.s.	n.s.	n.s.	n.s.	1.2 (0.3)
	290	n.s.	Regular gamblers	SOGS						
Productivity Commission (1999)	10,600	55	Phone survey	SOGS[a]	82	2.8	2.1	n.s.	n.s.	n.s.
Hong Kong										
Chen et al. (1993)	7,229	73	Phone survey	DIS	n.s.	n.s.	n.s.	n.s.	n.s.	1.6
Wong & So (2003)	2,004	57	Phone survey	*DSM*	n.s.	n.s.	n.s.	n.s.	4.0	1.8
Korea										
Lee et al. (1990)	3,134	84	Home survey	DIS	n.s.	n.s.	n.s.	n.s.	n.s.	1.0
New Zealand										
Abbott & Volberg (2000)	6,452	75	Phone and home survey	SOGS–R	86.2	0.8	0.6	94.0	1.9	1.0
Volberg & Abbott (1994)	4,053	66	Phone survey	SOGS	n.s.	n.s.	n.s.	95.0	4.2 (0.6)	2.7 (0.5)
Norway										
Gotestam & Johansson (2003)	2,014	48	Phone survey	*DSM*	68.8	0.45[b]	0.15[b]	n.s.	n.s.	n.s.

	N		Survey	Instrument						
Spain										
Becoña (1993)	1,615	n.s.	Home survey, Galacia	*DSM*	n.s.	n.s.	n.s.	n.s.	1.6	1.7
Becoña (1993)	1,028	n.s.	Home survey, Galacia	SOGS	n.s.	n.s.	n.s.	n.s.	2.0	1.4
Becoña (1993)	1,230	n.s.	Home survey, Catalonia	SOGS	n.s.	n.s.	n.s.	n.s.	2.5 combined	
Legarda et al. (1992)	598	60	Home survey, Seville	SOGS	n.s.	n.s.	n.s.	n.s.	5.2	1.7
Sweden										
Volberg et al. (2001)	7,139	77	Phone survey	SOGS	n.s.	1.4 (0.3)	0.6 (0.2)	n.s.	2.7 (0.4)	1.2 (0.3)
Switzerland										
Bondolfi et al. (2000)	2,526	59	Phone survey	SOGS	n.s.	2.2	0.8	n.s.	n.s.	n.s.
Taiwan										
Hwu et al. (1989)	11,004	96	Home survey	DIS	n.s.	n.s.	2.7–4.0	n.s.	n.s.	4.4–6.0
United Kingdom										
Sproston et al. (2000)	7,680	65	Home survey and question-naires by other family members	SOGS[a] DSM[a]	72	1.3 2.9	0.8 0.6	n.s.	n.s.	n.s.

Note. Numbers in parentheses indicate confidence intervals. If multiple surveys in a country were available, only nationally based ones are presented. SOGS = South Oaks Gambling Screen; DIS = Diagnostic Interview Schedule; *DSM = Diagnostic and Statistical Manual of Mental Disorders*; SOGS-R = Revised South Oaks Gambling Screen. n.s. = not stated.
[a]Individuals had to report having gambled regularly, or in the past year, before the SOGS or other diagnostic instruments were administered. [b]Timeframe over which problem gambling behaviors were measured was not stated.

Hong, & Cottrell, 1996). Most respondents were interviewed only about gambling participation, and a subsample of 290 individuals who gambled at least weekly was assessed for Level 3 gambling. Using estimates derived from the percentages of regular gamblers who then were classified as Level 3 gamblers, Dickerson et al. (1996) reported that just over 1% of Australian adults were lifetime Level 3 gamblers. A more recent national survey was conducted by the Productivity Commission (1999), which found that 2.8% of the respondents were current Level 2 gamblers and 2.1% were Level 3 gamblers.

In many European countries, electronic gaming machines have been available for a much longer time than in many North American countries. In the United Kingdom, Cornish (1978) estimated prevalence rates of individuals at risk for excessive gambling to be about 4% using the results of Gallup's (1976) criterion of gambling more often than weekly. Sproston, Ernst, and Orford (2000) conducted a more extensive survey. Using a standardized instrument to assess disordered gambling, they found substantially lower prevalence rates, as denoted in Table 2.2. Regional surveys of prevalence rates of disordered gambling have been also conducted in Spain and were reported by Becoña (1993). They reveal prevalence rates ranging from 1.6% to 2.0% for Level 2 gambling and 1.4% to 1.7% for Level 3 gambling.

In Switzerland, Bondolfi, Osiek, and Ferrero (2000) conducted a telephone survey prior to the introduction of casino-style gambling. They found current rates of Level 2 gambling to be 2.2% and 0.8% for Level 3. In Sweden, where legal and commercial gambling have existed since the 1930s, Volberg, Abbott, Ronnberg, and Munck (2001) found higher rates, whereas in a Norwegian study, Gotestam and Johansson (2003) reported that only a small proportion of the population was Level 2 or 3 gamblers. Gotestam and Johansson, however, created their own *DSM*-based questionnaire, and they did not indicate the timeframe over which gambling symptoms were assessed.

Several studies have also been conducted in Asian countries. Hwu, Yeh, and Chang (1989) found that rates of lifetime Level 3 gambling ranged from a low of 4.4% (+1.2) in rural villages to 6.0% (+1.4) in small towns in Taiwan. In Hong Kong and Korea, lifetime prevalence rates of Level 3 gambling were lower and estimated at 1.0% to 1.8% (Chen, Wong, Lee, Chan-Ho, & Lau, 1993; Lee et al., 1990; Wong & So, 2003).

Thus, prevalence rates of lifetime Level 3 gambling usually range from about 1% to 2% worldwide. Prevalence rates of Level 2 gambling are slightly higher in most studies, ranging from 2% to 5%. Past-year prevalence rates are about 40% to 60% of lifetime rates. The relative consistency of these estimates, despite the use of a variety of instruments administered in a number of languages, allows for some degree of confidence in this general estimation of prevalence rates assessed worldwide.

PREVALENCE RATES IN SPECIAL POPULATIONS

Gambling problems are of special interest for certain populations, either because they are thought to be particularly vulnerable to gambling problems or because gambling may have unique adverse effects among them. In the next section, I describe rates of gambling problems in four populations of interest: (a) substance abusers, (b) older adults, (c) employees in special fields, and (d) gaming patrons.

Substance Abusers

Substance abusers experience gambling problems at much higher rates than the general population. Shaffer, Hall, and Vander Bilt's (1999) meta-analysis provided estimates for surveys in substance-abusing samples. In 18 studies of adults in treatment for substance use disorders, lifetime rates of Level 2 gambling were 15.01% (CI: 8.94%–21.07%), and lifetime rates of Level 3 gambling were 14.23% (CI: 10.70%–17.75%). Since Shaffer, Hall, and Vander Bilt's (1999) review, a number of additional studies of disordered gambling in substance-abusing populations have been published (e.g., Hall et al., 2000; Langenbucher, Bavly, Labouvie, Sanjuan, & Martin, 2001; Lejoyeux, Loi, Solomon, & Ades, 1999; Toneatto & Brennan, 2002), and all suggest a relationship between the disorders. I describe specific hypotheses about this association, ranging from biological to environmental, in chapters 4 through 6, in which I discuss associations between substance use and pathological gambling.

In this section, I review prevalence rates of gambling problems from studies that surveyed patients seeking treatment for substance abuse. Data adapted from Petry and Pietrzak (2004) are summarized in Table 2.3.

First, 10 known studies have evaluated rates of disordered gambling among general substance abuse patients, not differentiated by substance use diagnoses (see Table 2.3). The prevalence rates of gambling disorders ranged from 5% to 33% for Level 3 gambling and from 6% to 22% for Level 2 gambling. These rates are substantially higher than the 1%–2% rates noted in general population surveys (Shaffer, Hall, & Vander Bilt, 1999).

Rates of gambling disorders appear to be high among all types of substance-abusing patients. Lesieur, Blume, and Zoppa (1986) differentiated patients by drug use diagnosis in their sample; for *alcohol-abusing patients*, 15% were lifetime Level 2 or 3 gamblers. Other studies of alcohol-abusing and -dependent patients, conducted in the United States (Elia & Jacobs, 1993; McCormick, 1993), France (Lejoyeux et al., 1999), Canada (Toneatto & Brennan, 2002), New Zealand (Sellman, Adamson, Robertson, Sullivan, & Coverdale, 2002), and Korea (Cho et al., 2002), have found rates of Level 3 gambling ranging from 4% to 13%.

TABLE 2.3
Lifetime Prevalence Rates of Gambling Problems in Individuals Seeking Substance Abuse Treatment

Substance use disorder	Study	Instrument	N	Level 2 (%)	Level 3 (%)
General substance use	Castellani et al. (1996)	SOGS	154	n.s.	14
	Ciarrocchi (1993)	SOGS	467	6	5
	Cunningham-Williams et al. (2000)	DIS	512	22	10
	Daghestani et al. (1996)	SOGS	276	n.s.	33
	Langenbucher et al. (2001)	SOGS	372	n.s.	13
	Lesieur et al. (1986)	SOGS	458	10	9
	McCormick (1993)	SOGS	2,171	n.s.	13
	Rupcich et al. (1997)	SOGS	328	11	14
	Shaffer et al. (2002)	DSM	171	12	5
	Toneatto & Brennan (2002)	SOGS	580	5 PY	11 PY
Alcohol	Cho et al. (2002)	DIS	5,176	n.s.	4[a]
	Elia & Jacobs (1993)	SOGS	85	n.s.	13
	Lejoyeux et al. (1999)	DSM	79	n.s.	9
	Lesieur et al. (1986)	SOGS	243	10	5
	McCormick (1993)	SOGS	581	n.s.	10
	Sellman et al. (2002)	SOGS	124	19	4
	Toneatto & Brennan (2002)	SOGS	n.s.	6 PY	9 PY
Cocaine	Hall et al. (2000)	DIS	313[b]	n.s.	8 (4 PY)
	Lesieur et al. (1986)	SOGS	113	16	14
	Steinberg et al. (1992)	DSM	298	n.s.	15
	Toneatto & Brennan (2002)	SOGS	n.s.	4 PY	12 PY
Opioids	Feigelman et al. (1995)	SOGS	220	3	7
	Ledgerwood & Downey (2002)	SOGS	62	11 P3mos	18 P3mos
	Lesieur et al. (1986)	SOGS	34	15	18
	Spunt et al. (1995)	SOGS	117	15	16
	Toneatto & Brennan (2002)	SOGS	n.s.	2 PY	5 PY
Cannabis	Tonneatto & Brennan (2002)	SOGS	n.s.	14 PY	24 PY

Note. SOGS = South Oaks Gambling Screen; n.s.= not stated; DIS = Diagnostic Interview Schedule; DSM = *Diagnostic and Statistical Manual of Mental Disorders*; PY = past year; P3mos = past 3 months. n.s. = not stated. From *Dual Diagnosis and Psychiatric Treatment: Substance Abuse and Comorbid Disorders* (p. 446), by H. R. Kranzler and J. Tinsley, 2004, New York: Marcel Dekker. Copyright 2004 by Marcel Dekker, Inc. Adapted with permission. [a]This percentage includes only men; the number of men in the original sample was not reported. [b]Two hundred patients were also opioid dependent.

Cocaine abusers also suffer from high rates of gambling disorders. Four reports of studies that have examined this population are available (Hall et al., 2000; Lesieur et al., 1986; Steinberg, Kosten, & Rounsaville, 1992; Toneatto & Brennan, 2002), and they found rates of Level 3 gambling ranging from 8% to 15%. Investigators have also studied rates of disordered gambling in *opioid-dependent patients*. Two studies were conducted in residential or inpatient settings (Lesieur et al., 1986; Toneatto & Brennan, 2002), and three were conducted in methadone maintenance clinics (Feigelman, Kleinman, Lesieur, Millman, & Lesser, 1995; Ledgerwood & Downey, 2002; Spunt, Lesieur, Hunt, & Cahill, 1995). Rates of Level 2 gambling ranged from 2% to 15%, and rates of Level 3 gambling varied from 5% to 18%, with combined rates of Level 2–3 gambling about 30% in three of these five studies (Ledgerwood & Downey, 2002; Lesieur et al., 1986; Spunt et al., 1995).

Only one known study (Toneatto & Brennan, 2002) evaluated rates of gambling disorders in patients seeking treatment for *cannabis problems*. This study found that patients with marijuana use disorders were more likely to suffer from gambling problems than patients with any other substance use disorder, but the number of patients within each drug abuse category was not stated. Therefore, these conclusions may be based on small samples in some of the categories and require replication in other samples of substance abusers.

In conclusion, gambling problems are common in individuals seeking treatment for substance use disorders. Chapter 5 focuses on issues related to psychiatric comorbidity. The data presented in this section, which were obtained from treatment-seeking populations, suggest that professionals in addiction treatment settings should routinely screen substance-abusing patients for gambling problems, because the prevalence rates of disordered gambling are so high.

Older Adults

In contrast to the high rates of disordered gambling found among treatment-seeking substance abusers, rates of gambling problems appear to be relatively low in another group of interest: older adults. General population surveys have revealed that Level 2–3 gambling is relatively rare among individuals over the age of 60 years. For example, in Welte et al.'s (2001) national survey, only 0.1% of respondents over age 61 years were classified as Level 3 gamblers, and only 2.2% were classified as Level 2 gamblers. In Gerstein et al.'s (1999) survey, only 0.1% of individuals over 65 years met lifetime criteria for Level 3 gambling, and only 0.2% met the criteria for Level 2 gambling.

Although these data may suggest that gambling is not a significant public health concern among older adults, this conclusion must be drawn with caution. Many studies have not broken out prevalence rates by age groups, and usually less than 20% of respondents are over 60 years. Only 400 to 500 respondents in Welte et al.'s (2001) and Gerstein et al.'s (1999) studies were in the oldest cohorts (over the ages of 60 and 65 years, respectively). These samples may not be large enough to derive accurate estimates of prevalence rates for a disorder that occurs at a low frequency.

Furthermore, although Gerstein et al. (1999) found that the proportion of adults aged 65 years and older who gamble is lower than the proportion of younger adults who gamble, the most dramatic increase in the percentage of individuals gambling has occurred in this older age group. In a 1975 study, only 35% of respondents over age 65 had gambled in their lifetimes (Kallick, Suits, Dielman & Hybels, 1976). In contrast, 80% of those over 65 who were interviewed in 1998 reported lifetime gambling (Gerstein et al., 1999). Past-year gambling also increased dramatically in the oldest age group, with only 23% of older adults reporting past-year gambling in 1975 versus 50% in 1998.

Few studies have focused exclusively on gambling problems in older adults. McNeilly and Burke (2000) surveyed a nonrandom sample of 315 older adults in Nebraska. Ninety-one of the respondents were recruited from gaming facilities (commercial and charitable bingo facilities or those on a shuttle bus day trip to a casino), and 224 were recruited from senior and retirement centers of AARP chapter members. Among the persons surveyed at gaming venues, 5.5% were Level 2 gamblers, and 11% were Level 3 gamblers. Among those surveyed from other community events, only 1.3% were Level 2 gamblers, and 2.7% were Level 3 gamblers. This study, despite its use of a nonrandom sample, suggests higher rates of gambling disorders in older adults than those reported in general population surveys. In fact, it found prevalence rates consistent with those noted in younger cohorts (see Table 2.1).

A similar study was recently completed in Connecticut (Ladd, Molina, Kerins, & Petry, 2003). In total, 492 adults over the age of 65 were recruited from senior centers ($n = 360$) or bingo parlors ($n = 132$). Not surprisingly, all the respondents recruited from bingo parlors had lifetime experience with gambling, and 86.6% of those recruited from senior centers reported lifetime gambling. In the full sample, 5.9% were classified as Level 2 gamblers, and 4.6% were classified as Level 3 gamblers. Even excluding individuals recruited from bingo halls, 9.7% were classified as Level 2 or 3 gamblers.

T. Moore (2001) conducted a telephone survey of 1,512 randomly selected Oregon adults age 62 and older and identified 1.1% of the respondents as Level 3 gamblers and an additional 2.3% as Level 2 gamblers. Among 80 independently living older adult African Americans in Los Angeles who frequented senior centers that provided bus trips to Las Vegas, 17% were classified as disordered gamblers (Bazargan, Bazargan, & Akanda,

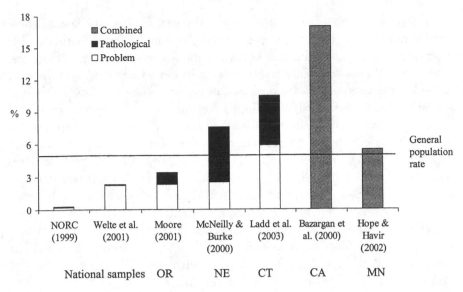

Figure 2.1 Prevalence rates of disordered gambling in studies of older adults

2001). In contrast, Hope and Havir (2002) reported that few older adults in Minnesota gambled problematically, but 5.5% of 146 individuals surveyed were "concerned" that they might have a gambling problem.

These studies are summarized in Figure 2.1, and they show a clinically significant rate of disordered gambling among older adults. Not surprisingly, studies that sampled some respondents at gaming venues revealed higher rates of gambling problems than those that sampled only from the general population. National studies, that include respondents who may not have easy access to certain forms of gambling or who are not physically active, appear to yield lower rates than regional surveys conducted in areas where casino gambling is available and relatively easily accessible.

I next describe a case example of an elderly gambler.

Case example. Betty is a 78-year-old widow living in a small town in northwestern Minnesota. She spent her life as a homemaker and raised three children, all of whom moved away after high school. Betty's husband was initially a farmer and later managed the local mill. He and Betty were both good savers, and he left her $400,000 when he passed away in his 60s.

A casino opened 40 miles from Betty's home in 1988. Initially, Betty went once or twice a week with friends, primarily for the all-you-can-eat buffet. As more of her friends passed away, Betty began going alone, catching rides with a young neighbor, Kate, who worked as a dealer. When her best friend died in 1996, Betty was lonely, and she preferred going to the casino to staying at home alone. She started going regularly with Kate and staying through Kate's work shift.

Betty was such a regular customer at the casino that all the staff knew her by name and greeted her every time she came. Betty cherished this attention and found all the staff very nice and accommodating. Sometimes, when her arthritis was really bad, she came in her wheelchair, and the staff helped her get around. Betty preferred bingo and slot gambling. Although she initially imposed a $10/day limit on gambling, this amount increased to $20 and even $50. Between her social security income and interest on her savings, Betty had a $32,000/year income. With a fully paid off home and food, utilities, and tax expenses of under $8,000/year, Betty saw no reason to limit her gambling, especially when the people at the casino were so nice to her. She quit worrying about the amount of cash she took with her. Although Betty never had a credit card in all her life and was suspicious of ATM machines, Kate insisted that it was like a checking account and very convenient. Kate went with Betty to the bank to arrange for an ATM card. Now, Betty could go to the casino with her ATM card and avoid making trips to the bank in the winter months.

Throughout the late 1990s and into 2000, Betty spent her entire annual income at the casino and also drew from her savings. The roof on her house began leaking in the winter of 2001, and repair estimates were $12,000. When Betty heard this estimate, she became irate and told the roofers to forget it. She had the grandson of an old friend patch it for $500. In 2002, the state sent her a bill for $9,000 in back taxes. Betty couldn't believe it. She always paid her taxes on time, or so she thought. She refused to pay the bill, even when served notice by the court. The sheriff knew Betty's son and called him in California. Her son came back home that summer for a week and went to the bank with his mother. There was only about $100,000 remaining across all her accounts, and he kept asking his mother where all the money had gone. Betty said she'd rather give it to the casino than the government. Betty never admitted to having problems with gambling. She insisted that gambling was entertainment and recreation for her and that she could spend the money she and her husband had saved any way she wanted.

Comment. This case is typical in that elderly gamblers often begin gambling as a recreational and social activity. Because casinos are generally safe places where older adults can go, they may begin going alone over time, as in Betty's case.

For many gamblers, gambling money is no longer considered "real money," and amounts that would never be considered reasonable for other forms of entertainment, or even for necessities, are rationalized for use in gambling. The financial consequences of gambling are often minimized in the early stages of the disorder.

Betty would be unlikely to admit to many of the symptoms of pathological gambling and, like Mary, the woman depicted earlier in this chapter, she may be classified as a Level 2 gambler, or possibly even a Level 1 gambler, depending on the instrument administered (see chap. 3 for a discussion of assessment instruments). In any case, Betty would be unlikely to seek treatment for gambling or to go to treatment even if pressured by her son.

Employees in Special Fields

Few companies routinely screen their employees for gambling problems (Lesieur, 1989), and only a handful of published studies have evaluated the prevalence of disordered gambling among employees in companies or institutional settings. Petry and Mallya (2004) evaluated disordered gambling in 904 employees of an academic health center and found rates of disordered gambling similar to that reported in the general population. Three percent of the respondents were classified as Level 2 gamblers, and an additional 1.8% were Level 3 gamblers. None of the Level 2–3 gamblers reported receiving treatment for gambling. Of the Level 3 gamblers identified in the survey, 80% had gambled in the past week, and 30% reported having missed work to gamble. These data suggest the potential need to include questions regarding gambling behaviors in employment health surveys.

From an employer perspective, gaming employees are another population of interest. In a study of 3,841 casino employees with a 74.9% response rate, Shaffer, Vander Bilt, and Hall (1999) found that 2.1% experienced Level 3 gambling in the past year, a rate significantly higher than past-year rates in general populations. Rates of Level 2 gambling in the sample, however, were lower than rates found in the general population. Only 1.4% of casino employees were current Level 2 gamblers. Despite their location and familiarity with gambling, employees and employee assistance programs at casinos were generally unfamiliar with screening and referral mechanisms for disordered gambling. This is currently an understudied phenomenon, and casino employers may begin to consider screening and providing early interventions for employees with gambling problems. Employment settings for individuals with high-risk demographic features (e.g., young, male, low education; see chap. 4) may also benefit from these efforts.

Gamblers or People Taking Exit Polls at Casinos

Surveys of individuals in gaming facilities are useful for determining rates of gambling disorders among individuals who gamble. Gerstein et al. (1999) conducted field interviews with 530 patrons of gaming establishments. The respondents included individuals purchasing lottery tickets; those visiting casinos, including tribal and riverboat casinos; and individuals attending pari-mutuel gaming establishments (a form of betting, usually on horse races, in which individuals holding winning tickets divide the total amount bet in proportion to their wagers, minus the proportion that goes to the house). An overall response rate of 50% was obtained. The lifetime rate of Level 3 gambling was 7.9%, and for Level 2 it was 5.3%. The past-year rate of Level 3 gambling was 5.3%, and for Level 2 gambling it was 4.9%. It is not surprising that rates of disordered gambling in interception surveys were higher than those obtained from general population surveys (see Table 2.1). Although the sample size was small ($n = 56$), persons interviewed at pari-mutuel gaming facilities had the highest rates of disordered gambling; 25% were lifetime Level 3 gamblers and 14% were Level 2 gamblers.

Intercept surveys are also available from two other countries. Fisher (2000b) administered a DSM-based questionnaire to 1,105 casino patrons in 40 casinos in the United Kingdom and achieved a near-100% response rate by providing the chance to win a prize for participation. Past-year prevalence rates were 5.1% for Level 2 gambling and 2.2% for Level 3 gambling. The bulk of disordered gambling was attributable to the nonregular casino patrons, who attended casinos less than weekly and who usually gambled on noncasino activities. Fisher (2000b) concluded that most disordered gambling in the United Kingdom is related to noncasino gamblers, as only about 3% of the British population gambles in casinos. In Brazil, Oliveria and Silva (2000) interviewed 171 adults at bingo clubs, a video poker club, and a horse racing club. They found a very high prevalence rate of disordered gambling: 43.8%.

Most of the above studies did not compare estimates derived from respondents gambling in different locations. However, data from Gerstein et al.'s (1999) study suggest that participation in some forms of gambling activities may be more likely to develop into disordered gambling or that certain forms of gambling may be more addictive. In the next section I address rates of participation in various forms of gambling activities and their association with disordered gambling.

PARTICIPATION RATES IN DIFFERENT TYPES OF GAMBLING ACTIVITIES

A variety of forms of gambling exist, ranging from legal to illegal. They include lottery tickets, instant lottery (scratch ticket, pull-tabs), electronic gaming machines (slots, video poker, video lottery terminals), card playing (blackjack, poker), dice games, sports betting, playing games of skill for money, bingo and charitable games, trading high-risk stocks and bonds, jai alai, racetrack (horse, dog), and Internet gambling. In a recent general population study conducted in Hong Kong, Wong and So (2003) found that respondents who gambled on horse races, soccer games, and casino games were significantly more likely to be classified as Level 2–3 gamblers than individuals who wagered on other forms of gambling.

The NRC (1999) reviewed data regarding whether certain types of gambling may be associated with higher rates of disordered gambling. They identified 11 studies from Shaffer, Hall, and Vander Bilt's (1999) meta-analysis that were conducted in the past 10 years and that indicated the various types of gambling in which the gamblers were most likely to participate. To determine whether some forms of gambling are more likely to be addictive than others, they compared proportions of respondents classified as Level 2–3 gamblers who participated in various forms of gambling with the proportion of Level 1 respondents who participated in them. Sports betting and instant lotteries/pull-tabs were examined in all 11 studies, with lottery, card games, and general casino games evaluated in at least half of the studies. Although the percentages of Level 2–3 gamblers participating in each type were higher than the percentage of Level 1 gamblers, Level 2–3 gamblers were disproportionately active in lotteries and instant tickets, sports betting and casino games. High rates of gambling on bingo and charitable games and racetrack betting were also noted among Level 2–3 gamblers, although only three studies were included in the analyses.

Data are also available on gambling participation in 904 employees (Petry & Mallya, 2004) and 488 general medical and dental patients (Ladd & Petry, 2002a) from the state of Connecticut. Level 3 gamblers were disproportionately active in six forms of gambling activities: (a) Internet gambling, (b) video poker, (c) dice games, (d) playing sports for money, (e) high-risk stocks, and (f) roulette. Of those who had ever sampled these gambling activities, a high percentage were classified as Level 3 gamblers. For example, although only 5.9% of the respondents were lifetime Level 3 gamblers, among the 49 respondents who had gambled on the Internet, 55.1% were Level 3 gamblers. Video poker was the type of gambling next most often played disproportionately by Level 3 gamblers. Whereas 163 respondents had played video poker in their lifetimes, 32.5% of those who reported this type of gambling were Level 3 gamblers. Two hundred eighty-four respondents had experience with dice games and, of these, 23.0% were Level 3 gamblers. Playing sports for money, trading high-risk stocks and bonds, and playing roulette were reported by 200 to 400 individuals. Rates of Level 3 gambling among those who had sampled these activities ranged from 15.5% to 19.0%.

In contrast, a much higher proportion of the overall sample had experience with other forms of gambling, including the lottery ($n = 1,225$), slot machines ($n = 1,114$), scratch tickets ($n = 992$), and card games ($n = 841$). Rates of Level 3 gambling among those who had tried each of these activities ranged from a low of 7.5%, for the lottery, to a high of 10.2%, for cards. Similarly, rates of Level 3 gambling averaged about 10% among those who had ever sampled other forms of gambling, such as betting on sporting events, horse races, and bingo, with about half of the sample indicating experience with each of these forms of gambling.

These data do not provide a definitive estimate of risk associated with any type of gambling. Although it is tempting to speculate that Internet and electronic machines are the most addictive forms of gambling, other explanations exist for these data. For example, individuals with gambling problems may be more likely to sample a variety of types of gambling and, therefore, activities in which individuals relatively rarely engage (Internet gambling, video poker in Connecticut) have a higher proportion of disordered gamblers participating in them. Future research, especially laboratory and longitudinal studies, are needed to better evaluate the addictive potential of various forms of gambling and whether preferred forms of gambling vary over time, by geographical region, or among individuals who go on to develop gambling problems.

EVIDENCE FOR INCREASES IN DISORDERED GAMBLING WITH THE SPREAD OF LEGALIZED GAMBLING

Legalized gambling has expanded steadily over the past 20 years in the United States. Currently, all states but Hawaii and Utah have some form of legalized gambling. Thirty-seven states have lotteries, and casinos are permitted in more than half the states (NRC, 1999). Whether rates of disordered gambling have increased with the spread of legalized gambling is a question of great interest.

Shaffer, Hall, and Vander Bilt's (1999) meta-analysis compared prevalence rates in studies conducted before 1993 with those in studies conducted between 1993 and 1997. They found a significant increase in disordered gambling in the latter studies. Combined lifetime prevalence rates of Level 2–3 gambling in studies conducted before 1993 were 4.4%, versus 6.7% in studies conducted between 1993 and 1997. However, as Shaffer, Hall, and Vander Bilt (1999) pointed out, many studies used different methodologies and a variety of tools to assess disordered gambling. The older studies were conducted when electronic gaming devices were not as widely available as they are today. Few longitudinal studies have traced changes in gambling problems over time within a specific population. A summary of studies evaluating the prevalence of problem gambling over time is presented in Figure 2.2.

Longitudinal surveys were conducted in three U.S. states using similar methods. In each, surveys were conducted immediately prior to, or in conjunction with, legalization of casino gambling and again several years later. The NRC (1999) summarized these data. Specifically, surveys were con-

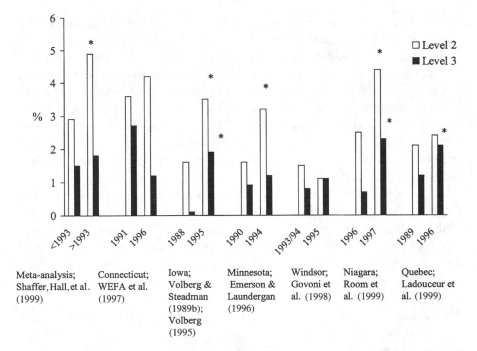

Meta-analysis;   Connecticut;   Iowa;   Minnesota;   Windsor;   Niagara;   Quebec;
Shaffer, Hall, et al.   WEFA et al.   Volberg &   Emerson &   Govoni et   Room et   Ladouceur et
(1999)   (1997)   Steadman   Laundergan   al. (1998)   al. (1999)   al. (1999)
     (1989b);   (1996)
     Volberg
     (1995)

Figure 2.2 Changes in prevalence rates with introductions of new forms of legalized gambling. See text for details and study descriptions. * = Statistically significant inversion in prevalence rates.

ducted in the state of Connecticut in 1991 and again in 1996 (WEFA Group, ICR Survey Research Group, Lesieur, & Thompson, 1997). About 1,000 respondents were surveyed each time. Foxwoods, now the world's largest casino, opened in Connecticut in 1992, and the Mohegan Sun Casino opened in Connecticut in 1996. Lifetime rates of Level 2 gambling rose nonsignificantly, whereas Level 3 gambling decreased nonsignificantly. Statewide surveys were also conducted in Iowa in 1988 (Volberg & Steadman, 1989b) and 1995 (Volberg, 1995), during which time interval riverboat casinos became operational. Significant increases in both Level 2 and 3 gambling were noted. In 1990 and 1994 surveys conducted in Minnesota (Emerson & Laundergan, 1996), rates of Level 2 gambling doubled, whereas rates of Level 3 increased nonsignificantly. In contrast, Govoni, Frisch, Rupcich, and Getty (1998) found no increase in disordered gambling within the year before and the year after the opening of Casino Windsor in Canada.

Room, Turner, and Ialomiteanu (1999) surveyed individuals residing in the Niagara Falls area with the opening of a local casino in 1996. Using random digit dialing, 1,002 adults were interviewed prior to the opening of the casino. Sixty-six percent of the sample (n = 662) was reinterviewed, along with 608 new respondents, about a year after the casino opened. In both cohorts, 86% reported gambling in the prior year. The proportion identified as Level 2 gamblers increased, as did the proportion classified as Level 3 gamblers. Ladouceur, Jacques, Ferland, and Giroux (1999) evaluated changes in gambling problems over a longer time interval in the province of Quebec. In 1989, 1,002 respondents were interviewed, and 54% reported past-year gambling, with 2.1% identified as lifetime Level 2 gamblers and 1.2% identified as Level 3 gamblers. In 1996, 1,257 individuals were surveyed. Past-year gambling rates had increased significantly, to 63%. Lifetime rates of Level 2 gambling remained relatively constant, but Level 3 gambling had increased significantly, to 2.1%.

Grun and McKeigue (2000) did not estimate prevalence rates of disordered gambling, but they found that the proportion of households in the United Kingdom that gambled more than 10% of their income increased significantly, from 0.4% to 1.7%, with the introduction of the national lottery in 1994. Among low-income households, this increase was even more dramatic, from 0.6% to 3.2%. In chapter 4, I address issues related to socioeconomic status and gambling.

Accessibility to gambling establishments also may be related to prevalence rates of disordered gambling. When combining the telephone and patron surveys, Gerstein et al. (1999) found that prevalence rates of Level 2 and Level 3 gambling were roughly double among persons who lived within 50 miles of a casino relative to those who lived farther away. However, this finding did not emerge when the telephone survey data were analyzed alone, perhaps because of the smaller sample size, or because people interviewed in the patron survey were more likely to live near gambling establishments than those interviewed over the telephone.

Together, these studies seem to suggest a modest but significant rise in the prevalence of gambling participation and disordered gambling as legalized gambling opportunities have spread. These conclusions are limited by the lack of large-scale longitudinal studies as well as the differences in response rates, sampling procedures, and instruments used across studies. Moreover, regular gambling may occur for 4 to 10 years before the gambler admits problems or seeks treatment (Petry & Oncken, 2002; Stinchfield & Winters, 2001). Rates of disordered gambling may rise in the forthcoming years, as individuals have more time to sample, and potentially develop problems with, various forms of gambling.

Most of the available data suggest an increase in rates of disordered gambling with the spread of legalized gambling opportunities. Rises in disordered gambling may have occurred over the relatively brief time intervals during which access to legalized gambling opportunities has spread, and they may continue to rise for the next several years, but prevalence rates may eventually stabilize. As more people are exposed to gambling opportunities throughout their lives, the proportion that develops gambling problems may rise rapidly initially and then taper off. Only longitudinal studies conducted with very large samples will be able to test this hypothesis.

SUMMARY AND CLINICAL IMPLICATIONS

Several clinical implications can be drawn from data presented in this chapter. Pathological gambling appears to have about a 1% to 2% prevalence rate worldwide, with problem gambling occurring even more frequently. Although these rates may not seem extraordinary, they are consistent with those associated with many other psychiatric disorders, including schizophrenia and bipolar disorder. They also translate into large numbers of people experiencing problems with gambling, and the rates are astounding in certain populations. In particular, all individuals seeking substance abuse treatment should be screened for gambling problems, as the comorbidity is so high in this patient population. Among older adults, data are mixed, but older adults who participate in community-organized gambling events (bingos, bus trips to casinos) may benefit from problem gambling screening efforts. Employee assistance programs may be well advised to consider assessing for gambling problems, especially in companies that employ large numbers of individuals with risk factors for problem gambling (see chap. 4). Finally, communities that are geographically proximate to gaming facilities, especially casinos and pari-mutuels, should probably invest in problem gambling screening, prevention, and treatment programs. In the next chapter, I describe methods for screening and diagnosing gambling problems.

3

ASSESSMENT

A variety of instruments have been developed for screening and classifying gambling behaviors (Shaffer, Hall, & Vander Bilt, 1997). The National Research Council (1999) identified 25 different instruments, but many of these were used in a single report and had no or very limited data about their psychometric properties. Rather than focusing on instruments that are rarely used, in this chapter I describe the most widely used instruments for screening and diagnosing Level 2–3 gambling. The instruments I cover are (a) the South Oaks Gambling Screen, (b) the Diagnostic Interview for Gambling Severity (Diagnostic Interview Schedule and its associated Gambling Assessment Module), (c) the National Opinion Research Center's *DSM–IV* Screen for Gambling Problems, (d) the Diagnostic Interview Schedule, (e) the Gambling Assessment Module for the *DSM–IV*, and (f) the Lie/Bet Questionnaire.

In addition to assessment tools, six instruments have been used to monitor gambling severity over time: (a) the Gambling Treatment Outcome Monitoring System, (b) the Addiction Severity Index—Gambling Severity Index, (c) the timeline follow-back method, (d) the Pathological Gambling Yale–Brown Obsessive–Compulsive Scale, (e) the Gambling Symptom Assessment Scale, and (f) the Global Clinical Inventory. I describe these instruments, their psychometric properties, and their advantages and disadvantages. Instruments are also available for screening for gambling problems in adolescents. I cover these issues in chapter 15, which is dedicated to gambling among youth and young adults.

South Oaks Gambling Screen

The most commonly used instrument for assessing disordered gambling is the 20-item, self-administered South Oaks Gambling Screen (SOGS; Lesieur & Blume, 1987). The items of the SOGS are shown in Exhibit 3.1. For a full description of the instrument, readers should consult the original source (Lesieur & Blume, 1987).

The SOGS is the instrument that has been used most often for classifying individuals with respect to disordered gambling. Scores range from 0 to 20, and individuals can be classified as Level 2 or Level 3 gamblers. However, definitions vary from study to study; some investigators classify individuals who endorse one to four items as Level 2 gamblers, whereas others use 3 or 4 points as cutoffs for classifying Level 2 gambling behaviors. A score of 5 or more typically is indicative of "probable pathological" or Level 3 gambling. Some researchers, however, include a higher cutoff value, of over 7 to 9. The average lifetime SOGS score of patients entering gambling treatment programs tends to be even higher, about 12 (Petry, 2002a).

In developing the SOGS, Lesieur and Blume (1987) incorporated a series of stages. First, using a gambling history instrument, they screened 458 patients entering the South Oaks Hospital in Long Island, New York, for treatment of drug or alcohol use problems. Patients who reported frequent or heavy gambling were queried more extensively about family, employment, and financial problems that may be associated with gambling. Lesieur and Blume (1987) also interviewed the patients' significant others to establish the external validity of responses. Finally, they collected counselors' impressions of the patients' gambling activities.

Using information gathered in this process, in the second stage Lesieur and Blume (1987) created 60 questions comprising the array of difficulties experienced by gamblers identified in the first stage. They administered this instrument to a second cohort of patients and eliminated low-frequency items, as well as redundant ones. Discriminant analysis further reduced the number of items down to the 20 now used. A score of 5 or more was selected as indicative of Level 3 gambling, because this cutoff value minimized the number of false-negative and false-positive codings.

In the third stage, Lesieur and Blume (1987) cross-validated the items of the SOGS. Along with *Diagnostic and Statistical Manual of Mental Disorders* (3rd ed., rev.; *DSM–III–R*; American Psychiatric Association, 1987) criteria, they administered the SOGS to 213 members of Gamblers Anonymous (GA), 384 university students, and 152 hospital employees. Among the GA members, 97% were appropriately classified as pathological gamblers. The concordance between classifications using the SOGS and *DSM–III–R*

EXHIBIT 3.1
Items From the South Oaks Gambling Screen

1. When you gamble, how often do you go back another day to win back money you lost?
   Responses: "Never"; "Some of the time (less than half the time) I lost"; "Most of the time I lost"; "Every time I lost"
2. Have you ever claimed to be winning money gambling but weren't really? In fact, you lost?
   Responses: "Never"; "Yes, less than half the time I lost"; "Yes, most of the time"
3. Do you feel you have ever had a problem with gambling?
   Responses: "No"; "Yes, in the past but not now"; "Yes, now"
4. Did you ever gamble more than you intended to?
   Responses: "Yes"; "No"
5. Have people criticized your gambling?
   Responses: "Yes"; "No"
6. Have you ever felt guilty about the way you gamble or what happens when you gamble?
   Responses: "Yes"; "No"
7. Have you ever felt like you would like to stop gambling but didn't think you could?
   Responses: "Yes"; "No"
8. Have you ever hidden betting slips, lottery tickets, gambling money, or other signs of gambling from your spouse, children or other important people in your life?
   Responses: "Yes"; "No"
9. Have you ever argued with people you live with over how you handle money?
   Responses: "Yes"; "No"
10. If yes, have money arguments ever centered on your gambling?
    Responses: "Yes"; "No"
11. Have you ever borrowed from someone and not paid them back as a result of your gambling?
    Responses: "Yes"; "No"
12. Have you ever lost time from work (or school) due to gambling?
    Responses: "Yes"; "No"

If you borrowed money to gamble or to pay gambling debts, who or where did you borrow from? (Check "yes" or "no" for each):

13. Household money?
14. Your spouse?
15. Other relatives or in-laws?
16. Banks, loan companies, or credit unions?
17. Credit cards?
18. Loan sharks?
19. Cashed in stocks, bonds, or other securities?
20. Sold personal or family property?
21. Borrowed on your checking account (passed bad checks)?

Note. To score the South Oaks Gambling Screen, Question 9 is not counted. If responses to Question 1 are "Most of the time I lost" or "Every time I lost," the person would score 1 point. For Question 2, responses of "Yes, less than half the time" or "Yes, most of the time" result in 1 point. For Question 3, 1 point is included if the response is "Yes, but in the past" or "Yes, now." The rest of the questions have "Yes" and "No" response categories, and each "Yes" response adds 1 point to the total score. Thus, 20 questions are included, resulting in a maximal score of 20. From "The South Oaks Gambling Screen (SOGS): A New Instrument for the Identification of Pathological Gamblers," by H. R. Lesieur and S. B. Blume, 1987, *American Journal of Psychiatry, 144*, pp. 1184–1188. Copyright 1987 by the American Psychiatric Association; http://ajp.psychiatryonline.org. Reprinted with permission.

criteria was 95.3% among students and 99.3% among hospital employees. To assess the reliability of the SOGS, Lesieur and Blume (1987) determined the internal consistency among the 749 surveys completed, and Cronbach's alpha was .97. Test–retest reliability was established among 74 inpatients and 38 outpatients who completed the instrument twice at least 30 days apart. The correlation was .71, using a dichotomous classification of pathological gambler or not.

The SOGS has good reliability and validity in clinical samples (Lesieur & Blume, 1987). It has been applied to samples derived from treatment settings, GA meetings, and the general population (Lesieur & Blume, 1987; Shaffer, Hall, & Vander Bilt, 1999). It is the instrument most frequently used for assessing gambling problems (Shaffer, Hall, & Vander Bilt, 1999). Other advantages include that it is self-administered and that the questions generally are easy to follow. It has adequate to good construct validity, internal consistency, and test–retest reliability. The SOGS has been translated into more than 20 languages, and it appears to demonstrate appropriate psychometric properties (e.g., Duvarci & Varan, 2001; Echeburúa, Baez, Fernandez, & Paez, 1994). The SOGS has also been adapted to identify recent gambling problems, such as over the past 6 months or past year (Stinchfield & Winters, 1996). However, the effect of these modifications on its psychometric properties is not known.

Despite its widespread use, some investigators have criticized the SOGS. The SOGS has never been updated for DSM–IV (American Psychiatric Association, 1994) criteria. Despite its frequent use as a diagnostic instrument, it was never intended for that purpose. Screening instruments developed for clinical settings require caution when used in general population surveys. In contrast to diagnostic interviews, screening tools are meant to identify possible problems, and they yield conservative scoring decisions, such as the phrase *probable pathological gambling,* recommended by Lesieur and Blume (1987).

Culleton (1989) questioned the appropriateness of applying the SOGS to establish prevalence rates of disordered gambling in the general population. Despite adequate sensitivity and specificity in treatment settings, its psychometric properties are not established in general populations. Because the base rate of pathological gambling is low in the general population, the predictive value of any screening instrument may be suspect. This problem is not unique for gambling. In estimating the prevalence of any disorder that is relatively infrequent, almost any screening instrument is likely to overestimate prevalence rates (J. M. Goldstein & Simpson, 1995). The SOGS overestimates the prevalence of pathological gambling in the general population compared with DSM criteria (Welte, Barnes, Wieczorek, Tidwell, & Parker, 2001).

Ladouceur, Bouchard, et al. (2000) found that many respondents misinterpret some items on the SOGS. Stinchfield (2002a) administered the SOGS to 803 individuals drawn from a general population sample and 1,589 individuals seeking gambling treatment. He found that it had adequate reliability in both samples—.69 and .86, respectively. It also correlated well with DSM–IV diagnostic criteria, and it differentiated the two samples. In the general population respondents, a SOGS cutoff value of 5 had a false-positive rate of only 0.5%. Nevertheless, this percentage was derived from an extraordinarily small sample, as only 3 individuals in the sample of 803 met criteria for pathological gambling using DSM–IV symptom counts, and only 4 general population respondents scored above 5 on the SOGS. Therefore, more research, with larger sample sizes in the general population, is needed to further evaluate sensitivity and false-positive rates. One recommendation for researchers and clinicians is to use the SOGS as an initial screening instrument and then to administer a clinical interview to verify the diagnosis.

Diagnostic Interview for Gambling Severity

The Diagnostic Interview for Gambling Severity (DIGS; Winters, Specker, & Stinchfield, 2002) is a comprehensive instrument that assesses gambling problems as well as other areas of functioning and consequences related to gambling involvement. These include psychiatric symptoms, financial difficulties, and legal problems. A trained professional administers the interview, and the diagnostic gambling section consists of 20 questions. The 10 DSM–IV criteria for pathological gambling are asked in two different forms, to ensure that the respondent understands the question and to maximize obtaining a positive response if the respondent meets the criterion. A positive answer to either form is counted as meeting that specific criterion.

The DIGS demonstrates good reliability and validity. When administered to 158 patients admitted to Minnesota outpatient gambling treatment programs, 87% met five or more DSM–IV criteria for Level 3 gambling. Internal consistency for the 20 DIGS questions was .92 and, when counting affirmative responses to the 10 DSM–IV criteria, it was .88. To examine convergent validity, Winters, Specker, et al. (2002) conducted correlations of the number of DSM–IV symptoms endorsed using the DIGS and the frequency of past-year gambling, the amount of gambling debt, and the number of financial problems experienced. For each variable, the correlation was positive and statistically significant. Correlations ranged from .39 to .47. The age of onset of gambling was negatively and significantly associated with the number of diagnostic symptoms endorsed (−.28), whereas the number of legal problems and social problems experienced were positively related to DIGS symptoms (.50 and .57, respectively).

To establish discriminant validity, Winters, Specker, et al. (2002) compared responses to other gambling items in the 138 individuals who met *DSM–IV* criteria for pathological gambling, using the DIGS with the responses of the 20 individuals who did not. On virtually every variable, individuals who met criteria endorsed more gambling-related problems than those who did not. For example, the diagnosed gamblers had a greater frequency of gambling in the past month (19 vs. 15 days), a larger gambling debt ($20,000 vs. $4,000), more financial problems (52% vs. 10%), and more legal difficulties (31% vs. 10%). They were more likely to have had an early onset of gambling (50% vs. 6%), and they were more likely to gamble at least weekly (93% vs. 65%).

Winters, Specker, et al. (2002) also conducted a principal-components factor analysis of the *DSM–IV* criteria as evaluated using the DIGS. Although two factors emerged with eigenvalues greater than 1, one factor seemed to be the most parsimonious explanation of the scale. The only questions that loaded most heavily on Factor 2 were those related to illegal activities, but such questions also loaded on Factor 1. The eigenvalue associated with Factor 1 was 5.0, and it explained 49.6% of the variance in responses. For Factor 2, the eigenvalue was only 1.1, explaining just 10.9% additional variance. Thus, the *DSM–IV* criteria as assessed by the DIGS seem to characterize a one-dimensional construct. The internal consistency and the convergent and discriminant validity of this instrument appear promising. The Minnesota treatment community uses this instrument extensively, and DIGS gambling questions are included in the Gambling Assessment Monitoring Treatment Outcomes Monitoring System.

Stinchfield (2003) extended evaluation of the psychometric properties of the DIGS to the general population. He administered a 19-item version of the DIGS to 803 adults in a telephone survey along with 259 individuals seeking gambling treatment. Internal consistencies for the 10 criteria were .81 for the general population and .77 for the treatment-seeking sample. The correlation between SOGS and DIGS scores were .77 and .75 in the respective samples, suggesting convergent validity. *Sensitivity* refers to the probability that a test result will be positive given that the person actually has the disorder. High sensitivity indicates the test is useful for screening purposes, identifying a high proportion of true positives while producing few false negatives. *Specificity* is the probability that a test result will be negative given that the person does not have the disorder. Tests with high specificity produce positive results almost only when the person has the disorder and not otherwise. Using a cutoff score of 5, Stinchfield found that sensitivity was .950 and specificity was .996. Thus, the DIGS appears to reliably and accurately classify pathological gamblers both in the general population and among treatment seekers.

National Opinion Research Center DSM Screen for Gambling Problems

The National Opinion Research Center DSM Screen for Gambling Problems (NODS) was developed as part of the National Gambling Impact Study Commission (1999). Like the DIGS, questions on the NODS are based on *DSM–IV* criteria for pathological gambling. One difference between the DIGS and the NODS is that the NODS does not have two questions for each of the 10 *DSM* criteria, but it does ask some of the criteria in two forms. Another difference between the instruments is that the NODS presents each of the criteria with respect to lifetime as well as past-year occurrence. The lifetime questions are shown in Exhibit 3.2.

Only limited data are available on the psychometric properties of the NODS. Prior to its use in the National Opinion Research Center survey (Gerstein et al., 1999), a sample of 40 individuals receiving outpatient treatment for pathological gambling responded to the NODS in a telephone survey. Of these individuals, 95% met criteria for a diagnosis of pathological gambling using the NODS. As expected, scores on the past-year version were slightly lower than the lifetime version. In addition, the NODS was administered over the telephone to a random sample of 45 respondents in the Chicago area. Test–retest reliability of the NODS across a 2- to 4-week period was evaluated in 44 cases (drawn from both the community and the treatment samples), and both the lifetime ($r = .99$) and the past-year ($r = .98$) versions were highly reliable.

Hodgins (2002) administered the past-year version of the NODS over the telephone to 86 individuals 1 year after they had completed a study evaluating brief treatments for gambling. Internal consistency was .79 when examining affirmative responses to the 10 *DSM–IV* items and .84 for the 17 items in the full scale, representing fair to good reliability. Principal-component analysis of the 10 *DSM* items revealed that three factors achieved eigenvalues greater than 1 and accounted for 59% of the variance. Four items reflecting negative behavioral consequences loaded on Factor 1 and explained 22% of the variance. The second factor consisted of items associated with preoccupation and impaired control and accounted for 19% of the variance. The items related to family, social, and employment problems loaded on both Factor 1 and Factor 2. Tolerance, withdrawal, and relief gambling loaded on the third factor, which accounted for 17% of the variance. Thus, the NODS has strong validity in identifying clinically confirmed, treatment-seeking pathological gamblers, and it has high retest

EXHIBIT 3.2
The National Opinion Research Center
DSM Screen for Gambling Problems

---

1. Have there been any periods lasting two weeks or longer   YES   NO
   when you spent a lot of time thinking about your gambling
   experiences or planning out future gambling ventures or bets?
   OR
   Have there been periods lasting two weeks or longer when   YES   NO
   you spent a lot of time thinking about ways of getting money to
   gamble with?

2. Have there been periods when you needed to gamble with   YES   NO
   increasing amounts of money or with larger bets than before in
   order to get the same feeling of excitement?

3. Have you tried to stop, cut down, or control your gambling?   YES   NO
   AND
   On one or more of the times when you tried to stop, cut down,   YES   NO   N/A
   or control your gambling, were you restless or irritable?

4. Have you tried *but not succeeded* in stopping, cutting down, or   YES   NO
   controlling your gambling?
   AND
   If so, has this happened three or more times?   YES   NO   N/A

5. Have you gambled as a way to escape from personal   YES   NO
   problems?
   OR
   Have you gambled to relieve uncomfortable feelings such as   YES   NO
   guilt, anxiety, helplessness, or depression?

6. Has there been a period when, if you lost money gambling on   YES   NO
   one day, you would often return another day to get even?

7. Have you more than once lied to family members, friends, or   YES   NO
   others about how much you gamble, or how much money you
   lost on gambling?
   AND
   If so, has this happened three or more times?   YES   NO   N/A

8. Have you written a bad check, or taken money that didn't   YES   NO
   belong to you from family members or anyone else in order to
   pay for your gambling?

9. Has your gambling caused serious or repeated problems in   YES   NO
   your relationships with any of your family members or friends?
   OR
   Has your gambling caused you any problems in school, such   YES   NO   N/A
   as missing classes or days of school or getting worse grades?
   OR
   Has your gambling ever caused you to lose a job, have trouble   YES   NO
   with your job, or miss out on an important job or career
   opportunity?

10. Have you needed to ask family members or anyone else to   YES   NO
    loan you money or otherwise bail you out of a desperate
    money situation that was largely caused by your gambling?

---

reliability. However, its reliability and validity in the general population are understudied.

A recent study examined some aspects of the NODS within the general population. Toce-Gerstein, Gerstein, and Volberg (2003) reanalyzed data obtained as part of the National Gambling Impact Study (Gerstein et al., 1999). They inspected the relationships between the distributions of responses to NODS items among the 399 people who responded affirmatively to at least one DSM criterion for pathological gambling using this instrument. They found that most gamblers who met only one or two criteria reported chasing their losses, or gambling in hopes of winning back lost money. Level 2 gamblers had extended problems indicative of gambling-related fantasy; they endorsed items associated with lying, escape, and preoccupation. Level 3 gamblers reported loss of control, withdrawal symptoms, risking social relationships, and the need for financial bailouts. Only the most severely disturbed gamblers committed illegal acts to support their gambling. Toce-Gerstein et al. (2003) concluded that chasing may represent a subclinical behavioral pattern and that pathological gambling may have two distinct levels of severity.

Diagnostic Interview Schedule

The Diagnostic Interview Schedule (DIS; Robins, Cottler, Bucholz, & Compton, 1996) is a structured instrument for assessing psychiatric diagnoses in epidemiological studies. A four-item scale of the DIS was used to evaluate disordered gambling during the 1980 Epidemiological Catchment Area Survey, conducted at the St. Louis site. Cunningham-Williams, Cottler, Compton, and Spitznagel (1998) published these data. To be classified as a Level 3 gambler, one had to report gambling at least twice in one's lifetime and have thoughts that one gambled too much. In addition, one had to endorse experiencing at least two of the following problems because of gambling: inability to pay bills, trouble at home or at work, and borrowing or stealing money to gamble. Level 2 gambling was defined as having gambled two or more times and experiencing at least one of the other symptoms. Although the DIS has been used in some large population surveys to assess disordered gambling (see chaps. 2 and 5), it has not been subject to extensive psychometric testing.

Gambling Assessment Module for the DSM–IV

The gambling items of the DIS have been updated to coincide with DSM–IV criteria. This newer version, which is undergoing development, is termed the Gambling Assessment Module (GAM–IV). It collects information on the number of diagnostic criteria met, frequency and reasons for gambling, problems associated with gambling, and treatment history. Its psychometric properties have not yet been published, but initial pretesting studies are promising (Cunningham-Williams, Cottler, & Books, 2002). A large study evaluating reliability and validity of this instrument is underway, and pencil-and-paper, interview, and computerized versions will be available.

Lie/Bet Questionnaire

Finally, because of its brevity, the Lie/Bet Questionnaire (E. E. Johnson et al., 1997) has been implemented in some clinical and screening settings. This is a very brief, two-item questionnaire. The two questions are as follows:

1. Have you ever had to lie to people important to you about how much you gambled?
2. Have you ever felt the need to bet more and more money?

These two items were selected from the 10 *DSM–IV* criteria because they emerged as the best predictors of pathological gambling status based on logistic regression. In the initial study, E. E. Johnson et al. (1997) studied samples consisting of 191 male GA members and 171 male nonproblem gambling control participants, who were employees at the Department of Veterans Affairs. A positive response to either or both questions seemed to accurately classify 95.3% of the respondents. In a follow-up study, E. E. Johnson, Hamer, and Nora (1998) administered the Lie/Bet Questionnaire to GA members and a control sample consisting of both sexes: 116 male GA members and 179 male control participants, and 30 female GA members and 98 female control participants.

The sensitivity was .99 in the first sample (E. E. Johnson et al., 1997) and 1.0 in the second sample (E. E. Johnson et al., 1998). The specificities were .91 and .85 in the first and second studies, respectively. The predictive values of a positive result were .92 and .78 in the two studies, meaning that, of the 206 or 188 people classified pathological gamblers by the Lie/Bet Questionnaire, 190 and 146, respectively, actually were pathological gamblers. The predictive values of a negative result were .99 and 1.00 in the two respective studies. These results indicate that, of the 156 or 235 people who were not classified as pathological gamblers by the Lie/Bet Questionnaire, 155 and 235, respectively, were actually not pathological gamblers (E. E. Johnson et al., 1997, 1998).

An advantage of the Lie/Bet Questionnaire is its brevity, especially for use as a brief screen. However, no other studies of the Lie/Bet Questionnaire have been published. Generalization of the initial promising findings in sensitivity and specificity may be limited to GA members, who are willing to admit a need for help. GA members may differ markedly from Level 3 gamblers in the community who have not sought help. More extensive psychometric testing of this instrument is necessary before it is implemented as a screening tool in general populations.

To illustrate the use of these instruments, and how they may differentially label gambling patterns, I next provide a case example.

Case example. John, a 36-year-old man, began gambling at age 10, when he and his father made small bets on games they watched together on television. During middle school, John bet about once a week with friends, starting with small amounts of change. In high school, he progressed toward wagering $10 and $20, and sometimes even up to $100, on a game. He saw gambling as a way of making spending money, and he never accumulated any real debt. Although he sometimes borrowed money from his brothers, he managed to pay them back the next time he won.

In college, gambling took over John's social life and was his primary source of income. He began loaning money to others during major sports seasons, and he also organized betting pools among his classmates. Although he was careful not to overdo it, John also bet on cards and sporting events himself from time to time. He lost a bit more than he won when actually gambling, but overall gambling was still profitable. He earned enough money as a bookie to buy a used sports car for himself and occasional expensive presents for his friends and family.

After college, John got a job as a stockbroker. Stock exchanging itself can be considered gambling, especially when it is done with one's own money and high-risk stocks are being traded regularly. However, John was engaging in stockbrokering as a profession, and at this early stage in his career, his own gambling was limited to occasional football games. He married Beth, who also had a high-paying job, and they had a child together. Beth quit work after the baby was born, and the bills became John's sole responsibility. John started going out with his friends more and more often on the weekends, and the evenings out always involved gambling—on cards, sports, or both. When he won, he would come home with large amounts of cash and buy something for his wife or baby later that weekend. When he lost, he sometimes was unable to pay the car loans or credit card bills. He borrowed money from his father at times, to tide him over until he won again.

Beth does not know the extent of John's gambling, and she pays little attention to the finances of the family. They feel they have a good relationship, and they rarely argue. John limits his gambling to off-work hours. Although he sometimes feels guilty about where his money goes when he loses, and he occasionally feels that he gambles too much, he generally enjoys his nights out gambling. He remembers all the times he has won, and whenever he's on a losing streak, he feels that he's bound to win again soon. When asked if he thinks he has a gambling problem, he says no.

Comment. The SOGS, NODS, DIS, and Lie/Bet Questionnaire can all be used to classify John's gambling behavior, but they yield different classifications. On the SOGS, John's gambling seems to fit the following criteria (see Exhibit 3.1): (1) he goes back most of the time to win back lost money, (4) he gambles more than he intends, (6) he feels guilty about gambling, and (15) he has borrowed money from relatives. According to his story, John does not seem to (2) claim to be winning when he is losing, (3) feel he has a problem with gambling, or (5) experience criticism about gambling. He (7) does not seem to feel unable to stop gambling, (8) does not hide his gambling, and (10) does not have arguments about money that center on gambling. He has not reported (11) being unable to pay people back or (12) losing time at work because of gambling. Also, according to his story, he has borrowed only from his relatives and not from other sources. Therefore, his SOGS score appears to be a 4, indicative of Level 2 gambling.

On the NODS, John seems to meet three or fewer criteria for pathological gambling: He gambles with increasing amounts of money, chases losses, and relies on others to relieve financial problems. Although observers may endorse those criteria in John's behavior, he may or may not have responded affirmatively when asked the questions directly. In any case, John would be unlikely to endorse other symptoms of pathological gambling, such as preoccupation, attempts to cut down, withdrawal symptoms when not gambling, gambling to escape negative moods, lying, committing illegal acts, or jeopardizing important relationships. Thus, according to the NODS, John is likely to be classified as a Level 2, or perhaps even a Level 1, gambler.

In contrast, on the DIS John would likely admit to three of the four symptoms: sometimes gambling too much, inability to pay bills, and borrowing money to gamble. Endorsing three of the symptoms on the DIS would classify John as a Level 3 gambler. Similarly, on the Lie/Bet Questionnaire, John may be classified as a Level 3 gambler. Although he has not lied to people important to him about how much he gambles, he does seem to feel the need to bet more and more money to make up for his prior gambling losses.

This exercise demonstrates how different instruments may classify the same gambling behaviors in different manners. No instrument is necessarily better than others, but the purpose of screening must be kept in mind. In a general population survey, John's responses may classify him in a high- or relatively high-risk category. For clinical screening, his responses to the briefer scales may warrant a closer examination of his gambling using diagnostic instruments.

INSTRUMENTS THAT ASSESS SEVERITY OF
GAMBLING PROBLEMS

In addition to screening and diagnosing individuals as Level 1, 2, or 3 gamblers, identifying the severity of gambling and gambling-related problems is necessary. As studies are developed and clinicians use techniques to treat pathological gamblers, the need to assess whether reductions in severity of gambling and gambling-related problems occur over time or in response to interventions is of paramount importance. A common approach to evaluating changes in gambling is to assess the number of *DSM* criteria endorsed over a specific time frame. However, this method will simply inform the researcher or clinician whether a person who once met diagnostic criteria no longer does. Another popular approach to assessing outcomes is to evaluate changes in past-month SOGS scores. The validity of this approach is questionable, because 1 month may be too short a time to accurately gauge changes in gambling-related problems. More specific instruments are being developed and used to assess changes in gambling and severity of gambling problems over time, as I describe next.

Gambling Treatment Outcome Monitoring System

Stinchfield and Winters (1996) developed a systematic way of assessing gambling severity using the Gambling Treatment Outcome Monitoring System (GAMTOMS). The DIGS (described earlier) is contained within the GAMTOMS, and the GAMTOMS also collects information in more depth than the DIGS on the types of gambling in which the individual engages; the frequency of the individual's gambling; and the severity of his or her gambling-related problems, including financial, social, and legal difficulties. The GAMTOMS can serve as a comprehensive assessment instrument at intake to gambling treatment facilities because it has sections on demographics, medical status, and treatment histories for psychiatric, substance abuse, and gambling problems. It collects information about other psychiatric symptoms as well, including substance use, anxiety, depression, mania, impulse control, and eating problems, as well as avoidant characteristics, attention-deficit/hyperactivity disorder, conduct disorder, and antisocial personality characteristics.

The GAMTOMS is administered as a structured interview, and information can also be obtained from significant others and treatment professionals. It can be used for screening, diagnosis, measurement of change over time, and posttreatment follow-up evaluations. Its wording was chosen to be understood by individuals with a sixth-grade reading level. Its scales have good reliability as measured by Cronbach's alpha coefficient; coefficients for the specific scales are as follows: SOGS Scores, α = .80, *DSM–IV* Diagnostic Criteria, α = .89, Financial Problems, α = .78, and Gambling Problem Recognition, α = .89. Convergent validity of the GAMTOMS was evaluated by comparing scores derived on it with scores obtained from other instruments, such as the SOGS. In addition, GAMTOMS scores were correlated with other measures, such as gambling frequency and debt. Discriminant validity was demonstrated by low correlations between scores and variables that should not be related to gambling problem severity, such as demographic characteristics (Stinchfield & Winters, 1996).

Addiction Severity Index

The Addiction Severity Index (ASI), created by McLellan et al. (1985), is the most widely used tool for evaluating problems related to drug use and monitoring changes in substance abusers. The ASI was developed in 1980, and it has been updated several times. It has seven sections that assess the severity of medical, employment, alcohol, other drug, legal, social, and psychiatric problems. Because many of these life areas are also affected by gambling disorders, the ASI has the advantage of assessing problems along a number of domains. Composite scores in each domain can be derived and range from .00, indicative of no problems in that area, to 1.00, indicative of very severe problems. Although originally developed as a structured interview, self- and computer-administered versions are available. Reliability and validity of the ASI in substance-abusing populations are established (Kosten, Rounsaville, & Kleber, 1983; McLellan, Arndt, Woody, & Metzger, 1993; McLellan et al., 1985), and scores are sensitive and responsive to treatment (Alterman et al., 1994; McLellan et al., 1993, 1996). Weisner, McLellan, and Hunkeler (2000) described normative data of the ASI in non-substance-abusing members of an HMO, suggesting widespread application of this instrument.

The ASI—Gambling Severity Index (ASI–G; Lesieur & Blume, 1991a) is a supplement to the ASI. In the original version, 30 items were added that examined such issues as fraud, embezzlement, and gambling offenses to the list of legal problems and a set of questions regarding frequency of gambling and gambling-related problems in the past month. Only five to six items are included in deriving the composite score. Lesieur and Blume (1991a, 1992) administered the ASI–G to 119 patients who scored greater than 5 on the SOGS at intake to an inpatient treatment program for substance abuse and pathological gambling. A follow-up interview was conducted 6 to 14 months later on 72 members of the original sample. The ASI–G had adequate internal consistency (Cronbach's alpha = .73) and good convergent validity with the SOGS (r = .57).

EXHIBIT 3.3
Questions Included in the Addiction Severity Index Gambling Subscale

1. How many days have you gambled in the past 30 days?
   Include days that you gambled in any form, including informal bets, purchases of lottery or scratch tickets, bets on sporting events, casino gambling, etc.

2. How much money have you spent on gambling in total in the past month?

3. How many days in the past 30 have you experienced gambling problems?

4. How bothered or troubled have you been by gambling problems in the past 30 days?
   (responses coded on 0–4 scale)

5. How important to you now is treatment for gambling problems?
   (responses coded on 0–4 scale)

The following formula is used to derive composite scores:

Composite score = (days of gambling in last 30 / 150) + (days experienced gambling problems in last 30 / 150) + (how troubled by gambling problems / 20) + (how important is gambling treatment / 20) + $\log_{10}$($ spent gambling in past 30 days) / 36.5.

For participants who report spending no money on gambling in the past month, a "0" is substituted in the last part of the equation where the log is located.

Note. From "Validity of a Gambling Scale for the Addiction Severity Index," by N. M. Petry, 2003c, *Journal of Nervous and Mental Disease, 191*(6), pp. 399–407. Copyright 2003 by Lippincott Williams & Wilkins. Reprinted with permission.

I (Petry, 2003c) further evaluated the ASI–G for assessing gambling and related problems in 597 participants from four different populations: (a) pathological gamblers enrolled in a treatment study, (b) pathological gamblers initiating outpatient treatment at a community-based program, (c) Level 2 gamblers recruited by means of advertisements, and (d) substance abusers. Each sample completed the ASI, along with the supplemental gambling subscale (ASI–G), the items of which are shown in Exhibit 3.3.

Internal consistency of the ASI–G was good (α = .90), and a principal-components analysis indicated that a single factor structure explained 73% of the variance in responses (Petry, 2003c). ASI–G scores demonstrated excellent convergent validity with other measures of gambling. For example, ASI–G scores correlated .75 with past-month SOGS scores and .58 with past-year *DSM–IV* criteria endorsed. ASI–G scores also correlated with collateral informant reports of days (r = .42) and amounts (r = .67) gambled, as well as clinician-rated reports of severity of gambling (r = .45), demonstrating external validity. ASI–G scores discriminated among the samples tested, with mean scores of .64 to .71 (*SD* = .22) in the two treatment-seeking samples, to scores of .30±.16 in Level 2 gamblers and scores of .04±.04 among individuals seeking substance abuse treatment. The temporal stability of ASI–G scores was high over a 1-month period for substance-abusing patients who were not seeking gambling treatment ($r = .76$). For treatment-seeking gamblers, ASI–G scores decreased over time, to an average of .37±25. Regression analyses revealed that the number of treatment sessions attended was significantly associated with reductions in ASI–G scores.

Together, these data suggest that the ASI–G may be useful for assessing the severity of gambling problems in a variety of populations, and it appears to be sensitive to changes in gambling severity over time. Use of the ASI also has the advantage of assessing problem areas along a number of other domains: employment, legal, substance use, family–social, and psychiatric. The ASI–G may be particularly useful for evaluating changes in gambling behavior in patients seeking substance abuse treatment, as the ASI is often used in these settings. However, as noted in Exhibit 3.3, and indicated in the case example detailed later in this chapter, ASI–G scores are relatively complicated to derive.

Timeline Follow-Back

The timeline follow-back procedure (TLFB) was first developed to assess alcohol consumption (M. B. Sobell et al., 1980). This interviewer-administered instrument uses calendar prompts to cue patients to remember the patterning of their alcohol consumption over time intervals. The TLFB typically assesses frequency and quantity of alcohol use over recent time intervals, such as 1 or several months. Data derived from the TLFB are often used as the primary outcome data for treatment studies of individuals with alcohol use disorders. The TLFB has been adapted to assess other drug use behaviors as well. Data suggest that these self-report instruments are highly correlated with objective indicators of drug use (Fals-Stewart, O'Farrell, Freitas, McFarlin, & Rutigliano, 2000). Some investigators (e.g., Del Boca & Noll, 2000; L. C. Sobell, Agrawal, & Sobell, 1997) have suggested that self-reports may be better indicators of drug use than biological markers such as urine, saliva, or blood testing. As long as confidentiality is ensured, and no consequences to reporting use are imposed, substance abusers seem to provide accurate self-reports of their drug use using TLFB methodology.

Taber, McCormick, Russo, Adkins, and Ramirez (1987) first suggested the use of the TLFB for assessing gambling. They found that treatment-seeking gamblers' self-reports of days and amounts gambled were highly related to reports obtained by collaterals, who were independently interviewed. Hodgins and Makarchuk (2003) evaluated the test–retest reliability of TLFB days and amounts gambled over a 6-month period. One year after completing a treatment study, 35 gamblers completed the TLFB twice, 2 to 3 weeks apart. Test–retest reliability coefficients ranged from good to excellent for all time periods ($rs = .42–.98$), for both days and dollars gambled. Collateral reports were highly correlated with patient reports for both days and dollars gambled, with correlations of about .60. These data suggest preliminary evidence of reliability and validity of the TLFB methodology for assessing gambling severity.

Pathological Gambling Modification of the Yale–Brown Obsessive–Compulsive Scale

On the basis of their conceptualization of gambling as an obsessive–compulsive spectrum disorder, DeCaria et al. (1998) developed the Pathological Gambling modification of the Yale–Brown Obsessive–Compulsive Scale (PG–YBOCS). It is a 10-item scale that assesses distress and interference in one's daily living caused by actual gambling behavior or thoughts related to gambling. The first 5 items reflect time occupied, interference, distress, resistance, and degree of control over gambling thoughts and urges, whereas the last 5 items relate to these same symptoms in terms of actual gambling behaviors. Preliminary data with a small sample of 8 pathological gamblers suggests that the PG–YBOCS has a high correlation ($r = .89$) with the Pathological Gambling Clinical Global Impression Scale (Guy, 1976), described in the section titled Clinical Global Impression Scales. The PG–YBOCS also seems to have good convergent validity with the SOGS ($r = .86$; Hollander et al., 1998), but further research is needed to confirm these initial results, given the small sample size. This instrument has primarily been used in trials evaluating pharmacotherapies (see chap. 7).

Gambling Symptom Assessment Scale

The Gambling Symptom Assessment Scale (G-SAS; Kim, Grant, Adson, & Shin, 2001) is a 10- to 12-item self-report scale that assesses gambling urges, thoughts, and behaviors during the prior week. Items reflect the frequency, intensity, and duration of gambling urges; the frequency and duration of gambling thoughts and behaviors; the degree of excitement caused by imminent gambling; and subjective distress and personal troubles caused by gambling. Each item is rated on a Likert scale. As with the PG–YBOCS, the G-SAS has been used primarily in medication studies. In a sample of 58 pathological gamblers, the test–retest reliability of the original 10-item version of the scale was .70. Cronbach's alpha of internal consistency was .89. The G-SAS demonstrated good convergent validity with the Clinical Global Impression improvement ratings (see the following section), with correlations ranging from .68 to .82. Principal-components analyses of the original scale indicated that both one- and two-factor solutions fit the model. In subsequent versions of the G-SAS, 1 of the original items was removed and others were added, resulting in a 12-item scale. This modified scale also appears to have concordance with Clinical Global Impression ratings in a small sample of patients (Kim et al., 2001), but additional psychometric testing of the modified version is not yet published.

Clinical Global Impression Scales

Clinical Global Impression (CGI) scales (Guy, 1976) are commonly used in measuring outcomes in pharmacological trials. Usually, these are two-item Likert scales assessing overall severity and improvement in symptoms, such as "How severe are the gambling symptoms?" and "To what extent have the gambling symptoms improved?" Responses to the latter question, for example, range from 1 (*"very much improved"*) to 2 (*"much improved"*) to 3 (*"minimally improved"*) to 4 (*"no change"*), and responses to the former question range from *none/mild* to *severe* on a similar Likert scale. Both patient and clinician (or researcher) ratings can be obtained. In studies of medications for pathological gambling, CGI scores were highly correlated with PG–YBOCS scores ($r = .89$; Hollander et al., 1998) and G-SAS scores ($rs = .78–.81$; Kim et al., 2001). This instrument has the advantages of brevity and construct validity; however, interrater reliabilities are not well established, and more indices of gambling involvement and outcome analyses would need to be assessed along with CGI results, as only 8 to 16 patients were included in the initial analyses.

The use of some of these instruments is illustrated in the case example of John, continued below.

Case example continued. One night, John came home after a long night of gambling with his friends, and Beth was still up, clearly very angry with him. She started yelling at him as he came toward her. "What are you doing? What did you do with my money?" she cried. She discovered that he had taken a couple thousand dollars from her personal savings account, without her knowledge. Beth also felt that John was dishonest with her about his whereabouts and his management of the family finances. John immediately admitted his guilt and told her he had only borrowed it— for gambling. He promised to pay it back and never to take money from her again.

For several weeks, their relationship was very shaky. Beth insisted that John seek treatment for his gambling, and she agreed to attend the initial session with him. At that session, the therapist asks John detailed questions about his gambling. The therapist discovers that he gambles about 4 days a week, and wagers an average of $1,200 a month. John does not feel he has a gambling problem because he claims he is eventually able to pay back any money that he loses. He does feel he needs gambling treatment, but only because it will help him appease his wife.

Comment. Given this new information, John's behavior results in new scores on the SOGS, NODS, DIS, and Lie/Bet Questionnaire; his ASI–G score can also be determined. On the SOGS, John's gambling seems to fit the same four criteria as before, although he may now also gain a couple of additional points. He may now be engaging in arguments over money with his wife (No. 10; see Exhibit 3.1). He has also now borrowed from his wife (No. 14). Therefore, his SOGS score may rise to 6, indicative of Level 3 gambling.

On the NODS, John's behaviors now may indicate Level 3 gambling. In addition to the three criteria that were fulfilled previously (gambles with increasing amounts of money, chases losses, and relies on others to relieve his financial problems), John now may also endorse the items related to lying and jeopardizing important relationships. Thus, John may now be classified as a Level 3 gambler on this instrument as well.

On the DIS and the Lie/Bet Questionnaire, John was already classified as a Level 3 gambler. Depending on the severity of his problems with his wife and whether he considers himself to have lied to her, he may now endorse all four items on the DIS and both of the Lie/Bet questions.

On the ASI–G, John's score would depend on his responses to questions related to the number of days he has experienced gambling problems, how troubled he is by gambling problems, and his desire for treatment. Most likely, he would state that he has not experienced any days of gambling problems and that he is not troubled by gambling problems per se but that his wife blew the issue out of proportion. His desire for treatment is minimal and only related to his marital problems. Referring to the scoring system for the ASI–G described in Exhibit 3.3, John's score would probably be $16 / 150 + 0 / 150 + 0 / 20 + 1 / 20 + \log_{10}(1200) / 36.5 = 0.35$. Note that this score is within the range of Level 2 gamblers and much lower than that of treatment-seeking Level 3 gamblers (Petry, 2003c).

Case example continued. After 2 months in weekly gambling treatment, John ceased gambling almost completely. He wagers now only about once or twice a month, spending $10 to $20 on a sporting bet. He does not feel that he needs gambling treatment and, once Beth's anger diminishes, John wants to stop seeing the therapist.

Comment. Given this change in circumstances, John's ASI–G score can be redetermined, and his improvement can be rated on the CGI scale. John's current ASI–G score would be $= 3 / 150 + 0 / 150 + 0 / 20 + 0 / 20 + \log_{10}(\$45) / 36.5 = 0.11$. This is a pretty substantial reduction in severity of gambling problems. On the CGI, the therapist may rate John as a 1 ("*very much improved*") or a 2 ("*much improved*").

The therapist may feel that John could continue to benefit from treatment, as he has not ceased gambling entirely. The therapist may feel that

John's gambling may again escalate now that the crisis has abated. Neverthe-less, convincing John of his continued need for treatment may be very difficult, especially considering that John's gambling problem was never severe and he never felt that he had hit rock bottom, or sunk to his lowest point and lost a lot of money, like other gamblers he knows. Although not addressed explicitly in this example, John's only psychosocial problems appear to be his strained relationship with his wife. Assuming that his marital and family situation remains intact and that he has no employment, substance abuse, or other psychiatric difficulties, John may decide he has no further need for therapy. I describe issues related to engaging Level 2 and early-stage Level 3 gamblers in treatment in chapter 14.

SUMMARY AND CLINICAL IMPLICATIONS

As demonstrated in the preceding sections and the case example, a number of different instruments have been developed to assess prevalence rates, diagnoses, and severity of problems related to gambling. No single instrument is best suited for any of these purposes; instead, a variety of possibilities are available, all with advantages and disadvantages. Clinicians deciding on a screening or diagnostic instrument should consider the sample to be studied, the purpose of assessment, and the length of the battery, as well as psychometric properties of available instruments. If a brief screen is intended for use in a clinical setting or for estimates of prevalence rates or comorbidity, the NODS or the DIGS may be the optimal choice.

For evaluation of clinical outcomes, the CGI, in conjunction with the TLFB or ASI–G, could be considered if only quantity and frequency variables are of interest. The PG–YBOCS or G-SAS can also be used, although these instruments focus more on thoughts, cravings, and urges and less on gambling behaviors relative to the other instruments. The ASI or GAMTOMS can be administered if a more comprehensive assessment of psychosocial func-tioning is of value to the research project or to the clinician. In addition, other clinical assessments may be included, such as depression or anxiety screens, as these clinical conditions share strong comorbidity with pathologi-cal gambling (see chap. 5) and may need to be addressed during the course of treatment.

In the next several chapters I describe the etiology and comorbidity of pathological gambling with other psychiatric conditions. Many of the studies outlined in the next chapters have used the instruments described in this chapter. The psychometric properties of the instruments should be considered to the extent that they can influence the relationships noted between pathological gambling and other disorders or conditions.

II

ETIOLOGY

4

DEMOGRAPHIC CORRELATES

In an attempt to understand the etiology of pathological gambling, I review the evidence suggesting a link between disordered gambling and some basic demographic variables. Investigators have evaluated the association of disordered gambling with several characteristics: younger age, minority ethnicity, lower socioeconomic class, single or divorced marital status, and male gender. For each potential risk factor, I first review general population surveys; then I detail evidence from individuals seeking treatment for pathological gambling. In the final section of this chapter, I synthesize data on gender and age differences in gambling.

GENERAL POPULATION SURVEYS

In this section I examine demographic risk factors using general population surveys.

Age

Age seems to be inversely related to gambling problems in studies conducted in North America as well as other regions worldwide. As I discuss in more detail in chapter 15, rates of disordered gambling are higher among adolescents and young adults than among older adults. Shaffer, Hall, and Vander Bilt (1999) found that lifetime prevalence rates of Level 2 and

Level 3 gambling were 9.5% and 3.9%, respectively, in adolescents, and 9.3% and 4.7%, respectively, in college students. In contrast, prevalence rates in general adult population surveys are about 3.8% for Level 2 gambling and 1.6% for Level 3 gambling. Thus, young people suffer from disordered gambling at about two to three times the rates of adults.

Similar findings are noted when rates of disordered gambling are determined independently across different age groups within a particular study. The National Research Council (NRC, 1999) reported that 17 of the studies identified in Shaffer, Hall, and Vander Bilt's (1999) meta-analysis provided breakdowns of prevalence rates across age groups. In 14 of these 17 studies, individuals under age 30 disproportionately suffered from gambling problems. Gerstein et al. (1999) also reported on prevalence rates of Level 2–3 gambling across age groups in their general population survey. Respondents aged 18 to 29 years experienced disordered gambling at a rate of about 3.1%, compared with 1.5% for the 30- to 39-year-olds, 2.4% for the 40- to 49-year-olds, and 2.8% for the 50- to 64-year-olds. Among those in the oldest cohort, over age 65, the prevalence rate was significantly lower: 0.3%. Welte, Barnes, Wieczorek, Tidwell, and Parker (2001) also noted an age-related trend. The odds ratio was 0.6, suggesting that for each decade of life one had a 40% decreased risk of gambling problems, but this age effect was no longer statistically significant when other demographic variables were included in the analyses. Nevertheless, the bulk of the studies suggest that younger age groups are overrepresented among individuals with gambling problems.

Prevalence studies from other countries lend further support for the negative association of age with disordered gambling. In Table 4.1, prevalence data are presented across different age groups from the two national surveys conducted in the United States, as well as surveys from other countries. In general, prevalence rates are derived from the South Oaks Gambling Screen (SOGS; Lesieur & Blume, 1987) in most of the European, New Zealand, and Australian surveys. Asian studies used the Diagnostic Interview Schedule (DIS; Robins, Cottler, Bucholz, & Compton, 1996), and U.S. studies used the National Opinion Research Center DSM Screen for Gambling Problems (National Gambling Impact Study Commission, 1999; Gerstein et al., 1999) or DIS (Welte et al., 2001). In chapter 2, I presented more specific information about the studies included in these tables, and readers should consult chapter 3 for a discussion of the development and psychometric testing of the instruments.

The Australian study (Productivity Commission, 1999) did not present data on prevalence rates per se, so instead ratios of Level 2–3 to nongamblers are reported within each age category. The age groups represented in Table 4.1 typically represent ages 18 to 30 years as the youngest cohort, 30 to 49 years as the younger middle, 50 to 65 years as the older middle, and over

TABLE 4.1
Prevalence Rates of Disordered Gambling in Adult Population Surveys, Based on Respondents' Ages

Country and study	Youngest cohort	Younger middle cohort	Older middle cohort	Oldest cohort	Instrument used	Lifetime (LT) or past year (PY)	Gambling level measured
Australia Productivity Commission (1999)[a]	42 : 20	26 : 28	25 : 28	7 : 24	SOGS	PY[c]	Ratio of Level 2–3 to nongamblers
Canada Ladouceur (1991)[a]	5.7	7.3	1.5[b]		SOGS	LT	Level 2–3
Hong Kong Chen et al. (1993)[a]	3.8	3.0	2.0[b]		DIS	LT	Level 3; men only
Korea Lee et al. (1990)	0.5	1.1	1.8[b]		DIS	LT	Level 3
New Zealand Abbott & Volberg (2000)[e]	3.8	3.1	2.9	0.7	SOGS	LT	Level 2–3
Volberg & Abbott (1994)[e]	13	7	4	4	SOGS	LT	Level 2–3
Norway Gotestam & Johansson (2003)[a]	1.97	0.19[b]			DSM	n.s.	Level 2–3
Spain Legarda et al. (1992)[a]	8.8	6.8	6.6	4.6	SOGS	LT	Level 2–3
Sweden Volberg et al. (2001)[a]	1.3	2.1	0.7	0.1	SOGS	LT	Level 2–3
Switzerland Bondolfi et al. (2000)[a]	6.4	2.1[b]			SOGS	PY	Level 2–3
United Kingdom Sproston et al. (2000)[a]	1.7	1.0	0.6	0.1	SOGS	PY[c]	Level 2–3
United States Gerstein et al. (1999)[a]	3.1	2.0	2.8	0.3	NODS	LT	Level 2–3
	0.9	0.7	0.0	0.2	NODS	PY	Level 2–3
Welte et al. (2001)	4.3	5.1	3.3	1.2	DIS	PY	Level 2–3

Note. All table values are percentages. SOGS = South Oaks Gambling Screen; DIS = Diagnostic Interview Schedule; *DSM* = *Diagnostic and Statistical Manual of Mental Disorders*; NODS = National Opinion Research Center *DSM* Screen for Gambling Problems. n.s. = not stated. [c]Only individuals who reported having gambled in the past year were asked SOGS questions. [a]Significant age effects. [b]Rates not broken down by other age categories.

65 years as the oldest cohort. In some cases, rates were averaged if two age cohorts overlapped in the original sources. Readers seeking further clarification of methods and results should consult the individual studies.

As seen in Table 4.1, all but 2 (Lee et al., 1990; Welte et al., 2001) of these 14 studies found that age was significantly and negatively associated with disordered gambling. Wong and So (2003) also found that age was not a significant predictor of Level 2–3 gambling in Hong Kong, although that study did not provide prevalence rates across age groups.

Several studies have evaluated the age of onset of gambling and its association with later development of problems. In general, these studies show that the earlier one initiates gambling, the greater the likelihood he or she will progress to disordered gambling. For example, Ladouceur (1991) found that 10% of 1,002 survey respondents had initiated gambling before the age of 15 years; among those identified as Level 2–3 gamblers, 26% had begun gambling before age 15. Volberg (1994) found that among respondents to general population surveys, only 7% to 8% had begun gambling before age 15. Of the Level 2–3 gamblers identified in the surveys, 23% to 36% had begun wagering before age 15. In Switzerland, Bondolfi, Osiek, and Ferrero (2000) found that respondents who had initiated gambling prior to age 21 were more likely to have Level 2–3 gambling than those who had initiated gambling after age 21. Thus, an apparent association exists between age of onset of gambling and development of disordered gambling in general population surveys. In contrast, few adolescents or young adults seek treatment services, as I describe in chapter 15. The relationship between age and onset of gambling becomes even more complex when one examines gender and age interaction effects in treatment-seeking gamblers, as the average age of treatment-seeking gamblers is in the mid 40s (Petry & Oncken, 2002; Stinchfield & Winters, 2001; see "Gender" section later in this chapter).

Ethnic Minorities

Another demographic feature that has been associated with increased risk of development of disordered gambling is non-White ethnicity. In Gerstein et al.'s (1999) survey, 71.5% of the respondents were Caucasian, with the rest of the sample comprising 11.1% African Americans, 10.2% Hispanics, and 7.3% individuals of other ethnicities. Among the Level 2–3 gamblers identified in the survey, African Americans were overrepresented. For example, 4.2% of African Americans were classified as lifetime Level 2–3 gamblers, compared with 1.7% of respondents in the other ethnic groups. Welte et al. (2001) found a similar effect for African American respondents, but they also found evidence for increased risk of developing gambling problems in members of other racial groups. With the exception of Asian Americans, all other ethnic groups had significantly higher rates of disordered gambling than Caucasians.

Smaller state and general population surveys have confirmed these relationships. From Shaffer, Hall, and Vander Bilt's (1997) database, 18 studies examined the prevalence of disordered gambling in Caucasians compared with at least one other racial group. In every study, the proportion of minorities identified as Level 2–3 gamblers was higher than the proportion of Caucasians. For example, Volberg (1994) reported that 80% of survey respondents were Caucasian, but only 64% of those identified as Level 3 gamblers were Caucasian. Volberg and Steadman (1988) found that although 23% of respondents in a New York State survey were non-Caucasian, 43% of the Level 2–3 gamblers were ethnic minorities. In New Jersey and Maryland, 19% of respondents, but 36% of Level 2–3 gamblers, were non-Caucasian (Volberg & Steadman, 1989a). African Americans were overrepresented in Level 2–3 gamblers identified in Cunningham-Williams, Cottler, Compton, and Spitznagel's (1998) study as well. The NRC (1999) evaluated these studies and concluded that a median of 31% of survey respondents were ethnic minorities and identified as Level 2–3 gamblers. Only a median of 15% of Level 1 gamblers were members of ethnic minorities. These data clearly indicate that members of ethnic minorities are at increased risk for developing gambling problems.

Since Shaffer, Hall, and Vander Bilt's (1999) review, two additional studies have focused on prevalence rates of disordered gambling in Native Americans in the United States. Volberg and Abbott (1997) described the results of a survey that included both telephone and in-person interviews of residents of North Dakota, and it overrepresented Native Americans, primarily from the Sioux and Chippewa tribes. The 367 Native Americans were compared with the 1,199 Caucasian respondents. The Native Americans were significantly more likely to participate in a variety of different gambling activities, including casino gaming, raffles, bingo, animal racing, and card and dice games. They also reported an overall higher monthly expenditure on gambling activities than the Caucasians (Ms = $91 and $31, respectively). The lifetime rates of Level 2 gambling were 7.1% among Native Americans versus 2.5% among Caucasians, whereas the rates of Level 3 gambling were 7.1% and 0.8%, respectively. Current rates of Level 2 gambling were 5.8% among Native Americans and 1.3% in Caucasians. For Level 3 gambling, respective rates were 6.6% versus 0.5%. All these rates differed significantly between the two ethnic groups.

One other study (Elia & Jacobs, 1993) examined rates of disordered gambling among Native Americans in a substance abuse treatment setting. Of 85 consecutive admissions to a VA alcohol clinic in South Dakota, 38% were Native Americans. Among the Caucasians, 14% were identified as

Level 2 gamblers, and an additional 7.3% were identified as Level 3 gamblers. A significantly higher percentage of the Native Americans had gambling disorders, with 19% identified as Level 2 gamblers and 22% identified as Level 3 gamblers. Wardman, el-Guebaly, and Hodgins (2001) conducted a literature review of gambling in Aboriginal and Native populations from the United States and Canada. They identified 11 studies and noted that the Aboriginal population had a rate of disordered gambling that was 2 to 15 times higher than the non-Aboriginal population.

Surveys from other countries confirm this association of increased rates of disordered gamblers among members of the nonmajority race. Data derived from national surveys in four countries that reported on the race or ethnicity of the respondents are presented in Table 4.2.

In New Zealand, Volberg and Abbott (1994) found that non-Caucasians comprised 15% of respondents to a national telephone survey, yet they represented 41% of the Level 2–3 gamblers. An older, non-nationally based survey found that Pacific Islanders and Maori respondents had a three- to six-fold increased risk of gambling problems relative to respondents of European descent (Abbott & Volberg, 1991). In a more recent New Zealand national survey, Abbott and Volberg (2000) confirmed an association between minority status and disordered gambling. The Productivity Commission (1999) in Australia found that living in a home in which English was not spoken increased the odds of meeting criteria for disordered gambling in that country as well.

Although they did not conduct a national survey, Blaszczynski, Huynh, Dumlao, and Farrell (1998) administered the SOGS to 2,000 students at a Chinese-speaking school in Australia, requesting that their parents fill it out; 548 surveys were returned. Although 60% of the parents reported that they had never gambled (a rate much lower than that for Caucasian Australians), a full 12% scored in the range of Level 3 gamblers. More striking is a small study from Connecticut that found rates of Level 3 gambling to be 59% among 96 refugees from Cambodia, Vietnam, and Laos (Petry, Armentano, Kuoch, Norinth, & Smith, 2003). Finally, even in Sweden, Volberg, Abbott, Ronnberg, and Munck (2001) found that respondents who were born outside of Sweden were more likely than native Swedes to develop gambling problems.

These studies suggest that rates of disordered gambling are significantly higher among members of ethnic minorities living in the United States, Canada, Australia, New Zealand, and Sweden. The reasons for this overrepresentation of gambling problems in minorities are unknown. The high rates may result from differential sensitivity and specificity of instruments in assessing gambling problems in these subgroups. It may be related to differences in the role and acceptability of gambling across cultures and ethnicities as well. Also, high rates of disordered gambling may be associated

TABLE 4.2
Prevalence Rates of Disordered Gambling in Adult National Population Surveys: Based on Respondents' Race or Ethnicity

Country and study	Country's majority race	Minority races combined	Specific minority populations
Australia			
Productivity Commission (1999)[a]	2.1%	8.2%[b]	
New Zealand			
Abbott & Volberg (2000)[a]	1.9%		11.0% Pacific Islander[a]
			7.1% Aboriginal[a]
			2.9% Asian
Volberg & Abbott (1994)[a]	6.9%[c]	17.0%	31% Pacific Islander[a]
			16% Aboriginal[a]
			11% Asian
Sweden			
Volberg et al. (2001)[a]	3.7%	6.6%[c]	
United States			
Gerstein et al. (1999) LT, PY[a]	1.8%, 0.3%		4.2%,1.2% African American[a]
			1.7%, 0.8% Hispanic
			1.7%, 0.8% Other
Welte et al. (2001)[a]	1.8%		7.7% African American[a]
			7.9% Hispanic[a]
			10.5% Native American[a]
			6.5% Asian

Note. See Table 4.1 for instruments used and timeframes over which disordered gambling was measured. LT = lifetime rates; PY = past-year rates.
[a]Minority groups differ significantly from majority groups. [b]English not spoken in home. [c]Not born in Sweden.

with the link between ethnic minority status and lower socioeconomic status (see next section). To date, little research has examined gambling patterns and problems in specific ethnic minority groups.

I now present a case example of a Southeast Asian refugee. Although this example is not meant to be representative of gambling patterns in general among this population, it provides some details of the cultural, familial, and personal issues faced by some ethnic minority pathological gamblers.

Case example. Thy was born in southern Cambodia, and he spent his early childhood in a refugee camp. His father was brutally murdered when he was just 5 years old. In the early 1980s, together with his mother and four sisters, Thy came to New York City, where he spent his teenage years. The family lived with his aunt, and Thy had difficulty integrating into American life. He had a hard time learning English, and he speaks softly, with a strong accent. He attended an integrated public school where some of the other students were also Cambodian, but he was a loner and made few friends. He dropped out of school at the age of 16, and he worked in the family supermarket from that age onward. When Thy turned 21, his older sister and her husband took him to Atlantic City for the weekend. He was immediately attracted to the roulette table. He watched the gamblers in awe for hours before placing his first $5 bet. The ball landed on his number, and he won $175. His luck was short lived, though, as he lost his next dozen bets. Thy returned to the number that was an early winner and, to his and fellow players' astonishment, he won again. He stayed at the roulette table all night, leaving with about $200 more than he came in with. This was a huge amount of money to Thy, and he could hardly contain his excitement as he told his sister of his good fortune. The next day, he again spent most of his time at the roulette table, but this time losing the previous day's wins. Still, he was hooked. He had won yesterday, and he felt lucky; he knew he could win again.

Atlantic City was only a few hours' bus ride from the family's apartment in New York. Thy started going to the casino on his days off. He worked extra hours at the supermarket whenever he could, so that he could get more money for his next trip. Soon Thy was going to the casino weekly, spending all that he earned. He no longer placed $5 bets—each wager had to be at least $50.

After a few years of regular gambling, Thy felt certain that he was about to win really big, but he knew that, to win big, he needed to bet big. He had only $200 to take to the casino that week. He borrowed $1,500 from the supermarket's register, certain that he would win and replace what he borrowed, plus more. When he arrived at the casino, he did win—at first. The $1,700 quickly grew to over $5,000. But Thy couldn't stop. He placed it all on the number 3, his lucky number. When the winning number came up a 9, Thy stood in shock. He just stared at the wheel. The world was spinning all around him, and he couldn't move. A security guard eventually escorted him away from the table. Thy didn't know where to go or what to do. He was too embarrassed to go home. He was too ashamed to tell his family that he had taken the money. While spending the next several nights on the streets, Thy considered suicide, but he felt too afraid to do it. Eventually, he started hitchhiking and ended up in Seattle. He now cleans an office building there. After 5 years, Thy has still not contacted his family.

Comment. This case describes how a young man, after escaping a terrorist regime and then growing up in a somewhat impoverished environment, began his gambling career. The lure of his first "big win," although not astronomical by monetary standards, made him feel special. The casino was a place, perhaps one of the only places, where he felt accepted. His gambling started in the form of recreation, gradually turned into his only form of regular entertainment, and eventually became the focal point of his life. Although he had never engaged in prior criminal activity, Thy took money to support his gambling, fully intending to pay it back. However, he could not control his gambling. When he lost his family's money, he chose to leave rather than experience the dishonor of facing his family.

Lower Socioeconomic Status

Lower socioeconomic status is a third demographic characteristic that is rather consistently associated with increased rates of disordered gambling. This is a difficult variable to isolate in terms of its association with mental health conditions. Socioeconomic status is often confounded with other variables that may be independently or interactively related to psychiatric disorders. For example, members of ethnic minority groups are overrepresented in the lower socioeconomic classes, and therefore it is difficult to determine whether increased risk is related to ethnicity or to socioeconomic status. Less education is also associated with lower socioeconomic status (as well as with nonmajority ethnicity). Therefore, the unique or shared risk these variables exert with respect to disordered gambling is difficult to ascertain. In this section, I present socioeconomic status in its broadest sense. I discuss data associated with income, education, and socioeconomic rankings, depending on how they are defined within the specific prevalence surveys.

The NRC (1999) identified 15 studies that were included in Shaffer, Hall, and Vander Bilt's (1997, 1999) meta-analysis and that provided information on income distributions for Level 1 versus Level 2–3 gamblers. These studies had found that individuals with incomes under $25,000 per year were likely to be overrepresented among the problem gambling groups.

Only seven studies identified by Shaffer, Hall, and Vander Bilt (1997, 1999) compared employment status among Level 1 and Level 2–3 gamblers. Across these studies, employed individuals were represented in relatively equal proportions in Level 2–3 gamblers (*Mdn* = 64%) and Level 1 gamblers (*Mdn* = 61%). Individuals receiving disability compensation, however, seem to be at an increased risk for developing gambling problems: Disabled persons made up a median of only 2% of respondents who were classified as Level 1 gamblers, but they represented a median of 6% of respondents who were classified as Level 2–3 gamblers. Unfortunately, these data were derived from only three studies, and the number of disabled persons surveyed was very small.

The NRC (1999) also reviewed the results of Shaffer, Hall, and Vander Bilt's (1999) meta-analysis with respect to education and found 18 studies that provided breakouts of educational achievement for Level 1 versus Level 2–3 gamblers. Across these studies, a median of only 13% of Level 1 gamblers had a high school education or less, compared with 23% of Level 2–3 gamblers.

In terms of some individual studies, Ladouceur (1991) found that the two lowest income groups had disproportionably high rates of disordered gamblers in a large survey in Quebec. In New Jersey and Maryland, Volberg and Steadman (1989a) found that individuals who had not graduated from high school were overrepresented among Level 2–3 gamblers. Such individuals were also overrepresented in the Massachusetts, Maryland, New Jersey, California, and Iowa surveys (Volberg, 1994). In a New York state survey, Volberg (1988) found that whereas 45% of all respondents earned less than $25,000 per year, 60% of the Level 2–3 gamblers were in this income group.

Although the association between socioeconomic status, education, and income and disordered gambling is fairly consistent, some notable exceptions to this relationship can be found in the literature. Cunningham-Williams et al. (1998) found no differences in gambling problems among individuals with or without a college degree. In the New York state survey, Volberg (1988) did not note a difference in educational achievement among Level 2–3 gamblers compared with Level 1 gamblers.

Nevertheless, data from the two nationally based U.S. studies, as well as those from other countries, show that lower socioeconomic status appears to be associated with disordered gambling in most studies, as demonstrated in Table 4.3. All of the studies that conducted statistical testing of prevalence rates of disordered gambling across socioeconomic groupings found a statistically significant relationship. In every study except the one from Switzerland (Bondolfi et al., 2000), this relationship was inverse, such that lower socioeconomic status was related to increased rates of disordered gambling, but the nature and rationale behind this association are not well understood.

TABLE 4.3

Prevalence Rates of Disordered Gambling in Adult Population Surveys, Based on Respondents' Income, Education, or Employment Status

Country and study	Variable studied	Lowest	Middle	Highest
Australia Productivity Commission (1999)[a,b]	College graduate Full-time employed Mean income	31% : 24% 54% : 42% $30,050 : $31,100		
Canada Ladouceur (1991)[c]	Income	7.4%	2.9% all others	
Hong Kong Wong & So (2003)[c]	Education	7.6%	4.9% all others	
New Zealand Abbott & Volberg (2000)[c]	Education Employment status Income	4.1% 5.9% Unemp 3.4%	2.8% 3.0% Emp 2.6%	1.5%
Volberg & Abbott (1994)[c]	Employment status	22.5% Unemp	6.9% Emp	2.3%
Norway Gotestam & Johansson (2003)[b]	Education Employment status	0.5% 0.5% Unemp	0.6% 0.7% Emp	0.7%
Spain Legarda et al. (1992)[b]	Education Employment Income	5.2% 8.4% Unemp 5.0%	7.1% 11.6% Occasional emp 8.5%	8.8% 4.8% Regular emp 8.4%
Sweden Volberg et al. (2001)[c]	Education	5.3%	4.2%	2.9%
Switzerland Bondolfi et al. (2000)[c]	Employment Income	1.6% Nonwage earners 1.3%	4.1% Wage earners 3.6% all others	
United Kingdom Sproston et al. (2000)[c]	Income	1.5%	1.0%	0.2%
United States Gerstein et al. (1999)[c]: Rates presented for lifetime, past year	Education Employment Income	2.6%, 0.9% 2.1%, 0.4% Unemp 2.0%, 0.5%	2.5%, 0.7% 0.6%, 0.5% PT 2.3%, 0.6%	1.0%, 0.0% 2.3%, 0.6% FT 1.5%, 0.2%
Welte et al. (2001)[c]	SES category	4.6%	3.2%	1.6%

Note. Unemp = unemployed; Emp = employed; PT = part time; FT = full time. SES = socioeconomic status. [a]Ratio of Level 2–3 gamblers to nongamblers. [b]Statistical testing was not conducted on prevalence rates. [c]Statistically significant effects.

One hypothesis is that the relationship may be based in part on a poorer ability to understand the probabilities associated with gambling among less educated individuals, but little empirical evidence is yet available to support this hypothesis (see chap. 12). Related theories are sociobiological or socio-economical in nature. Individuals in more desperate situations may be more risk prone (e.g., Friedman & Savage, 1948), resulting in an increased propensity to gamble. Economic status may also have an effect on the development of some psychiatric symptoms (e.g., Costello, Compton, Keeler, & Angold, 2003). The *downward-drift theory* argues that impaired functioning can lead to a decline in social status (e.g., Cooper, 1961; Dohrenwend, 1990), and a competing theory maintains that low social class may cause or exacerbate some psychiatric disorders (e.g., J. G. Johnson, Cohen, Dohrenwend, Link, & Brook, 1999). Although these associations are not well studied in the case of gambling, biological and genetic mechanisms may interact with the social and environmental context. Some individuals, especially those with biological or genetic risk factors (see chap. 6), may be more susceptible to the reinforcing effects of gambling when in these more deprived situations and therefore may be more likely to develop problems with gambling.

Marital Status

Marital status may also be associated with gambling problems. In a regional study, Cunningham-Williams et al. (1998) found that Level 2–3 gamblers were more likely to be divorced or separated than were nonproblem gamblers. Volberg (1994) reported that Level 3 gamblers were less likely than nonproblem gamblers to be married. Ladouceur (1991) noted that only 37% of Level 2–3 gamblers were married, compared with 54% of all respondents. In studies of employees (Petry & Mallya, 2004) and medical and dental patients in Connecticut (Ladd & Petry, 2002b), my colleagues and I also have found that Level 1 gamblers were more often married (61%) than Level 2 (43%) or Level 3 (25%) gamblers.

Prevalence rates of disordered gambling based on marital status in surveys conducted throughout the world are shown in Table 4.4. Nine of these 10 studies conducted statistical testing of prevalence rates based on marital status. Six of these noted that married people had lower prevalence rates of disordered gambling than divorced or separated individuals or those who had never married. Divorce or separation may result as a consequence of disordered gambling, or disordered gamblers may be less likely to get married because of an inability to form stable relationships. Another possible explanation is that nonmarried status may be confounded by other variables that also are more common among Level 2–3 gamblers, such as younger age.

TABLE 4.4

Prevalence Rates of Disordered Gambling in Adult Population Surveys, Based on Respondents' Marital Status

Country and study	Married or common law	Divorced or separated	Never married
Australia Productivity Commission (1999)[a,b]	47.3 : 66.3	8.1 : 4.6	43.2 : 21.9
Canada Ladouceur (1991)[b]	2.6	5.2 all others	
New Zealand Abbott & Volberg (2000) Volberg & Abbott (1994)[b]	3.0 5.5	2.4 8.0	3.2 13.0
Norway Gotestam & Johansson (2003)	0.4	1.0 all others	
Spain Legarda et al. (1992)[c]	5.2	10.0	10.4
Sweden Volberg et al. (2001)[b]	2.0	4.0	6.9
Switzerland Bondolfi et al. (2000)[b]	2.0	4.2 all others	
United Kingdom Sproston et al. (2000)[b]	0.5	2.4	1.8
United States Gerstein et al. (1999): lifetime, past year	1.7, 0.7	2.2, 0.0	2.9, 0.5

Note. All table values are percentages. See Table 4.1 for instruments used and timeframes over which disordered gambling was measured. [a]Ratio of Level 2–3 gamblers to nongamblers. [b]Prevalence rates differ significantly across marital groups. [c]Statistical testing was not conducted.

Male Gender

Male gender has been repeatedly demonstrated to be a risk factor for gambling problems. Eighteen of the general population surveys identified by Shaffer, Hall, and Vander Bilt (1999) provided breakdowns of prevalence rates of disordered gambling by gender. In 17 of these studies, the proportion of men was greater among Level 2–3 gamblers compared with Level 1 gamblers.

The overrepresentation of men among disordered gamblers is confirmed in one of the two national U.S. surveys. The overall sample included in Gerstein et al.'s (1999) survey did not find a statistically significant effect of gender among individuals identified as Level 2 and Level 3 gamblers. However, using both the SOGS and the DIS, and regardless of whether prevalence rates were current or lifetime, Welte et al. (2001) noted a significant gender effect: Men had an approximately 40% increased risk of developing disordered gambling relative to women.

Nationally based studies from every other country in which data are available confirm an association between gender and disordered gambling. In the Swiss study, Bondolfi et al. (2000) found that 73% of the Level 2–3 gamblers identified in the survey were male, although men comprised only 49% of the total respondents. In Norway (Gotestam & Johansson, 2003), men had 0.74% and 0.21% rates of Level 2 and 3 gambling, respectively, versus rates of 0.19% and 0.09% for women. Studies from Asian countries (Chen, Wong, Lee, Chan-Ho, & Lau, 1993; Hwu, Yeh, & Chang, 1989; Lee et al., 1990; Wong & So, 2003) have found a very pronounced gender effect as well. Rates of disordered gambling in surveys worldwide are shown in Table 4.5.

Although notable gender differences exist with respect to prevalence rates of disordered gambling, gender effects may also be influenced by age. Shaffer et al. (1997) found that male adolescents and college students had a threefold increased risk of disordered gambling compared with female peers, whereas in adult samples the increased risk was only twofold. In the oldest cohorts, this gender difference may diminish even more. Sproston, Ernst, and Orford (2000) provided an Age × Gender breakdown and found that younger age was significantly associated with Level 3 gambling among men in the United Kingdom, although age effects were less pronounced in women.

Mok and Hraba (1991) discussed age and gender effects in a survey conducted in Iowa. They reported not only that men and women often exhibit different patterns and preferences for gambling activities but also that these effects may vary by age cohort. General population surveys typically find that women and older adults wager more often on electronic

TABLE 4.5
Prevalence Rates of Disordered Gambling in Adult Population Surveys, Based on Respondents' Gender

Country and study	Male	Female
Australia		
Productivity Commission (1999)[a]	60 : 45	
Canada		
Bland et al. (1993)[b,c]	0.7	0.2
Ladouceur (1991)[c]	6.3	1.7
Hong Kong		
Chen et al. (1993)[c]	2.9	0.2
Wong & So (2003)[c]	9.5	2.1
Korea		
Lee et al. (1990)[c]	1.9	0.2
New Zealand		
Abbott & Volberg (2000)[c]	4.0	2.0
Volberg & Abbott (1994)[c]	11.2	4.3
Norway		
Gotestam & Johansson (2003)[c]	1.0	0.2
Spain		
Legarda et al. (1992)[c]	10.4	3.8
Sweden		
Volberg et al. (2001)[c]	6.6	1.9
Switzerland		
Bondolfi et al. (2000)[c]	4.4	1.6
Taiwan		
Hwu et al. (1989)[b,c]	7.9–10.2	0.0–1.4
United Kingdom		
Sproston et al. (2000)[c]	1.3	0.5
United States		
Gerstein et al. (1999):		
Lifetime, past year	2.5, 0.5	1.7, 0.6
Welte et al. (2001)[c]		
Lifetime SOGS, DIS	14.3, 5.7	8.9, 3.9
Past-year SOGS, DIS	6.4, 4.1	4.7, 3.0

Note. All table values are percentages. See Table 4.1 for instruments used and timeframes over which disordered gambling was measured. SOGS = South Oaks Gambling Screen; DIS = Diagnostic Interview Schedule.
[a]Ratio of Level 2–3 gamblers to nongamblers presented. [b]Lifetime Level 3 gamblers determined by the DIS. For the Hwu et al. (1989) study, ranges across different geographical locations are presented. [c]Prevalence rates differ significantly between genders.

gaming machines and bingo, whereas men are more likely to bet on animal races, cards, and sports. Studies detailing gender differences have been conducted primarily with treatment-seeking gamblers, as I describe in the following sections.

TREATMENT-SEEKING GAMBLERS AND HELP-LINE CALLERS

The five risk factors for disordered gambling identified in general population surveys that I have just discussed can also be examined for concordance in gambling treatment-seeking samples. In comparing individuals identified in general population surveys with treatment-seeking gamblers, a number of important points must be kept in mind. First, few individuals seek gambling treatment. The National Gambling Impact Study Commission (1999) found that less than 10% of Level 3 gamblers ever present for professional treatment. Second, those who do seek treatment may be different in some fundamental ways from gamblers who do not seek treatment. Treatment-seeking gamblers may have developed more severe gambling-related problems, including employment, social, or legal difficulties. Treatment-seeking pathological gamblers may also suffer from higher rates of other psychiatric conditions than their non-treatment-seeking counterparts, an issue I address in chapter 5. Comparing demographic characteristics of treatment-seeking gamblers with those of Level 3 gamblers identified in general population surveys may provide an indicator of whether certain groups of individuals are underrepresented in treatment settings. Also in this section I elucidate the profile of patients whom clinicians treating pathological gamblers are likely to encounter.

Younger Age

Younger age is associated with increased risk of developing disordered gambling in general population surveys, but younger age groups appear underrepresented in treatment populations. Volberg (1994) presented general demographic characteristics of Level 3 gamblers who have sought treatment for gambling compared with those of Level 3 gamblers who were identified in general population telephone surveys. The treatment population represented programs from the states of New Jersey, Maryland, Massachusetts, Iowa, and California. Whereas the median age of the Level 3 gamblers identified in the telephone surveys was 34 years, the median age of the treatment-seeking gamblers was 37 years. These age differences were not statistically significant, although a trend toward underrepresentation of young gamblers in the treatment-seeking population was noted. In Connecticut, respondents to a statewide gambling survey (WEFA Group, ICR Survey

Research Group, Lesieur, & Thompson, 1997) were about equally divided in the age groups of 18 to 34 years (36%), 35 to 54 years (33%), and over 55 years (31%). The youngest age group was more likely to be identified as Level 3 gamblers, with 46% being younger than 35 years. However, only 33% of treatment-seeking gamblers in Connecticut were under 35 years of age, and only 6% were under 25 years (Petry & Oncken, 2002).

Thus, a trend toward reduced treatment seeking is noted in the youngest age groups, with most treatment-seeking gamblers between age 35 and 54 years. Demographic characteristics of patients receiving gambling treatment at state-funded treatment programs in the United States (Petry & Oncken, 2002; Stinchfield & Winters, 2001) and Canada (Wiebe & Cox, 2001), as well as of some gambling treatment programs in Australia (Jackson, Thomas, Ross, & Kearney, 2000) and New Zealand (Paton-Simpson, Gruys, & Hannifin, 2002), are depicted in Table 4.6. Results from an analysis of callers to a gambling help line in the United Kingdom (Griffiths, Scarfe, & Bellringer, 1999) also are presented, as are characteristics of patients seeking treatment in programs located in Germany (Schwarz & Lindner, 1992), Brazil (Tavares, Zilberman, Beites, & Gentil, 2001), and Spain (Ibàñez, Mercade, Sanroma, & Cordero, 1992; Legarda, Babio, & Abreu, 1992).

These data suggest that middle-aged gamblers are more likely to be in treatment than younger gamblers. Special outreach efforts may need to be directed toward attracting younger gamblers into treatment settings and developing treatment programs specifically targeted toward the youth and younger adults (see also chap. 15).

Ethnicity

In Volberg's (1988) study, 64% of Level 3 gamblers identified in the general population survey were Caucasian, but between 89% and 94% of treatment-seeking gamblers were Caucasian. These differences were statistically significant. Although Level 3 gamblers in Connecticut are more likely to be ethnic minorities (WEFA Group et al., 1997), a full 86% of treatment-seeking gamblers identified their race as Caucasian (Petry & Oncken, 2002), suggesting again that minorities are underrepresented in gambling treatment programs. The Minnesota treatment programs likewise have high rates of Caucasians seeking treatment (Stinchfield & Winters, 2001), as does a large program in Canada (Wiebe & Cox, 2001). In contrast, a higher proportion of non-Caucasians appear to present for treatment in Australia and New Zealand (see Table 4.6). In Florida, Cuadrado (1999) compared Hispanic ($n = 209$) and non-Hispanic ($n = 5,311$) callers to the state-funded help line for problem gamblers. Non-Hispanic callers were twice as likely to have sought prior gambling treatment, and they had more legal and employment problems, than did Hispanic callers. Although non-Hispanics may have

TABLE 4.6
Characteristics of Treatment-Seeking Gamblers

Location and study	N	Age	Ethnicity (Caucasian)	Education (% < HS)	Income (in 1,000s)	Employment (% Full time)	Marital status	Gender (% Male)
Australia Jackson et al. (2000)	3416	35[a]	76% AU born	n.s.	$30K[a]	42%	48% M 26% S	45%
Austria Horodecki (1992)	237	35[a]	n.s.	n.s.	$24K (U.S.)	77%	60%M 24% S	90%
Brazil Tavares et al. (2001)	71	43	89%	n.s.	n.s.	56% Reg 6% Occ 38% Unem	58% M	49%
Canada (Manitoba) Wiebe & Cox (2001)	1376	39	n.s.	7%	<$10K 12% >$50K 20%	52%	53% M 20% S	63%
Germany (inpatient program) Schwarz & Lindner (1992)	58	32	14%	12%	n.s.	n.s.	33% M 48% S	100%
New Zealand Paton-Simpson et al. (2002) Help line callers	2363	36[a]	58%	n.s.	n.s.	n.s.	n.s.	50%
Therapy clients	1801	37	58%					59%
Spain Ibáñez et al. (1992)	45	41	n.s.	25%	n.s.	n.s.	65% M 22% S	89%
Legarda et al. (1992)	24	37[a]	n.s.	0%	46% low 33% middle 17% high	54% Reg 13% Occ 17% Unem	71% M 13% S	88%

	N	Age						
United Kingdom (help line)								
Griffiths et al. (1999)	882	26–39[b]	n.s.	n.s.	n.s.	n.s.	n.s.	90%
United States								
Petry & Oncken (2002): Connecticut	345	42	86%	15%	$37K	68%	45% M 20% S	60%
Stinchfield & Winters (2001): Minnesota	586	35[a]	86%	7%	$25K[a]	64%	48% M 25% S	59%
Reported in Volberg (1994)								
Maryland	276	38	89%	16%	n.s.	n.s.	40% M	91%
New Jersey	155	38	90%	11%	n.s.	n.s.	59% M	93%
Massachusetts	137	37	93%	7%	n.s.	n.s.	71% M	93%
Iowa	135	35	92%	13%	n.s.	n.s.	51% M	86%
California	71	33	94%	2%	n.s.	n.s.	31% M	93%

Note. HS = high school; AU born = born in Australia; Reg = regular employment; Occ = occasional employment; Unem = unemployed; M = married; S = single; n.s. = not stated.
[a] Modal values reported. [b] Modal age range; includes individuals who called about someone else's gambling problem.

more severe gambling problems, the results may have been confounded by ethnic differences in help-seeking behaviors or willingness to endorse psychosocial problems. More effort is needed to attract and tailor gambling treatment to the needs of ethnic minorities.

Socioeconomic Status

Volberg (1994) found that better educated gamblers might be overrepresented in treatment settings. Although 79% of Level 3 gamblers identified in the general population samples were high school graduates, 84% to 98% of treatment-seeking gamblers had at least a high school education. This education effect was significant. In Connecticut, 85% of treatment-seeking gamblers had a high school degree or more (Petry & Oncken, 2002), but this level of educational achievement was consistent with that found in the general population survey. In terms of other socioeconomic variables, the Connecticut survey found that 59% of respondents were employed full time (WEFA Group et al., 1997). In contrast, 75% of those in treatment for gambling were employed on a full-time basis (Petry & Oncken, 2002).

Finally, in terms of income, in the earlier part of this chapter I suggested that lower income might be related to gambling problems. Lower income also seems to be associated with increased treatment seeking. Almost half of the treatment-seeking gamblers in Connecticut earned less than $30,000 per year, and only 6% earned more than $75,000 (Petry & Oncken, 2002). In contrast, nearly one fifth of Connecticut residents have incomes in this highest category (WEFA Group et al., 1997). However, these studies of treatment-seeking gamblers were conducted in a state-supported treatment program and a research clinic. Level 3 gamblers with high incomes may be more likely to seek private gambling treatment and therefore not be represented in these samples.

Because treatment-seeking Level 3 gamblers seem to be employed full time, but perhaps more often in low-income positions (cf. M. W. Abbott & Volberg, 2000), this pattern may suggest a need to introduce screening and treatment services in certain company settings. Manufacturing and other industries that employ primarily men with high school education may have relatively high proportions of gamblers, and therefore perhaps these settings should be targeted for screening and prevention efforts. Enhancing screening and prevention efforts in employment settings may reduce some of the adverse effects associated with gambling, as 30% to 70% of Level 3 gamblers report missing work because of gambling (Ladouceur, Boisvert, Pepin, Loranger, & Sylvain, 1994; Lesieur & Anderson, 1995; Petry & Mallya, 2004), and about one third have lost a job because of gambling (Ladouceur, Boisvert, et al., 1994; Lesieur & Anderson, 1995; Thompson, Gazel, & Rickman, 1996).

Marital Status

In general population surveys reviewed by Volberg (1994), 62% of Level 3 gamblers were not married. Percentages of treatment-seeking gamblers who were not married varied widely across studies, ranging from 29% to 69%, with a median of 49%. Treatment-seeking gamblers were more likely to be married than Level 3 gamblers identified in population surveys.

In Minnesota, 38% of 944 gamblers entering the treatment programs were married, whereas 26% were divorced or separated, and 25% were single. Only 2% were widowed. In Connecticut, a slightly higher proportion of treatment-seeking gamblers were married (45%; Petry & Oncken, 2002). Jackson et al.'s (2000) Australian study found that rates of separation and divorce are higher in treatment-seeking gamblers than in the general population but consistent with the marital status rates of Level 3 gamblers identified in the national survey (Productivity Commission, 1999).

The fact that about half of Level 3 gamblers are married, and that married gamblers may be more willing to seek treatment than unmarried ones, suggests that treatment focusing on marital issues may be useful. To date, no known research has focused on married versus unmarried gamblers, and the degree to which the family should be the focus of treatment for pathological gamblers is unclear. I describe the role of the spouse in treatment of pathological gamblers in chapter 9.

Gender

At the time of Volberg's (1994) study, men were overrepresented in treatment programs. Although 76% of Level 3 gamblers identified in general population surveys were men, 86% to 93% of treatment-seeking gamblers were men. Early reports of treatment-seeking gamblers ubiquitously reveal high rates of men in the United States (Lesieur & Blume, 1991a; Ramirez, McCormick, Russo, & Taber, 1983; Russo, Taber, McCormick, & Ramirez, 1984; Taber, McCormick, Russo, Adkins, & Ramirez, 1987) and Europe (Horodecki, 1992; Ibàñez et al., 1992; Legarda et al., 1992; Schwarz & Lindner, 1992).

In the past 10 years, this gender gap has narrowed. Although male gender generally is still a risk factor for development of disordered gambling, men and women who are Level 3 gamblers appear to be equally likely to seek treatment for their gambling problems. In Connecticut, 62% of Level 3 gamblers identified in the telephone survey (WEFA Group et al., 1997) were men, and 60% of those who sought treatment for gambling were men (Petry & Oncken, 2002). These results seem consistent with other states and countries. In Minnesota, 59% of the treatment-seeking gamblers were men (Stinchfield & Winters, 2001), a rate similar to those noted in recent studies of treatment-seeking gamblers in Canada (Wiebe & Cox, 2001), Brazil (Tavares et al., 2001), Australia (Jackson et al., 2000), and New Zealand (Paton-Simpson et al., 2002).

Some studies have reported on gender differences in gambling patterns and preferences. Mark and Lesieur (1992) pointed out the dearth of literature on gambling in women. Getty, Watson, and Frisch (2000) evaluated depression and coping styles in 20 male and 10 female GA members. Despite high rates of depression and poor coping relative to control participants, no gender differences in gamblers were found. However, the sample size was so small that only very large effect sizes could be detected.

A couple of studies have used larger samples to identify similarities and differences between the genders. Crisp et al. (2000) compared 1,520 male and female gamblers seeking treatment in Australia. They found that men were more likely to present with external concerns, such as employment and legal matters, whereas women were more likely to express concerns about physical symptoms and emotional issues. Crisp et al. reported that therapists were more likely to deem treatment "successful" for women, but standardized assessments with known psychometric properties were not administered to ascertain changes in gambling or other psychosocial domains. Both genders attended a similar number of counseling sessions (slightly over three sessions), but women were more likely to receive systemic or supportive counseling, whereas men more often received referrals to other services, such as legal services.

Grant and Kim (2002a) compared 53 men and 78 women seeking pharmacological treatment for gambling (see chap. 7) in Minnesota. They found that men were younger and had an earlier age of onset of gambling, whereas women progressed to problem gambling more quickly once they started gambling. Gender differences in preferred gambling activities (slots and bingo relative to cards, sports, and track) were noted. Loneliness was more often a precipitant of gambling in women than men, but other measures of severity of gambling problems generally were similar between the genders. In Brazil, Tavares et al. (2001) likewise found that women began gambling later in life and progressed more rapidly to disordered gambling than men. Female gamblers were also less often married and less likely to be regularly employed than men.

Some similar gender effects were noted among gamblers calling into help lines or presenting at treatment programs in Connecticut. Potenza et al. (2001) compared characteristics of 349 male and 213 female callers to a gambling help line. Relative to women, men were younger, had higher incomes, and were less likely to be African American. Male gamblers reported a longer duration of gambling problems, and the types of preferred gambling activities differed between genders, similarly to that noted by Grant and Kim (2002a). Although both genders reported similar numbers of problems related to gambling, the types of problems varied. Women had more financial problems and more credit card debt, whereas men were more likely to be indebted to bookies and to report recent drug use. Men were more likely to have been arrested for a gambling-related crime, whereas women were more likely to report gambling-related illegal activities, without arrest. Women also were more likely to have received mental health treatment and report a suicide attempt subsequent to gambling.

Such differences were noted among callers to a help line, and about one third of callers actually present for professional treatment. Ladd and Petry (2002b) examined gender differences in 115 treatment-seeking gamblers. Similar to the other studies, men were younger and had higher incomes than women. After controlling for these demographic characteristics, men initiated gambling at a younger age, began gambling regularly, and first tried to stop gambling and first entered treatment at younger ages than women. Men also had more severe legal difficulties and alcohol problems than women, but women were more likely to be living with someone with a gambling or drinking problem. These gender differences are depicted in the following case examples.

Case example. Ned is a 45-year-old man with a long history of gambling. He started gambling with his father and older brothers on card games, and he frequented horse and dog races with them. Gambling was a part of his family and social circle—all the men did it.

Ned got married when he was 20, to his high school girlfriend, Angela. They had three children, the first just a year after their wedding. They had a hard time early in life, because they were both so young and didn't have much money. Throughout the marriage, Ned felt that Angie was always nagging him—trying to keep tabs on him. He hated that. They argued a lot, and he often lost his temper with her. Still, she was a good mother to their children. As the children grew up, Ned spent less and less time at home. He had a problem with alcohol in his 20s and 30s, but after a car wreck and a couple of weeks in the hospital, he vowed never to drink again. When he quit drinking, he started spending more and more time at the track. While at home, Ned studied the sports section, especially the statistics on football games and the horses. This angered Angie almost as much as his drinking, but what could she do? He said it was none of her business.

After the children grew up, Angie and Ned had very little in common, and she spent much of her time visiting the children or her parents. Ned spent more and more of his time betting on sports with his buddies or at the track. When his construction business took a turn for the worse in the early 1990s, Ned had a lot of free time on his hands, and he spent almost all of it gambling. Little money was coming in, and Ned was furious with Angie for her excessive spending on the new grandchild. He took all the credit cards away and would give her only $30 per week for groceries. She threatened to leave. She did move in with their son for a couple of weeks, but she always came back to him.

The financial problems became more serious, and the mortgage company foreclosed on their second mortgage a few years ago. Ned and his wife now live in a small apartment, and he tries to do some temporary work, when he can find it. Ned still goes to the track several times a week, claiming that it is his only form of relaxation. When Ned got caught stealing cash and blank checks from the office at a temporary job, his public defender urged him to seek gambling treatment. Ned, however, insisted he did not have a gambling problem.

Case example. Sarah is a 58-year-old retired schoolteacher from Connecticut. She was married for more than 30 years, but she and her husband separated, and then divorced, about 7 years ago. He was an alcoholic, and after all those years, she couldn't take it any more and left him. They had one daughter. When her son-in-law got transferred to Denver in 1995, soon after Sarah retired early to stay at home with her granddaughter, Sarah became very lonely. She considered going back to work, but the school system told her that a hiring freeze was in effect.

Sarah's days seemed long, and she became depressed the year after her daughter moved away. She went to visit them for a month, but when she returned, she was more down than ever. She took a depression screen during a doctor's appointment, and he recommended that she start taking an antidepressant. Sarah took it for a few weeks, but then stopped, because she didn't think it was helping. She found little reason to get up in the mornings. Her daughter suggested that she get involved in some volunteer activities, and after much prodding, Sarah started helping out at a senior center that summer.

Sarah arranged social activities at the center, including monthly bus trips to the casino. She met some other people her age through this, and together they attended every casino trip. One of them suggested a trip to Las Vegas that winter, and Sarah went along. The Vegas casinos were even more exciting to Sarah than the ones in Connecticut. She spent more than $3,000 that week in Vegas, and for the first time in a long time, she felt like she was having fun.

When Sarah returned to Connecticut to face the long winter, the casino became a more attractive place to be. She could go alone and not feel self-conscious. Whenever she was playing slots, she forgot about how unhappy she was. She lost track of time, and the money didn't seem to matter. She had enough to spend as she chose. However, within 3 years, Sarah had accumulated more than $30,000 in credit card debt, and she didn't know how she could pay it back. She had picked up a card about a gambling help line at the casino 6 months earlier. She finally got the courage to call it.

Comment. As depicted in the above examples, male and female gamblers often differ with respect to the onset and patterns of their gambling.
Ned started gambling as a young boy, whereas Sarah did not begin gambling
until after she retired. Ned's gambling appears to be related to thrill seeking,
whereas for Sarah it fills a void associated with depression.

Gender differences noted among pathological gamblers appear to be
related to age effects. I (Petry, 2002a) categorized 343 gamblers initiating
treatment in Connecticut into young adults (ages 18–35 years, n = 97),
middle-aged adults (ages 36–55 years, n = 197), and older adults (ages 56
years or higher, n = 55). They all completed the Addiction Severity Index
(McLellan et al., 1985) and the SOGS (see chap. 3). Differences in gambling
variables, demographics, and Addiction Severity Index composite scores
were compared across the age groups. Middle-aged and older gamblers were
more often women (46%–50%) than were the younger gamblers (23%),
but the groups were similar with respect to almost all other demographic
characteristics. After controlling for gender, older age was associated with
more employment problems but fewer alcohol, drug, legal, social, and psychiatric difficulties. Older gamblers had less severe gambling problems, and
lower SOGS scores, relative to younger gamblers. Older female gamblers
did not begin gambling regularly until late in life, at an average age of 63
years, whereas older men generally reported a lifelong history of gambling.
Middle-aged and older gamblers were also more likely to report problems
with slot machines. Grant, Kim, and Brown (2001) compared 16 treatment-
seeking gamblers over the age of 60 years with 56 younger gamblers. The
older cohort had a later age of onset of gambling and developed gambling
problems over a longer duration of time than did the younger gamblers.
Older gamblers were less likely to wager on multiple types of gambling,
and they overwhelmingly preferred slot gambling. They also reported fewer
gambling-related marital problems relative to the younger groups.

The results from these studies suggest that older adults comprise a
minority of treatment-seeking gamblers, and the data are consistent with
general epidemiological data showing older age to be a protective factor in
development of disordered gambling. Nevertheless, differences in psychosocial problems noted across age groups, such as financial, family, legal, and
substance abuse problems, may suggest the need for interventions tailored
to specific issues encountered by older gamblers. Compared with younger
and middle-aged gamblers, older gamblers may have less need for family
therapy or concurrent substance abuse treatment in conjunction with gambling treatment.

In part based on age and gender differences, a great deal of clinical
interest has centered on subtyping gamblers (Blaszczynski, McConaghy, &
Frankova, 1990; Blaszczynski & Nower, 2003; McCormick, 1988, 1996).
Gamblers have primarily been classified on the basis of their putative reasons

for gambling. These reasons have ranged from boredom, to depression, to a mixture of both (Blaszczynski et al., 1990), or to the presence of narcissistic tendencies (McCormick, 1996). Alternate subtyping includes *action* or *escape* gamblers, characterizations that are somewhat analogous to the boredom and depressed subtypes. *Action gambling* generally refers to engaging in forms of gambling that involve some elements of skill and suspense, such as sports betting, racetracks, or card playing. *Escape gambling,* in contrast, usually consists of slot machine gambling and lottery or scratch tickets (e.g., Petry, 2003a; Potenza et al., 2001).

To date, little empirical research exists with respect to subtypes of gamblers, in terms of either classification, types or severity of problems experienced, or the need to intervene differentially with patients on the basis of their preferred gambling activity. However, women and older gamblers are more likely to experience problems with electronic gaming machines compared with men and younger gamblers, who are more likely to report problems with cards and sports betting (Petry, 2003a). Comorbid psychiatric symptoms vary on the basis of these gambling preferences as well (Petry, 2003a). Underlying biological dispositions may also differ on the basis of age, gender, or gambling preferences, although the data available addressing these issues are far from conclusive. I discuss these and related issues in the subsequent two chapters.

SUMMARY AND CLINICAL IMPLICATIONS

In this chapter, I have reviewed the evidence suggesting that certain demographic characteristics are associated with the development of problem and pathological gambling. In particular, younger age, ethnic minority status, lower socioeconomic standing, marital situation, and gender all appear to be related to disordered gambling behaviors. Clinicians may consider enhancing gambling screening efforts or providing outreach services to individuals with these risk factors.

Although people with these risk factors may develop gambling problems at rates higher than the population norms, and may benefit from prevention and intervention services, not all of the groups with high risk factors are adequately represented in gambling treatment settings. Instead, the typical profile of a treatment-seeking gambler is middle aged, married, and employed, with a relatively low level of education and Caucasian ethnicity. Efforts may need to be extended to populations (e.g., ethnic and racial minorities) that do not readily seek gambling services. In addition, treatment services may need to be adapted or tailored to better suit the needs of some gamblers.

Although subtyping treatment-seeking pathological gamblers on the basis of age, gender, or preferred gambling activities has received some clinical attention, little empirical data exist on methods for classifying gamblers or on the utility of subtyping in terms of better understanding etiologies or treatments for gamblers. The only thing that is clear is that many pathological gamblers suffer from a wide variety of other psychiatric conditions that may also need to be addressed during the course of gambling treatment. In the next chapter, I specifically address issues related to comorbidity.

5

COMORBIDITY OF DISORDERED GAMBLING AND OTHER PSYCHIATRIC DISORDERS

Comorbidity is the term used to describe the co-occurrence of two or more disorders. Each disorder can occur independently, a pattern that constitutes *lifetime comorbidity*, or the two disorders can occur at the same time, a pattern known as *current comorbidity*. Because many psychiatric disorders have some similar symptoms, both disorders must demonstrate the standard etiology and characteristic presentation of symptoms for a comorbid diagnosis to be made. A sophisticated understanding of comorbidities in the gambling field is lacking, because few large studies have been conducted. Nevertheless, some data exist regarding prevalence rates of gambling with other mental health disorders (e.g., Crockford & el-Guebaly, 1998b).

In this chapter, I first review comorbidities of pathological gambling and substance use disorders. I next provide details about studies of affective disorders and pathological gambling, and then I describe the relationship between anxiety disorders and pathological gambling. Some other psychiatric disorders have also been investigated in conjunction with pathological gambling, but only in a few studies. These include psychotic, somatization, eating, alexithymia, and attention-deficit disorders. Last, I review studies that have examined the comorbidity of gambling and personality disorders.

Within each section, I first describe general population surveys, as they represent the most accurate account of comorbidity. Few general population

85

surveys, however, have evaluated comorbidities. I also present studies of the prevalence of other psychiatric disorders in treatment-seeking pathological gamblers. In some cases, rates of pathological gambling have been investigated among individuals seeking treatment for other psychiatric disorders, but this type of research primarily has been limited to substance abusers. Because these issues were detailed in chapter 2, I review them only briefly in this chapter.

SUBSTANCE USE DISORDERS

In this section I review the prevalence of problem gambling in the general population and among various substance use subpopulations and then look more closely at the onset of gambling problems in comorbid populations.

Comorbidites in General Population Surveys

Any Substance Use Disorder

Results from general population surveys that have evaluated the relationship between gambling and substance use disorders were reviewed by Petry and Pietrzak (2004) and are summarized below as well as in Table 5.1.

In a general population survey, Bland, Newman, Orn, and Stebelsky (1993) conducted interviews with adults in Edmonton, Alberta, Canada. Over half the Level 3 gamblers identified in the survey had a substance use disorder, compared with less than 20% of nongamblers. In a phone survey in Texas, Feigelman, Wallisch, and Lesieur (1998) found that among all respondents identified with lifetime Level 2–3 gambling, over one third also had a substance use problem. Feigelman et al. (1998) also explored the converse relationship; among respondents with a current substance use problem (n = 412), 20.1% also had a gambling problem. Thus, this study provides evidence for a bidirectional association between gambling and substance use disorders, broadly defined. In the next sections I review the relationship between disordered gambling and specific substance use problems.

Alcohol Use Disorders

Two nationally based surveys (Gerstein et al., 1999; Welte, Barnes, Wieczorek, Tidwell, & Parker, 2001) have suggested a strong association between alcohol and gambling disorders. A very recent nationally-based study, results from which are not yet published, likewise demonstrated this relationship (Petry, Stinson, & Grant, manuscript submitted for publication). Surveys from specific geographical locations corroborate these findings, with rates of alcohol abuse or dependence being four or more times higher

TABLE 5.1
Prevalence Rates of Substance Use Disorders in General Population Surveys

Disorder	Sample N	No. Level 2–3 (L2–3) gamblers in sample	Lifetime substance use diagnosis in L2–3 gamblers (%)	Lifetime substance use diagnosis in nongamblers (%)
General or any substance use disorder (16.7%)[a]				
Bland et al. (1993)	7,214	30 L3	63.3[b]	19.0
Feigelman et al. (1998)	6,308	265 L2–3	35.2[b]	6.5[c]
Alcohol abuse or dependence (13.5%)[a]				
Bland et al. (1993)	7,214	30 L3	63.3[b]	16.5
Cunningham-Williams et al. (1998)[d]	2,954	161 L2–3	44.1[b]	7.5
Gernstein et al. (1999)	2,417	21 L3	9.9[b,e]	1.1[e]
Petry, Stinson, & Grant (manuscript submitted for publication)	43,093	195 L3	73.2[b]	25.0
Smart & Ferris (1996)	2,016	151 "Heavy"	8.5[e]	4.4[e]
Welte et al. (2001)	2,638	36 L3	25.0[b,e,f]	1.4[e,f,g]
Drug abuse or dependence (6.1%)[a]				
Bland et al. (1993)	7,214	30 L3	23.3[b]	6.3
Cunningham-Williams et al. (1998)[d]	2,954	161 L2–3	15.5	3.5
Petry, Stinson, & Grant (manuscript submitted for publication)	43,093	195 L3	38.1[b]	8.8
Nicotine dependence (25%)[h]				
Cunningham-Williams et al. (1998)[d]	2,954	161 L2–3	54.7[b]	27.2
Petry, Stinson, & Grant (manuscript submitted for publication)	43,093	195 L3	60.4[b]	n.s.
Smart & Ferris (1996)	2,016	151 "Heavy"	41.6[b]	21.3

Note. n.s. = nct stated. From *Dual Diagnosis and Psychiatric Treatment: Substance Abuse and Comorbid Disorders* (p. 439), by H. R. Kranzler and J. Tinsley, 2004, New York: Marcel Dekker. Copyright 2004 by Marcel Dekker, Inc. Adapted with permission. [a]Lifetime general population rate (Regier et al., 1990): *N* = 20,291. [b]Level 2–3 gamblers differ from the comparison group in the same study (*p* < .05). [c]Percentage of non-Level 2–3 gamblers. [d]Refers to unweighted percentages. [e]Current prevalence rate. [f]Percentage of non-Level 3 gamblers. [g]Estimated current general population rate according to the *Diagnostic and Statistical Manual of Mental Disorders* (4th ed.; American Psychiatric Association, 1994).

among individuals identified as having a gambling disorder compared with those without a gambling disorder (e.g., Bland et al., 1993; Cunningham-Williams, Cottler, Compton, & Spitznagel, 1998; Smart & Ferris, 1996).

Illicit Drug Abuse or Dependence

Studies have also noted a relationship between gambling and other drug use disorders but, perhaps because of the relatively low prevalence rates of disordered gambling and illicit drug use disorders, only studies that surveyed large numbers of people have found statistically significant relationships. In Gerstein et al.'s (1999) study, formal drug use diagnoses were not made, but 8.1% of lifetime Level 3 gamblers, and 16.8% of lifetime Level 2 gamblers, reported illicit drug use in the past year, versus 4.2% of Level 1 gamblers and 2.0% of nongamblers. Of the Level 2–3 gamblers identified in Cunningham-Williams et al.'s (1998) study, 15.5% demonstrated illicit drug use disorders, compared with 7.8% and 3.5% of Level 1 and Level 0 gamblers, respectively. Bland et al.'s (1993) survey found that the prevalence of illicit drug abuse and dependence was about four times higher in Level 3 gamblers than in nongamblers, and the most recent study, which included an even larger sample size, found very high rates of comorbidity of pathological gambling and drug use disorders (Petry, Stinson, & Grant, manuscript submitted for publication).

Nicotine Use and Dependence

Smoking occurs at relatively high rates in the general population, and some studies have examined comorbidity of smoking or nicotine dependence with disordered gambling. Cunningham-Williams et al. (1998) noted that rates of nicotine dependence were higher in Level 2–3 gamblers than in Level 0 gamblers, and intermediary rates of smoking (43.7%) were noted among Level 1 gamblers. Smart and Ferris (1996) found that 41.6% of heavy gamblers were smokers, compared with 30.1% of recreational gamblers and 21.3% of nongamblers.

In sum, general population surveys from national samples, as well as some specific regional studies, suggest a strong relationship between disordered gambling and virtually all substance use disorders. Because these surveys focused primarily on issues related to diagnoses, details about onset and patterns of the symptoms or disorders were rarely available. Research in treatment-seeking samples tends to corroborate these patterns of comorbidity between substance use and gambling disorders. Some of the studies also provide added information about comorbidity, severity, and onset of the disorders, as I describe below.

Substance Use Disorder Comorbidity in Treatment-Seeking Pathological Gamblers

Prevalence Rates of Substance Use Disorders

Compared with the general population, treatment-seeking gamblers are more likely to have alcohol and other drug diagnoses, with lifetime rates ranging from about one quarter to over two thirds across studies, as shown in Table 5.2. For example, Ramirez, McCormick, Russo, and Taber (1983) assessed substance use disorders in admissions to a Veterans Administration gambling treatment program and found that 39% met criteria for past-year drug or alcohol use disorders, and 47% met lifetime criteria for an alcohol or drug use disorder. Studies conducted of Gamblers Anonymous (GA) members (Lesieur & Blume, 1991b; Linden, Pope, & Jonas, 1986), inpatient gambling treatment programs (McCormick, Russo, Ramirez, & Taber, 1984), and outpatient clinics (Ibàñez et al., 2001; Ladd & Petry, 2003; Maccallum & Blaszczynski, 2002; Specker, Carlson, Edmonson, Johnson, & Marcotte, 1996; Stinchfield & Winters, 1996) ubiquitously have found high rates of alcohol and other drug abuse and dependence.

Cigarette smoking is common in treatment-seeking gamblers, but little research has been published on this topic. Maccallum and Blaszczynski (2002) reported that 65.3% of poker players seeking gambling treatment in Australia smoked cigarettes, but only 37% met nicotine dependence criteria. Other studies have not used formal criteria to determine nicotine dependence, but Petry and Oncken (2002) found that 62% of treatment-seeking gamblers in Connecticut were current smokers. Similarly, in a group of 944 treatment-seeking gamblers from Minnesota, Stinchfield and Winters (1996) found that 69% were current daily cigarette smokers. In summary, substantial evidence, and no contradictory data, indicates that substance use disorders are prevalent in treatment-seeking pathological gamblers.

Other Difficulties Experienced by Dual-Diagnosis Pathological Gamblers

Thus, individuals who seek treatment for gambling have high rates of substance use disorders. In most cases, substance use diagnoses were past, not current. In studies of patients seeking outpatient treatment for gambling in Connecticut (Ladd & Petry, 2003), for example, only about 10% reported current use of illicit drugs or regular, heavy use of alcohol. Similarly low rates of current substance abuse have been noted among gamblers seeking outpatient treatment in Minnesota programs (Specker et al., 1996; Stinchfield & Winters, 1996, 2001).

Despite the fact that most substance use problems occurred in the past and not at the time of seeking gambling treatment, some differences emerge rather consistently when comparing pathological gamblers with and without

TABLE 5.2
Prevalence Rates of Substance Use Disorders in Treatment-Seeking Pathological Gamblers

Disorder	Study	N	Lifetime substance use disorder (%)	Current substance use disorder (%)
General or any substance use disorder (16.7%)[a]	Black & Moyer (1998)	30 ad respondents	63	7
	Ladd & Petry (2003)	341 outpatients	31[b]	5
	Ramirez et al. (1983)	51 inpatients	47	39
	Specker et al. (1996)	40 outpatients	60	8
	Stinchfield & Winters (1996)	944 outpatients	33[b]	
	Stinchfield & Winters (2001)	592 outpatients	35	
Alcohol abuse or dependence (13.5%)[a]	Black & Moyer (1998)	30 ad respondents	63	10
	Ibáñez et al. (2001)	69 outpatients	35	23
	Ladd & Petry (2003)	341 outpatients	26[b]	4
	Lesieur & Blume (1991b)	50 female GA members	26	
	Linden et al. (1986)	25 male GA members	48	24
	Maccallum & Blaszczynski (2002)	75 outpatients	32	
	McCormick et al. (1984)	50 inpatients	50	8
	Specker et al. (1996)	40 outpatients		
Any illicit drug abuse or dependence (6.1%)[a]	Black & Moyer (1998)	30 ad respondents	27	13
	Ladd & Petry (2003)	341 outpatients	14[b]	1
	Ibáñez et al. (2001)	69 outpatients		3
	McCormick et al. (1984)	50 inpatients	4	
Cannabis abuse or dependence (4.3%)[a]	Maccallum & Blaszczynski (2002)	75 outpatients	23	11
	Specker et al. (1996)	40 outpatients		0
Cocaine abuse or dependence (0.2%)[a]	Ladd & Petry (2003)	341 outpatients	8[b]	<1
	Specker et al. (1996)	40 outpatients	5	0
Heroin abuse or dependence (0.7%)[a]	Ladd & Petry (2003)	341 outpatients	1[b]	0
	Maccallum & Blaszczynski (2002)	75 outpatients	0	0
Nicotine dependence (25%)[c]	Maccallum & Blaszczynski (2002)	75 outpatients		37
	Petry & Oncken (2002)	345 outpatients		62
	Stinchfield & Winters (1996)	944 outpatients		69

Note. GA = Gamblers Anonymous. From *Dual Diagnosis and Psychiatric Treatment: Substance Abuse and Comorbid Disorders* (p. 443), by H. R. Kranzler and J. Tinsley, 2004, New York: Marcel Dekker. Copyright 2004 by Marcel Dekker, Inc. Adapted with permission. [a]Lifetime general population rate (Regier et al., 1990): *N* = 20,291. [b]Past history of treatment. [c]Estimated general population rate according to the *Diagnostic and Statistical Manual of Mental Disorders* (4th ed.; American Psychiatric Association, 1994).

substance use diagnoses. Treatment-seeking gamblers with a history of substance use disorders tend to have more severe gambling problems, psychiatric symptoms, and other psychosocial difficulties than gamblers without substance use problems. Ladd and Petry (2003) compared the 31% of gamblers with substance abuse histories with the remainder without such histories. Those with substance abuse histories had more years of gambling problems and more frequent gambling activity. They were also more likely to be receiving treatment for mental health problems and reported greater psychiatric distress than gamblers without prior substance abuse problems.

Even cigarette smoking appears to be related to severity of psychosocial problems in gamblers. An analysis (Petry & Oncken, 2002) of Ladd and Petry's (2003) same sample of treatment-seeking gamblers found that, after controlling for substance abuse treatment histories, gender, and age, smokers had more severe gambling, family, and psychiatric problems. Compared with nonsmokers, smokers gambled more often and spent more money gambling; they also craved gambling more and had lower perceived control over gambling. The smokers were more likely to be taking psychiatric medications, and they experienced psychiatric symptoms, especially anxiety, more often than nonsmokers.

These studies call for further examination of the role of drug use (both past and present) in the development and course of pathological gambling. Substance abuse may also affect the course of treatment or outcomes of gambling treatment. One report found that treatment-seeking gamblers with a history of a substance use disorder were less likely to relapse to gambling than were individuals without other addictions (Zion, Tracy, & Abell, 1991). Perhaps having overcome another addiction may assist a gambler in ceasing gambling. However, another study of 169 treatment-seeking gamblers (Toneatto, Skinner, & Dragonetti, 2002) found that only about 10% had used illicit drugs in the month before entering gambling treatment, and outcomes were not influenced by drug use status.

Gambling Problems in Substance Abusers: Onset and Severity of Problems

As I reviewed in chapter 2, studies have noted high rates of gambling problems in treatment-seeking substance abusers. Prevalence rates of Level 2–3 gambling are about 2 to 10 times higher in substance abusers relative to the general population (see Table 2.4). In studies of treatment-seeking substance abusers, dually addicted patients have more severe problems than individuals with a substance use diagnosis alone. These problems range from family and legal difficulties to increased psychiatric symptoms and more severe drug use problems.

Treatment-seeking substance abusers identified as having gambling problems evidence more severe employment, legal, and family difficulties than their counterparts without gambling problems. For example, Hall et al. (2000) found that cocaine-dependent patients diagnosed as Level 3 gamblers were more likely to be unemployed, engage in illegal activities for profit, and serve time in prison than were cocaine-dependent patients without gambling problems. In another sample of cocaine abusers, Steinberg, Kosten, and Rounsaville (1992) reported that those identified as engaging in Level 3 gambling had more arrests, were convicted on more occasions, and spent more time in prisons than those without gambling problems. Langenbucher, Bavly, Labouvie, Sanjuan, and Martin (2001) found that substance abusers who were also pathological gamblers scored higher on indexes of social impairment than did nonpathological gamblers. I (Petry, 2000b) found that severity of gambling problems in substance abusers was significantly and independently predictive of engaging in risky sexual activities that spread infectious diseases.

Psychiatric symptoms also appear to be more severe in substance abusers identified with gambling problems. Langenbucher et al. (2001) reported increased rates of conduct disorder and attention-deficit disorder symptoms, and Hall et al. (2000) reported higher rates of antisocial personality disorder among substance abusers with gambling problems compared with those without. Steinberg et al. (1992) noted increased rates of attention-deficit disorder among cocaine abusers with gambling problems. Compared with substance abusers without gambling problems, McCormick (1993) found that dually diagnosed substance abusers scored higher on measures of impulsivity, aggression/hostility, and negative affect, and I (Petry, 2000c) found they had increased symptoms of somatization, obsessive–compulsive disorder, interpersonal sensitivity, hostility, and paranoia.

Severity and number of drug use problems are also elevated in substance abusers with gambling problems relative to those without. Hall et al. (2000) found that cocaine patients identified as pathological gamblers had higher rates of tobacco dependence than cocaine abusers not identified as such. In a mixed sample of substance abusers, Langenbucher et al. (2001) noted higher nicotine dependence scores, more frequent use of alcohol, and more alcohol and other drug dependence symptoms in pathological versus non-pathological gamblers. Steinberg et al. (1992) reported increased rates of alcohol dependence in cocaine abusers identified with gambling problems. They also had made more drug abuse treatment attempts, reported a greater number of overdoses, and used drugs more frequently than nonpathological gambling cocaine abusers. McCormick (1993) found that substance abusers with gambling problems abused a greater number of substances than did nongamblers, and Daghestani, Elenz, and Crayton (1996) found that drug-abusing veterans who also had a gambling problem began drug and alcohol use at an earlier age and reported more frequent current alcohol use than their counterparts without a gambling problem.

Although the evidence is strong that gambling problems among substance abusers are associated with increased problems along a number of dimensions, very little research has addressed issues related to onset and patterning of the disorders. Cho et al. (2002) found that alcohol problems preceded gambling problems in most dually diagnosed alcohol-dependent and alcohol-abusing men in Korea. Hall et al. (2000), in contrast, found that onset of gambling preceded onset of cocaine dependence in 72% of their cocaine-dependent sample from the Baltimore, Maryland, area. Cunningham-Williams, Cottler, Compton, Spitznagel, and Ben-Abdallah (2000) found that most pathological gamblers began smoking cigarettes, using marijuana, and drinking alcohol prior to developing gambling problems, but pathological gambling often preceded dependence on other drugs, especially stimulants.

Regardless of which comes first, pathological gambling and drug abuse may perpetuate one another. Spunt, Lesieur, Hunt, and Cahill (1995) found that methadone patients combined gambling and drug use to make money to buy drugs, increase their high from drugs, and celebrate gambling wins. In laboratory studies with healthy participants, Baron and Dickerson (1999) found that alcohol reduced resistance to begin and end a gambling session, and Kyngdon and Dickerson (1999) noted that alcohol prolonged the duration of gambling episodes and amount wagered. Thus, the use of substances while gambling may impair judgment and lead to increased problems in one or both areas.

Only a couple of studies have been published regarding the relationship of disordered gambling with outcomes of substance abuse treatment. Ledgerwood and Downey (2002) found that pathological-gambling methadone patients were more likely than their nonpathological-gambling counterparts to use cocaine during treatment and to drop out of the clinic prematurely. In contrast, Hall et al. (2000) did not find that gambling status was associated with increased cocaine or opioid use or treatment retention in samples of cocaine-dependent patients in drug-free or methadone treatment. Thus, more research is needed to ascertain whether gambling status influences outcomes of substance abuse patients.

I now present a case example of a substance abuser who also has a gambling problem.

Case example. Luis is a 24-year-old heroin addict with a long history of drug problems and gambling. After his mother was institutionalized for schizophrenia and alcoholism when he was about 9, Luis was placed in a series of foster homes. In the first of these, he was introduced to gambling by one of his foster brothers. They played cards, dice, and marbles for money and cigarettes, which were usually stolen from the foster parents. Luis loved the excitement of beating the foster brother, even though the brother often wouldn't give him what Luis had won. It was the feelings of control and specialness that appealed to Luis more than the actual winnings.

Luis left that family after about a year, following an incident in which he got in a fight with one of the other, younger foster children. His next situation was even worse, and he was sexually molested by one of the foster mother's boyfriends. He moved again and again, and he spent some time in a psychiatric hospital as an adolescent. He managed to avoid serious troubles, though, and left the state system at the age of 18. After dropping out of high school, he got a job pumping gas and made enough to rent a small apartment with some friends.

Luis's job lasted only a few months before he was fired for theft from the cash register. He needed extra money that week because he was behind on the rent, and he had spent his last paycheck on alcohol and drugs. By this time, Luis was drinking and smoking pot regularly, and he occasionally used cocaine. He quickly found a new job, stocking shelves at a grocery store.

One of Luis's drug suppliers was also a big gambler. Once, when Luis came to buy his supply, he found a group of dealers in a serious poker game, where thousands of dollars were at stake. They teased him as he walked in, treating him like a kid. This angered Luis. Instead of getting his drugs and leaving, he asked to get in on the next hand. They told him it was too high stakes for him, but Luis insisted. Luis was dealt a bad hand initially, and the others mocked him for his bet. On the third hand, Luis thought he had a good chance, and he was going to show them. He bet everything he had—$200. But he lost. He asked one of the others to borrow $50 more so he could stay in the game, determined that his luck would change. He lost that, too, and by the end of the night he owed $500. The others laughed at him and told him to stay in his own league. Luis was so angry he could hardly control himself. After ridiculing him, the guy who'd lent him the money said he could wait a week before he had to pay, but there would be an interest charge. Luis slammed the door and left.

Two days later, the guy who had lent him the money told Luis he had a deal for him. He'd forget about the $500 if Luis would serve as a decoy in a drug deal. Luis thought his role seemed easy, so he said yes. When the deal went off without a hitch, the dealer gave Luis an extra $100. Luis asked if they were planning another poker game. The dealer laughed, and said, "Yeah, come to the Outpost Motel tomorrow at about 10. Room 14." Luis came, with his $100 and another $50 he had saved from his paycheck. That night, Luis's luck changed. They played until 4 or 5 in the morning. Luis left the next day with over $3,000.

Over the next couple years, Luis's life consisted of poker playing and taking harder and harder drugs. Luis gradually got hooked on heroin. When he felt that the withdrawal symptoms were interfering with his game, he eventually entered a methadone maintenance clinic. Once he got on the right dose of methadone, he was able to refrain from doing any hard drugs while playing cards, but a bit of Jack Daniels helped him keep a level head and hide any emotions during the game. He had his ups and downs but somehow managed to get by. He felt he was gaining respect in his circle. After a couple of weeks of bad luck in poker, Luis broke into a store and stole a television, which he planned to give to his bookie in exchange for interest on his gambling debt. However, the police caught Luis. Luis is now awaiting sentencing for breaking and entering. In addition, he still owes over $10,000 to bookies and drug dealers.

OTHER PSYCHIATRIC DISORDERS

In this section I discuss other psychiatric disorders that may be comorbid with gambling. I focus on affective disorders, anxiety disorders, some other Axis I disorders, and personality disorders.

Mood Disorders and Suicidality

Depression, other mood disorders, and suicide seem to be related to disordered gambling as described in the following sections.

General Population Surveys

Only two published general population surveys (Bland et al., 1993; Cunningham-Williams et al., 1998) have evaluated comorbidities of psychiatric conditions and disordered gambling. Both studies used the Diagnostic Interview Schedule (Robins, Cottler, Bucholz, & Compton, 1996) to assess disordered gambling as well as rates of affective disorders, including major depression, dysthymia, bipolar disorder, and suicidality. The results of these studies are summarized in Table 5.3.

Cunningham-Williams et al. (1998) found that being a gambler increased the chances of having major depression. Rates of major depression were higher in Level 2–3 gamblers than in Level 0 gamblers. Level 1 gamblers (who accounted for 41.6% of the sample) were not included in this analysis. Cunningham-Williams et al. (1998) also examined the risk of psychiatric disorders in Level 1 compared with Level 0 gamblers and found that Level 1 gamblers were more likely to have both major depression (odds ratio [OR] = 1.7, 95% confidence interval [CI] = 1.1–2.6) and dysthymia (OR = 1.8, 95% CI = 1.0–3.0). Therefore, simply gambling, without any gambling-related problems, was related to depressive disorders in that sample. Bland et al. (1993) also found increased rates of affective disorders and dysthymia in

TABLE 5.3

Prevalence Rates of Affective Disorders in General Population Surveys and Treatment-Seeking Gamblers

Group and disorder	Study	Sample N	No. disordered gamblers	Lifetime prevalence in Level 2–3 (L2–3) gamblers (%)	Lifetime prevalence in nongamblers (%)
General population					
General/any affective disorder (8.3%)[a]	Bland et al. (1993)	7,214	30 L3	33.3[b]	14.2
	Petry, Stinson, & Grant (manuscript submitted for publication)	43,093	195 L3	49.6[b]	18.5[f]
Major depression (4.9%)[a]	Bland et al. (1993) Cunningham-Williams et al. (1998)	7,214 2,954	30 L3 161 L2–3	20.0[b] 8.8[b]	12.4 5.2
	Petry, Stinson, & Grant (manuscript submitted for publication)	43,093	195 L3	37.0[b]	12.3[f]
Dysthymia (3.3%)[a]	Bland et al. (1993) Cunningham-Williams et al. (1998)	7,214 2,954	30 L3 161 L2–3	20.0[b] 4.2	4.9 3.4
	Petry, Stinson, & Grant (manuscript submitted for publication)			13.2[b]	3.8[f]
Bipolar/manic episodes (1.3%)[a]	Bland et al. (1993)	7,214	30 L3	3.3	0.6
	Cunningham-Williams et al. (1998)	2,954	161 L2–3	3.1	0.8
	Petry, Stinson, & Grant (manuscript submitted for publication)	43,093	195 L3	22.8[b]	2.5[f]
Suicidality/suicide attempt(s)	Bland et al. (1993) Cunningham-Williams et al. (1998)	7,214 2,954	30 L3 161 L2–3	13.3 2.0	1.6
	Ladouceur, Dubé, & Bujold (1994)	1,471	41 L3 college students	26.8[b]	7.2

Treatment-seeking gamblers

		Lifetime rate	Current rate
General/any affective disorder (8.3%)[a]			
Black & Moyer (1998)	30 ad respondents	60.0	8.7
Ibáñez et al. (2001)	43 outpatients	15.9	52.0[c]
Linden et al. (1986)	25 male GA members		58.3
Roy, Adinoff, et al. (1988)	24 (20 inpatients; 4 outpatients)	75.0	35.7
Specker et al. (1996)	40 outpatients	77.5	16.0
Stinchfield & Winters (2001)	592 outpatients		
Major depression (4.9%)[a]			
Black & Moyer (1998)	30 ad respondents	50.0	
Linden et al. (1986)	25 male GA members	76.0	
McCormick et al. (1984)	50 inpatients	76.0	
Ramirez et al. (1983)	51 inpatients	52.9[d] 97.0[e]	
Specker et al. (1996)	40 outpatients	70.0	35.0
Taber, McCormick, Russo, et al. (1987)	66 inpatients	33.3	
Dysthymia (3.3%)[a]			
Specker et al. (1996)	40 outpatients	7.5	7.5
Bipolar disorder (1.3%)[a]			
Bellaire & Caspari (1992)	51 inpatients	3.9	3.9
Black & Moyer (1998)	30 ad respondents	20.0	
Linden et al. (1986)	25 male GA members	24.0	
Specker et al. (1996)	40 outpatients	5.0	0.0
Hypomanic disorder			
McCormick et al. (1984)	50 inpatients	38.0	
Suicidal ideation			
Frank et al. (1991)	162 GA members	47.5	
Ibáñez et al. (1992)	45 inpatients	42.2	
McCormick et al. (1984)	50 inpatients	80.0	
Petry & Kiluk (2002)	345 outpatients	48.8	22.5
Specker et al. (1996)	40 outpatients	40.4	
Sullivan (1994)	329 hotline callers	92.0	
Suicide attempt(s)			
Ibáñez et al. (1992)	45 inpatients	13.0	11.1
Frank et al. (1991)	162 GA members	12.0	
McCormick et al. (1984)	50 inpatients	17.0	
Petry & Kiluk (2002)	345 outpatients		2.3
Schwarz & Lindner (1992)	58 inpatients	36.7	
Sullivan et al. (1994)	329 hotline callers	4.0	

Note. GA = Gamblers Anonymous.

[a]Lifetime general population rate (Regier et al., 1990): N = 20,291. [b]L2–3 gamblers differ from comparison group ($p < .05$). [c]Percentage of patients with recurrent affective disorders. [d]Patients reporting no problem with substance abuse. [e]Patients reporting problems with substance abuse. [f]Derived from odds ratios comparing pathological gamblers with nonpathological gamblers.

Level 3 versus Level 0 gamblers. However, neither Cunningham-Williams et al. (1998) nor Bland et al. (1993) found an association between gambling and bipolar disorder.

Another large scale study of comorbidities in the general population of the United States has recently been completed. The National Epidemiologic Survey on Alcohol and Related Conditions (NESARC) is the largest comorbidity study ever conducted. It assessed *DSM–IV* substance use disorders, nine mood and anxiety disorders, and seven personality disorders in a nationally representative sample of 43,093 adults. It also included a *DSM–IV* based assessment of pathological gambling. Although results of the gambling-based assessment are not yet published, preliminary analyses of the data suggest high rates of comorbidity between pathological gambling and major mood disorders (Petry, Stinson, & Grant, manuscript submitted for publication).

Cunningham-Williams et al. (1998) found no increased rates of suicidality across individuals with differing levels of gambling problems. Bland et al. (1993) asked a question regarding suicide attempts to only the Level 3 gamblers identified in that survey and found that 13.3% had attempted suicide. In Ladouceur, Dubé, and Bujold's (1994) survey of 1,471 college students, 26.8% of those identified as Level 3 gamblers had attempted suicide, compared with 7.2% of students without gambling problems. A sociological study conducted by Phillips, Welty, and Smith (1997) evaluated rates of suicide in Las Vegas and Atlantic City and concluded that Las Vegas has the highest rate of suicide in the United States, among both its residents and its visitors. In Atlantic City, they found high rates of suicide among residents and visitors, but only since the casinos opened. Campbell, Simmons, and Lester (1999) examined the impact of increasing opportunities to gamble in Louisiana. They compared suicide rates between 1989 and 1990 and between 1994 and 1995, and found that high rates of unemployment and per capita spending on the lottery were associated with increased rates of suicide over this time period. McCleary, Chew, Merrill, and Napolitano (2002) compared rates of suicide in 148 U.S. metropolitan areas before and after the advent of casinos and found a modest positive correlation between the presence of casinos and suicide rates.

Thus, suicide rates may be associated with increased access to gambling. Affective disorders seem to occur at higher rates among disordered gamblers than control participants in general population surveys, but often only trends of increased rates have been noted. Because only two general population surveys evaluating comorbidity have been published to date, research in large general population surveys is needed to confirm these relationships.

Mood Disorders in Treatment-Seeking Pathological Gamblers

Studies that have used structured diagnostic instruments to assess the presence of affective disorders in treatment-seeking pathological gamblers are also summarized in Table 5.3. Several studies have evaluated rates of major depression in gamblers who were treated on inpatient units (McCormick et al., 1984; Ramirez et al., 1983; Taber, McCormick, Russo, Adkins, & Ramirez, 1987) and found lifetime major depression rates ranging from 33% to 76%. In outpatient treatment (Ibàñez et al., 2001; Specker et al., 1996), GA (Linden et al., 1986), and samples recruited from advertisements (Black & Moyer, 1998), rates of mood disorders were high as well.

McCormick et al. (1984) examined the etiology of depression and gambling disorders. In 38 treatment-seeking gamblers who met criteria for a major depressive episode, gambling preceded depression in 86% of cases. These results suggest that depression may stem from, rather than contribute to, gambling, at least for most treatment-seeking gamblers in that sample.

In Black and Moyer's (1998) sample, 20% of Level 3 gamblers had bipolar disorder. Some studies (Linden et al., 1986; McCormick et al., 1984), but not others (Bellaire & Caspari, 1992), have found elevated rates of hypomania, manic episodes, or bipolar disorder. Some rates were higher than in the general population (Regier et al., 1990), but these differences are confounded by the fact that the patients were receiving inpatient psychiatric treatment. Patients receiving outpatient treatment have less severe problems. In gamblers seeking outpatient treatment, Specker et al. (1996) found no differences in rates of bipolar disorder between gamblers and control respondents.

Other studies have compared scores on psychological tests that measure mood in treatment-seeking pathological gamblers. These studies tend to concur that depressive symptoms are high in pathological gamblers (e.g., Blaszczynski & McConaghy, 1989; Gerstein et al., 1999; Moravec & Munley, 1983). Studies also have reported on significant life events (e.g., trauma, divorce) in gamblers. Taber, McCormick, and Ramirez (1987) and Roy, Custer, Lorenz, and Linnoila (1988) have noted more significant life events in gamblers than in control respondents. According to retrospective analyses, these events occurred before the onset of both the disordered gambling and the major depressive episode, and therefore they may be considered contributory to psychiatric problems.

High rates of suicidal ideation and attempts have also been reported in treatment-seeking gamblers. An early study by Kennedy, Phanjoo, and Shekim (1971) found that gamblers who had attempted suicide reported betting more money than did nonsuicidal gamblers. Subsequent studies in GA members (Frank, Lester, & Wexler, 1991), inpatient treatment programs (McCormick et al., 1984), help-line callers (Sullivan, 1994), and outpatient samples both in the United States (Petry & Kiluk, 2002) and throughout the world (Ibàñez, Mercade, Sanroma, & Cordero, 1992; Schwarz & Lindner, 1992), all suggest high rates of suicidal ideation and attempts in gamblers. Thus, strong evidence exists for a depressive component to pathological gambling, with substantial rates of suicidality in treatment-seeking gamblers. However, a better understanding of the directionality of the relationship is needed.

Anxiety Disorders and Pathological Gambling

Anxiety Disorder Comorbidity in General Population Surveys

Many of the studies outlined above also assessed anxiety disorders, and these results are summarized in Table 5.4.

Cunningham-Williams et al. (1998) found that being a Level 2–3 gambler significantly increased the odds of having phobias (OR = 2.3, 95% CI = 1.2–4.3). Obsessive–compulsive disorder, panic disorder, and generalized anxiety disorders were no more likely to occur in Level 2–3 gamblers compared with nongamblers in their sample. Bland et al. (1993) found that pathological gamblers were more likely than nongamblers to have any anxiety disorder. Rates of agoraphobia were also higher in Level 3 gamblers compared with nongamblers, but rates of phobias and panic disorders did not differ between groups in their sample. Bland et al. (1993), unlike Cunningham-Williams et al. (1998), also noted a relationship between Level 3 gambling and obsessive–compulsive disorder. The NESARC study (Petry, Stinson, & Grant, manuscript submitted for publication) found elevated rates of all anxiety disorders among pathological gamblers, but that study did not evaluate obsessive–compulsive disorder.

Anxiety Disorders in Treatment-Seeking Samples

The main results from published studies that have examined anxiety disorders in treatment-seeking gamblers are summarized in the lower portion of Table 5.4. With the exception of agoraphobia, investigators have noted high rates of generalized anxiety disorders as well as specific anxiety disorders (Black & Moyer, 1998; Linden et al., 1986; Roy, Adinoff, et al., 1988; Specker et al., 1996). However, some studies report contradictory findings, with low rates of comorbidity between gambling and anxiety disorders. Ibàñez et al. (2001) found that less than 10% of treatment-seeking gamblers had a lifetime or current anxiety disorder. Blaszczynski and McConaghy (1989) administered an inventory assessing anxiety symptoms and reported that scores in 75 inpatient gamblers were no different from normative scores.

Some of the features of disordered gambling are thought to share similarities with obsessive–compulsive disorder (OCD; see Blanco, Moreyra, Nunes, Sáiz-Ruiz, & Ibàñez, 2001; Hollander & Wong, 1995). Linden et al. (1986) found that 5 of the 25 (20%) male GA members met criteria for OCD. However, in each case the patient suffered from at least one other major psychiatric disorder, such as bipolar or an anxiety disorder. Black and

TABLE 5.4

Prevalence Rates of Anxiety Disorders in General Population Surveys and Treatment-Seeking Gamblers

Group and disorder	Study	Sample N	No. disordered gamblers	Lifetime prevalence in Level 2–3 (L2–3) gamblers (%)	Lifetime prevalence in nongamblers (%)
General population					
General/any anxiety disorder (14.6%)[a]	Bland et al. (1993)	7,214	30 L3	26.7[b]	9.2
	Cunningham-Williams et al. (1998)	2,954	161 L2–3	7.7	9.0
	Petry, Stinson, & Grant (manuscript submitted for publication)	43,093	195 L3	41.3[b]	15.5
Any phobia (12.6%)[a]	Bland et al. (1993)	7,214	30 L3	16.7	6.8
	Cunningham-Williams et al. (1998)	2,954	161 L2–3	14.6[b]	9.5
Agoraphobia (5.2%)[a]	Bland et al. (1993)	7,214	30 L3	13.3[b]	2.4
	Petry, Stinson, & Grant (manuscript submitted for publication)	43,093	195 L3	5.1[b]	1.0[e]
Social phobia (2.8%)[a]	Bland et al. (1993)	7,214	30 L3	0.0	1.2
	Petry, Stinson, & Grant (manuscript submitted for publication)	43,093	195 L3	10.6[b]	4.6[e]
Simple phobia (10.0%)[a]	Bland et al. (1993)	7,214	30 L3	10.0	5.4
	Petry, Stinson, & Grant (manuscript submitted for publication)	43,093	195 L3	23.5[b]	7.8[e]
Panic (1.6%)[a]	Bland et al. (1993)	7,214	30 L3	3.3	1.8
	Cunningham-Williams et al. (1998)	2,954	161 L2–3	3.1	1.6
	Petry, Stinson, & Grant (manuscript submitted for publication)	43,093	195 L3	18.1[b]	4.2[e]
Obsessive–compulsive (2.5%)[a]	Bland et al. (1993)	7,214	30 L3	16.7[b]	2.3
	Cunningham-Williams et al. (1998)	2,954	161 L2–3	0.9	2.1

(continued)

TABLE 5.4 (Continued)

Group and disorder	Study	Sample N	No. disordered gamblers	Lifetime prevalence in Level 2–3 (L2–3) gamblers (%)	Lifetime prevalence in nongamblers (%)
				Lifetime rate	Current rate
Treatment-seeking gamblers					
General/any anxiety disorder (14.6%)[a]	Black & Moyer (1998)	30 ad respondents		40.0	27.0
	Ibáñez et al. (2001)	43 outpatients		7.2	4.3
	Linden et al. (1986)	25 male GA members		28.0	
	Roy, DeJong, et al. (1989)	24 (20 inpatients, 4 outpatients)		12.5[c]	
	Specker et al. (1996)	40 outpatients		37.5	22.5
Agoraphobia (5.2%)[a]	Linden et al. (1986)	25 male GA members		4.0	
	Specker et al. (1996)	40 outpatients		5.0	0.0
Social phobia (2.8%)[a]	Linden et al. (1986)	25 male members		4.0	
	Specker et al. (1996)	40 outpatients		5.0	5.0
Simple phobia (10.0%)[a]	Black & Moyer (1998)	30 ad respondents		30.0	20.0
	Linden et al. (1986)	25 male GA members		8.0	
	Roy, DeJong, et al. (1988)	24 (20 inpatients, 4 outpatients)		12.5	
	Specker et al. (1996)	40 outpatients		12.5	10.0
Panic (1.6%)[a]	Black & Moyer (1998)	30 ad respondents		10.0	10.0
	Linden et al. (1986)	25 male GA members		16.0	
	Specker et al. (1996)	40 outpatients		20.0	10.0
Obsessive–compulsive (2.5%)[a]	Black & Moyer (1998)	30 ad respondents		10.0	6.7
	Linden et al. (1986)	25 male GA members		20.0	
	Specker et al. (1996)	40 outpatients		2.5	2.5
Posttraumatic stress (8.0%)[d]	McCormick et al. (1989)	59 male inpatients		29.0	
	Specker et al. (1996)	40 outpatients		12.5	5.0

Note. GA = Gamblers Anonymous, n.s. = not stated.
[a]Lifetime general population rate (Regier et al., 1990): *N* = 20,291. [b]L2–3 gamblers differ from the comparison group in the same study (*p* < .05). [c]Percentage of patients with generalized anxiety disorder or simple phobia. [d]Lifetime general population rate according to the *Diagnostic and Statistical Manual of Mental Disorders* (4th ed., text rev.; American Psychiatric Association, 2000). [e]Derived from odds ratios comparing pathological gamblers with nonpathological gamblers.

Moyer reported slightly lower rates of OCD in Level 3 gamblers recruited from community advertisements, whereas Specker et al. (1996) found that only 1 of 40 gamblers had OCD.

Blaszczynski (1999) compared 40 treatment-seeking gamblers with 40 control respondents on an inventory that assesses OCD symptoms. Gamblers had higher total scores, with elevations on factors related to impaired control over mental activities (exaggerated doubts, ruminative thinking, and difficulties with simple thinking) and worries of losing control over motor behaviors (e.g., concern about violent impulses). No differences were found in regard to fears of contamination or excessive checking and counting.

Familial studies are another method of assessing possible associations between conditions. If two conditions are genetically linked, one would expect higher rates of one disorder among family members with the putatively related disorder. In a familial association study of individuals with OCD, Black, Goldstein, Noyes, and Blum (1994) found that relatives of patients with OCD were no more likely than healthy control respondents to have gambling problems. However, this study included only 32 diagnosed OCD cases. In a larger study, Bienvenu et al. (2000) likewise reported no increased risk of pathological gambling in 343 family members of OCD patients; less than 1% had gambling problems. Thus, these data do not support a link between OCD and pathological gambling.

Only two known studies have examined the co-occurrence of pathological gambling and posttraumatic stress disorder (PTSD). McCormick, Taber, and Kruedelbach (1989) found that 29% of 59 gamblers in a Veterans Administration hospital had PTSD. Using the SCID, Specker et al. (1996) found much lower rates of PTSD (12.5%) in an outpatient sample from Minnesota.

The data published are far from conclusive in terms of establishing a relationship between gambling and anxiety disorders. However, they suggest that rates of certain anxiety disorders and phobias may be higher in Level 3 gamblers relative to the general population. In addition, results from the recent NESARC study reveal high rates of comorbidity between pathological gambling and panic disorder, social and specific phobias, and generalized anxiety disorders (Petry, Stinson, & Grant, manuscript submitted for publication). The NESARC study did not include modules on OCD or PTSD, but other published studies are mixed with respect to the association of OCD or PTSD and gambling disorders.

Other Axis I Psychiatric Disorders

The comorbidity of pathological gambling with other psychiatric conditions has not been well studied, and the few studies that exist for each disorder are detailed in Table 5.5. Because very limited research in this area

TABLE 5.5
Prevalence Rates of Other Psychiatric Disorders in General Population Surveys and Treatment-Seeking Gamblers

Group and disorder	Study	Sample N	No. disordered gamblers	Lifetime prevalence rate in Level 2–3 (L2–3) gamblers (%)	Lifetime prevalence rate in nongamblers (%)
General population					
Schizophrenia (1.5%)[a]	Bland et al. (1993)	7,214	30 L3	0.0	0.7
	Cunningham-Williams et al. (1998)	2,954	161 L2–3	3.9[b]	1.1
Somatoform disorder (0.2%–2.0%)[c]	Cunningham-Williams et al. (1998)	2,954	161 L2–3	8.6[b]	4.0
Eating disorders					
Anorexia (0.5%)[c]	Bland et al. (1993)	7,214	30 L3	0.0	0.1
Alexithymia	Lumley & Roby (1995)	1,147	35 L3	31.4	11.1[d]

Treatment-seeking gamblers	Study	Sample N	No. disordered gamblers	Lifetime rate	Current rate
Schizophrenia/psychosis	Bellaire & Caspari (1992)		51 inpatients	5.9	
	Black & Moyer (1998)		30 ad respondents	3.3	0.0
	Taber, McCormick, Russo, et al. (1987)		66 inpatients	3.0	
Schizoaffective disorder (<1%)[c]	Specker et al. (1996)		40 outpatients	2.5	2.5
	McCormick et al. (1984)		50 inpatients	2.0	
Somatoform disorder (0.2%–2.0%)[c]	Black & Moyer (1998)		30 ad respondents	10.0	10.0
	Specker et al. (1996)		40 outpatients	0.0	
Eating disorders (any)	Specker et al. (1996)		40 outpatients	0.0	
Bulimia (1.0%–3.0%)[c]	Black & Moyer (1998)		30 ad respondents	16.7	0.0
Anorexia (0.5%)[c]	Black & Moyer (1998)		30 ad respondents	0.0	0.0
Adjustment disorder (2.0%–8.0%)[c]	Ibáñez et al. (2001)		43 outpatients	17.4	
Attention-deficit/hyperactivity disorder (3.0%–7.0%)[c]	Specker et al. (1995)		40 outpatients	20.0	
Impulse control (any)	Specker et al. (1995)		40 outpatients	35.0	
Compulsive buying	Specker et al. (1995)		40 outpatients	25.0	
Compulsive sexual behavior	Specker et al. (1995)		40 outpatients	10.0	
Intermittent explosive	Specker et al. (1995)		40 outpatients	7.5	
Kleptomania	Specker et al. (1995)		40 outpatients	5.0	
Compulsive exercise	Specker et al. (1995)		40 outpatients	2.5	

[a]Lifetime general population rate (Regier et al., 1990); N = 20,291. [b]L2–3 gamblers differ from the comparison group in the same study (p < .05). [c]Lifetime general population rate according to the Diagnostic and Statistical Manual of Mental Disorders (4th ed., text rev.; American Psychiatric Association, 2000). [d]Percentage of non-Level 3 gamblers with alexithymia

is available, both community sample surveys and treatment studies are described together for each disorder.

A small number of studies have reported on the co-occurrence of psychotic disorders with pathological gambling. In a community sample, Cunningham-Williams et al. (1998) found that being a Level 2–3 gambler increased more than threefold the odds of having schizophrenia (95% CI = 1.3–9.7). In contrast, Bland et al. (1993) found no relationship between Level 3 gambling and schizophrenia in another community survey. In treatment-seeking samples, Bellaire and Caspari (1992), Black and Moyer (1998), Specker et al. (1996), McCormick et al. (1984), and Taber, McCormick, et al. (1987) reported that only 3% to 6% of Level 3 gamblers had a psychotic disorder. Blaszczynski and McConaghy (1988) administered an inventory assessing psychiatric symptoms to treatment-seeking gamblers and found that they scored higher than community-based norms on scales assessing paranoia and psychoticism, but the scores of the gamblers did not differ from those of other samples of psychiatric outpatients.

Thus, little evidence suggests that individuals who seek gambling treatment are any more likely than the general population to suffer from psychotic disorders. Of course, this conclusion is limited by the small sample sizes of patients identified with gambling problems and psychotic disorders, both of which occur at relatively low base rates. Results from treatment-seeking samples may underestimate the association, because individuals with severe mental health disorders, such as schizophrenia, may be unlikely to receive treatment for a concomitant disorder like pathological gambling at the programs that treat gamblers. Studies investigating gambling participation and problems among schizophrenic individuals are needed to better address comorbidities between these disorders.

Cunningham-Williams et al. (1998) found that somatization syndrome, a disorder characterized by focusing on bodily ailments, was more prevalent in Level 2–3 gamblers than in nongamblers (OR = 3.0, 95% CI = 1.6–5.8). Black and Moyer (1998) reported somatoform disorder in 10% of Level 3 gamblers, but Specker et al. (1996) found that none of the 40 gamblers they evaluated suffered from somatoform disorder. Using scores on a psychiatric symptom inventory, Blaszczynski and McConaghy (1988) and Petry (2000c) have reported that problem gamblers had higher scores of somatization than control respondents.

Although a relationship between eating disorders and pathological gambling has been speculated (Lesieur & Blume, 1993), most empirical reports are based on small samples and have used questions about eating problems rather than psychometrically validated instruments. Lesieur and Blume (1991b) found that 20% of 50 female GA members called themselves "compulsive overeaters," and 1 (2%) referred to herself as "anorexic." Lesieur et al. (1991) found that college students identified as Level 3 gamblers were more likely to report a problem with "overeating" than students who were not identified as Level 3 gamblers, but no differences were noted in terms of "overeating then vomiting." Ladouceur, Dubé, and Bujold (1994) reported an increased rate of self-reported "compulsive eating" in gamblers identified in another survey of college students. However, these findings are limited by the lack of psychiatric diagnosis for identifying eating disorders. Black and Moyer (1998) used the Diagnostic Interview Schedule (Robins et al., 1996) and found that none of the Level 3 gamblers they interviewed had anorexia, but 17% had bulimia. Bland et al. (1993), in a general population survey, and Specker et al. (1996), in a treatment sample, found that none of the Level 3 gamblers met diagnostic criteria for eating disorders.

A survey of young adults examined symptoms of *alexithymia*, a disorder characterized by difficulty in describing or recognizing one's own emotions, and its co-occurrence with disordered gambling. Lumley and Roby (1995) administered an alexithymia scale and a screen for gambling disorders to 1,147 young adults, of whom 3.1% were classified as Level 3 gamblers. Alexithymia was noted in about three times as many Level 3 gamblers as control respondents.

Specker, Carlson, Christenson, and Marcotte (1995) found that 20% of treatment-seeking gamblers met criteria for attention-deficit/hyperactivity disorder (ADHD). Carlton and Manowitz (1992) evaluated attention-deficit disorder symptoms, conduct disorder symptoms, and behavioral restraint in 12 GA members, 12 Alcoholics Anonymous (AA) members, and 15 control respondents. They found that AA and GA members scored higher than control respondents on the attention-deficit disorder symptoms, whereas only AA members differed from control respondents on conduct symptoms. GA members did not differ from control respondents on the behavioral task, but AA members did. Rugle and Melamed (1993) compared retrospective reports of childhood ADHD symptoms and performance on attention tasks in 33 treatment-seeking gamblers (without substance abuse) and 33 nonaddicted control respondents. Gamblers scored higher than control respondents on the childhood ADHD scale. On attention measures, gamblers performed worse than control respondents on three tasks that tap executive frontal functions, but no differences were found on tasks that reflect lower order attention.

Specker et al. (1995) examined rates of impulse control disorders in treatment-seeking gamblers. Although the sample size was small, their data are suggestive of increased rates of compulsive buying and sexual behaviors, intermittent explosive behaviors, and kleptomania in gamblers. More research from general population surveys and clinical samples is needed to establish rates of comorbidity between disordered gambling and these psychiatric conditions.

Rates of Disordered Gambling in People Seeking Treatment for Other Psychiatric Conditions

Surprisingly few investigators have evaluated rates of disordered gambling among individuals seeking treatment for mental health disorders other than substance abuse (see chap. 2). Lesieur and Blume (1990) administered the South Oaks Gambling Screen (Lesieur & Blume, 1987) to 105 hospitalized psychiatric patients with a range of diagnoses and found that 6.5% were Level 3 gamblers. Lejoyeux, Arbaretaz, McLoughlin, and Ades (2002) examined gambling disorders in 107 inpatients in France who met criteria for major depressive disorders. Only 3 were diagnosed with Level 3 gambling, a rate that cannot be considered higher than general population norms. Hollander et al. (1997) surveyed 701 members of the Obsessive Compulsive Foundation and found that fewer than 1% had a current or past history of pathological gambling. Similarly, in a report from India, none of the 231 OCD patients interviewed met criteria for pathological gambling (Jaisoorya, Reddy, & Srinath, 2003). As noted earlier, disordered gambling also does not appear to be higher among family members of patients with OCD (Bienvenu et al., 2000; Black et al., 1994). However, a study of 43 compulsive shoppers (Schlosser, Black, Repertinger, & Freet, 1994) revealed that 11% met lifetime criteria for Level 3 gambling, and 9% met current criteria, which is suggestive of a possible relationship between this impulse control disorder and pathological gambling.

Lepage, Ladouceur, and Jacques (2000) administered the South Oaks Gambling Screen (Lesieur & Blume, 1987) to 87 individuals who received community assistance (food kitchen attendees or people staying at homeless shelters) and found a rate of pathological gambling of 17.2%. Similar rates of Level 2–3 gambling were noted among 171 consecutive admissions of homeless people in Boston with substance use disorders (Shaffer, Freed, & Healea, 2002); 12.8% were Level 2 gamblers, and 5.5% were Level 3 gamblers. Finally, Muelleman, DenOtter, Wadman, Tran, and Anderson (2002) evaluated 61 women receiving emergency room treatment for intimate partner violence and found that 23% of these women had a partner who may be a Level 3 gambler.

No other known studies have examined rates of pathological gambling among individuals seeking treatment for other psychiatric disorders, and it is clear that much more research is needed among specific populations of interest. For example, patients presenting at emergency rooms for suicide attempts may experience high rates of Level 3 gambling, as may patients receiving treatment for depression and other affective disorders. Given a putative association between schizophrenia and gambling disorders, a study of the prevalence rate of gambling problems among schizophrenic individuals would also be of interest. People with somatoform disorders and hypochondriasis may also experience elevated levels of gambling disorders, as would individuals with certain personality disorders, as I describe in the next section. In the absence of large-scale general population surveys, examination of gambling problems among individuals seeking treatment for these conditions may further elucidate the relationships among these disorders.

Personality Disorders

The concept of an "addictive personality" has intuitive appeal in explaining the high comorbidity between addictive behaviors, such as alcohol and drug abuse, cigarette smoking, pathological gambling, eating disorders, and even compulsive spending and sexual disorders. Indeed, many Level 3 gamblers describe themselves in this manner, reporting their addictions and tendencies to go to extremes. The construct of an addictive personality, however, has not been operationally defined, and no standardized manner of assessing an addictive personality has been established. Nevertheless, a number of personality disorders are described in the *Diagnostic and Statistical Manual of Mental Disorders* (4th ed.; American Psychiatric Association, 1994), and these are termed *Axis II disorders*. Prevalence rates of Axis II disorders have been evaluated in some studies of gamblers, as I detail in the following sections.

Antisocial Personality Disorder

The most evidence exists for an association between pathological gambling and antisocial personality disorder (ASPD). ASPD is considered part of the Cluster B personality disorders, which also include borderline, histrionic, and narcissistic personality disorders. In community samples, Cunningham-Williams et al. (1998) and Bland et al. (1993) have found significant increases in ASPD among individuals identified with a gambling disorder compared with those without gambling problems. Slutske et al. (2001) examined rates of ASPD in more than 7,000 male veteran twin pairs, and increases in rates of ASPD were noted among veterans identified with disordered gambling compared with those without gambling problems.

In samples of treatment-seeking gamblers, Blaszczynski, McConaghy, and Frankova (1989), Ibàñez et al. (2001), Steel and Blaszczynski (1998),

Blaszczynski and McConaghy (1994a), and Kroeber (1992) all have reported high rates of ASPD, but Specker et al. (1996) did not. Cunningham-Williams et al. (2000) found that gambling status was associated with ASPD among drug users recruited from drug treatment and community settings. In Langenbucher et al.'s (2001) sample of 372 substance users, the 13% (n = 49) of patients who were identified as pathological gamblers scored higher than nonpathological gamblers (n = 323) on measures of conduct disorder symptoms, impulsivity, and ASPD symptoms.

Other Personality Disorders

Although ASPD is the personality disorder for which most data are available, some studies have examined prevalence rates of other personality disorders in gamblers. Ibàñez et al. (2001) found that 27.5% of treatment-seeking gamblers had a personality disorder other than ASPD. Specker et al. (1995) reported the lowest rates of personality disorders (25%) using SCID diagnoses, whereas Bellaire and Caspari (1992) found intermediary rates of about 50% of "severe personality disorders" in a sample of 51 inpatients. In a very small sample of 7 inpatients who were identified as Level 3 gamblers when seeking other psychiatric treatment, Lesieur and Blume (1990) found that almost 75% had a personality disorder. These rates are reported in Table 5.6. These rates are higher than the rates in general population surveys, but conclusions should be drawn with caution because so few studies have been conducted.

A personality disorder that has gained a lot of attention clinically among gambling treatment providers is narcissistic personality disorder. A case example, continued from chapter 4, provides an example of this type of gambler.

Case example continued. Ned, a 45-year-old married man, presented for treatment at an outpatient gambling clinic in Maryland. He had been indicted on several charges of stealing and passing checks from an employer and is now on probation. His probation officer insisted he attend treatment. Ned walks into the clinic for his first appointment, and the receptionist hands him some forms to complete. Ned asks her how long she's been working there and why they have such a dumpy looking building. He tells her that she is the only bright thing in the office and that she is too pretty to be working there. After complimenting her dress and hair, Ned asks her what it's like working with these losers who don't know how to control their gambling.

Sally, the receptionist, does not respond to a lot of his comments but reminds him that the therapist will need the forms. Ned starts on Questions 1 and 2 and then tells her that Question 3, related to his address, is ambiguous. He says:

> Well, I'm moving to a big house by the shore next week, so which address do you want? My old one or my new one? My ex is staying in the old house, and she stays home all the time, so you can find me through her. She's just been devastated since I told her I couldn't take it any more and I was leaving her. I don't even think she's got anything to live for now that I left her. And I stayed with her for a long time. Because she's the mother of my three children. I bet you know my son. He plays for the Pittsburgh Steelers. He's on television all the time, and he's got so much money. I could set you up with him, you know. Are you single? He would really like you. Here, let me show you a picture.

Sally says, "Sir, we really need you to complete the form. I can't call the therapist until you finish that form." Ned says:

> OK, sure. But what about Question 6 here, about my income. I don't know why you need to know that. I make a lot of money, and it's not anybody's business how much I make. Last year, I grossed over $200,000. My wife, she just wants to spend it all, too. I let her, you know. I bought her a mink coat last winter, and a huge diamond ring. But not any more. She needs to figure out how she's going to make it on her own. I've had it with her.

Sally says, "Sir, you don't have to answer that question if you don't want to, but you do have to fill out the rest of that form before I can have you see the therapist." Ned says:

> I don't need to see a therapist. My lawyer told me I should come here. Just a bad business deal, a misunderstanding, that's why I'm here. Not what you see here most of the time, I'm sure. You probably see all sorts of losers here. I make more than everyone here combined. I'm going to tell them a thing or two, too.

Ned laughs: "They'll be paying me for my advice. I bet these therapists have never met anyone like me before."

Comment. Ned's description is fairly typical of that of a narcissistic gambler. He brags and exaggerates his perceived successes, many of which are not based in reality. He is showy and acts in a very disrespectful manner to the receptionist. He may also have aspects of antisocial personality disorder, evidenced by his theft behavior and possibly familial violence (see chap. 9). He has a prior history of alcohol dependence (see chap. 4). He does not feel that he has a gambling problem and denies the relationship between his gambling and his financial, legal, and marital situation. Ned's story is continued in chapter 10, in which I describe the use of psychodynamic therapy for treating gamblers.

TABLE 5.6
Prevalence of Personality Disorders in General Population Surveys and Treatment-Seeking Gamblers

Group and disorder	Study	Sample N	No. disordered gamblers	Lifetime rate in Level 2–3 (L2–3) gamblers (%)	Lifetime rate in nongamblers (%)
General population					
Conduct disorder	Slutske et al. (2001)	7,869 men	615 L2–3	41.0[a]	7.0
Antisocial personality (2.6%)[d]	Bland et al. (1993)	7,214	30 PGs	40.0[a]	3.1
	Cunningham-Williams et al. (1998)	2,954	161 L2–3	35.0[a]	4.6
	Petry, Stinson, & Grant (manuscript submitted for publication)	43,093	195 L3	23.3[a]	2.8[e]
	Slutske et al. (2001)	7,869 men	615 L2–3	24.1[a]	2.0
Avoidant (0.5–1.0%)[d]	Petry, Stinson, & Grant (manuscript submitted for publication)	43,093	195 L3	14.0	2.0[e]
Dependent	Petry, Stinson, & Grant (manuscript submitted for publication)	43,093	195 L3	3.2[a]	0.5[e]
Obsessive–compulsive (1.0%)[d]	Petry, Stinson, & Grant (manuscript submitted for publication)	43,093	195 L3	28.5[a]	6.0[e]
Paranoia (0.5–2.5%)[d]	Petry, Stinson, & Grant (manuscript submitted for publication)	43,093	195 L3	24.1[a]	3.4[e]
Schizoid	Petry, Stinson, & Grant (manuscript submitted for publication)	43,093	195 L3	15.0[a]	2.7[e]
Histrionic (2.3%)[d]	Petry, Stinson, & Grant (manuscript submitted for publication)	43,093	195 L3	13.1[a]	1.5[e]

(continued)

TABLE 5.6 (Continued)

Group and disorder	Study	Sample N	No. disordered gamblers	Lifetime rate in Level 2–3 (L2–3) gamblers (%)	Lifetime rate in nongamblers (%)	Lifetime rate
Treatment-seeking gamblers						
Any personality disorder	Bellaire & Caspari (1992)		51 inpatients			49.0
	Ibáñez et al. (2001)		43 outpatients			27.5[b]
	Lesieur & Blume (1990)		7 inpatients			71.4
	Specker et al. (1995)		40 outpatients			25.0
	Steel & Blaszczynski (1998)		82 outpatients			92.7
	Taber, McCormick, Russo, et al. (1987)		66 inpatients			19.7
Cluster A (any)						
Paranoid	Specker et al. (1995)		40 outpatients			5.0
	Specker et al. (1995)		40 outpatients			2.5
	Steel & Blaszczynski (1998)		82 outpatients			40.2
Schizoid	Kroeber (1992)		43 outpatients			9.3[c]
	Specker et al. (1995)		40 outpatients			2.5
	Steel & Blaszczynski (1998)		82 outpatients			20.7
Schizotypal	Lesieur & Blume (1990)		7 outpatients			28.6
	Steel & Blaszczynski (1998)		82 outpatients			37.8
Cluster B (any)						
Borderline	Specker et al. (1995)		40 outpatients			7.5
	Kroeber (1992)		43 outpatients			4.7
	Specker et al. (1995)		40 outpatients			2.5
	Steel & Blaszczynski (1998)		82 outpatients			69.5
Conduct disorder	Black & Moyer (1998)		30 ad respondents			40.0
	Blaszczynski & McConaghy (1994a)		306 (152 inpatients; 154 GA members)			32.1
Antisocial	Black & Moyer (1998)		30 ad respondents			33.3
	Blaszczynski et al. (1989)		109 (77 inpatients; 32 GA members)			14.6
	Blaszczynski & McConaghy (1994a)		306 (152 inpatients; 154 GA members)			15.4

Disorder	Study	Sample	%
	Ibáñez et al. (2001)	43 outpatients	14.5
	Kroeber (1992)	43 outpatients	20.9
	Specker et al. (1996)	40 outpatients	0.0
	Steel & Blaszczynski (1998)	82 outpatients	29.3
Histrionic	Specker et al. (1995)	40 outpatients	0.0
	Steel & Blaszczynski (1998)	82 outpatients	65.9
Narcissistic	Kroeber (1992)	43 outpatients	11.6
	Specker et al. (1995)	40 outpatients	5.0
	Steel & Blaszczynski (1998)	82 outpatients	57.3
Cluster C (any)	Specker et al. (1995)	40 outpatients	17.5
Passive–aggressive	Lesieur & Blume (1990)	7 outpatients	14.3
	Specker et al. (1995)	40 outpatients	2.5
	Steel & Blaszczynski (1998)	82 outpatients	35.4
Dependent	Kroeber (1992)	43 outpatients	7.0
	Specker et al. (1995)	40 outpatients	5.0
	Steel & Blaszczynski (1998)	82 outpatients	48.8
Obsessive–compulsive	Lesieur & Blume (1990)	7 outpatients	14.3
	Specker et al. (1995)	40 outpatients	5.0
	Steel & Blaszczynski (1998)	82 outpatients	31.7
Avoidant	Specker et al. (1995)	40 outpatients	12.5
	Steel & Blaszczynski (1998)	82 outpatients	36.6
Not otherwise specified	Lesieur & Blume (1990)	7 outpatients	14.3
	Specker et al. (1995)	40 outpatients	2.5

Note. PG = pathological gambler, GA = Gamblers Anonymous, n.s. = not stated. [a]Level 2 and 3 gamblers differ from the comparison group in the same study (p < .05). [b]Excludes individuals also diagnosed with antisocial personality disorder [c]Schizoid and paranoid combined. [d]Estimated lifetime general population value reported in the *Diagnostic and Statistical Manual for Mental Disorders* (4th ed.; American Psychiatric Association, 1994). [e]Derived from odds ratios comparing pathological gamblers with nonpathological gamblers.

SUMMARY AND CLINICAL IMPLICATIONS

Studies suggest high rates of comorbidity between pathological gambling and some Axis I and Axis II psychiatric disorders. Evidence is unequivocal for the relationship between substance use and gambling disorders. Whether samples are drawn from the general population or from people seeking treatment for either gambling or for substance use disorders, high rates of comorbidity are found, and virtually no negative findings are noted. Thus, clinicians treating substance abusers should screen for gambling problems, and patients initiating treatment for gambling should be questioned about their past and current substance use. The secondary disorder may require specialized treatment in conjunction with the presenting problem(s).

For other psychiatric conditions, less information is available. Data are strong regarding an association between affective and gambling disorders, although little is understood about the bidirectionality of the two disorders. In evaluating the presence of disordered gambling and other psychiatric conditions, future studies should ascertain the onset of symptoms for both disorders and the dynamic relationships among multiple disorders.

The relationship between anxiety and gambling disorders is not yet well established, although the recent NESARC study (Petry, Stinson, & Grant, manuscript submitted for publication) should shed further light on this association. Comorbidity between obsessive–compulsive and impulse control disorders with pathological gambling is also debatable, and more studies with larger samples are necessary to further elucidate these relationships. Clinicians specializing in treatment of these other psychiatric conditions should consider inquiring about gambling problems, although it is unclear whether rates will be substantially higher than those noted in the general population. Clinicians who treat pathological gamblers would be well advised to consider assessment of other psychiatric symptoms, which may require concomitant treatments.

Data are fairly convincing that treatment-seeking pathological gamblers have high rates of personality disorders, but whether personality disorders are better accounted for via their association with psychiatric disorders other than pathological gambling itself is unclear. In other words, high rates of ASPD among pathological gamblers may be secondary to the relationship between ASPD and substance abuse. Pathological gamblers without substance use disorders may be no more likely to have ASPD than the general population. Studies with much larger samples are needed to better examine these patterns of comorbidity.

Finally, more research related to the onset and patterning of comorbid disorders is needed. As I describe in the remaining chapters, studies of treatment outcomes of gamblers are fairly limited, and whether comorbidity influences outcomes is an important issue that can be addressed only in large studies containing sufficient numbers of gamblers with varying psychiatric comorbidities.

6

NEUROBIOLOGY AND GENETICS

In this chapter I focus on the limited, but developing, research on the biological basis of pathological gambling. First I summarize data on familial histories of gambling problems and twin studies. In the second section, I review evidence of biological abnormalities in pathological gamblers. Last, I describe possible abnormalities in serotonin, norepinephrine, dopamine, and opioid systems in pathological gamblers. I also review studies of the molecular genetics of pathological gambling.

FAMILIAL AND GENETIC STUDIES

Family Studies

Family studies have demonstrated that problem and pathological gambling tends to run in families. In one study of 9- to 14-year-olds ($N = 477$) who reported regular gambling, for example, 86% stated that they had gambled with family members (Gupta & Derevensky, 1997). Evaluations of lottery play in college students (B. A. Browne & Brown, 1994) and disordered gambling in 15- to 28-year-olds (Winters, Stinchfield, & Fulkerson, 1993) suggest a relationship with parental gambling, but whether the relationship is dependent on socialization or genetics cannot be ascertained from these types of studies.

Studies of adults confirm the association between familial exposure to gambling and disordered gambling. In community samples, adults identified as Level 2–3 gamblers are more likely than Level 0–1 gamblers to report having a parent with gambling problems (Volberg & Steadman, 1989a; Winters & Rich, 1998). Hraba and Lee (1995) found that, in more than 1,000 adults, Level 2–3 gambling was associated with childhood exposure to gambling. Black, Moyer, and Schlosser (2003) found that 9% of first-degree relatives of pathological gamblers had a gambling problem themselves. In samples of treatment-seeking substance abusers or psychiatric patients, approximately 10% to 44% of those identified as Level 3 gamblers also stated that one or more of their parents had a gambling problem (Daghestani, Elenz, & Crayton, 1996; Gambino, Fitzgerald, Shaffer, Benner, & Courtnage, 1993; Lesieur & Blume, 1990; Lesieur, Blume, & Zoppa, 1986; Lesieur & Heineman, 1988). Walters (2002) conducted a meta-analysis of family studies and estimated that the heritability of Level 3 gambling is about 16%. More severe forms of the disorder appeared to have greater familial liability than less severe forms, and the familial effects were more reliably inferred for men than for women.

Although these studies suggest that familial patterns of disordered gambling exist, family histories of gambling problems were often measured by a single-item question. This method has unknown reliability and validity in assessing gambling problems and therefore may over- or underestimate this association. Furthermore, these studies were all cross-sectional in nature, assessing retrospective reports of familial gambling that were not confirmed by interviews with the family members. Finally, these types of studies are unable to distinguish the extent to which gambling among family members results from genetic or environmental influences.

Adoption and Twin Studies

Adoption and twin studies can tease out the role between shared environment and genetics. In adoption studies, the behavior of individuals adopted shortly after birth can be compared with that of their biological and adoptive parents. A genetic influence on the behavior of interest can be inferred if the individual's behavior is more consistent with that of the birth parents rather than the adoptive parents. To date, no known adoption studies of pathological gambling have been published.

Twin studies can also be used to ascertain the relationship between genes and behavior. Identical or monozygotic twins share all of their genes, whereas fraternal or dizygotic twins share only about half their genes. If monozygotic twins exhibit a behavior of interest at higher rates than dizygotic twins, then a genetic influence is suggested. Winters and Rich (1998) reported a greater similarity of gambling behaviors among 42 monozygotic twin pairs compared with 50 dizygotic twin pairs, but this effect was noted only among men and only for games with high potential payoffs, such as casino cards, gambling machines, pull-tabs, and lotteries. The association was not significant for lower payoff games, such as informal card betting, bingo, and games of personal skill. In 63 female twin pairs, the differences in gambling behaviors between monozygotic and dizygotic twin pairs were not significant for any types of gambling. Similar to the results of studies of alcoholism (McGue, Pickens, & Svikis, 1992), the genetic risk for gambling appeared stronger in men than in women. Winters and Rich evaluated frequency of gambling behaviors, rather than Level 2–3 gambling, because the prevalence rate of disordered gambling was too low to be accurately reflected in a sample size of under 100 twin pairs. No increased risk of any gambling, monthly or more frequent gambling, or early-onset gambling (prior to age 18 years), was noted for the monozygotic relative to dizygotic twins.

In a much larger study of 6,718 male members of the national Vietnam Era Twin Registry, Eisen et al. (1998) examined vulnerability from inherited factors, environment experiences shared by twins, and environmental experiences not shared by twins. Shared environmental experiences are such things as exposure to parental gambling or alcohol use and having the same childhood friends. These experiences are assumed to contribute similarly to risk in monozygotic and dizygotic twins. Unique environmental influences include parental experiences and peers who were not shared by the twins, as well as differential experiences outside the family. Of the twins who reported gambling at least 25 times in a 1-year period over their lives, 29% (7.9% of the total cohort) reported at least one symptom of pathological gambling and are henceforth referred to as *Level 2 gamblers*. An additional 1.4% of the full cohort met diagnostic criteria and are referred to as *Level 3 gamblers*.

In Eisen et al.'s (1998) study, inherited factors explained 35% of the variance in having gambled more than 25 times in a year without developing any symptoms of disordered gambling and 48% of the risk for developing Level 2 gambling. Familial factors (inheritance, experiences shared by twin siblings during childhood, or both) explained 62% of the variance in development of Level 3 gambling. The low prevalence rate of the full disorder prevented quantification of the contribution of inherited versus experiential familial factors, but familial factors clearly were shown to influence symptoms of disordered gambling in this sample of men.

In another study with this same sample, a linear relationship was observed between a history of alcohol abuse or dependence and severity of disordered gambling (Slutske et al., 2000). Five percent of individuals with no history of alcohol problems were Level 2 gamblers, compared with 9% of those with mild alcohol dependence, 12% with moderate dependence, and 16% with severe alcohol dependence. The percentages of men with no, mild, moderate, and severe alcohol dependence who met criteria for Level 3 gambling were 0.7, 0.8, 2.5, and 4.5, respectively. Level 3 gambling was also significantly associated with age of onset of alcohol use, heavy drinking (7 or more drinks/occasion), and frequent drinking (11 or more days per month), with odds ratios of 0.6, 2.4, and 1.6, respectively.

Slutske et al. (2000) used biometric modeling to examine the basis for the comorbidity of gambling and alcohol disorders in this same sample. Depending on how disordered gambling was classified, between 64% and 75% of the co-occurrence was attributable to genes that simultaneously influenced both disorders. No contribution was noted from shared family environment to the association between Level 3 gambling and alcohol dependence. In contrast, nonshared environmental experiences influenced both gambling and alcohol dependence. However, the nonshared environment was responsible for considerably less of the overlap between Level 3 gambling and alcohol dependence than were genetic factors. Between 3% and 8% of the nonshared environmental variation in the risk for disordered gambling was accounted for by the risk for alcohol dependence. On the other hand, between 12% and 20% of the genetic variation in the risk for disordered gambling was accounted for by genetic variation in common with the risk for alcohol dependence. Thus, risk for alcohol dependence predicted a significant proportion of the risk for gambling problems, possibly explaining, at least in part, the high rates of comorbidity of alcohol use and gambling disorders described in chapters 2 and 5.

Using this same twin registry, Slutske et al. (2001) also evaluated the relationship between antisocial personality disorder and disordered gambling; I reviewed this study in chapter 5. They found that Level 3 gambling was associated with antisocial personality disorder, for both the adult manifestation of the syndrome and the childhood version (conduct disorder). The association between antisocial behavior and disordered gambling was primarily explained by genetic factors rather than environmental ones. Slutske et al. (2001) concluded that the antisocial and illegal behaviors observed among some individuals with Level 3 gambling are probably not simply a consequence of pathological gambling. However, these interpretations may hold true only for male gamblers, as women were not included in this study.

Although the above-mentioned studies suggest some role of familial factors in the development of disordered gambling, it clearly is a multifaceted disorder, and both familial and environmental factors are important. The consistent association of pathological gambling with substance use disorders may suggest that the two disorders share some genetic linkage, but more than one gene may be involved, and these genes may influence the expression of neurochemicals or result in structural or functional abnormalities. In the next sections I review some of the research on biological aspects of gambling.

BIOLOGICAL ABNORMALITIES

Arousal

Early research on the biological basis of gambling revealed that participation in games of chance might influence physiological states, primarily stimulation and arousal. Anderson and Brown (1984) reported that heart rate is increased when an individual plays blackjack and that increases in heart rate correlated with the magnitude of the stakes. Subsequent studies found that heart rates rise when gamblers bet at poker machines (Coulombe, Ladouceur, Desharnais, & Jobin, 1992; Dickerson, Hinchy, England, Fabre, & Cunningham, 1992; Leary & Dickerson, 1985), fruit machines (D. Carroll & Huxley, 1994; Griffiths, 1993), and horse racing (Coventry & Norman, 1997). Leary and Dickerson (1985) reported that heart rate responses were greater in frequent gamblers than in infrequent gamblers. Blanchard, Wulfert, Freidenberg, and Malta (2000) demonstrated that pathological gamblers had increased heart rates relative to control respondents when exposed to a gambling-related scenario, but other physiological measures of arousal (blood pressure, skin resistance) did not differ between the samples in that study. In yet another study, Sharpe, Tarrier, Schotte, and Spence (1995) found no differences between problem and nonproblem gamblers with respect to gambling-associated changes in heart rates, but problem gamblers displayed greater physiological arousal in other domains, such as muscular activity and skin conductance. Still other investigators failed to confirm any relationship between gambling status and physiological measures of arousal in response to gambling situations (Coulombe et al., 1992; Coventry & Norman, 1997; Dickerson et al., 1992; Griffiths, 1993).

One explanation for the different findings across studies may be related to the gambling situations to which participants were exposed. In some cases, participants made "fake" or low-stakes wagers in laboratory settings, whereas others were conducted in real life gambling situations. Meyer et al. (2000) examined heart rate and salivary cortisol, a stress hormone, in 10 pathological gamblers playing blackjack. In one setting, blackjack was played for points rather than money, and in the other setting actual money was used. Only in the actual wager condition did heart rates increase substantially and were cortisol levels elevated. Anderson and Brown (1984) noted similar effects on heart rate depending on the stakes, as did Ladouceur, Sevigny, Blaszczynski, O'Connor, and Lavoie (2003). Meyer et al. (2000) hypothesized that cortisol secretion may enhance a positive mood state, at least in the short term, which may be associated with the reinforcing effects of gambling (see chap. 11). However, they did not evaluate cortisol responses in nonproblem gamblers, so whether physiological and emotional effects differ on the basis of problem severity is not yet clear.

Although many studies have shown that gambling may lead to increased physiological arousal—at least, as measured by some indexes—the specificity of these effects to gambling itself, and pathological gambling in particular, is not well established. Effects appear to be related at least in part to the populations studied, the tasks administered, and the physiological measures assessed. Arousal, in a general sense, may be influenced by a number of variables.

Indeed, Brunelle, Assaad, Phil, Tremblay, and Vitaro (2003) found that increased heart rates in response to some situations might be a possible marker for addictive disorders. Research on the etiology of alcohol dependence suggests that individuals with a family history of alcoholism have an elevation in heart rate following alcohol consumption (e.g., Wilson & Nagoshi, 1988), which appears to be linked to a potentiation of positive mood in response to the alcohol administration (Martin, Earleywine, Musty, Perrine, & Swift, 1993). One hundred five healthy young men consumed a moderate dose of alcohol in a laboratory setting (Brunelle et al., 2003). Those with greater ethanol-induced heart rates had significantly higher scores on the South Oaks Gambling Screen (Lesieur & Blume, 1987), confirming the well-established link between alcohol and gambling problems and suggesting a possible physiological marker related to both disorders. Whether or how these effects may be linked to increased arousal in response to gambling situations is not yet unknown.

Some investigators have attempted to link aspects of arousal in decision-making tasks to neurobiological mechanisms. Stojanov et al. (2003) examined 17 pathological gamblers and 21 age- and gender-matched control respondents in a passive listening task and another task involving the need to make discrimination decisions about auditory stimuli. The gamblers evidenced enlarged startle responses, indicative of higher levels of arousal, and they had impaired sensorimotor gating relative to the control respondents. The authors hypothesized that these effects may be related to increased noradrenergic activity and disruptions in dopamine neurotransmission. The evidence for and against hypotheses related to altered neurotransmission in pathological gamblers is reviewed in the "Neurobiology" section of this chapter.

Structural and Functional Abnormalities

Data from some other studies suggest that pathological gamblers may have structural or functional abnormalities that may be related to deficits in sensory or information processing. L. Goldstein, Manowitz, Nora, Swartzburg, and Carlton (1985) found that pathological gamblers had reduced levels of hemispheric differentiation relative to control respondents when EEG readings were recorded. Similarly diffuse abnormalities, however, are noted in other populations, and Goldstein et al.'s study failed to indicate whether any of the eight pathological gamblers tested suffered from concurrent substance abuse or psychiatric conditions that may have been associated with the abnormalities. Rugle and Melamed (1993) noted frontal lobe dysfunction in pathological gamblers relative to control respondents, even when the pathological gamblers did not evidence any history of substance use disorders. However, the presence of other psychiatric conditions was not assessed. Regard, Knoch, Gütling, and Landis (2003) found impaired concentration, memory, and executive function and nonleft hemispheric language dominance in gamblers compared with control respondents. In addition, EEG dysfunction was noted in significantly more gamblers than control respondents. The results from this study suggest that the abnormalities may have resulted subsequent to brain damage, as 81% of the 17 gamblers tested had a traumatic brain injury, primarily early in life in the pre- or perinatal period, although the nature and severity of these events was not specified. The results from this study nevertheless point to the need to rule out other possible explanations for brain function abnormalities in pathological gamblers.

The Stroop task is a popular method for evaluating attention and information processing in psychiatric patient populations. This task involves, for example, frequent presentation of matched color–word stimuli (e.g., the word *green* written in a green-colored typeface) and occasional presentation of mismatched color–word stimuli (e.g., the word *green* written in blue type). Respondents are asked to categorize the stimuli by, for example, responding by pressing a computer key whenever the color green appears on the screen. Presentation of the mismatched stimuli requires response inhibition. Boyer and Dickerson (2003) administered three versions of this task to 60 individuals with varying levels of gambling involvement. The tasks differed with respect to the types of words presented: neutral, drug, or gambling. Individuals with more impaired gambling behaviors had an increased response latency in responding to words related to gambling, whereas those without gambling problems evidenced no difference across the three types of word categories. Potenza, Leung, et al. (2003) evaluated the neural correlates associated with response inhibition on the standard word–color Stroop task. They conducted functional magnetic resonance imaging while 13 pathological gamblers and 11 control participants performed the task. Compared with control participants, pathological gamblers demonstrated reduced activity in the left ventromedial prefrontal cortex, a brain region implicated in impulse regulation. However, other patient populations also evidence somewhat similar deficits on this task (e.g., Blumberg et al., 2003), suggesting that the alteration may not be unique to pathological gambling.

Potenza, Steinberg, et al. (2003) conducted another functional magnetic resonance imaging study in which 10 gamblers and 11 control participants viewed videotapes of happy, sad, or gambling content while brain function was assessed. During the gambling scenes, gamblers had *decreased* activity in some brain regions, including frontal and orbitofrontal cortex, caudate/basal ganglia, thalamus, and ventral anterior cingulate. Studies of analogous videotapes of cocaine cues in cocaine abusers have found *increased* activity in some of these same brain regions (Childress' et al., 1999; Wexler et al., 2001). The differential results across studies and populations are perplexing. Furthermore, in Potenza, Steinberg, et al. (2003), gamblers and control participants evidenced differential activation of brain regions when viewing all three types of videos, so the effects may not be limited to gambling situations.

Other studies of neural processing have found that gains and losses may be processed differentially in certain brain regions, primarily the frontal lobe (e.g., Bechara, Damasio, Tranel, & Damasio, 1997; Breiter, Aharon, Kahneman, Dale, & Shizgal, 2001). Gehring and Willoughby (2002) found that choices made subsequent to losses may be riskier and associated with greater loss-related brain activity than choices made after gains, but this study was conducted primarily with healthy control participants, so it failed to explain why some people gamble excessively and others do not. I (Petry, 2001b) showed that substance abusers who also have a gambling problem performed more poorly on a gain–loss decision-making task than did substance abusers without a gambling problem, and both groups performed more poorly than control participants. Cavedini, Riboldi, Keller, D'Annucci, and Bellodi (2002) replicated my results and noted that even "pure" pathological gamblers performed more poorly on this task than control participants. No known studies have yet conducted functional brain imaging of pathological gamblers participating in this task, so localization of these effects to particular brain regions in this population is still speculative.

Thus, evidence is emerging that attention and arousal states, as well as neural processing, may differ in pathological gamblers and control individuals. However, the specificity of many of these effects to gambling-related tasks, and the unique relationship of some of these abnormalities to pathological gambling, as opposed to other psychiatric conditions or premorbid biological conditions, is not well established at this time. Still, this is a fruitful area for further investigation, and additional studies are attempting to link some of these physiological effects to neurobiology, as I describe below.

NEUROBIOLOGY

Serotonergic, noradrenergic, and dopaminergic neurotransmitters, as well as the endogenous opioids, have all been implicated in pathological gambling. Each system may play a role in mechanisms that underlie behavioral disinhibition, reward mechanisms, and arousal associated with impulse control and addictive disorders, including disordered gambling, but results from these studies are still far from conclusive.

Serotonin

Serotonin, or 5-hydroxytriptomine (5-HT), is linked to initiation and inhibition of behavior, aggression, and suicide (Soubrie, 1986). Cell bodies are located in particular brain regions, known as the *raphe nuclei, midbrain,* and *hindbrain.* The anatomy and functioning of the serotonin system is complex, and many receptors exist. For psychiatric disorders, some of the most important receptors are the 1a, 1d, 2a, and 2c receptors, which are preferentially distributed in certain brain areas (e.g., Stahl, 2000). For example, 5-HT1a receptors are found in the hippocampus, raphe nuclei, septum, and neocortex, and selective serotonin reuptake inhibitors, such as fluvoxamine, activate these sites. 5-HT2c receptors are present in areas of the brain known as the *globus pallidus, substantia nigra, hypothalamus, cortex,* and *choroid plexus.* Those in the limbic system are associated with mood, whereas those in the hypothalamus affect appetite, thermoregulation, sleep, sexual behavior, and neuroendocrine function. Meta-chlorophenylpiperazine (m-CPP), a postsynaptic receptor agonist, activates 5-HT2a and 5-HT2c receptors, which are linked to release of prolactin, a protein hormone.

Measurement of Seratonin in Gamblers

Some pharmacological challenge studies and platelet studies suggest possible 5-HT dysfunction in pathological gamblers. Moreno, Sáiz-Ruiz, and López-Ibor (1991) compared serum levels of cortisol, growth hormone, and prolactin in gamblers and control respondents. No differences were noted in cortisol or growth hormone levels, but gamblers had low baseline serum prolactin. They also demonstrated a blunted plasma prolactin response after intravenous administration of 12.5 mg clomipramine, a 5-HT reuptake blocker. The results are indicative of a hypoactive serotonin system. DeCaria et al. (1997) examined responses to an oral dose of m-CPP in 10 pathological gamblers and control respondents. Prolactin release in response to a postsynaptic 5-HT receptor agonist such as m-CPP provides a dynamic index of central 5-HT function. Gamblers showed increased prolactin response and reported greater feelings of "high" than did control respondents. Euphoric responses to m-CPP have been noted in individuals with other impulse control disorders (Moss, Yao, & Panzak, 1990). Results from DeCaria et al.'s (1997) study suggest 5-HT postsynaptic hypersensitivity in gamblers that may be related to decreased availability or release of 5-HT. Gambling severity was correlated with changes in prolactin levels during the challenge, suggesting that more severe gamblers may have more dysregulated 5-HT systems, but these results have not been replicated.

Platelet monoamine oxidase activity, a peripheral marker of 5-HT function, has also been examined in several studies of pathological gamblers. Low-platelet monoamine oxidase (MAO) activity is linked to impulsivity (Oreland, Ekblom, Garpenstrand, & Hallman, 1998), and a defect in the structural gene for MAO-A has been associated with impulsive behaviors (Brunner et al., 1993). Carrasco, Sáiz-Ruiz, Hollander, Cesar, and Lopez-Ibor (1994) and Blanco, Orensanz-Muñoz, Blanco-Jerez, and Sáiz-Ruiz (1996) found decreased platelet MAO activity in pathological gamblers compared with control respondents. These findings suggest low 5-HT functioning in pathological gamblers. Another study in support of this hypothesis found that 5-HT metabolite levels in the cerebral spinal fluid (CSF) were lower among 10 pathological gamblers compared with 12 control respondents (Nordin & Eklundh, 1999).

Although these data suggest the possibility of a presynaptic serotonin deficiency, and a possible postsynaptic hypersensitivity of 5-HT receptors, not all studies of gamblers demonstrate abnormalities in the serotonin system. Roy, Adinoff, et al. (1988); Roy and Linnoila (1989); and Bergh, Eklund, Sodersten, and Nordin (1997) measured serotonin metabolites in the CSF of pathological gamblers and control respondents. These studies found similarities in serotonin metabolites between groups, but differences in metabolite levels of other neurotransmitters, as detailed later in this chapter. The contradictory results across studies may be related to the different samples of gamblers used or methods for obtaining and measuring metabolites.

Molecular Genetics

Studies on the molecular genetics of disordered gambling are in their infancy. Comings, Gade, et al. (1996) initially suggested an association of mutations in the serotonin tryptophan 2,3-dioxygenese (TDO2) gene with Level 3 gambling. In a subsequent study, Comings et al. (2001) used a genetic technique (multivariate analysis of associations) to evaluate the additive effects of multiple genes in 139 Level 3 gamblers and 139 control respondents. Seven serotonin genes were examined, and four were included in the regression analysis. Together, they explained about 7% of the variance. Two of the specific serotonin genes were independently associated with Level 3 gambling—the tryptophan hydroxylase (TPH) and TDO2 genes. The TPH gene is associated with suicidality and alcoholism (Nielsen et al., 1998). A greater association of the TPH gene was noted among the gamblers with a history of substance abuse (53% of the sample) than among the gamblers without a history of substance use disorders. In contrast, the TDO2 gene was noted primarily among the gamblers with no history of substance abuse, consistent with a prior study demonstrating that this gene was not associated with alcoholism (Comings, Gade, et al., 1996). Although these data suggest that serotonin genes have a role in pathological gambling, their effects are not necessarily unique to gambling disorders. As I describe in later sections of this chapter, genes associated with other neurotransmitter systems have been equally associated with gambling.

Nevertheless, support for a genetic contribution of serotonin genes to pathological gambling has been noted in another sample from Spain. Pérez de Castro, Ibàñez, Sáiz-Ruiz, and Fernández-Piqueras (1999) found an association between the less efficient variant of a functional polymorphism at the serotonin transporter gene and pathological gambling in men but not women. A second study (Ibàñez, Pérez de Castro, Fernández-Piqueras, Blanco, & Sáiz-Ruiz, 2000) isolated the effects to the MAO-A gene and found that severity of gambling was associated with a polymorphism in this gene in men. That same study found no association between a polymorphism in the MAO-B gene and gamblers versus control respondents.

Another report (Pérez de Castro, Ibàñez, Sáiz-Ruiz, & Fernández-Piqueras, 2002) noted an association between pathological gambling and functional DNA polymorphisms at the MAO-A gene and the 5-HT transporter gene. The same 68 gamblers and 68 control respondents from the prior study were screened by molecular analysis of a region of the MAO-A gene. The investigators looked for polymorphisms in this MAO-A gene, consisting of a genetic sequence present in 3, 3.5, 4, and 5 copies. Alleles (or forms of the gene) with 3.5 or 4 copies are transcribed 2 to 10 times more efficiently than those with either 3 or 5 copies. Allelic frequency of three- and five-copy alleles was significantly higher in gamblers than control participants, and the difference was most pronounced in male gamblers with severe gambling problems. The gender-specific effects suggest possible gender differences in the pathophysiology of disordered gambling, which in turn have led to a hypothesis that different pharmacotherapies may be useful in treatment. Studies evaluating serotonin reuptake agents in treating pathological gambling are described in chapter 7, and one study indicated differential efficacy of these medications in male and female gamblers.

Noradrenergic Function

Norandrenergic function mediates arousal and is activated in response to novel or aversive stimuli (Siever, 1987). The greatest concentration of norepinephrine (NE) is found in the locus ceruleus region of the brain. Axons from NE neurons project to various brain regions, including the limbic system, basal ganglia, and cortex. These regions mediate arousal, mood, and impulse control. Plasma 3-methoxy-4-hydroxyphenylglycol (MHPG) is an NE metabolite. Plasma MHPG, along with plasma NE and CSF levels of MHPG, are measured as indices of NE function.

Measurement of Norepinephrine in Gamblers

Roy, Adinoff, et al. (1988) found lower plasma MHPG levels in pathological gamblers relative to control respondents. The gamblers also had greater urinary outputs of NE, even after covarying age and weight. Although CSF levels of MHPG were not different between gamblers and control respondents, gamblers demonstrated a higher centrally produced fraction of CSF MHPG than did control respondents, after adjusting for peripheral MHPG levels. In a subsequent study, Roy, DeJong, and Linnoila (1989) found correlations between personality measures of extroversion and CSF levels of MHPG, plasma levels of MHPG, and urinary NE output. Together, these studies suggest possible dysregulation of NE in pathological gamblers, and this dysregulation may be related to personality features. However, no replication of these interesting results has been published.

Some pharmacological challenge studies have revealed abnormalities in the NE system in pathological gamblers. Clonidine is an NE alpha-2 adrenergic receptor agonist that increases growth hormone release via postsynaptic receptor stimulation. In a small study of 5 male pathological gamblers and 8 control participants, oral clonidine (0.15 mg) resulted in nonsignificant increases in growth hormone over time in the gamblers, and the results reached significance at peak time (DeCaria et al., 1997). Severity of pathological gambling was correlated with growth hormone responses to clonidine, and self-reported control of thoughts or urges to gamble correlated with peak change in growth hormone response. These results suggest an increase in arousal or response to readiness to gamble among the more severe Level 3 gamblers.

Galanin is an amino acid peptide that enhances NE release from peripheral sympathetic nerves. In a study examining CSF levels of galanin in 19 pathological gamblers, 48 alcoholics, and 13 control participants (Roy, Berrettini, Adinoff, & Linnoila, 1990), no differences in levels of galanin were observed among the groups. Nevertheless, a nonsignificant trend was noted between CSF galanin and NE levels and between galanin and corticotropin-releasing hormone levels in the gamblers. These correlations were not apparent in the other groups. This study gives modest support for the possibility of altered NE function in gamblers, but the results need to be replicated. Because CSF levels of MHPG were not correlated with galanin levels in any of the groups, mechanisms of action of these putative relationships need to be better delineated.

Neurons releasing gamma-aminobutyric acid (GABA) have an inhibitory effect on the release of central NE. Diminished release of central GABA is reported in the pathophysiology of depression (Berrettini & Post, 1984), and pathological gamblers may also have a disturbance of the GABA system that affects the NE system. One way of assessing GABA dysregulation is by measuring diazepam-binding inhibitor, a neuromodulator of GABA present in GABA neurons. In one study, Roy, Adinoff, et al. (1988) found that depressed gamblers had higher CSF levels of diazepam-binding inhibitor than did nondepressed gamblers. Although this finding suggests a possible association of GABA dysregulation in a subset of gamblers, whether it is related to the depression or the gambling could not be ascertained. In a second study, Roy, DeJong, et al. (1989) found no differences in CSF levels of GABA in gamblers and control participants.

The relationship among GABA, NE, and pathological gambling requires further study. Most of the reports described above were conducted with very small numbers of gamblers. The inclusion of gamblers with comorbid conditions increases generalization, but it also reduces ability to attribute specifically to gambling any differences that are found between gamblers and controls participants.

Molecular Genetics

As mentioned earlier, in the "Serotonin" section, Comings et al. (2001) examined the role of a variety of genes in disordered gambling. This study included examination of seven norepinephrine genes. Four of them did not demonstrate any increased variance in the gamblers relative to the control participants and were excluded from further analyses. The remaining three—dopamine beta-hydroxylase, adrenergic alpha2c receptor, and catechol-o-methyltransferase—accounted for 8% of the variance in pathological gambling, with only the adrenergic alpha2c receptor gene significant on its own. This gene is also associated with attention-deficit disorder and conduct disorder (Comings et al., 2000), two conditions that share comorbidity with disordered gambling (see chap. 5). Further evaluation of the association of this gene with gambling is needed.

Dopamine

Dopamine function is associated with reward and reinforcement mechanisms, and dopamine is implicated in most drug use disorders (e.g., Koob, 1992). On the basis of the conceptualization of disordered gambling as a behavioral addiction (Moreyra, Ibàñez, Liebowitz, Sáiz-Ruiz, & Blanco, 2002), some investigators have examined the role of dopamine in disordered gamblers.

Measurement of Dopamine in Gamblers

Two studies compared CSF levels of dopamine in gamblers and control participants, but they yielded different results. Roy, Adinoff, et al. (1988) found no differences between groups in plasma, urinary, or CSF dopamine levels. However, Bergh et al. (1997) measured monoamines and their metabolites in the CSF of 10 pathological gamblers and 7 control participants and found a decrease in dopamine and increase in 3,4 dihydroxyphenylacetic acid and homovanillic acid (metabolites of dopamine). NE and its metabolite 3-methoxy-4-hydroxyphenylglycol were also elevated, whereas 5-HT and 5-hydroxyindoleacetic acid were unchanged in gamblers compared with control participants. These differences between studies may be attributed, at least in part, to the techniques used to obtain CSF and measure the metabolites.

Several case reports have pointed to an association between pathological gambling and Parkinson's disease, a disorder in which the dopamine neurons deteriorate. In these cases, Parkinson's patients who are treated with agents that mimic or increase the synthesis of dopamine began gambling in a pathological manner during dopamine agonist treatment. In one case report (Seedat, Kesler, Niehaus, & Stein, 2000), treatment with risperidone (a dopamine antagonist) resulted in a complete cessation of gambling and a reduction in hypomanic symptoms, but additional dopaminergic agents (levodopa/carbidopa) were necessary to abate the Parkinsonian symptoms. Two other cases were described by Gschwandtner, Aston, Renaud, and Fuhr (2001). In both of these cases, the gambling behavior emerged subsequently to l-dopa treatment for Parkinson's disease; in one case, it remitted spontaneously after 5 months of excessive gambling, and in the second, a reduction in the dopaminergic drugs was associated with a cessation of gambling. In these last two cases, the gambling appeared without any other manic or hypomanic symptoms, whereas in the former case it may have been related to a hypomanic state, which is an exclusionary criterion for the diagnosis of pathological gambling. In Spain (Molina et al., 2000), 12 patients in a sample of 250 patients with Parkinson's disease were diagnosed with pathological gambling, and in 10 of these 12 the onset of gambling occurred after Parkinson's symptoms and levodopa treatment began.

However, a contradictory report also exists. In the largest of all studies to date, Driver-Dunckley, Samanta, and Stacy (2003) found an overall incidence rate of pathological gambling of only 0.05% in 1,884 Parkinson's patients treated in a clinic in Arizona. Eight of the nine patients who developed symptoms of pathological gambling while being treated for Parkinson's disease were taking the dopamine agonist pramipexole but, even among all patients treated with this drug, the overall incidence rate of pathological gambling was only 1.5%, a rate that cannot be considered substantially higher than population norms. Thus, the relationship between dopamine agonist therapy and development of pathological gambling should still be considered speculative.

Molecular Genetics

Some studies have investigated the role of dopamine genes in pathological gambling. In one of the earliest studies, Comings, Rosenthal, et al. (1996) reported an association between an allele of the D2 dopamine receptor gene (known as the *Taq-A1 allele*) and gambling. The Taq-A1 allele is also associated with other impulsive, addictive, and compulsive behaviors and may be suggestive of a reward deficiency system (Blum et al., 1995). Other studies suggest a role of the dopamine D1 (Comings et al., 1997) and D4 receptor genes (Comings et al., 1999).

A particular gene sequence, referred to as the *7 repeat allele of the 48 bp repeat polymorphism of the third cytoplamic loop of the D4 dopamine receptor gene* (DRD4), is related to a variety of psychiatric conditions, including attention-deficit disorder, Tourette syndrome, and substance abuse (e.g., Comings et al., 1999). Pérez de Castro, Ibàñez, Torres, Sáiz-Ruiz, and Fernández-Piqueras (1997) examined 68 pathological gamblers and 68 control respondents and found that the less efficient variant of this polymorphism in the DRD4 gene was common among female gamblers but not male gamblers. As described earlier, another pattern of a polymorphism in the MAO-A gene was found among men with severe gambling problems (Ibàñez et al., 2000). Together, these results may suggest that genetic contributions may differ between men and women, with 5-HT dysfunction more common in the pathophysiology of the disorder in men, and dopamine dysregulation more common in women. However, more research is needed to confirm these findings in larger samples.

Comings et al.'s (2001) recent study found that DRD2, DRD4, and the dopamine transporter gene DAT1 were all associated with pathological gambling in a study of 139 gamblers and 139 control respondents. The dopamine genes accounted for about 8% of the total variance. The overall regression analysis suggested that the 16 genes, including dopamine, NE, and 5-HT, together accounted for 15% to 21% of the variance of pathological gambling. The authors concluded that dopamine, serotonin, and norepinephrine all play a role in pathological gambling, but none are unique to the disorder; rather, they all are also associated with a variety of other psychiatric conditions. Individuals who inherit a threshold number of these genes may be at increased risk of developing a number of impulsive, compulsive, and addictive disorders. The specific disorder that occurs may be influenced by environmental factors or other genes that have not yet been investigated. A better understanding of the molecular genetics of pathological gambling may be useful for identifying individuals at risk for the disorder and for testing pharmacotherapies that directly modulate the affected neurotransmitter system(s).

Opioids

Opioids may play a role in the development and maintenance of gambling behaviors as well. One study (Shinohara et al., 1999) found elevated levels of beta-endorphin, the endogenous μ-opioid receptor agonist, in habitual players of Pachinko, a common gambling activity in Japan. This study further found that levels of endorphins peak during winning periods. Relative to control participants, Blaszczysnski, Wintor, and McConaghy (1986) noted low plasma levels of beta-endorphin in a small sample of pathological gamblers who preferred horse race betting. However, these effects were not found among the gamblers who preferred poker machine gambling, and the act of betting itself did not result in changes in beta-endorphin levels among horse race gamblers in that study.

Although only limited data exist on abnormalities in opioid systems in gamblers, the opioid receptor system has been investigated as a target for pharmacotherapies of other addictive disorders, including opiate, alcohol, and nicotine (Petry, 2002b). This system is thought to influence regulation of the mesocortical limbic system, which modulates reward and reinforcing behaviors. Opioid antagonists, such as naltrexone, are used to treat a variety of drug use disorders as well as other psychiatric conditions (Modesto-Lowe & van Kirk, 2002). As I describe in the next chapter, they may also have beneficial effects in treating gamblers.

SUMMARY AND CLINICAL IMPLICATIONS

The available data suggest that a familial component of gambling problems clearly exists, and this familial component may be at least in part genetically influenced. Thus, clinicians may consider screening and providing early interventions for family members of pathological gamblers who may have gambling problems themselves.

Biological abnormalities, as varied as increased activation and arousal to changes in functioning of brain regions, are reported in pathological gamblers relative to control respondents. Studies examining the molecular genetics of disordered gambling are now emerging as well. Together, the data suggest that serotonin, norephinephrine, dopamine, and opioid systems all may be involved in the pathogenesis of disordered gambling. Genetic abnormalities may result in functional and physiological changes that may influence an individual's propensity to gamble problematically. Indeed, a number of possible neurophysiological abnormalities in pathological gamblers have been described, via measurement of neuropsychological performance and neurotransmitters and their metabolites as well as responses to challenge studies. Most studies, however, have not provided conclusive evidence of biological abnormalities in pathological gamblers relative to control respondents, and independent investigators have not yet replicated many of the preliminary results. Although this research is still in its infancy, a better understanding of the physiological and genetic factors underlying disordered gambling ultimately may aid clinicians in early identification of individuals at high risk for development of the disorder as well as in the investigation of pharmacotherapies.

III

RESEARCH ON INTERVENTIONS

7

PHARMACOTHERAPIES

As I reviewed in chapter 6, some physiological and genetic abnormalities have been identified in disordered gamblers. Changes have been noted in serotonin, norepinephrine, dopamine, and opioid systems, although many of these findings have not yet been replicated in independent samples. Nevertheless, if physiological abnormalities are present in disordered gamblers, then medications that act on these systems may be useful in abating the symptoms. In the first section of this chapter, I describe pharmacotherapy studies that have been conducted with pathological gamblers. In the second section, I relate the use of pharmacotherapies in treatment of gambling to those used in the treatment of substance use disorders.

PHARMACOTHERAPIES

Abnormalities in serotonin, norephinephrine, dopamine, and opioid systems have been noted in gamblers (see chap. 6), making these systems putative targets for pharmacotherapies. To date, no studies evaluating norepinephrine or dopaminergic agents have been published. Drugs acting on serotonin and opioid systems have been evaluated in case reports and double-blind controlled trials. Some studies that have investigated mood stabilizers have been published. These reports are summarized in Table 7.1 and are detailed below.

TABLE 7.1

Pharmacotherapy Trials for the Treatment of Pathological Gambling

Medication (mean dose)	Study	No. enrolled/ completers	Design	Duration	Results
Serotonin reuptake inhibitors					
Clomipramine (125 mg)	Hollander et al. (1992)	1/1	Double-blind cross-over	10 weeks per phase	25% reduction on placebo vs. 90% reduction on drug.
Citalopram (35 mg)	Zimmerman et al. (2002)	15/9	Open label	12 weeks	53% (87% of completers) reduced gambling; depressed and nondepressed responded similarly.
Nefazodone (346 mg)	Pallanti et al. (2002)	14/12	Open label	8 weeks	62% (75% of completers) reduced gambling.
Paroxetine (57 mg)	Kim et al. (2002)	45/41	Placebo lead in; then randomized double blind	1 week; 8 weeks	12% placebo lead-in response; 23% later placebo responders vs. 60% drug responders.
Paroxetine (10–60 mg)	Grant et al. (2003)	76/45	Placebo lead in; then randomized double blind	1 week; 16 weeks	8% placebo lead-in response; 49% later placebo responders vs. 59% drug responders.
Fluvoxamine (220 mg)	Hollander et al. (1998)	16/10	Single-blind exposure to both	8 weeks on each	42% responders to placebo vs. 70% responders to drug.
Fluvoxamine (195 mg)	Hollander et al. (2000)	15/10	Placebo lead in; double blind randomized crossover	1 week; 8 weeks on each	Among completers, 46% responders to placebo phase vs. 70% responders to drug phase; significant order effect.
Fluvoxamine (200 mg)	Blanco et al. (2002)	32/13	Double blind randomized	24 weeks on drug or placebo	59% placebo responders vs. 73% drug responders at Month 2; but much higher dropout rate in drug (80%) vs. placebo (41%); overall beneficial effects in men and

Mood stabilizers

Drug	Study	N	Design	Duration	Results
Lithium (1,800 mg)	Moskowitz (1980)	3/3	Open label	1.5–2.5 years	Reductions in gambling; all had bipolar disorder.
Lithium (796 mg) or Valproate (874 mg)	Pallanti et al. (2002)	42/31	Single blind	14 weeks	65% completed in lithium arm (61% were responders); 84% completed in valproate arm (68% were responders).
Carbamezapine (600 mg)	Haller & Hinterhuber (1994)	1/1	Double blind	12 weeks on each	No change on placebo; At week 2 on drug, gambling cessation began.

Opioid antagonists

Drug	Study	N	Design	Duration	Results
Naltrexone (100 mg)	Kim (1998)	1/1	Open label	36 weeks	At 100 mg, no gambling urges or behaviors.
Naltrexone (50 mg) + Fluoxetine (20 mg)	Crockford & el-Guebaly (1998b)	1/1	Open label	4 weeks	Decreased urges to gamble and drink.
Naltrexone (157 mg)	Kim & Grant (2001)	17/14	Open label	6 weeks	Decreased gambling behaviors and urges.
Naltrexone (188 mg)	Kim et al. (2001)	89/45	Double blind randomized	1 week lead-in; 12 weeks on drug or placebo	27% responders at placebo lead in; 24% placebo responders vs. 75% drug responders.

Serotonin Reuptake Inhibitors

Several studies have investigated the role of serotonin reuptake inhibitors in treating gamblers. Much of this work was based initially on the hypothesis that pathological gambling may have some obsessive–compulsive elements (Hollander & Wong, 1995; but see chap. 5). Medications that are useful in treating obsessive–compulsive spectrum disorders were hypothesized to have potential for abating gambling symptoms.

A case report describing double-blind, placebo-controlled clomipramine treatment suggested that there were beneficial effects of this serotonin reuptake inhibitor (Hollander, Frenkel, DeCaria, Trungold, & Stein, 1992). The patient was on a placebo and an active drug (125 mg/day) for 10 weeks each. A 25% reduction in gambling was noted during the placebo phase, and a 90% reduction in gambling was noted during the clomipramine treatment phase. Clomipramine was continued in an open manner for an additional 28 weeks, during which time abstinence from gambling was maintained. Despite beneficial effects, subsequent evaluations of clomipramine have not been published. Other serotonin reuptake inhibitors, however, have been investigated for treatment of pathological gambling in larger trials, as described below.

Zimmerman, Breen, and Posternak (2002) reported on an open-label administration of citalopram (Celexa) to 15 patients, 9 of whom completed the 12-week treatment period. Doses of citalopram began at 10 mg/day and were titrated up to 60 mg/day, with a mean dose of 34.7 mg/day. Decreases in gambling urges and behaviors were noted, and 87% of completers (53% of the full sample) were considered treatment responders on the basis of clinician-rated Clinical Global Impression scales (CGI; Guy, 1976) of "improved" or "very much improved." Most responders improved by the first assessment evaluation, which was conducted 2 weeks after treatment started. Depressed and nondepressed gamblers responded equally well, suggesting that any medication effects on gambling were unrelated to antidepressive properties of the medication.

Another open-label study was conducted using nefazodone (Serzone), a 5-hydroxytriptomine-2 (5HT2) receptor antagonist with mixed norepinephrine/serotonin reuptake inhibitor effects. Pallanti, Quercioli, Sood, and Hollander (2002) administered nefazodone to 14 gamblers for up to 8 weeks. The drug was administered at doses starting at 50 mg/day and increased up to 500 mg/day, or until a 25% reduction in Pathological Gambling Modification of the Yale–Brown Obsessive–Compulsive Scale (PG–YBOCS; DeCaria et al., 1998) scores or a CGI score of "improved" or "very much improved" was achieved. The average dose was 346 mg/day. Of the 14 enrolled patients, 12 completed the study, and 9 of these were considered responders. Because no comparator groups were included in these two studies, and because high rates of response to placebos have been noted in other studies as detailed below, these results should be interpreted with caution.

Other pharmacotherapies that act on the serotonin system have also been tested for treating pathological gamblers using placebo-controlled designs. Kim, Grant, Adson, Shin, and Zaninelli (2002) evaluated the efficacy of a selective serotonin uptake inhibitor, paroxetine (Paxil), in a randomized, double-blind trial of 45 pathological gamblers. After a 1-week placebo lead-in period, patients received a placebo or paroxetine for 8 weeks. Paroxetine doses started at 20 mg/day and could be increased 10 mg/week up to a maximum of 60 mg/day, with a mean dose of 57.1 mg/day. A 12% response rate to placebo was noted in the first week, prior to randomization. Continued reductions in gambling symptoms were noted throughout the first 5 weeks of the randomized phase in the group that received the placebo. The paroxetine-treated group showed a more precipitous reduction of gambling initially, which was maintained throughout the 8 weeks of treatment. Beneficial effects of medication were noted in terms of responses on the Gambling Symptom Assessment Scale (Kim, Grant, Adson, & Shin, 2001) in the final 2 weeks of the study. Significantly more of the paroxetine-treated patients (60%) than the placebo-treated patients (23%) were considered "responders." However, this study was conducted with pathological gamblers who had no other Axis I disorders and low baseline levels of depression and anxiety. Thus, these results may be of limited generalizability in the treatment of disordered gambling, because so many Level 3 gamblers have a comorbid psychiatric disorder.

Furthermore, a larger follow-up study called these initially positive effects of paroxetine into question. Grant et al. (2003) randomized 76 pathological gamblers to flexible doses of paroxetine or placebo for 16 weeks. Both groups evidenced comparable improvement on CGI, PG–YBOCS, and Gambling Symptom Assessment Scale (Kim et al., 2001) scores. Thus, paroxetine was not efficacious in reducing gambling in this study.

The most extensive research with selective serotonin reuptake inhibitors is related to fluvoxamine (Luvox). Both a single-blind and two double-blind trials have been conducted. Hollander et al. (1998) initially entered 16 pathological gamblers in a trial consisting of an 8-week placebo lead-in period followed by 8 weeks of fluvoxamine. Ten gamblers completed the study, and 7 were classified as responders because they reduced their gambling by 25% or more. The dose was adjusted upward until improvement occurred, and the mean dose was 220 mg/day. A beneficial effect of the placebo was noted in the 8-week placebo lead-in phase, with scores on the PG–YBOCS scale dropping an average of 33%. Five of the 12 patients who completed the placebo phase were judged to be treatment responders. Further reductions in PG–YBOCS scores and clinician-rated improvements were noted among the 10 individuals who completed the 16-week trial, although the 70%

improvement rate with fluvoxamine did not differ significantly from the 42% improvement in the placebo phase. Two of the 3 nonresponders had a history of cyclothymia, a condition that worsened with higher doses of fluvoxamine.

This same group of investigators conducted a second study of this medication. Hollander et al. (2000) used a 16-week double-blind cross-over design in which each patient received fluvoxamine and placebo, in a randomized order, for 8 weeks each. There was a 1-week placebo lead-in period before the randomization phase. Two of 15 patients dropped out during the initial lead-in period, and an additional 3 withdrew within the first 4 weeks of randomization. Thus, data were available from 10 respondents who completed at least 4 weeks of each condition. Dosing was similar to that in the single-blind study described earlier. Again, placebo responses were evident in the 1-week lead-in period, and both groups improved equally during the first 8-week randomized phase of the study. In the latter 8 weeks of the study, a beneficial effect of fluvoxamine over the placebo emerged, but this was limited to the final 2 weeks of the study. Although it demonstrated the possible efficacy of fluvoxamine in treating gamblers, this study was limited by the small sample size, a relatively homogenous patient population, and a short duration of medication treatment.

Blanco, Petkova, Ibàñez, and Sáiz-Ruiz (2002) conducted a 6-month randomized, double-blind trial of fluvoxamine in 32 pathological gamblers. The overall analyses did not reveal a beneficial effect of drug over placebo, and again, a very high placebo response rate (59%) was observed. When data from men and younger patients were analyzed separately, a beneficial effect of fluvoxamine emerged. Because of the gender differences noted in 5-HT transporter genes in male but not female gamblers (Pérez de Castro, Ibàñez, Sáiz-Ruiz, & Fernández-Piqueras, 1999), Blanco et al. (2002) hypothesized that the efficacy of fluvoxamine may be gender specific, related to a gene deficiency that is more likely to occur in men. Larger scale studies are needed to further evaluate fluvoxamine's efficacy in treating gamblers and to ascertain whether the effects are truly gender specific.

Thus, several serotonin reuptake inhibitors have been used to treat pathological gamblers. The results from double-blind studies are mixed, with most finding no or only modest benefits of active drugs. In particular, the high placebo response rates noted thus far in every double-blind medication study for pathological gambling may limit the ability to detect anything but an extremely large effect size of a medication. The reasons for the high placebo response rates are unknown. They may result from nonspecific factors (e.g., a therapeutic relationship with treatment staff, or wanting to please staff), greater attention to one's own gambling by frequent monitoring, or motivational effects. That is, patients who initiate a treatment program may be aware of and attuned to the problems caused by gambling, and they may have already begun the process of changing their gambling behaviors (see chap. 8). The *transtheoretical model* (DiClemente et al., 1991) posits that motivation to change problem behaviors may be a robust predictor of outcomes in substance use disorders. In a recent study, I (Petry, in press) evaluated motivation to change among 234 treatment-seeking pathological gamblers. Those with higher motivation to change evidenced significantly greater reductions in gambling, including complete gambling abstinence, relative to those with lower motivation, regardless of the psychotherapy condition to which they were assigned. Whether motivation to change gambling behavior is associated with placebo response rates in medication trials remains to be determined.

Other problems with medication trials are the rates of study dropout. Attrition, which often is in the range of 30% to 50%, mitigates against finding a drug effect when intent-to-treat analyses, the gold standard in most research trials, are used. The need for further large-scale, well-designed studies that limit attrition and conduct follow-up evaluations even among individuals who withdrew from the study are needed to better evaluate the efficacy of medications in treating pathological gamblers.

The role of medication in the treatment of an individual pathological gambler, Sarah, a depressed, retired woman with relatively late-onset gambling problems, is described in the following case example, which is continued from chapter 4.

Case example (continued from chap. 4). Sarah, a 58-year-old woman with problems with depression and slot machine gambling, called a gambling help line and was referred to Gamblers Anonymous and a gambling treatment program. Sarah knew she would never go to Gamblers Anonymous, but she felt so desperate that she decided to try the treatment program. At her first meeting, the therapist thought that Sarah may be depressed, given her mannerisms and slowness of speech. He suggested that she meet with the staff psychiatrist for an assessment of depression. He also recommended that she attend a group therapy session at the center. Although she was embarrassed to go, she told herself she would just never come back if she didn't like it. Sarah attended her first group session 2 days later. The group members spoke primarily about how much they missed gambling, but they also knew their lives were better without it. Sarah did not say much at the group, but she was pleasantly surprised that there were other women like her in the group.

The next week, Sarah decided that she would follow through with the psychiatrist's appointment. The psychiatrist suggested that she start taking Luvox (fluvoxamine), and he told her that it should help her feel better and not want to gamble so much. Sarah was skeptical, and during the first couple of weeks she didn't feel like it was helping with anything. She was still depressed, and she went back to the casino one day when she felt really discouraged about her life. Fortunately, she stayed at the casino for only a couple of hours. While there, she observed some women who looked like they were glued to the slot machines and were clearly losing lots of money. She felt disgusted by it all and just didn't feel the desire to gamble, so she went home. There was a support group at the treatment center that night, and she decided to go. Again, she didn't say much at the group, but afterward, a young woman in the group invited everyone to join her at a coffee shop. All the women were going, so Sarah decided to go, too.

Sarah actually had fun that night. They didn't talk about gambling at the coffee shop. Instead, they spoke about their families, childhoods, and jobs. She had an appointment with the psychiatrist the next day, and she admitted to him that she had gone to the casino. He suggested that they increase the dose, and Sarah said she'd give it a try. The weeks went by, and Sarah started going to two groups per week at the treatment center. After the Thursday night meeting, she always went out with some of her new friends from the group. She was gradually feeling better, and although she still felt down from time to time, she knew that the casino was not the answer.

Sarah stayed on the medication for 8 months. Although she was a little worried about coming off it, she had gained new confidence in herself. She had taken a part-time volunteer job at the local library, working in the children's room. She really liked it, and she continued going to groups at the treatment center for about a year. Sarah has not gambled in over 3 years.

Comment. This case example does not demonstrate the efficacy of antidepressants in the treatment of pathological gambling; that is, Sarah may have ceased gambling without the antidepressant. Similarly, the psychosocial treatment provided may or may not have been responsible for Sarah's improvements. Simply by presenting for treatment, Sarah may have made a personal decision to reduce or stop her gambling. The psychosocial treatment may have given her a background of extra support, and the medication may have alleviated the depressive symptoms, which may or may not have been related directly to the gambling.

Most antidepressants do not reduce depression until several weeks after treatment begins. In Sarah's case, her initial skepticism about the benefits of the therapy may have been related to this delayed onset of action. She also may have been on too low of a dose, or she may not had yet garnered the appropriate social resources to stop gambling. These, or other as-yet-unknown variables, may individually or collectively lead to gambling cessation. Most likely, the reasons for long-term reductions in Sarah's gambling behaviors are related to her engagement in new hobbies and social relationships that she finds fulfilling.

Mood Stabilizers

A couple of reports have described the use of carbamazepine and lithium in the treatment of patients with comorbid gambling and bipolar disorders. As in many of the initial evaluations of medications, the first publications of mood stabilizers were based on case reports. Carbamazepine, an anticonvulsant with properties similar to tricyclic antidepressants, was tried in the treatment of one gambler (Haller & Hinterhuber, 1994). After a 12-week placebo period, the patient reported no change from baseline levels of gambling. A gradual increase to a dose of 600 mg/day resulted in a complete cessation of gambling by Week 2, and abstinence was maintained throughout 10 weeks of double-blind treatment and persisted during a 30-month period of continued treatment. Likewise, reductions in gambling were noted in three gamblers with bipolar features who were treated with lithium (1,800 mg/day; Moskowitz, 1980).

Pallanti et al. (2002) treated 42 pathological gamblers with no other major psychiatric disorders with either lithium carbonate (n = 23) or valproate (n = 19), a mood stabilizer used in bipolar, borderline, and other personality disorders with aggressive and impulsive features. The two medications were administered in a single-blind manner for 14 weeks. The mean doses achieved were 796 mg/day in the lithium group and 874 mg/day in the valproate group. Fewer patients treated with lithium completed the study (15 of 23, or 65%) than patients treated with valproate (16 of 19, or 84%). In both groups, an initial positive response to the medication was achieved in the first week of treatment, perhaps indicative of a placebo response. Although these reductions in gambling dissipated slightly in Weeks 2 to 3, decreases in gambling relative to baseline were still noted in the last 10 weeks of the study for patients treated with both medications. The two drugs had the same time course of effect, and no differences were noted in terms of the percentages considered responders using CGI scores of "improved" or "very much improved." In the lithium-treated patients, 14 of 23 patients (61%) were considered responders, and in the valproate group 13 of 19 patients (68%) were considered responders. Reductions in gambling were not considered to be secondary to alteration in mood, because no changes were noted in depression scale scores relative to baseline. Although this study suggests the possible use of mood stabilizers in the treatment of pathological gambling, the results are limited by the lack of a placebo control group as well as the small sample size. Furthermore, the mechanism of action of these drugs is speculative. Lithium may affect serotonin, and valproate is thought to have anxiolytic or other inhibitory effects by potentiating gamma-aminobutyric acid and thereby affecting other neurotransmitter systems secondarily. Research evaluating the efficacy and mechanisms of actions of these drugs is needed.

Opioid Antagonists

Two case reports of naltrexone initially were published. In one, 100 mg/day of naltrexone resulted in clinically significant decreases in gambling (Kim, 1998). The other report described beneficial effects of naltrexone in addition to fluoxetine in reducing urges to gamble in a patient with comorbid alcohol dependence and pathological gambling (Crockford & el-Guebaly, 1998a). These reports were followed by an open-label administration of naltrexone to 17 patients with pathological gambling but no other psychiatric comorbidity (Kim & Grant, 2001). Reductions in gambling behaviors and urges were noted over the 6 weeks of treatment.

Kim et al. (2001) subsequently published results from a 10-week, double-blind study of naltrexone in treating pathological gamblers. Eighty-three gamblers were enrolled in the study. After a 1-week placebo lead-in period, gamblers were randomized to receive placebo or naltrexone. The naltrexone dose was gradually adjusted upward until a maximal beneficial effect or 250-mg dose was achieved. Thirty-eight of the 83 gamblers (46%) were excluded from the analyses, primarily because of a response during the 1-week placebo lead-in period ($n = 22$, or 27%). Of the remaining 45 patients, 20 were randomized to naltrexone, and 25 were randomized to placebo. The patients in the naltrexone group demonstrated improvements on three outcome measures: (a) patient-rated CGI, (b) clinician-rated CGI, and (c) a gambling symptom scale. At the end of the 11-week treatment period, 75% of the patients in the naltrexone group, versus 24% of the patients in the placebo group, were "much" or "very much" improved. The mean dose of naltrexone was 188 mg/day, approximately three to four times the standard daily dose use in treatment of other addictive disorders. Certain side effects were common, including nausea, dry mouth, and vivid dreams. Elevated liver transaminases developed in 4 patients in the naltrexone-treated group, but this effect occurred almost exclusively in patients who were taking analgesics concurrently, and their levels normalized following discontinuation of the medication. Patients with more gambling urges at baseline responded better to naltrexone than patients with low levels of urges. Kim et al. (2001) suggested that opioid antagonists may best be suited for gamblers with strong gambling urges, but replication of this result in a prospective manner is necessary before treatment decisions will be based on this hypothesis.

This study, along with others (Blanco et al., 2002; Hollander et al., 2000; Hollander et al., 1998), suggests a significant placebo effect in the treatment of pathological gambling. However, it also suggests the possible efficacy of naltrexone in the treatment of pathological gambling. Future studies are needed to replicate these results. Other opioid antagonists with a lower side-effect profile, such as nalmafene, may also be useful.

The following case example describes the use of naltrexone in the treatment of a pathological gambler with comorbid alcohol abuse.

Case example. Brad is a 37-year-old man who is in the Army. He has been gambling and drinking regularly since adolescence. During football season, he especially likes to gamble, sometimes placing hundreds of dollars on big games. Brad doesn't consider his gambling to be a problem, and he can go weeks, or even months, without betting at certain times of the year, such as in the off season. He considers his drinking to be normal. All his friends had always like to party as much as he did, and Kelley, his long-term girlfriend, used to go out drinking with him.

Throughout his 30s, while many of his friends were outgrowing the party scene, Brad continued gambling and drinking. With his position in the Army, there always seemed to be people to go out with. Kelley eventually grew tired of Brad's absences because of his work assignments and, when he was at home, his long evenings and weekends out with the boys. She left him about 3 years ago and moved in with her parents. She took their 14-year old son and 11 year-old daughter with her. Brad now sees his children only once a month.

During a recent football season, Brad was gambling a lot, placing bets at work, and spending almost every evening in a local bar. Whenever there was a game, Brad felt he just had to bet on it, and he no longer limited his wagering to professional football, betting also on college games. His supervisor, whom Brad had known for a long time and was an old drinking buddy, started noticing Brad arriving to work late and seeming to be hung over. He spoke with Brad about it several times, but Brad denied any problems. Finally, after he failed to show up for work one day, his supervisor insisted that he take a leave of absence to "get his head straightened out."

As part of the absence, Brad was required to have a physical examination and meet with a psychiatrist, who felt Brad was drinking too much. The psychiatrist also inquired about his family history and learned that Brad's father had had both a drinking and a gambling problem. Brad denied any serious problems with gambling, but he admitted that he bet weekly and felt the need to gamble sometimes when he didn't even think it was going to be a good game. The psychiatrist prescribed naltrexone. At doses of 50 mg/day, Brad felt no differently and continued gambling and drinking as before. The doctor gradually increased the dose up to 150 mg/day, at which time Brad stated that he felt less desire to drink and that his urges to bet on games were also not as strong as they once were. When at a bar, he would drink two or three beers and didn't feel the need to continue drinking like he used to. If a sports game was on the television at the bar and others were betting, he didn't feel the excitement or the urge to put money on it. Sometimes, he would just watch without wagering at all. Other times, he would place a small $10 bet.

Brad returned to duty after a month and was glad to find out he had been assigned to a new unit, where he could have a fresh start. Brad continued taking the naltrexone, on and off, for 4 months. Although he still drinks and gambles occasionally, he has not encountered any troubles with gambling or drinking in over a year.

Comment. As in the previous example of Sarah, this case description does not demonstrate the efficacy of naltrexone in treating Brad's gambling problems. Rather, the naltrexone may have diminished Brad's desire to drink alcohol, which in turn may have decreased his urge to gamble. Alternatively, the naltrexone may not have engendered any specific effects, and Brad's modification in lifestyle may have been responsible for his changes in gambling and drinking.

COMPARISONS WITH MEDICATIONS FOR TREATING SUBSTANCE USE DISORDERS

As reviewed above, three types of medications have been used to treat pathological gamblers: (a) serotonin reuptake inhibitors, (b) mood stabilizers, and (c) opioid antagonists. Although some positive effects have been noted, the results are far from conclusive, and no medication has yet been approved by the Food and Drug Administration for treating gamblers. Replication in double-blind studies needs to be conducted by independent researchers, and thus far such efforts have revealed inconsistent results.

In investigating putative pharmacotherapies for gambling, consideration of medications used in treatment of substance use disorders may provide some guidance (Petry, 2002b). Four types of pharmacotherapies exist for treating substance use disorders. First, medications that alleviate withdrawal symptoms have been useful in treating some substance use disorders. Examples of these medications include benzodiazepines for alcohol withdrawal; nicotine replacement therapy for nicotine dependence; and clonidine, benzodiazepines, or tapering doses of opioids for opioid withdrawal. Drugs such as cocaine and marijuana that do not induce significant physiological dependence do not necessitate such medications. Because pathological gambling is associated with only a mild withdrawal syndrome and no physical dependence (Rosenthal & Lesieur, 1992), such medications are unlikely to be useful for treating gambling.

A second type of medication for substance use disorders is drugs that mimic effects of the abused drug. These are often referred to as *maintenance* or *substitution* drugs. Examples include methadone, L-alpha-acetyl-methadol (LAAM), or buprenorphine for treatment of opioid dependence. These drugs are longer acting than the abused substance, thereby permitting patients to function without experiencing withdrawal symptoms. Because pathological gambling does not exert a significant physiological dependence, such medications are unlikely to be useful in treatment of gamblers.

A third class of medication is that which prevents consumption of the abused drug by blocking reinforcing effects or exerting aversive effects when combined with the abused drug. For opioids, naltrexone is the classic example. A detoxified heroin addict maintained on naltrexone cannot experience the effects of opioids, because naltrexone prevents opioids from binding. Naltrexone has also been approved for the treatment of alcohol dependence, and it is thought to block the subjectively reinforcing effects of alcohol (O'Malley et al., 1992; Volpicelli, O'Brien, Alterman, & Hayashida, 1992). As I described earlier in this chapter, naltrexone has been used to treat pathological gambling, and its effects are thought to be mediated by blocking urges to gamble, or possibly abating the stimulating and positive subjective effects experienced when gambling. To the extent that opioid antagonists are found efficacious in treating disordered gamblers in future studies, researchers should carefully assess the drug's mechanisms of action on influencing urges to gamble or on the actual pleasurable effects of gambling.

Some drugs induce aversive effects when an abused drug is ingested. Disulfiram is used to treat alcohol dependence (Fuller et al., 1986). Rather than blocking effects of alcohol on receptor systems, this drug works by preventing degradation of acetaldehyde, a toxic by-product of alcohol. Beneficial effects of apomorphine, a drug that produces vomiting, to induce conditioned aversion to gambling, were reported in a case report (Salzmann, 1982). These aversion effects are not unique to gambling but can be applied to any problem behavior. Poor compliance with such treatments, however, limits effectiveness.

Finally, another class of medication for treating substance use disorders is those that alleviate a common comorbid condition and thereby reduce drug abuse indirectly. The rationale for this approach comes from the *self-medication hypothesis*. For example, high rates of depression are noted in alcohol-dependent patients, and some theories posit that individuals drink to mask depression (Khantzian, 1975). Antidepressants improved outcomes in studies of cocaine addicts (Ziedonis & Kosten, 1991) and methadone-maintained patients (Kleber, Weissman, Rounsaville, Prusoff, & Wilber, 1983; Nunes, Quitkin, Brady, & Stewart, 1991). In other studies, however, antidepressants seemed more efficacious than placebos in treating depression symptoms, but they had no beneficial effect on reducing substance use (Kranzler et al., 1995). As described earlier, antidepressants have been used to treat gamblers, as have some mood stabilizers. It is interesting that the beneficial effects of these medications in reducing gambling appear to be unrelated to their effects on mood. Patients with major mood disorders generally have been excluded from these studies and, as I discussed earlier, reductions in gambling have not been correlated with changes in mood. These findings underscore the need to better assess the medications' mechanisms of actions in reducing gambling if they are found efficacious in larger, double-blind trials.

Although the efficacy and mechanisms of action of medications for treating gamblers are not well understood, the development of pharmacological treatments for gambling may be guided by research in the treatment of substance use disorders. To date, only drug use disorders with substantial physiological dependence—such as nicotine, alcohol, and opioid dependence—have been managed by pharmacotherapy. In contrast, cocaine and marijuana dependence, both of which induce relatively mild withdrawal, have not yet been treated reliably with medications. Pathological gambling may more closely resemble these disorders, as its withdrawal syndrome is modest. Therefore, the most fruitful area for investigating pharmacotherapy for pathological gambling may be related to management of concomitant psychological symptoms, such as alleviating gambling urges or depressive symptoms.

Furthermore, an examination of pharmacological studies in the area of substance abuse treatment reveals that rates of long-term favorable response are modest (Kranzler, Amin, Modesto-Lowe, & Oncken, 1999). Relapse rates are high, and pharmacotherapies typically exert effects over a narrow band of symptoms. Pharmacotherapies in general, and antagonist medications in particular, suffer from a lack of compliance, which limits their clinical utility (Elkin, Pilkonis, Docherty, & Sotsky, 1988; Kranzler, Escobar, Lee, & Meza, 1986). Thus far, in the treatment of pathological gambling, medication compliance has been generally poor, and treatment attrition rates are high (Blanco et al., 2002; Hollander et al., 1998; Kim et al., 2001).

Unlike in the treatment of substance use disorders, strong placebo effects have been reported in pathological gamblers (Hollander et al., 1998, 2000; Kim et al., 2001). Some medications (e.g., naltrexone) are also associated with significant side-effect profiles (A. C. King, Volpicelli, Gunduz, O'Brien, & Kreek, 1997). Finally, pharmacotherapies do not address the psychosocial difficulties common in substance abusers and pathological gamblers.

Most of the research in pharmacotherapy for disordered gambling has been conducted without concurrent psychosocial treatment. Patients participating in medication studies generally have been forbidden from receiving concomitant psychotherapy. The rationale for this is to isolate any beneficial effects to the medication alone. However, if administered in a clinical context, medication is likely to be provided in conjunction with psychosocial therapy. In the treatment of substance use disorders, some studies have found additive beneficial effects when pharmacotherapies and psychotherapies are combined (for a review, see K. M. Carroll, 1997). The addition of psychotherapy to a medication regimen may enhance patient retention and abate urges or cravings as well as address related psychosocial difficulties. No published studies of combined pharmacotherapy and psychotherapy treatments for pathological gambling exist, but de la Gandera (1999) reported on a 6-month, open-label trial of fluoxetine (Prozac, 20 mg/day) for 6 months. In this study, 11 patients received fluoxetine plus psychotherapy, and 9 received psychotherapy alone. The combined group demonstrated improvements relative to the psychotherapy-alone group, but the lack of a placebo medication control condition, and of a group receiving medication alone, limits the interpretation of the findings. If an efficacious medication is found, research must evaluate the independent and interactive effects of pharmacotherapy and psychotherapy in large and diverse samples of pathological gamblers.

SUMMARY AND CLINICAL IMPLICATIONS

Some initial results of pharmacological treatments of pathological gambling are encouraging, but more research is needed to evaluate the short- and long-term efficacy of pharmacotherapies before they should be considered the initial treatment of choice among gamblers. At this point, given that no pharmacotherapy has received approval from the Food and Drug Administration, the most conservative and safest recommendation may be to treat concomitant psychiatric disorders with medications. Thus, if a gambler presents to treatment with concurrent major depressive disorder, then serotonin reuptake inhibitors may be a reasonable option. If a gambler presents for treatment with bipolar features or cyclothymia, then mood stabilizers such as lithium or valproate may be justified, whereas fluvoxamine may exacerbate the symptoms (Hollander et al., 1998). A patient with concurrent alcohol dependence and pathological gambling may respond to naltrexone treatment, although the necessary doses may be high and require frequent safety monitoring for liver functioning. One case report (Crockford & el-Guebaly, 1998a) found that a comorbid patient who did not respond to fluoxetine at 20 mg/day experienced remission from gambling after naltrexone at 50 mg/day was added. Optimal durations of pharmacotherapies have yet to be investigated. If psychotherapy is provided concurrently, it should probably be continued beyond cessation of any medication treatment.

As more pharmacotherapies for pathological gambling are developed and tested in controlled trials, some issues should be considered. In the treatment of gambling, as in the treatment of substance use disorders, engagement in treatment may be one of the greatest challenges. As I review in the next chapter, few pathological gamblers receive professional treatment. The availability of multiple treatment options, including both pharmaco-therapies and psychotherapies, may enhance participation in treatment and reduce the negative personal and societal consequences of pathological gambling.

8

RECOVERY WITHOUT
PROFESSIONAL INTERVENTIONS

The National Research Council (NRC, 1999) and the National Gambling Impact Study Commission (1999) have estimated that only about 8% of Level 3 gamblers receive treatment for gambling, and virtually no Level 2 gamblers seek or receive assistance. These data suggest one of two possibilities: Either (a) disordered gamblers rarely stop gambling, or (b) they overcome gambling problems without help. In this chapter, I explore rates of recovery from gambling problems and the research that has examined methods and processes of natural recovery. I also describe some putative methods for maintaining gambling abstinence and why so many gamblers do not seek outside assistance. In the second half of the chapter, I describe Gamblers Anonymous (GA), the most commonly used intervention for gamblers who do seek help, although not a professionally-guided one.

NATURAL RECOVERY

Estimating Rates of Resolution of Gambling Problems

As I described in chapter 2, lifetime rates of Level 2–3 gambling are higher than past-year rates. Shaffer, Hall, and Vander Bilt (1999) reviewed 22 general population surveys in which both lifetime and past-year prevalence rates were measured. Dividing past-year rates by lifetime rates and then subtracting this value from 1 is a common method for estimating the proportion of individuals who have been diagnosed as disordered gamblers who have overcome their problems with gambling. Using this formula and the 22 surveys cited by Shaffer, Hall, and Vander Bilt (1999), Hodgins, Wynne, and Makarchuk (1999) estimated that 36% to 46% of Level 3 gamblers would be considered in recovery or resolved gamblers. For Level 2 gambling, resolution rates across studies similarly ranged from 32% to 46%. These data suggest that between one third and one half of people who ever had problems with gambling are no longer experiencing gambling problems.

Although rates of resolution are fairly consistent across studies, this approach may overestimate actual rates of recovery from gambling. In most of these studies, the South Oaks Gambling Screen (SOGS; Lesieur & Blume, 1987) was used to estimate lifetime rates, but the SOGS does not require all of the symptoms to occur at the same time to classify an individual as a Level 2 or 3 gambler (see chap. 3). For example, imagine a scenario in which a person borrows gambling money from his or her parents during the teenage years, from his or her spouse during one's 20s, and from a credit card account after a divorce. This person may endorse these three lifetime symptoms, and therefore be classified as a Level 2 gambler, even though the gambling itself and the amounts the person borrowed may not have increased at all over the 20-year time span. In other words, at any one time this person would have endorsed only a single item on the SOGS (indicating that he or she is a nonproblem gambler), but over his or her lifetime would endorse three items (indicating that he or she is a Level 2 gambler). When all the items of the SOGS refer to a more limited time period (e.g., the past year), the symptoms would have to occur more or less in an overlapping time frame for a person to be classified as a disordered gambler. Thus, rates of resolution would be overestimated if one used the formula described earlier, because the lifetime classification system may have overestimated the presence of disordered gambling in the above example.

Only one known study confirmed rates of recovery from individuals identified in a general population survey. Hodgins et al. (1999) attempted to reinterview respondents from a general population survey who were classified as Level 2–3 gamblers on the SOGS. In the initial survey of 1,821 individuals from Alberta, Canada, 7.9% were classified as lifetime Level 2–3 gamblers, and 4.8% were classified as past-year Level 2–3 gamblers. Thus, according to the formula presented earlier, 39% are considered recovered, a rate consistent with the surveys reviewed by Shaffer, Hall, and Vander Bilt (1999). Approximately 4 months after the first survey, Hodgins et al. (1999) contacted 42 (76%) of these individuals. Although all of them had earlier responded affirmatively to at least three SOGS items, the vast majority (N = 36, or 86%) denied "ever having a gambling problem" (Item 3 on the SOGS). Only 6 of the 42 acknowledged a lifetime gambling problem, and all 6 of these individuals stated that they no longer gambled to a problematic degree. This rate of resolution is clearly much different than the rate reported in other studies, thereby raising doubts regarding the rates of resolution from gambling problems reported in other studies.

Reasons for Ceasing Gambling

Hodgins et al. (1999) inquired about why and how the six individuals identified in a general population survey as resolved gamblers had reduced their gambling, including questions about involvement with treatment services. Only two of the six reported seeking professional treatment for gambling. Not seeking treatment is not limited to North American gamblers. A Swiss study (Bondolfi, Osiek, & Ferrero, 2000) noted that only one respondent identified as a Level 2–3 gambler had sought treatment. Similarly, in Brazil, only 4.9% of the Level 2–3 gamblers reported having sought treatment (Tavares, Zilberman, Beites, & Gentil, 2001).

The reasons for ceasing gambling appear to be primarily financial and emotional in nature. Most of the resolved gamblers in Hodgins et al.'s (1999) study reported that a bad monetary loss precipitated their desire to stop gambling, one reported a bankruptcy, and several indicated not having enough money. Emotional reasons ranged from stress and depression to arguments with spouses. In a follow-up study, Hodgins and el-Guebaly (2000) used media advertisements to recruit 43 resolved Level 3 gamblers (with a median of 14 months abstinence) and 63 Level 3 gamblers who were actively gambling. For the former group, the advertisement began, "Have you successfully overcome a gambling problem without formal treatment?", and for the latter it started with "Do you have a gambling problem now?" No differences in demographics, SOGS scores, or psychiatric comorbidity were noted between resolved and active gamblers. Both groups appeared to be similar to Level 3 gamblers identified in other general population surveys. Half were women, the average age was about 42 years, about half were married, and slightly over half were employed full time. Lifetime SOGS scores averaged about 12 in each group, indicative of relatively severe gambling problems.

Over half the full sample (Hodgins & el-Guebaly, 2000) reported no experience with gambling treatment, either professional treatment or involvement with GA. A small minority reported minimal involvement in some form of treatment, and 16% of active gamblers and 33% of resolved gamblers had substantial (five or more sessions) experience with some form of treatment. Those with significant treatment involvement had more severe gambling problems, as assessed by higher SOGS scores or *Diagnostic and Statistical Manual of Mental Disorders* (4th ed.; American Psychiatric Association, 1994) symptom counts. Among the resolved group, 81% reported that their goal was to quit gambling completely, and 19% stated that their initial goal was to cut back on gambling. Eighty-four percent said that they had quit gambling cold turkey, and the rest said they had tapered their gambling over time. Approximately two thirds of the resolved gamblers said that their decision to stop or cut down their gambling was a conscious one, as opposed to something that simply happened.

As with the resolved gamblers identified in the general population survey (Hodgins et al., 1999), these resolved gamblers indicated that the most common reasons for ceasing gambling were financial and emotional in nature. Other reasons were related to family influences or demands and feeling that gambling was incompatible with desired images or goals. In other words, the resolved gamblers said that they felt they wanted to be a role model for their children and that gambling was inconsistent with this image. Spiritual reasons, hitting "rock bottom," experiencing a humiliating or traumatic event, and evaluating pros and cons were some other reasons endorsed by approximately one third to one half of the gamblers. Less than half noted health, work, or legal problems; a change in another addictive behavior; or a major lifestyle change as reasons for ceasing gambling.

In another study, Hodgins, Makarchuk, el-Guebaly, and Peden (2002) recruited through advertisements an additional 101 gamblers who had recently quit gambling, with an average of only 19 days of abstinence. Similar open-ended questions and checklists were administered to assess reasons for stopping gambling in this group, compared with the group of individuals who had abstained from gambling for a longer time. Again, the majority reported that the decision to stop gambling was "completely conscious," and about one third reported that the decision was prompted by a crisis. Reasons for quitting appeared to be similar between long-term resolved and recent quitters. Financial concerns were most prevalent, followed by negative emotions. Family influence, incompatibility with desired self-image, and cognitive appraisals (evaluating pros and cons) also were frequently cited. The long-term resolved gamblers and recent gamblers differed only with respect to the frequency of two items. Long-term resolved gamblers were more likely to report social support and reasons "out of their awareness" for ceasing gambling. About 50% of both samples reported a current or previous attempt at gambling treatment, via GA or professional programs. Those who had received treatment reported a greater number of reasons to stop gambling than those who had not.

Reasons for ceasing addictive behaviors can be categorized into *internal* and *external* ones. In a study of smoking cessation, Curry, Wagner, and Grothaus (1990) found that intrinsic motivations to quit were more predictive of successful cessation than were external motivations. Similarly, alcoholics are more likely to attribute reasons for terminating relapses to internal factors than to external ones (Hodgins, Ungar, el-Guebaly, & Armstrong,

TABLE 8.1
Reasons for Ceasing Gambling

Reason	% Endorsing reason	Internal or external
Financial concerns	96	Internal
Emotional factors	92	Internal
Concern about family/children	69	Internal
Hit "rock bottom"	61	Internal
Evaluated pros and cons	54	Internal
Humiliating event	50	External
Physical health	48	External
Work problems	43	External
Confrontation	43	External
Major lifestyle change	43	External
Problems with spouse	39	External
Traumatic event	39	External
Incompatible with desired self-image	31	Internal
Legal problems	26	External
Spiritual reasons	22	Internal
Change in another addictive behavior	22	Other
Lack of financial resources	12	External
Rational appraisal	10	Internal
Fear of future negative consequences	7	Internal
Social support	4	External
Out of awareness	3	Other

Note. Data from "Why Problem Gamblers Quit Gambling: A Comparison of Methods and Samples," by D. C. Hodgins, K. Makarchuk, N. el-Guebaly, and N. Peden, 2002, *Addiction Research and Theory, 10*, pp. 203–218.

1997). Hodgins et al. (2002) had independent evaluators rank gamblers' reasons for quitting as internal, external, or other. The proportions of the total sample endorsing each item are shown in Table 8.1.

As noted in this table, the majority of the most popularly recalled reasons for stopping gambling were internal in nature. Although these reports may be influenced by the retrospective nature of recall, they nevertheless give some insight into why people stop gambling. Whether these reasons hold as predictors of long-term change among gamblers remains to be determined.

The following case example describes a man's development of gambling problems and the circumstances under which he resolved to stop gambling.

Case example. Bob is a 38-year-old automotive worker who lives in a suburb of Detroit. He is divorced, but he maintains a good relationship with his ex-wife, and he has two sons, ages 12 and 14. Bob started gambling when he was a boy, on cards and sports games with his friends. During his teens and 20s, he continued wagering from time to time, but never problematically.

When he first got married and his boys were young, Bob had little interest in gambling. When the Windsor Casino opened nearby, Bob was in his 30s, his sons had grown older, and he and his wife had drifted apart.

Bob started going to the casino after work with friends and played blackjack. It was just a night out, a couple times a month. In his mid-30s, his wife had an affair with a mutual friend of theirs. Although Bob was very angry, he also knew that their marriage wasn't going well, and Bob had been seeing other women. They divorced amicably, and Bob moved out of the house. He found it lonely at first and started spending more and more time at the casino. Soon he was going two or three nights per week and spending several hundred dollars at a time.

Although Bob felt he was coming out ahead enough of the time, he also started noticing that he didn't like how he was feeling. He sometimes woke up the next day regretting the previous night, having stayed far later at the casino than he had intended. On a couple of months he was late with child support payments, and he had to ask his father for help. Although his ex-wife was understanding about the late payments, Bob felt guilty. He realized that he didn't have a dime in savings. His car was getting old, and he couldn't afford a new one, although he had a good salary. He came home from work one day and opened his credit card statement: He owed over $10,000 and was 2 months late on his payments. That day, Bob decided that enough was enough—he was going to stop gambling.

Methods for Maintaining Gambling Abstinence

In addition to understanding the reasons for an individual's initial decision to cease gambling, evaluating the processes by which that person maintains his or her abstinence is important. Hodgins and el-Guebaly (2000) recruited 43 resolved gamblers through advertisements and asked them about how they maintained their abstinence from gambling. Both open-ended and checklist assessments were used and revealed that the respondents used similar methods to maintain abstinence.

The most commonly cited ways for maintaining abstinence were recalling past gambling problems and engaging in new activities. Each reason was cited by over half the sample. Other common factors for maintaining abstinence were the use of self-control or willpower and feeling a sense of pride or accomplishment about the resolution. Treatment, cognitive strategies (e.g., remembering negative aspects of gambling), and social support also were relatively frequently cited methods, mentioned by about one quarter of the sample. Spiritual reasons, limiting one's access to money, and rewarding oneself for not gambling were infrequently endorsed reasons.

Hodgins (2001) administered the Processes of Change Questionnaire (Prochaska, Velicer, DiClemente, & Fava, 1988) to the 43 long-time abstinent gamblers from Hodgins and el-Guebaly's (2000) study. This questionnaire has been widely used in other addiction populations, and 10 processes of change have been identified. They cluster into two groups: (a) cognitive–experiential and (b) behavioral.

Cognitive–experiential processes include *raising consciousness*, which consists of recalling negative information about gambling and thinking about financial problems from gambling. Another process is *self-reevaluation*—getting upset when thinking about one's gambling or being ashamed of one's own gambling behaviors. *Dramatic relief* is exemplified by being frightened by situations in which one finds oneself because of gambling and feeling scared about the strength of one's urges to gamble. *Social liberation* refers to noticing societal recognition of the dangers of gambling via advertisements or news stories and recognizing others who have stopped gambling. Last, *environmental reevaluation* is related to thinking about how one's gambling has caused problems for friends or family members.

Five behavioral processes are reported in the literature on overcoming addictive behaviors. The first of these, *helping relationships*, means having people to talk with about gambling and related problems. *Stimulus control* refers to avoiding people or places associated with gambling and controlling access to money. *Counterconditioning* is keeping oneself busy to avoid gambling, distracting oneself, or doing exercise when urges arise. *Reinforcement management* means spending time with people who reward or make one feel good for not gambling, or rewarding oneself for not gambling. *Self-liberation* is making a commitment to not gamble, using willpower, and reminding oneself that one does not need to gamble to feel good.

The most frequently reported processes of change were cognitive–experiential in nature (Hodgins, 2001). In descending order, they were self-reevaluation, environmental reevaluation, and dramatic relief. Thus, feelings of shame and struggling with one's self-image were common processes, as were acknowledging the impact of gambling on others and experiencing strong negative feelings about one's gambling. Two of the three least common methods endorsed by the resolved gamblers were behavioral in nature: reinforcement management, stimulus control, and social liberation. The other four methods (raising consciousness, counterconditioning, self-liberation, and helping relationships) were used to intermediary degrees. Gamblers who had experience with professional treatment used all the strategies more often than gamblers who were never in treatment. Thus, treatment may have availed gamblers of new strategies. However, gamblers who attend treatment may use more strategies to begin with, in part because they may have more severe gambling problems. Longitudinal studies of naturally and treatment-assisted resolved gamblers are needed to test these possibilities.

The results of these studies are consistent with those of studies conducted with other populations. Research on other addictive disorders suggests that cognitive–experiential methods are more often used in early stages of abstinence, whereas abstinence is maintained by behavioral processes. For example, Snow, Prochaska, and Rossi (1994) found that Alcoholics Anonymous (AA) members and nontreated abstinent alcoholics reported similar use of cognitive–experiential processes, but the AA members used more behavioral change processes. It is clear that more research on the methods and processes used to initiate and maintain abstinence in gamblers is needed.

The case of Bob, continued from earlier in this chapter, describes how one gambler stopped gambling on his own and how he maintained abstinence.

Case example continued. Four years later, Bob can still remember vividly how he gave up gambling. After getting the credit card statement, and having the choice of either asking his father for money again or figuring this mess out on his own, he resolved to stop. He decided not to go to the casino any more after that day, no matter what. The first couple of weeks were hard for him, and he didn't know what to do with his free time. He started working on his car on the weekends and in the evenings, but he was determined to not go back to the casino.

Bob is proud of his ability to stop on his own. He says he is not ashamed of himself anymore, and he has nothing to hide from his family. He managed to pay off his debts over the next several years, and he recently bought a new car. He said he doesn't miss the gambling at all.

Bob saw his younger son playing cards for money with his friends one day, and he discussed it with him. He told him that working was a better way to earn money and that people can get into trouble by expecting to win at gambling. Bob said he knew his son had to learn for himself, but he was glad that he was able to set a good example for him.

Comment. This is an example of a person who developed moderate to severe gambling problems, recognized his difficulties with gambling, and resolved to change on his own. Bob may not have realized that treatment for gambling was available, but even if he did, he may not have felt that he needed outside assistance to stop gambling. Indeed, he managed to stop successfully on his own.

Reasons Why Gamblers Do Not Seek Treatment

Recovery from addictive problems without formal treatment is an increasingly recognized phenomenon (Institute of Medicine, 1990; McCartney, 1996). In fact, natural recovery for alcohol problems is the most typical pathway to recovery (L. C. Sobell, Cunningham, & Sobell, 1996), and most former smokers also quit on their own (DiClemente & Prochaska, 1982). Similarly, the available data suggest that few Level 2–3 gamblers ever seek or receive help for gambling (NRC, 1999; National Gambling

Impact Study Commission, 1999). Hodgins and el-Guebaly (2000) asked both resolved and nonresolved gamblers about why they had not sought treatment. The most frequently endorsed reason was that they wished to handle the problem on their own; over 80% indicated that this was the primary reason for not seeking treatment. Five other factors were listed by about half the gamblers as at least moderately important in their decision to not seek treatment: (a) embarrassment or pride, (b) not considering their gambling to be sufficiently problematic to necessitate treatment, (c) being unaware of the availability of treatment, (d) inability to share their problems with others, and (e) concern about stigma. Less than one quarter of the gamblers had negative attitudes toward treatment, and treatment cost was endorsed as a variable by only a minority of participants. Of course, this study was conducted in Canada, where out-of-pocket costs for medical and mental health treatments are less of a concern because of socialized health care.

Section Summary

Although comparisons between lifetime and past-year prevalence rates of disordered gambling indicate that a fair number of gamblers resolve their problems with gambling, researchers still know little about how or why individuals stop gambling once they develop problems. Both internal and external reasons for ceasing gambling have been identified, and cognitive–experiential and behavioral reasons appear to be important in the maintenance of abstinence. Reasons why gamblers seek or do not seek treatment need further exploration. As demonstrated in this chapter, a significant proportion of gamblers are able to resolve their problems on their own. Identifying predictors of unassisted abstinence may be useful in determining patients for whom treatment may not be necessary or even recommended. Conversely, treatment could be targeted toward individuals who are unlikely to abstain successfully on their own. With the growth of GA meetings and professional treatment options, more gamblers may begin to access services in upcoming years.

GAMBLERS ANONYMOUS

As described earlier, and in the case example, some pathological gamblers recover on their own. For those who seek assistance, the most popular intervention is GA. GA began in Los Angeles in 1957. By 1960, 16 chapters existed. This number grew to 130 by 1970 and to over 600 by 1990. At present, more than 1,000 GA chapters are available in the United States alone, with an increase of 36% between 1995 and 1998 (NRC, 1999). At

EXHIBIT 8.1
The 12 Steps of Gamblers Anonymous

1. We admitted we were powerless over gambling—that our lives had become unmanageable.
2. Came to believe that a Power greater than ourselves could restore us to a normal way of thinking and living.
3. Made a decision to turn our will and our lives over to the care of this Power of our own understanding.
4. Made a searching and fearless moral and financial inventory of ourselves.
5. Admitted to ourselves and to another human being the exact nature of our wrongs.
6. Were entirely ready to have these defects of character removed.
7. Humbly asked God (of our understanding) to remove our shortcomings.
8. Made a list of all persons we had harmed and became willing to make amends to them all.
9. Made direct amends to such people wherever possible, except when to do so would injure them or others.
10. Continued to take personal inventory and when we were wrong, promptly admitted it.
11. Sought through prayer and meditation to improve our conscious contact with God as we understood Him, praying only for knowledge of His will for us and the power to carry that out.
12. Having made an effort to practice these principles in all our affairs, we tried to carry this message to other compulsive gamblers.

Note. From Gamblers Anonymous International, http://www.gamblersanonymous.org/recovery.html. Reprinted with permission.

least 1 GA chapter is available in each of the 50 states, with the number of chapters per state ranging from 1 to 129 (NRC, 1999). GA has chapters worldwide, with meetings available in such countries as Spain, Germany, Austria, the United Kingdom, Australia, New Zealand, Brazil, Israel, Kenya, Korea, and Japan, as well as elsewhere.

GA is a self-help fellowship modeled after AA. The structure and philosophy of GA are somewhat similar to those of AA. GA proposes that pathological gambling is a disease that can never be cured but only arrested by complete abstinence from gambling. As in AA, 12 principles or steps are followed, and members "work the steps." These steps include accepting their problem and powerlessness over gambling and surrendering to a "higher power." Many of the slogans and philosophies used in AA have been adapted by GA, including "take one day at a time" and the serenity prayer: "God, grant me the serenity to accept the things I cannot change, the courage to change the things I can, and the wisdom to know the difference." The 12 steps of GA are listed in Exhibit 8.1.

GA attendees are asked to identify themselves only by their first names, and meetings typically begin with introductions of "My name is John S., and I'm a compulsive gambler." Often, the length of abstinence is stated

EXHIBIT 8.2
The 20 Questions from Gamblers Anonymous

1. Did you ever lose time from work or school due to gambling? .... YES NO
2. Has gambling ever made your home life unhappy? .... YES NO
3. Did gambling affect your reputation? .... YES NO
4. Have you ever felt remorse after gambling? .... YES NO
5. Did you ever gamble to get money with which to pay debts or to otherwise solve financial difficulties? .... YES NO
6. Did gambling cause a decrease in your ambition or efficiency? .... YES NO
7. After losing, did you feel you must return as soon as possible and win back your losses? .... YES NO
8. After a win, did you have a strong urge to return and win more? ...... YES NO
9. Did you often gamble until your last dollar was gone? .... YES NO
10. Did you ever borrow to finance your gambling? .... YES NO
11. Have you ever sold anything to finance gambling? .... YES NO
12. Were you reluctant to use "gambling money" for normal expenditures? .... YES NO
13. Did gambling make you careless of the welfare of yourself or your family? .... YES NO
14. Did you ever gamble longer than you had planned? .... YES NO
15. Have you ever gambled to escape worry or trouble? .... YES NO
16. Have you ever committed, or considered committing, an illegal act to finance gambling? .... YES NO
17. Did gambling cause you to have difficulty in sleeping? .... YES NO
18. Did arguments, disappointments or frustrations create within you an urge to gamble? .... YES NO
19. Did you ever have an urge to celebrate a good fortune by a few hours of gambling? .... YES NO
20. Have you ever considered self-destruction or suicide as a result of your gambling? .... YES NO

Note. From Gamblers Anonymous International, http://www.gamblersanonymous.org/20questions.html. Reprinted with permission.

during introductions, such as "I've haven't gambled in 63 days." Newcomers may be asked to respond to the 20 Questions (Exhibit 8.2). Pins are awarded to members for hallmark periods of abstinence, such as a 1-year period without gambling. Attendees are encouraged to have sponsors, who may serve as resource links and support systems outside of the formal meetings. Call lists are also provided. Members are encouraged to telephone one another in times of emergencies, or whenever they are tempted to gamble.

Differences Between Gamblers Anonymous and Alcoholics Anonymous

B. R. Browne (1991, 1994) has outlined the differences between GA and AA. Although many similarities exist between these self-help groups, he noted some important differences. One of the most striking differences is that GA is less spiritual, and the role of a higher power is de-emphasized. As shown in Exhibit 8.1, a reference to God is qualified with the phrase, "as we understood Him." Little emphasis is placed on church attendance, and the Lord's Prayer is not read at meetings. GA tends to be pragmatic rather than spiritual.

Another major difference between AA and GA is related to consequences of the disorders and reasons for seeking assistance. As shown earlier in this chapter, gamblers tend to have financial stressors that serve as an impetus to seeking help. To assist with managing debt, some GA chapters offer "pressure relief" sessions to assist new members with managing gambling debts. In pressure-relief meetings, members with a defined period of abstinence and regular GA attendance (usually 30–90 days) are provided help arranging detailed budgets and repayment plans, for both legal and illegal creditors. Usually, long-term GA members with personal experience in managing large debts conduct these pressure-relief sessions. GA is strongly opposed to the concept of bankruptcy, believing that repayment of debt is a continuous reminder of what happens when one gambles. GA members' spouses are encouraged to attend pressure-relief meetings, with the recommendation that the gambler turn over all finances to his or her partner or another trusted friend or relative.

GA meetings also tend to be more family oriented than many AA meetings. If available, GamAnon meetings (directed at significant others of pathological gamblers; see chap. 9) may be held in the same venue, and on the same night, as GA meetings, but in a different room. Joint meetings may also be held. Cross-availability encourages attendance of both members of the couple and other concerned family members.

Another difference between GA and AA is that GA meetings are smaller. Whereas AA meetings can often have in excess of 50 to 100 people, GA meetings typically have between 5 and 30 attendees. Despite the smaller size, GA meetings are usually longer, and they can last upward of 3 to 4 hr. The longer length appears to be related in part to the practice of allowing everyone to "give therapy," or share their feelings. In some of the larger meetings that have 40 or so attendees, each person's therapy may be limited to 5 min, with one individual designated the timekeeper.

Despite their recent growth, GA meetings are not as widely available as AA meetings. Only in selected areas (e.g., Nevada) can members attend "90 meetings in 90 days." In rural areas, attendance at more than 1 meeting a week may be impractical, if not impossible. AA meetings outnumber GA meetings by 20- to 100-fold or more, depending on the city. The relative dearth of GA meetings may also make it difficult for new attendees who do not feel comfortable with a particular meeting to find another one in the local area. With the exception of Nevada, attending GA meetings during both day and evening hours usually is not possible.

Efficacy and Effectiveness of GA

Identifying with other people who are experiencing similar problems can be a powerful experience, offering hope and relief. Custer (1982) proposed several reasons for the popularity of GA. He suggested that GA provides a nonjudgmental approach that demands honesty and responsibility. It identifies and corrects character problems and can undercut denial and rationalization. At the same time, friendships formed in GA can provide affection, concern, and support. They can also fill a void that is left by the cessation of gambling.

Despite the popularity of GA, little published literature exists on its efficacy. Of the observational work, most concurs that a vast number of GA attendees fail to become actively involved in the fellowship (Preston & Smith, 1985; Rosecrance, 1988; Taber & Chaplin, 1988; Turner & Saunders, 1990). The most comprehensive study of GA attendance was conducted in Scotland. Stewart and Brown (1988) reviewed attendance records from three meetings, spanning a 16-year period. Of the 232 attendees, 52 (22.4%) never came back for a second meeting, and another 36 (15.5%) attended only 2 meetings. Of the full sample, 161 (69.4%) attended 10 or fewer meetings, and only 7.5% earned a 1-year abstinence pin.

Stewart and Brown (1988) also conducted a small prospective study. In 14 GA groups that met over a 3-month period, they asked all new members to complete a questionnaire. After 3 months, they distributed a second questionnaire to the groups; this questionnaire asked about each person who had filled out the first questionnaire—whether the new attendee had returned for more meetings and whether the regular GA members knew of any relapses or changes in the new attendees' circumstances. Only 60% of new attendees agreed to participate, so a response bias is likely. Nevertheless, 20 questionnaire sets were available, the first one completed by the new attendee and the second by the GA group he or she had first attended. Of the 20 attendees, 11 (55%) returned to at least one more GA meeting; the remaining 9 attended only once. These results are similar to the retrospective study in that they demonstrate high rates of attrition. Other longitudinal studies of GA attendance are unavailable. Despite self-help groups' focus on anonymity, some studies of effectiveness are emerging (Weiss et al., 2000), and similar studies are needed to evaluate GA.

Reasons for dropout in GA were detailed in a series of articles by Brown (1986, 1987a, 1987b, 1987c). He presented information obtained from interviews from two groups of GA attendees: (a) those who attended more than once but did not become actively involved in the fellowship and (b) those who earned a 1-year pin. The people who dropped out and who were interviewed comprised only 13% of all-comers to GA, as a substantial proportion never attended more than one meeting. Only about half of attendees responded to a mail survey and, of those, half declined participation. Thus, both groups appear unrepresentative of GA attendees in general.

Nevertheless, Brown (1986, 1987a, 1987b) observed some interesting results. No differences in demographics were noted, but the children of people who continued to attend GA meetings were older than children of individuals who dropped out. Older children may better understand the gambling, resulting in increased familial stress, which in turn may prompt continued involvement in GA. However, semistructured interviews revealed no differences in familial or other external pressures (legal, financial) to attend. Although income was similar between people who dropped out and those who continued, the individuals who dropped out had lower debts. In general, the people who dropped out considered their own situations to be less severe than those of other members.

Retrospectively endorsed reasons for first attending GA were similar between the groups. They ranged from subjective feelings of despair to external pressures (domestic, financial, legal) and awareness of harm done to others. Both groups reported positive feelings about their first GA meeting, but the feelings reported by people who eventually dropped out tended to be more unrealistic, such as references to their first meeting as "fantastic" and feelings of "thought I was cured." In contrast, retrospective reports of memories from the first meeting of the people who continued to attend GA meetings tended to be more realistic and motivating for further personal development, such as "there was hope" and "a great deal to be learned." The people who continued also were more likely to have spouses who were active in GamAnon than were the people who dropped out. Most of the people who dropped out who were interviewed (10 of 12) reduced their gambling, at least temporarily. Half eventually resumed gambling, but 5 of these regarded their present level of gambling as "satisfactory." Ten of the 12 people who dropped out reported that they would likely return to GA at some point.

Thus, even people who dropped out from GA felt they had benefited from GA. Reasons for nonattendance ranged from feeling cured, to changes in external circumstances, to concerns about personality clashes within the fellowship. People who dropped out were more likely to endorse the concept of "controlled gambling," and they did not identify with the severity of problems of some members (Brown, 1986, 1987c). People who continued with GA tended to have more severe gambling problems and were more likely to endorse an abstinence-oriented goal. Brown (1987c) suggested that GA may be less effective with gamblers at an earlier stage of gambling problems (Level 2, or early-stage Level 3). Moreover, about two thirds of both people who dropped out and those who continued reported concern about how slips to gambling were handled in GA. The majority of attendees felt that some members were dishonest about slips and that the stance of the group was unsympathetic or punishing toward those who slipped. People who dropped out also were more likely to be dissatisfied with irrelevant talk at meetings, excessive time spent on administrative matters, and domination of cliques.

The general interpretation of this study is that GA may be more effective for severe gamblers. It may be more helpful in preventing relapse as opposed to dealing with slips. However, the data were gathered from a very small and unrepresentative sample of GA attendees in Scotland more than 10 years ago. Further evaluation is needed to better understand the reasons for initial attendance, rates of attrition, and reasons for discontinuation at GA meetings.

The following case example describes how a female pathological gambler became involved with GA.

Case example. Connie is a 42-year-old married woman who developed substantial problems with slot machine and lottery gambling. One day, while in the casino, having spent her last dime from her paycheck, Connie saw a phone number to a gambling help line. Afraid to go back home and face her husband again, Connie called the number from the casino. She got in touch with Alice, a recovering gambler, who spoke with her for almost an hour. Alice gave Connie hope. Alice listened to her concerns and told Connie her own, similar story. Connie realized that if Alice could overcome her problem with gambling, then maybe she could, too. Alice convinced Connie to come to a GA meeting the next night. It was being held just a couple towns away from Connie's home. Alice also suggested that Connie tell the truth about her gambling to her husband. Her husband could come to a GamAnon meeting, to better understand his wife's gambling.

Connie went home that evening and found her husband, Jim, asleep in front of the television. She woke him up and told him everything. He knew that she had been gambling, and he had some idea of how bad it was, but he had not realized the full extent of the problem. She cried as she told him about how embarrassed she was, how guilty she felt, and how sorry she was. She promised him that she was going to get help, and that she was going to a meeting the next night. To her relief, Jim seemed supportive.

The next evening Connie went to her first GA meeting. She was anxious and worried that someone might recognize her, but everyone assured her that everything said at the meetings was confidential. People went around the table in turns, stating their first names, welcoming her, and telling their stories. Connie was mesmerized by some of the stories. Some people had lost their spouses, and even their children, over gambling. Others had spent all their savings, and some had lost their homes. Connie didn't identify with all these people, but she got a good sense of how addicting gambling can be. She was furious that the casinos were allowed to open and that the state was doing nothing to help these people. Connie left that evening resolved to stop gambling. She just had to quit cold turkey—and she did. Whenever Connie became tempted to gamble, she thought about how it would affect her husband and about the people she met at GA that evening.

Comment. In this example, Connie called an informational number that she found at the casino after having a long losing streak at gambling. In the state of Connecticut, most of the phone calls to the gamblers' help line come from postings at the local casinos, and many casinos throughout the country likewise display the phone number of gambling help lines. Connie felt a bond with the woman she spoke with on the help line, which may have been responsible for her decision to attend the GA meeting. In Connie's case, a one-time visit to a GA meeting was useful for her. Perhaps this meeting, her honesty with her husband, or her own resolution were responsible for success in overcoming her gambling problem. This case also exemplifies how attendance at one meeting does not necessarily demonstrate failure—in contrast, one brief meeting appeared to be all that Connie needed to arrest her gambling problems.

Differences Between Gamblers Who Attend Gamblers Anonymous Versus Those Who Receive Professional Treatment

Despite the limited research on GA and the rather disappointing results from observational and retrospective studies, some individuals who attend GA do become actively involved in the fellowship and clearly benefit from it. Others, however, seek treatment at professional programs either in addition to, or instead of, GA. Some studies have compared gamblers who sought treatment at GA with those who presented at professional programs. Blaszczynski and McConaghy (1994b) found that GA members were significantly older (39 years) than gamblers who sought professional therapy (37 years), but no other demographic differences emerged between the groups. That study focused on comparing criminal activities in the two samples, but no differences between the groups were noted. Ciarrocchi and Richardson (1989) compared 186 pathological gamblers seeking treatment at a private psychiatric hospital with 150 GA members. Again, the GA members were older than the gamblers seeking other treatment. GA members were also more likely to be married, and a higher proportion were employed full time than the private hospital patients. The private hospital patients were more likely than the GA members to have a substance use problem (71% and 10%, respectively), and they were also more likely to have a history of outpatient psychiatric treatment (62% vs. 42%). The proportion of private hospital patients who had a parent who was an alcoholic (43%) or a compulsive gambler (28%) exceeded that noted in the GA sample (18% and 14%).

The private hospital patients were more likely to have been incarcerated (19%) or arrested (40%) than the GA sample (9% and 21%, respectively). These data suggest that gamblers who seek treatment exclusively at GA seem to vary from patients who seek professional treatment, with those who seek professional treatment evidencing poorer overall psychosocial functioning.

Case example. Al is a 62-year-old man who has been coming to GA for more than 25 years. He began his gambling career at about age 12, when he helped clean the horse stables near his home in Kentucky. As a boy, Al would make small bets with his friends and with some of the men working at the stables. The horses fascinated him, and he felt proud when his horses won.

Al enlisted in the Army on his 18th birthday and was soon sent to Vietnam. He was in an infantry troop for awhile, but he never saw much action. Instead, much of the time was spent hanging out and playing cards. A lot of guys in his unit were big gamblers—there didn't seem to be much else to do. Al became pretty good at poker, and he was able to significantly supplement his Army income at the card table. When he returned to the United States, Al got a union job at the same factory where his father worked. His weekends were spent at the track or playing cards.

Al never considered himself a professional gambler, but he knew he was good at it. His gambling winnings went toward buying new cars (he never let his get older than 2 or 3 years) and taking out women. He would buy them expensive gifts and enjoy their reactions.

Although he never married, Al did somewhat settle down in his 30s with a woman whom he really loved. He was taken with Kay the first time he saw her—at the Kentucky Derby. She was clearly from a wealthy family, and Al wanted to impress her. It was several months before she would even agree to go out with him, but eventually they got together and seemed to have a lot in common, including their love of horses. Kay seemed quite impressed with Al's knowledge of the track. They moved in together after about a year of dating, and for the first time in his life, Al was committed. He wanted to have a family with her.

Things went well for the first year, but then financial problems set in. Al's company was going under, and people were getting laid off. Al avoided the layoffs but was forced to take a pay cut. At the same time, his luck at the track seemed to take a turn for the worse. The whole 1976 season was bad for him. He couldn't seem to win a single race. As he got more and more desperate, he was more and more sure that his luck was about to turn, so he bet larger amounts. He couldn't even make the mortgage payments, and Kay was used to living in style. Al borrowed a couple thousand dollars from his father, but soon that, too, was gone. Kay continued spending as if there were no tomorrow, and it angered him. They started arguing and fighting. She threatened to leave him. He couldn't stand the thought of losing her, and he continued gambling to try to get his old life back.

By 1977, Kay was fed up, and she left him. Al found out that she soon moved in with another, older man, and he was furious. Al then spent all his free time at the track, and sometimes he couldn't even bring himself to go to work in the mornings. He just wanted to watch the races. He figured that he made more money gambling than he ever did working. After several absences, Al was fired from his job. Within a few months, the bank threatened foreclosure on his house, and neither his father nor his brothers had enough money to bail him out, although they gave him what they could. Al packed up his clothes one day, left his house, and decided to stay in a rundown stable. That night, he made a decision: He would take all the money his father and brother gave him, and put it all down on a long shot. If he won, he could go on. If he lost, it was all going to be over.

Al made the bet and walked to the track with a combination of anticipation and dread. His horse was behind from the start. He could feel his life closing in on him as his horse continued lagging behind. Al's head was spinning, and he felt like he was in a trance. Later that night, sitting alone in the stable, he tied a hangman's knot and looped the rope over a beam. He broke down sobbing, and cried for hours, not certain if he could end his life but not seeing any way out. A neighbor saw a light on in the old barn that night, and called the police, suspicious of burglars. They found Al and took him to the hospital.

After 7 days in a locked psychiatric unit, Al was released. He moved in with his brother and his wife in Ohio, and he started going to GA meetings at the Veterans Administration hospital. There were only two other regulars at Al's first GA meeting. Both were men much older than Al, and they too had very serious gambling problems. They met once a week, every week, and talked about their gambling, the problems it had caused them, and how they were managing their lives now without gambling. Through one of them, Al got a job at a mill, and after about a year, he had saved enough money to rent a small apartment in town. Although occasionally other people would attend the meeting, Al and his two friends comprised the core. Al considered them to be like fathers to him.

It is now 25 years later, and Al's friends have long since passed away. Al still goes to GA meetings religiously, every Wednesday night. Each time a young man comes in and looks desperate, Al goes out of his way to offer him hope.

Comment. Al's case, although perhaps not typical of the vast majority of GA attendees, is one not unusual for a lifelong gambler who developed severe gambling problems. Al's only experience with professional treatment interventions was during his brief hospital stay following his suicide attempt.

Because that event occurred decades ago, it is unlikely that any specific treatment for gambling was available. Nowadays, a person like Al may have become involved in both GA and professional therapy, as I describe in the next section.

Al was fortunate that he relocated to Ohio, where one of the few GA meetings were held at that time. Al fit in with this small group of GA attendees, and he found solace and support in his friendships with these men. Gradually, this meeting expanded over time, and the gender composition changed. Al identifies best with the young men who share similar difficulties as he once did. It is also interesting to note that, unlike Connie, Al continued attending GA meetings even decades after he ceased gambling.

Gamblers Anonymous in Combination With Professional Therapy

Whereas the above-mentioned studies and case examples refer exclusively to individuals seeking one form of treatment over another, some gamblers receive assistance from both professional and self-help modalities. Some data suggest that the effectiveness of GA can be enhanced by concurrent participation in professional treatment programs. Russo, Taber, McCormick, and Ramirez (1984) conducted an evaluation of 124 patients who completed a Veteran's Administration program that combined individual and group psychotherapy with GA. Of the 60 patients who were assessed at the 12-month follow-up, 33 (27% of the full sample) reported abstinence from gambling. Attendance at GA and engagement in professional therapy were associated with abstinence. Taber, McCormick, Russo, Adkins, and Ramirez (1987) reported on 6-month outcomes of 57 of 66 consecutive admissions to the same facility. Abstinence was reported by 56% of the patients at follow-up, and again GA attendance was associated with abstinence. Lesieur and Blume (1991a) contacted 72 of 119 (61%) gamblers who attended an inpatient treatment program that combined professional and 12-step treatment for gambling and substance use disorders. GA engagement was not assessed in this study, but 46 (39% of the full sample) reported abstinence from gambling in the 6 to 14 months after treatment completion. These reports demonstrate that a sizable proportion of pathological gamblers who received combined professional and GA treatment were able to maintain abstinence. However, in all these studies, professional treatment was provided in an inpatient setting, and the vast majority of gamblers (>95%) were male. Generalization of these results to outpatient settings and to women is unclear. Moreover, sample sizes were small, and study-refusal rates were high.

Stinchfield and Winters (1996) reported on characteristics and outcomes of approximately 1,000 patients entering outpatient treatment programs in Minnesota. About 40% were female, the average age was 39 years, and over two thirds were employed full time. Of the full sample, 658 (49%) became actively engaged in professional therapy, and 452 (34%) attended GA at least once. Those who completed the professional therapy treatment demonstrated reductions in gambling and psychosocial problems. GA attendance was not a significant independent predictor of outcomes in that study but, because of missing data, less than 25% of the full sample was included in the analyses.

I (Petry, 2003b) evaluated prior GA participation rates in 342 consecutive admissions to professional gambling treatment programs in Connecticut. Fifty-four percent ($n = 184$) attended GA before initiating professional treatment. Compared with non-GA attendees, GA attendees were older, had higher incomes, and were less likely to be single. GA attendees also had more severe gambling problems, as evidenced by higher SOGS scores, more years of gambling problems, and larger debts. Gamblers with a history of GA attendance also differed on several dimensions from those who had never attended GA. Gamblers who had attended GA reported more severe family and social problems than gamblers who had not attended GA. A trend toward greater psychiatric problems was noted in those who went to GA, and GA attendees had a higher rate of suicidal ideation. More severe problems along a range of domains may enhance treatment engagement, and those with the most severe problems may seek multiple forms of treatment.

Gamblers who had never attended GA had more drug problems than gamblers with GA experience (Petry, 2003b). Approximately 14% of non-GA attendees, versus 7% of GA attendees, reported illicit drug use in the month prior to gambling treatment entry. These data suggest that substance-abusing pathological gamblers may be less likely than non-substance-abusing gamblers to attend GA. This finding may relate only to current drug use problems, though, because both groups were equally likely (about 30%) to report a history of substance use disorders.

In terms of treatment participation, almost half of patients with a history of GA attendance became re-engaged in GA once they initiated professional therapy (Petry, 2003b). Gamblers who had been involved in GA also were more likely to become active in professional therapy. A 2-month follow-up evaluation revealed that 41% of gamblers with a history of GA attendance came to five or more professional therapy sessions, compared with only 24% of people who had never attended GA. Moreover, GA attendees had a higher rate of gambling abstinence (48% vs. 36%) 2 months after starting treatment. The number of GA meetings attended since treatment initiation was significantly and independently associated with gambling abstinence, even after controlling for demographic variables, gambling severity, and number of professional treatment sessions attended.

Although these conclusions have practical implications, they are limited by shortcomings of the study design. Only a short follow-up period was used, and potential biases exist with respect to data collection procedures. The global outcome measure of abstinence versus any gambling fails to account for meaningful reductions in gambling. Generalization of the results is also limited by the nature of the population sampled. These data were derived from individuals seeking professional treatment for gambling, who may differ from pathological gamblers in the community who never seek treatment as well as from gamblers who seek treatment only from GA (Hodgins & el-Guebaly, 2000). Most likely, GA attendees in the study represented gamblers at the most severe end of the continuum—those who had sought treatment previously and failed.

The studies I have just reviewed suggest the potential effectiveness of GA, but they do not demonstrate its efficacy in reducing gambling, because random assignment procedures were not used. The data simply suggest that gamblers who choose to attend GA along with professional treatment experience more positive outcomes than those who present for professional therapy but do not become actively engaged in either modality. A better understanding of the frequency and patterns of GA attendance through the use of longitudinal designs may also provide information on the impact of GA in reducing gambling problems, either alone or in combination with professional treatment.

SUMMARY AND CLINICAL IMPLICATIONS

Few pathological gamblers present for treatment, and many appear to recover from gambling problems on their own. Of those who do present for treatment, GA is the most popular modality. The gamblers who do attend GA seem to differ from gamblers who do not go to GA. GA attendees are generally older, and they are more likely to be married. Although only about 10% of attendees become actively involved in GA, regular members appear to have severe gambling problems. GA attendance seems to be associated with improved outcomes, but controlled studies are needed to further confirm these impressions. In terms of treatment recommendations, referral of gamblers who present for professional treatment to also attend GA may assist in maintaining abstinence, but at the same time therapists should recognize that only a minority of patients, and only those with abstinence-oriented goals, are likely to become involved in the 12-step program.

9

THERAPY FOR FAMILIES AND SIGNIFICANT OTHERS

Pathological gambling affects not only the individual but also his or her family. In fact, family members of pathological gamblers may be more likely to seek assistance than gamblers themselves. Much of the literature on partners of problem gamblers is observational in nature, based on clinical impressions of partners who present to treatment (e.g., Franklin & Thoms, 1989; Heineman, 1994; Steinberg, 1993). Clinical impressions, although useful in initially studying a phenomenon, may be biased by unique or memorable cases. Empirical studies of the characteristics and psychosocial problems of partners of problem gamblers are lacking. Furthermore, little is known regarding effective interventions for partners of gamblers. In this chapter, I review the literature, which is brief, on the influence of gambling on family members. I also review various forms of treatment, including GamAnon, individual therapy, and conjoint and couples therapy.

INFLUENCE OF PATHOLOGICAL GAMBLING ON THE SPOUSE

Estimates indicate that every pathological gambler directly affects the lives of 8 to 10 other people (Lobsinger & Beckett, 1996). The affected individuals range from spouses to other immediate family members (children, parents, and siblings) to employers and coworkers. Gamblers can also directly

175

influence more distant relatives, neighbors, and even strangers, who may be negatively affected by illicit activities related to gambling. It is clear, however, that the people closest to the gambler are the most often adversely affected. Spouses are affected by financial losses, which may include large credit card debt, informal loans from friends and relatives, and even illegal debt to bookies. Failure to pay mortgages or rent may result in loss of homes or evictions. It is not uncommon to hear stories about gamblers withdrawing all the family's savings or retirement funds, monies that may be irreplaceable.

In addition to these financial consequences, communication and trust are usually severely impaired in couples in which one partner is a pathological gambler. Early reports described marital problems among gamblers and their spouses (Boyd & Bolen, 1970; Custer & Milt, 1985). Couples may argue excessively, or they may be hardly speaking to one another. Chronic lying to hide the extent of gambling, financial difficulties, and legal concerns may underlie the problems. Similar to alcoholics, pathological gamblers may be in denial about their gambling. They may claim that the gambling is not really the problem, but instead the economy, or their bad luck at getting and keeping jobs, is at the heart of the matter. They may also claim that their spouse is making an issue out of nothing. *Enabling,* a communication style that characterizes alcoholic couples, is common in spouses of pathological gamblers as well. The spouse may help cover up gambling losses, provide bailouts, or put his or her own needs secondary to that of the affected spouse.

Violence seems to occur in families afflicted by gambling problems. In 6 of 10 communities surveyed, the advent of casinos was associated with an increase in domestic violence cases (Gerstein et al., 1999). In a survey of Level 3 gamblers identified in a community sample (Bland, Newman, Orn, & Stebelsky, 1993), 23% admitted to "hitting or throwing things more than once at [their] spouse or partner." Lorenz and Shuttlesworth (1983) found that almost half of the 144 spouses of pathological gamblers they interviewed reported physical or verbal abuse from the gambler. A study of 286 admissions of women to an emergency room noted that partner violence occurred in 26% of the cases. Presence of gambling problems in the partner, alone or in conjunction with alcohol problems, was a significant and independent predictor of violence (Muelleman, DenOtter, Wadman, Tran, & Anderson, 2002). These rates of violence may be related, at least in part, to the high rates of antisocial personality disorders in pathological gamblers, which I reviewed in chapter 5.

Relationship difficulties may be attributed directly to the gambling, but another possibility is that communication difficulties and even aggressive behaviors may predate the gambling. Lorenz and Shuttlesworth (1983) reported that in many of the couples they interviewed gambling did not become problematic until after the marriage. They proposed that pathological gambling may surface in response to a poor relationship. Problem gamblers, as well as the partners of gamblers, often grow up in addictive families, and parents of partners of pathological gamblers have high rates of addictive disorders (Heineman, 1987). Exposure to troubled familial relationships may be intergenerational. Poor patterns of communication developed in childhood may be modeled and perpetuated in adult relationships.

Only a few studies have examined psychosocial problems in spouses of gamblers. The largest known report was based on 18 programs in Australia that provide services to problem gamblers and their partners. Crisp, Thomas, Jackson, and Thomason (2001) reported on 440 partners of gamblers who sought treatment at these centers over a 12-month period. The majority (70%) were married to the gambler, with 62% having dependent children. Partners of gamblers had a higher employment rate than that noted in the general population, with 80% of men and 61% of women employed. Psychosocial problems of partners of gamblers were identified by the counselors after the initial intake evaluation. The most common were interpersonal difficulties (>70%), followed by emotional problems (48%) and family issues (38%). Financial concerns were noted in more female (42%) than male partners (30%). Physical symptoms and legal or employment issues affected only a small percentage of the treatment-seeking partners; however, these problem areas were assessed by clinician impressions, not standardized instruments, so reliability and validity are questionable.

Lorenz and Yaffee (1988, 1989) have collected data from individuals attending national Gamblers Anonymous (GA)/GamAnon conferences, but again, instruments with established psychometric properties were not used. For 151 couples, information was obtained from both the spouses (exclusively women) and the gamblers, who were exclusively men (Lorenz & Yaffee, 1989). The gamblers' most common emotions during heavy gambling periods were desperation for money (69%), guilt (38%), depression (38%), and isolation (23%). The spouses' recollections of their feelings were similar. The most frequently endorsed feelings were anger (70%), depression (42%), isolation (38%), and guilt about contributing to the gambling (26%). Physical symptoms also were noted, with headaches and stomach complaints reported by more than one third of both groups. Pathological gambling has also been associated with a lack of interest in sex and impotence (Daghestani, 1987). Lorenz and Yaffee (1988, 1989) have found that during periods of excessive gambling, less than one third of partners reported a satisfactory sexual relationship, but two thirds reported satisfaction after gambling ceased. Other types of conflict may also diminish with gambling abstinence. Bergh and Kuehlhorn (1994) and Lorenz and Yaffe (1988) have found poor family cohesion in families of pathological gamblers, but Ciarrocchi and Reinert (1993) noted that long-term GA members demonstrated less family distress than did shorter term members.

Although the results from these studies suggest some areas of concern among partners of gamblers, the data are limited by the samples surveyed. In most studies, the spouses were seeking professional treatment or were members of GamAnon. In some, the gamblers were also actively involved in GA. As discussed previously, only a minority of pathological gamblers become actively involved in GA or professional treatment, and therefore these results may be generalizable only to those gamblers who participate actively in some form of treatment. Such gamblers, and their spouses, may be more motivated to solve their problems, or have better relationships, than spouses who divorce during the gambling or who do not seek treatment or attain abstinence. The results are also limited by the retrospective reports of feelings endorsed during episodes of gambling, which may have occurred years or even decades in the past. That reliable and valid instruments were not used to assess psychosocial problems also is problematic.

More studies on the spouses of gamblers, especially from community-based samples that are not confounded by the severity and comorbidity of treatment-seeking samples, are needed. Examinations of the impact of gambling during active phases of gambling as well as longitudinal studies assessing changes in psychosocial functioning during initial and later stages of abstinence also are needed. Finally, much of the research in this area has been conducted primarily with male gamblers and their female spouses. Because the number of female pathological gamblers has been rising, research is needed on the male spouses of female gamblers.

The following case example describes a man who is married to a pathological gambler.

Case example. Henry is a 49-year-old man who has been married to Judy for over 20 years. They have a 17-year-old son, Andy, who is finishing high school. Henry is a middle manager in an insurance company and has worked hard throughout his life to support his family. Judy works part time as a day care teacher. When the casinos opened about 5 years earlier, Henry and Judy went together several times a year. Judy liked the slot machines, and Henry preferred blackjack. They had fun going, and they took visitors there as well.

When Andy started high school, Judy felt less needed around home. If Andy had a sports game or practice after school, Judy would have to try to find something else to do in the afternoons and early evenings. Henry never came home from work before 6:30 or 7:00. She started going to the casino on some afternoons, but never more than once or twice a week, and she always made it home in time to make dinner for Henry. As Andy got older and spent more and more evenings away from home, Judy's trips to the casinos became more frequent.

Henry never even noticed his wife's absences. He came home every night about the same time, and Judy was always there. Dinner was always prepared.

Unbeknownst to Henry, Judy's gambling had gotten out of control. She gained access to the couple's $100,000 in retirement savings and the $20,000 they had saved for Andy's college. All of it was gone, but only Judy knew that. In her desperation to win back the money, Judy started opening up credit card accounts. Their house was paid off, so she had good credit. She opened up 11 accounts over an 8-month period and took the maximum cash advance from each one. When tax time was approaching, Judy knew Henry would be looking closely at all the account statements, but there was nothing left. She didn't know what to do. Judy began drinking heavily in an attempt to cope with her anxiety about Henry finding out about her gambling.

Judy started drinking a couple of glasses of wine while cooking and eating dinner, and then she needed more to sleep at night. Their sex life, which had not been good for some time, became nonexistent, and Henry began complaining about her drinking. Judy tried to get more credit cards, but she was now being rejected. The day after Henry announced he was about to start preparing tax forms for the accountant, Judy panicked. This was her last chance. She wrote out ten $50 checks, all to different grocery stores, and bought a couple of small items at each store. She went to the casino with the $480 left over. In 40 minutes, all the money was gone. Judy didn't know what to do. She stayed out all that night, and Henry had no idea where she was. He was terrified. He was certain she'd been kidnapped or in an accident. He called the police, but they said they couldn't do anything but call the hospitals until she had been away for at least 24 hours.

Comment. This example depicts a marriage that had gradually been failing. Henry, preoccupied by his work, was unsuspecting of his wife's unhappiness and her gambling problems. It is hard to imagine how one spouse can gain sole access to a joint account, but gamblers who are desperate go to extremes to get money. This case continues later in the chapter.

TREATMENT FOR SPOUSES OF GAMBLERS

There are a number of treatment approaches for helping spouses of gamblers, including help lines, GamAnon, and individual and couples therapy. In the sections that follow, I discuss the research supporting these approaches and provide some case examples that involve these treatments.

Initial Help Seeking and Gambling Help Lines

Often it is the spouse of the gambler who first initiates help seeking, either for him- or herself or for the gambler. The best indication of this phenomenon is from gambling help lines. Reports of help lines from the

United States, the United Kingdom, and New Zealand indicate that over 40% of calls are from partners of gamblers rather than from gamblers themselves (Cuadrado, 1999; Griffiths, Scarfe, & Bellringer, 1999; Potenza et al., 2001; Sullivan, Abbott, McAvoy, & Arroll, 1994). Help line staff typically refer spouses to GamAnon or professional treatment. Many state-funded treatment programs for gamblers provide services for the spouses of gamblers as well. These may include individual and group psychotherapy as well as referrals to GamAnon. Although virtually no information is available regarding the efficacy or effectiveness of these services, the different forms of treatment applied, and the limited research on these interventions, are described in the following sections.

GamAnon

GamAnon is the counterpart of AlAnon for GA. Although not as widely available as GA, most states have at least one GamAnon chapter, and its availability is roughly proportional to the number of GA meetings within a location. GamAnon, like AlAnon, educates attendees about the nature and progression of pathological gambling. It also helps the partners cope with their own feelings and provides guidelines for interacting with the gambler.

Although no controlled studies of GamAnon are available, one retrospective report compared outcomes of gamblers whose wives participated in GamAnon with those whose wives did not. E. E. Johnson and Nora (1992) collected 90 surveys that were distributed to GA members. The spouses of 44 gamblers (48.8%) participated in GamAnon. Almost half of the gamblers (45%) whose wives participated in GamAnon reported abstinence for 4 or more years, compared with only 28% of the gamblers whose wives did not attend GamAnon. This difference was not statistically significant, but it demonstrated a trend in favor of spousal participation in GA. However, these results are limited by a self-selection bias, as the gamblers surveyed represent only a small proportion of pathological gamblers and their spouses. Participation in GamAnon was not operationalized and may have ranged from attending once to years of participation. Furthermore, durations of abstinence were not independently confirmed.

Zion, Tracy, and Abell (1991) administered a survey to 43 members of GA to determine whether spousal involvement in GamAnon was associated with reduced relapse to gambling among the gamblers. Each respondent was required to have been involved in GA for at least 6 months, with a range of 7 months to 24 years. Sixty percent of the gamblers had spouses involved in GamAnon. Across the full sample, 40% of gamblers reported one or more lapses to gambling during their time in GA. The percentage who had relapsed, the number of times they relapsed, and the duration they had been abstinent prior to relapse did not differ between gamblers with and without spouses involved in GamAnon. More research, with large samples and prospective designs, is needed to clarify the relationship between spousal involvement in self-help groups and outcomes, for both the spouse and the gambler.

Below, the case of Judy and Henry is continued. Although they did not receive professional gambling therapy, they did try couples counseling, and Henry obtained the support he needed from his physician.

Case example continued. Judy called Henry at work the next day. He was vastly relieved to hear her voice, but then she started sobbing. As she confessed what had happened, Henry's emotions ranged from scared to furious. He couldn't believe Judy's betrayal, or how this could have happened without his noticing. At the end of the conversation, Judy said she was going to stay with her sister for a couple of days. Henry wasn't sure if he wanted to see her or not, or how he would explain it to Andy. It took Henry several weeks to sort through the finances, and things were even worse than he thought. He couldn't imagine what had possessed Judy to do this.

Henry told Andy that Judy was needed to help her sister and that she wouldn't be back for awhile. Andy knew something was wrong, but he didn't say much. Three weeks later, Henry and Judy met for lunch for the first time since she left. Henry wasn't sure how he was going to respond to her, or where they were going to go from here. They talked at lunch and agreed that she would move back home and that they would go to couples counseling.

When Judy came home, Henry knew he was being cold to her. They went to therapy, but Henry had a hard time opening up. He was very angry, but he didn't like to show his anger, especially not in front of a stranger. They became more and more estranged. Henry went to a lawyer, who recommended that Judy file for personal bankruptcy. At least all the credit cards were in her name only, and that debt could be removed. The $120,000 of savings, though, could not be replaced.

Henry had a history of high blood pressure, and during this period it was not responding to any of the usual medications. He went to the doctor's office almost weekly, and eventually he started telling his physician about the problems with his wife. Henry was confused—he felt guilty for causing or allowing the gambling, and at the same time he was angry about it.

After 6 months of trying to work it out, Henry decided to file for divorce. He felt he could never trust Judy again, and although she was no longer gambling (as far as he could tell), she continued drinking. It took 8 months for the divorce to be finalized, and they lived together during this period. Henry didn't think that he should have to give up the house when Judy was the one who had spent all their money. Judy had nowhere to go and little money available to her. Fortunately, Andy had gone off to college, so he did not have to live in the house during much of these tense times.

Individual Therapy With Spouses of Gamblers

Steinberg (1993) provided a framework for delivering therapy to spouses of gamblers. He described the initial stages of therapy as being focused on basic survival rather than emotional intimacy issues. Because financial problems are often overwhelming, they should be addressed. The therapist must have adequate knowledge of loan consolidation, consumer credit bureaus, and bankruptcy so that he or she can refer the gambler and spouse as needed. As in GA and GamAnon, Steinberg encouraged the spouse to maintain control of the family's finances. Because control and power are posited to be at the heart of the struggle between the spouse and gambler, Steinberg provided suggestions for reframing the potentially negative experiences of turning over financial control. These may include suggesting a trial period, or allowing the gambler to come up with the idea on his or her own. Once the imminent financial issues are resolved, the therapy can address issues related to marital communication and intimacy. Heineman (1994) described the content of five initial sessions with the spouse, with the goal of engaging the gambler in treatment. For a more detailed description, a book is available (Heineman, 2001). However, the descriptions are based on experiences of particular therapists, and these therapies have not been subjected to scientific testing to evaluate efficacy.

Only one known study has evaluated treatments for spouses of gamblers. Makarchuk, Hodgins, and Peden (2002) adapted the Community Reinforcement and Family Training (CRAFT) approach, developed for spouses of alcoholics (e.g., Meyers & Smith, 1997; W. R. Miller, Meyers, & Tonigan, 1999), for use with spouses of gamblers. This is a cognitive–behavioral approach that teaches family members to use behavioral strategies to reduce the gambling behavior and to encourage the gambler to seek treatment. It also addresses areas of stress in the family members' lives and teaches them to better recognize and cope with the consequences of gambling. In the treatment of spouses of alcoholics, CRAFT produces favorable results relative to Al-Anon or other individual interventions (W. R. Miller et al., 1999).

Makarchuk et al. (2002) adapted CRAFT to use in a workbook format. In this manner, no face-to-face contact with the spouses was necessary, and individuals from rural areas could participate. Thirty-one concerned others of gamblers who were actively gambling were randomized to the CRAFT workbook condition or to a standard treatment condition in which they were provided with informational brochures commonly used by gambling help lines and treatment programs. The two groups did not differ in terms of proportions who lived with the gambler (68%), estimated days of gambling in the prior 3 months (M = 35 days), psychiatric symptoms of the concerned other, or measures of relationship satisfaction at study initiation.

Ninety percent of the concerned others were interviewed 3 months after having received the materials. Those who received the CRAFT manual were more likely to be satisfied with the treatment, and 77% reported that they had read the entire workbook, with the remainder saying that they had read at least some sections. Over half stated that they used the strategies from the workbook regularly. Psychiatric symptoms and relationship satisfaction improved over the 3-month time interval in both groups. However, time by group interaction effects were not significant. Only about 20% of the gamblers in either group had sought treatment by the 3-month follow-up evaluation. A greater proportion of concerned others who had received the CRAFT manual noted reductions in the gamblers' gambling (47%) relative to those who had received the informational brochures only (19%). These data suggest modest but possibly beneficial effects of this treatment approach for concerned others of gamblers. Larger sample sizes will be necessary to assess whether this treatment has beneficial effects for reducing levels of distress in the concerned others and decreasing gambling behaviors of the gamblers.

Couples Therapy in Groups

Although little outcome data are available on individual psychotherapy with spouses of gamblers, a couple of reports about professionally led groups for gamblers and their spouses have been published. Boyd and Bolen (1970) described outcomes of 9 male pathological gamblers and their wives, who were seen within the context of two marital therapy groups. They portrayed the gamblers as experiencing antisocial personality disorder, depression, dependency, and schizoid personality. The mental status of the wives was described as even worse. The marriages were depicted as long lasting but chaotic, with repeated separations and threats of divorce. The initial phase of the group therapy involved discussions of "war stories" about gambling and rehashing of old arguments and disagreements. The therapist was subsequently able to move the couples to discussions of relationship patterns. The therapy focused on identifying thoughts and feelings of the other partner and understanding the nature of the gambling within the context of the relationship. Of the 8 couples who remained in treatment, 3 of the gamblers ceased gambling entirely, and the remaining 5 reduced their gambling.

Tepperman (1985) conducted a nonrandomized study that examined 10 couples who agreed to participate in a 12-step oriented group therapy for couples and 10 others who did not. All gamblers were members of GA, and all spouses were involved in GamAnon. Thus, the difference between groups was that half the couples participated in a professionally led group in addition to GA. A comparison of pre- and posttreatment scores revealed that no significant differences occurred between groups on measures of depression, communication, or interpersonal relationships, but both groups improved on these indexes. All participants in the study were self-selected for both GamAnon and GA involvement and willingness to undergo the group couples therapy. The analyses included data only from treatment completers, so it is possible that even less impressive results would be obtained had an intent-to-treat analysis been included. Despite the problems associated with the experimental design and a small sample size that would preclude detection of only very strong effect sizes, Tepperman suggested that the group therapy was successful, and the groups continued after the expected duration of 12 weeks. Two years after the formal treatment study ended, all but one of the couples involved in the group therapy was still involved with GA/GamAnon, and all the gamblers in the couples group reported maintaining gambling abstinence. More research on such professionally led couples groups is necessary. Development of written materials and manuals describing the content of the therapy is also needed so that efficacious therapies can be delivered by different therapists across settings.

Case example continued. Henry never knew about couples therapy for gambling, or even about GamAnon. He spoke with his physician about his personal problems regularly, and that served as needed support for him during the next couple of turbulent years. After about a year and a half of severe stress, Henry's blood pressure finally got under control with a new medication.

Henry and Judy got divorced. Although there weren't many assets to split, Henry was forced to pay her alimony for 10 years. He was upset about that, but at least he got to keep the house, so Andy had some stability during his college years. Henry was determined to get back on his feet financially. He was able to work overtime, and that helped a bit.

About 5 years after this all began, Henry had managed to save some toward retirement again and began to feel settled. Andy finished college, and he quickly moved in with, and then married, a young woman. Henry was certain his son was making a big mistake—this girl had many similarities to Judy, and Henry could see much of himself in Andy.

Comment. This case example describes a couple who broke up because of the wife's gambling. Other problems clearly preceded the gambling and, given the amount of joint money that Judy lost to gambling, it is not surprising that she and Henry did not reconcile. Their son was remarkably quiet about his mother's gambling problems and his parents' divorce. Fortunately, Andy was older when his mother began gambling, and he did not exhibit any outward problems as a result of the turmoil in his family. Although little empirical research exists, many children of pathological gamblers appear to suffer from a variety of adverse consequences, as I describe next.

CHILDREN OF PATHOLOGICAL GAMBLERS

As suggested earlier, little is known regarding the psychological well-being and the efficacy of treatment interventions of spouses of pathological gamblers. Even less is known about their children, although the presence of pathological gambling in a parent is likely to distort the home life and the upbringing of children.

Early descriptions (Custer & Milt, 1985; Wanda & Foxman, 1971) have detailed accounts of a see-saw relationship in which parents switch back and forth from doting on their children, lavishing them with gifts and praise, to virtually ignoring them at other times. Some accounts suggest that pathological gamblers may engage in aggressive and even violent outbursts toward their children, or steal from them in an attempt to gain more money for gambling. Children of pathological gamblers are portrayed as feeling angry, hurt, lonely, guilty, and abandoned (Custer & Milt, 1985; Wanda & Foxman, 1971). These outcomes clearly are not limited to children of pathological gamblers, but they may be sequelae of growing up in a variety of adverse environmental conditions and with parents who have been diagnosed with any number of psychiatric conditions. The strongest evidence of comorbidity in problem gamblers is related to substance use disorders; these data were reviewed in chapters 4, 5, and 6. Both substance use disorders and pathological gambling appear to have environmental and genetic components that may be transmitted independently or in an additive manner to the children. Thus, it is not difficult to imagine that the teenage years of the children of pathological gamblers may be troubled by psychological problems and early onset of gambling and substance use.

Lorenz and Yaffee (1988) asked spouses of gamblers about their children's psychosomatic illnesses, but no differences were noted between the children of gamblers and children from the general population. Because this study was conducted with families who were actively engaged in GA, any adverse effects of the gambling may have been diminished in scope because these gamblers were seeking treatment and, in many cases, had been abstinent for years.

In a study of high school students, Jacobs et al. (1989) found that youth who had a parent with a gambling problem were more likely to report abusing stimulant drugs and overeating than youth who did not have a parent with a gambling problem. Children of gamblers were also more likely to describe their childhood as unhappy, be depressed or suicidal, and have a legal action pending. Lesieur and Klein (1987) found that children of pathological gamblers were more likely to have a gambling problem themselves than were children of nonpathological gamblers.

Lesieur and Rothschild (1989) administered questionnaires to GA rooms, asking the GA members to distribute them to their children. A stamped, preaddressed envelope was included, and the children were instructed to mail the questionnaires themselves in an anonymous manner. One hundred five questionnaires were returned; approximately half of the respondents were female, and the mean age was 17 years. In 95% of the cases, the gambler was the father. Comparisons were made between children of "pure" pathological gamblers and children from multiple-problem families in which other drug or alcohol use disorders were also present. Drinking alcohol in a moderate to heavy manner and overeating were more prevalent in children from families with multiple problems compared with those from families with only a gambling disorder present. In addition, the children from families with multiple disorders were more likely to report poor sleeping, unhappy early childhoods, and feeling insecure or inadequate.

Using a measure of parental violence, Lesieur and Rothschild (1989) found that parents from both groups were likely to throw things and engage in abuse at rates higher than community norms, and multiple-problem parents (substance abuse and gambling) engaged in more violence than did "pure" gambling parents. Likewise, a study of 413 sixth-grade students in Thailand found that children who lived with a parent who had a gambling problem were more likely to be victims of parental aggression than those who did not (Isaranurug, Nitirat, Chauytong, & Wongarsa, 2001). Together, these data suggest that children of pathological gamblers experience more volatile and unhappy childhoods than children from non-problem-gambling families, and the presence of both pathological gambling and other addictive disorders may compound the adverse effects. However, more research is needed with larger and representative samples to further elucidate the effects of pathological gambling on the children.

Gam-Ateen is available in some locations, although the number of locations in which this fellowship is available is limited. No outcome evaluations or clinical trials of treatments for children of pathological gamblers have been published.

SUMMARY AND CLINICAL IMPLICATIONS

In this chapter, I have described the limited research that has examined how gambling affects the spouses and children of pathological gamblers. Most of the studies used nonstandardized questionnaires, often asking the spouses to reflect on problems experienced years earlier. Obvious methodological problems are associated with this type of research. Similarly, in identifying problems that children of pathological gamblers experience, a myriad of psychological difficulties are suggested, but systematic research in this area is in its infancy.

Little controlled research exists on family or couples treatment for pathological gambling. Some reports with relatively small sample sizes indicate that treatment for the significant other alone may help him or her manage his or her own problems, but these approaches as yet appear ineffective in inducing gamblers to enter treatment. In terms of couples or family treatment, there is little evidenced-based treatment to recommend at this point, but this area has been identified as an important topic for intervention studies. As with many forms of treatment used with pathological gamblers, including psychoanalytical and psychodynamic therapies which I describe in the following chapter, recommendations are based primarily on clinical experience.

10

PSYCHOANALYTIC AND
PSYCHODYNAMIC TREATMENTS

In chapter 9, I described how gambling can affect the family, and I begin this chapter by addressing issues related to childhood and how early life experiences may influence the onset of pathological gambling as well as its treatment. I then briefly describe psychoanalytic and dynamic approaches in treating pathological gamblers. Empirical studies of psychoanalytic or psychodynamic therapy are not available, so these descriptions should not be taken as evidence of their efficacy. Instead, I review these theories as they dominated initial psychotherapeutic approaches of treatments for pathological gambling and continue to influence therapy for this disorder. These theories may also be helpful for understanding some aspects of interactions that may occur between therapists and patients, regardless of the therapeutic stance of the former. In the last section of this chapter, I describe issues that commonly arise in the patient–therapist relationship, and I suggest methods of handling them.

EARLY LIFE EXPERIENCES

The early life experiences of pathological gamblers have rarely been studied, but in chapter 6 I reviewed data suggesting that gamblers are more likely than nonproblem gamblers to have a parent and other relatives with psychiatric conditions, including pathological gambling. I have also described some evidence for a genetic contribution to pathological gambling. Environmental factors are likely to contribute to the development of pathological gambling as well, with gamblers often reporting wagering within the family, at a very early age (see chaps. 6 and 15).

In addition to putative biological and exposure factors, parenting factors may play a role in development of pathological gambling. Grant and Kim (2002b) administered an instrument assessing bonding between parents and adult children to 33 pathological gamblers and found that gamblers had significantly lower scores than control participants. The modal perceived parenting style was one of low parental care and affection as well as low protection, which is indicative of neglectful parenting.

Individuals with a host of psychiatric conditions report turbulent childhoods, and pathological gamblers may be no exception. On the basis of anecdotal accounts, pathological gamblers are also thought to experience trauma and abuse at high rates (Niederland, 1967, 1968), and excessive gambling has been characterized as a way of coping with trauma and abuse (Jacobs, 1989a, 1989b; Specker, Carlson, Edmonson, Johnson, & Marcotte, 1996). Female gamblers, in particular, are portrayed as "escape gamblers," who are hypothesized as gambling in an attempt to cope (Lesieur & Blume, 1991b; Trevorrow & Moore, 1998). Whitman-Raymond (1988) described interviews with eight Gamblers Anonymous (GA) members and pointed out a pattern of early life losses, in terms of parental death or loss through divorce.

Only a couple of studies, however, have evaluated rates of trauma and abuse in pathological gamblers. Taber, McCormick, and Ramirez (1987) reported that 23% of 44 male gamblers experienced sexual or physical traumas, and Specker et al. (1996) found that 32.5% of 40 pathological gamblers acknowledged some form of sexual or physical abuse. A recent study of 149 treatment-seeking pathological gamblers from sites across North America (Petry, Steinberg, & The Women's Problem Gambling Research Group, in press) found that pathological gamblers experienced higher rates of childhood maltreatment than community control participants. This study used an instrument with well-established psychometric properties. Not only were gamblers' scores higher than those of control participants, but also gamblers exceeded scores obtained from substance abusers on certain subscales, such as Emotional Neglect and Emotional Abuse. Moreover, scores on the trauma questionnaire were significant and independent predictors of age of onset of gambling problems, severity of gambling problems, and frequency of gambling episodes, even after controlling for age, gender, depression, and substance use. Although childhood maltreatment may be associated with disordered gambling, more research is needed to determine the specificity and mechanisms underlying this relationship.

Current research about the role of early childhood experiences as related to the development of later life pathological gambling is quite distinct from earlier theorizing of these relationships. This early work was more clearly grounded in psychoanalytic theory, as I discuss next.

PSYCHOANALYTICAL PERSPECTIVE

Early work with gamblers was based on the psychoanalytic perspective. Simmel (1920) focused on narcissistic fantasies of gamblers, involving grandiosity and entitlement, whereas Bergler (1958) felt that gamblers had an unconscious desire to lose. Galdston (1960) proposed a theory that gamblers had been subjected to early and severe deprivation by their parents; they then presumably turned to fate for the love and approval they were denied as children. Boyd and Bolen (1970) viewed pathological gambling as a manic defense against helplessness and depression, secondary to early loss. Several researchers have reviewed this early psychoanalytic perspective of pathological gambling (Rabow, Comess, Donovan, & Hollos, 1984; Rosenthal, 1987), but none have used scientific methods to ascertain the existence of these personality profiles or the contribution of childhood experiences to the onset of pathological gambling.

In terms of treatment, a few case reports have described how psychoanalytic therapy can be delivered to pathological gamblers (Harris, 1964; Lindner, 1950; Victor & Krug, 1967). Bergler (1958) wrote the most extensive report on outcomes of analytic treatments, although the methods that he used are flawed by today's standards. Using subjective clinical criteria, he claimed a success rate of 75% among 60 gamblers. However, these 60 cases on which outcomes were reported had been selected from a total of 200 referrals for whom no outcome data were provided.

Although early writings were based on case reports and theoretical discussions, they lay the groundwork for some methods of treating gamblers. Rosenthal and Rugle (1994) wrote one of the most comprehensive descriptions of psychoanalytic and psychodynamic treatments for pathological gamblers. They suggested that the initial approach focus on abstinence and recommended that the therapist be supportive and nonjudgmental and at the same time confront the gambler with the consequences of his or her behavior, calling attention to inconsistencies in stories. Because gamblers are often ambivalent about treatment (see chap. 8), therapists may experience adversarial relationships at least some of the time (Taber & Chaplin, 1988). According to Rosenthal and Rugle's theory, the therapist should consider helping the gambler better understand what gambling means for him or her.

Rosenthal and Rugle (1994) suggested that gamblers can be classified into seven types. The classifications are not mutually exclusive, and some gamblers may demonstrate features of several types. Furthermore, these proposed categorizations are not empirically validated. I review them here only to provide some insight as to why some people may gamble problematically and into the types of feelings that may be addressed within the context of therapy.

Rosenthal and Rugle (1994) suggested that, for some gamblers, *excitement* may underlie the disorder, with winning possibly representing a fantastic triumph. A desire for success may be driven by a strong need to impress others, especially a critical parent. A second, somewhat similar, possible reason for gambling is related to control. Rosenthal (1986) described the concept of *omnipotent provocation*, or flirting with fate. This behavior may involve engaging in high-risk activities and placing extraordinarily high wagers. Strong sensations may be desired, perhaps to compensate for feelings of emptiness and depression. *Competitiveness* may be a third reason that some people gamble. Growing up feeling unappreciated or neglected may prompt a need to excel, with gambling being the one thing a person feels that he or she is good at. *Rebelliousness* may be a fourth reason people gamble; some individuals may gamble to break conventional norms, and an aggressive tendency may underlie this type of gambling. Winning may be associated with fantasies of getting back at others, by purchasing expensive cars or clothes and flaunting them. A fifth reason may be a desire to win independence; these gamblers may believe that a big win will allow them to quit working, get a divorce, or gain independence from parents. *Social acceptance* is a sixth possibility. Some gamblers may be impressed by the perks they receive in both tangible (free hotel rooms or meals) or intangible forms (staff remembering their names, or sitting next to a famous person at a blackjack table). Finally, the *self-medication hypothesis* is yet another potential reason: For individuals who are lonely and depressed, gambling may relieve isolation and depression.

Next is a case example, continued from chapters 4 and 5, of Ned, a competitive gambler who also demonstrates aspects of gambling to win independence, to gain social acceptance, and to self-medicate.

Case example (continued from chaps. 4 and 5). Recall that Ned displayed anxious and objectionable behaviors to the receptionist, Sally, when he first arrived at the gambling clinic. He was declaring his successes in life and his lack of need for therapy. When Steve, the therapist, comes out to meet Ned for the first time, Ned says, "What, don't I get her to be my therapist?" while he winks at Sally. Steve ignores the comment and asks Ned how he's doing. Steve tries to maintain some structure to the session, asking Ned how he got to the clinic and about his gambling. Ned doesn't want to focus on the gambling; instead, he complains bitterly about the legal system, decrying the injustices that have been done to him. Steve lets him talk and at the same time asks occasional questions to better understand inconsistencies in Ned's stories, how his gambling started, and what it means for Ned. Finally, Steve summarizes the situation and ends with:

> So, I understand that you're here not because you want to be, but because your probation officer is making you come. That's OK. But, because we do have to meet once a week for the next couple of months, what do you think you'd like to work on while you're here? How can we best use your time?

This initial session makes Ned feel less defensive. Although competition drives most of Ned's interpersonal interactions, he does not feel threatened by Steve. Ned responds to Steve's question with "Well, I'm sure I can teach you a thing or two about gambling." In response to this, Steve says, "I'm sure you will help me learn more about gambling. But, what about you? What can we discuss so that you feel like you are learning something about yourself?"

Comment. In this example, the therapist did not feed into Ned's desires to feel special; neither did he fall into a competitive trap with Ned. Instead, he tried to place a positive spin on the session and left it to Ned to make the time useful for himself.

According to psychoanalytic theory, once a person better understands the reasons for gambling, defenses can be confronted. *Denial* is a common defense. Freud (1928/1961) described denial as a disavowal of external reality. He proposed that selected perceptions are rejected to avoid the pain associated with them. Inherent in denial may be the use of fantasy. While gambling, some people's fantasies may relate to a sense of invulnerability or specialness. In regard to addictions, denial can be extended to mean the common failure to admit that one has problems with the behavior (Boutin, Dumont, Ladouceur, & Montecalvo, 2003) and the associated ambivalence about one's behaviors (Shaffer, 1994). Because denial can be considered a defense against pain, psychodynamic therapy may focus on teaching the patient to accept feelings of guilt, shame, and ambivalence about gambling within the context of therapy.

Chasing, the act of continued betting in hopes of winning lost money, is considered a crucial aspect of pathological gambling (Lesieur, 1977). Rosenthal and Rugle (1994) suggested that chasing is related to narcissistic entitlement rather than the financial reasons that many gamblers verbalize. They stated that some gamblers may believe that winning is owed to them. Competitive gamblers in particular may feel that winning may make up for the early deprivation and unfairness they experienced in life. Other gamblers, however, may keep chasing because of feelings of guilt and shame. Rosenthal and Rugle suggested that these gamblers may be trying desperately to hide their gambling, the extent of financial losses, and their embarrassment associated with their gambling problem (see the case of Judy in chap. 9). They may gamble to conceal what they consider to be their own intolerable weaknesses. If family members of these gamblers do find out about the gambling and are supportive of treatment, they may feel enormous relief (see the case of Connie in chap. 8).

Making an active change in one's lifestyle can be one step toward overcoming gambling problems (see chap. 13). Often, however, gamblers insist that they can stop on their own and do not need the advice of others, including GA members, their family, or a therapist (Rosenthal & Rugle, 1994). For example, some gamblers may feel that they can continue watching sports on television, buying gas at the station where they have purchased lottery tickets, or maintaining control over their finances. Rosenthal and Rugle (1994) suggested that exploring gamblers' reactions to and rejections of various ideas, including the underlying resistance to options, may help them in treatment.

W. Miller (1986) described specific dynamic approaches toward treating gamblers, and he focused on the need for gamblers to maintain a dynamic equilibrium. He suggested that gamblers may simultaneously desire a level of stimulation, and at the same time they may gamble to escape problems and worries. Gambling may provide temporary relief and comfort, and to give it up can represent a significant loss of a "love" object. According to this theory, a grief process may ensue when gambling ceases, and this loss may be worked through in therapy.

Psychodynamic therapy is based on the concept that what the patient says and does is meaningful. The relationship between present statements and actions and underlying causal connections may be uncovered in the context of therapy (Rosenthal, 1986). Rosenthal and Rugle (1994) suggested that the therapist seek to provide a balance between pushing the patient toward examining his or her emotional vulnerabilities and connections between past events and current behaviors and proactively manage his or her emotions and memories. They further recommended that the therapist help the patient identify adverse emotional states that may have been relieved by gambling to understand the defensive functioning of gambling. Although in some contexts these processes can be considered in a psychodynamic manner, emotions and their relationship to gambling can also be addressed within the context of cognitive–behavioral therapy, which I describe in chapter 13.

Some of these aspects of psychodynamic therapy are described in the following continuation of the case of Ned.

Case example continued. Steve can immediately see that Ned is in denial about his gambling. In the first session, it becomes apparent that Ned gambles extensively and even lost his home because of gambling. Ned is primarily a sports and track bettor and is in legal trouble related to some gambling-related theft from an employer. He has been desperately chasing his losses for years and has never been honest with his wife, or anyone else, about the extent of his gambling. After a couple of sessions, consciously avoiding any form of competition with this patient, Steve asks Ned directly, "What would make you really happy in life? Not material things, but what kind of relationships and feelings would you like to have more often in your life?" For the first time, Ned really thinks before answering.

"I guess I want people to care about me," Ned says and then pauses. He quickly continues,

> People do care about me—my wife is just crazy about me. She can't stand that I left. And my kids, they think I'm the best dad in the world. Did I show you the card my daughter sent me for Father's Day? Do you see, she said I was "the best dad in the world."

Steve says,

> So, I see that your family is very important to you. How they perceive you matters a lot to you. How do you think your gambling has affected them? How do you think your relationship with them would be different if you had never gambled?

Comment. As depicted in this case, the therapist was able to get Ned to admit that his family, and their impressions of him, are very important to him. Ned's case is one of a patient with narcissistic personality disorder (see chap. 5), perhaps leading to his subsequent comments about how much his wife and children care for him. As the therapy progresses, Steve may continue to gradually nudge Ned into considering his family members' reactions to Ned's gambling.

PATIENT–THERAPIST RELATIONSHIPS

Freud (1912/1953) first described *transference* and *countertransference* in psychotherapy in general, and Rugle and Rosenthal (1994) related these concepts to the treatment of gamblers. As I mentioned earlier, some gamblers grew up in abusive, addictive, or otherwise deprived environments that may contribute to their poor ability to form relationships (Jacobs, 1989a, 1989b; Jacobs et al., 1989; Rugle, 1993; Steinberg, 1993). Krystal (1978) suggested that, in working with addictive patients, transference can be diluted by having cotherapists in group therapy and by using different therapists for individual and group sessions. Diluting transference in this way may allow the primary therapist to help the gambler recognize the reactions he or she elicits in others. *Splitting*, or focusing all the good feelings on one therapist and all the negative feelings on another, also may occur in this context (see Kaufman, 1989). Given the limited resources and expertise in treating gamblers, only relatively large and specialized treatment programs will have the luxury of having two therapists available to provide concurrent group and individual treatment.

Because of narcissistic personality traits in at least a subset of gamblers (see chap. 5), an issue with these gamblers may be a desire to maintain control over the therapeutic relationship (Custer & Milt, 1985; Rosenthal, 1986; Taber & Chaplin, 1988). Some gamblers appear overly reliant on external sources of reinforcement; they may lack the ability to manage their own negative affect. Reliance on external reinforcement may lead to extreme reactions. For example, if a therapist cancels a session, the gambler may take it personally and refuse to come again. Another way narcissism plays out is by soliciting approval from the therapist or group members. If criticized or confronted, such patients may express extreme anxiety or anger. As noted in Ned's case, therapists should be careful to not compete with or confront narcissistic patients, except in the gentlest manner. On the other hand, some gamblers, especially women, may take an overly protective role of either the therapist or a group member who is perceived as vulnerable. If the gambler feels that other patients are criticizing the therapist or another group member, this caretaking role may be elicited. It may also manifest in behaviors such as bringing food or gifts to sessions or providing transportation for other patients to the group sessions.

An extreme form of positive transference is *idealization* (Imhoff, 1991; Rosenthal, 1986), in which the patient may feel that if she praises the therapist, she may maintain control over the relationship and thereby minimize fear of rejection or abandonment. The patient may unconsciously desire to find the perfect therapist who will take care of her completely, thereby compensating for all the problems she has experienced in life. In its most blatant form, idealization may manifest early in therapy, with the patient proclaiming extreme insight on the part of the therapist. In more subtle forms, it may result in the patient complimenting the therapist's attire or office. An observation by the therapist about how much the gambler must want someone to like her may begin to address these vulnerabilities.

Taber and Chaplin (1988) suggested that a switch from positive transference to negative transference often occurs during the course of therapy. It might result from critical feedback, a change in a scheduled session, or an enforcement of limits. The patient may react with depression, anxiety, or extreme anger. Competition may also drive negative transference. Because of their competitive nature (Custer & Milt, 1985), some gamblers may view much of life, including the therapeutic relationship, as something to win or lose. Competition can manifest in passivity, withholding information, or arguing. Intellectual competition, in which the therapist's knowledge is questioned, also may occur. For highly competitive patients such as Ned,

Rugle and Rosenthal (1994) recommended that the therapist acknowledge at the outset that the patient can outsmart any therapist but that what is important is for the patient to learn to work with the therapist.

Pseudo-independence, in which the patient presents as arrogant or overly self-confident and extremely sociable, is another type of negative transference (Derby, 1992). The therapist may recognize this superficiality and help the patient acknowledge the fears that underlie his or her façade. Hostile attitudes are also common and may represent a fear of closeness. These feelings may be demonstrated as anger expressed over concern that the therapist disclosed personal information to others or as criticisms of the therapists' lack of experience. In traditional addiction treatment, negative transference may be viewed as denial or resistance (Nowinski, Baker, & Carroll, 1995).

Confrontation, or directly pointing out the patient's problem behaviors, is common in some forms of treatment for substance abusers (e.g., Forman, Bovasso, & Woody, 2001), but it may intensify a gambler's feelings of abandonment. In dynamic approaches, examples of negative transference are pointed out objectively, in a nonconfrontational manner (Rugle & Rosenthal, 1994). For example, the therapist may say, "I see you are upset that I spoke about your absence last week with Sally. What concerns you about what Sally thinks?" The patient's reactions may be used as a method for recognizing his or her relationship to gambling and its emotional and interpersonal consequences.

Countertransference—the therapist's reactions toward the patient—also should be considered (Imhoff, 1991; Kaufman, 1989, 1992). At times, the therapist may be pulled into challenges with the patient or become weary of being conned by some patients. Concerns may arise that the gambler is not telling the truth or is using therapy for some external gain, such as for a letter to the court. If the therapist can recognize and accept his or her own feelings, he or she may be less likely to act out in a manner that is harmful to the patient (Kaufman, 1989). Contact with other therapists and supervision may be helpful.

Case example continued. In Ned's case, therapy will progress slowly. Ned does a lot of talking, and much of it appears, at least on the surface, to be unrelated to gambling. Steve will eventually help Ned examine the meaning of gambling for him. Ned clearly has a lot of problems, and it is unlikely that his relationship with his family is as rosy a picture as he paints it. However, because of his defensiveness, Ned is unlikely to admit to understanding feelings of others.

Steve will walk a balancing act between trying to open Ned's interpretations of his own behaviors in the sessions and at the same time not confront Ned directly. Steve is bound to occasionally experience some countertransference with a patient like Ned, especially on days when Ned's narcissism is intense, or when he acts aggressively. Steve finds it best in these situations to just let Ned talk and to gradually steer the discussions back to gambling. In a couple of sessions, Steve asks Ned to role play, with each taking the turn of the wife and then of Ned. At first, these situations focus on other communication issues, not necessarily related to gambling per se. Steve asks Ned to consider how his wife may feel when these interactions take place. After a time, he gets Ned to imagine how his wife would react to his being honest about when he gambles. Although Ned is unlikely to change his communication patterns dramatically, he may begin to recognize some of his own defensiveness.

Comment. Ned may be among the most difficult of clients to treat, because of his underlying personality disorder. Such difficulties are not uncommon in treating gamblers, especially some of the old-time male gamblers. Because Ned was mandated to therapy, Steve might may be able to engage in some of these longer term, psychodynamic approaches. Gamblers like Ned may be unlikely to continue in therapy long term without some external pressures.

SUMMARY AND CLINICAL IMPLICATIONS

Little research has investigated outcomes, and no studies have examined the efficacy, of psychoanalytic or psychodynamic treatment of pathological gamblers. Instead, the use of these therapeutic techniques has been described within the context of treating gamblers. Today, some treatment programs for gamblers continue to use these techniques and frameworks through an eclectic approach that may also incorporate GA, family therapy, and cognitive–behavioral techniques, all of which I describe in the remaining chapters.

11

EARLY BEHAVIORAL TREATMENTS

At present, much of the therapy provided for gamblers, as well as for individuals diagnosed with other mental disorders, is cognitive–behavioral in nature. The foundation of this type of treatment stems from early behavioral theories and basic research in behavioral analysis. In this chapter, I describe the theoretical basis for behavioral therapy. I review, in relation to gambling, the concepts related to basic and laboratory research in behavioral analysis, and then I describe some of the early case reports of behavioral therapies.

BEHAVIORAL ACCOUNTS OF GAMBLING

The similarities of gambling to behaviors maintained by intermittent schedules of reinforcement have long been recognized. This association resulted in attempts to treat disordered gambling from a behavioral perspective. In this section, which is adapted from Petry and Roll's (2001) article, I describe aspects of behavior theory as related to gambling.

Variable Ratio Schedules of Reinforcement

A variable ratio schedule of reinforcement is a powerful technique for maintaining behaviors. Variable ratio schedules provide a reinforcer after an average number of responses has been made (Ferster & Skinner, 1957). A common example in animal research is when, on average, every fifth lever press is reinforced with a piece of food. The similarities between variable ratio schedules and certain types of gambling, such as slot machines and scratch tickets, are apparent. Although payouts vary by individual games, approximately every second or third scratch ticket or pull of the slot machine handle results in a win.

Variable ratio schedules engender a response pattern characterized by very high response rates. For example, rats who have been trained with these schedules will respond at rates of two or more presses per second. High response rates occur across species and reinforcers (Ferster & Skinner, 1957), suggesting the widespread generalization of the effects of the schedules. Furthermore, variable ratio schedules maintain behavior patterns that are difficult to extinguish (Ferster & Skinner, 1957). An individual whose behavior has been shaped through a variable ratio schedule may continue to respond hundreds of times without receiving reinforcement. Given the similarities between variable ratio schedules and the payouts arranged in many types of gambling, it is not difficult to understand gamblers' high response rates and continued gambling after multiple losses.

The term *variable interval* describes schedules that reinforce the first behavior that occurs after a predetermined time interval has elapsed. For example, a variable interval 2-minute schedule would provide a reinforcer every 2 minutes, on average. After the specified time period elapses, the next lever press that occurs results in the reinforcer. Skinner (1948) described how variable interval schedules engender superstitious behaviors in pigeons. By receiving reinforcement for a peck on a key on a schedule of every 2 minutes, on average, for example, pigeons develop strange behavior patterns. If a pigeon was flapping its right wing when a reinforcer was delivered, the pigeon may begin flapping its right wing whenever placed in the operant box, even though flapping does not influence reinforcement.

Gamblers are also known for their superstitious behaviors—they may feel compelled to bet if they see their son's birthdate on a license plate, or when they are holding a lucky charm. These superstitions may have developed in response to random pairings, such as having won on someone's birthday or while holding a particular item. Skinner (1948) demonstrated the long-term maintenance of superstitious behaviors in pigeons. Gamblers may affirm their superstitions in a similar manner, even in the face of repeated nonreinforcement (see chap. 12).

Response Cost

Response cost refers to the amount of effort needed to obtain a reinforcer (Weiner, 1962). Learning new behaviors depends on how much effort is required. For example, a pigeon may readily learn to peck a key to obtain food if the force required to press the key is minimal. If a great deal of force is necessary to press the key, then the pigeon may never peck it hard enough to obtain the reinforcer, and learning will occur much more slowly, if at all (L. K. Miller, 1970).

In the case of gambling, response cost may refer to the cost of a bet or the amount of effort needed to gamble. The gaming industry recognizes the association of response cost with gambling behavior. The popularity of slots, bingo, lotto, and scratch tickets is related to their low response cost—$0.25 or $1 per bet. Marketing techniques reduce the response cost of gambling even further. Often, free bus rides to the casino are provided, $10 in tokens may be furnished to riders, and dinner coupons are given to attract regular or new patrons to facilities. Casinos also offer preferred-member cards that track wagering and reward it with overnight hotel stays, room upgrades, or vouchers for use in casino stores. These techniques reduce the response cost of gambling, perhaps making it more likely that individuals will begin to gamble or will continue gambling.

Response cost can also be considered in terms of travel to gamble. With casinos now available in 27 states, the National Gambling Impact Study Commission (1999) estimated that over three quarters of Americans live within a 1-day drive of a casino. Even more remarkable is the abundance of lottery outlets. One may not need to travel more than 1 or 2 miles to purchase a lottery ticket. As I discussed in chapter 2, the prevalence rate of disordered gambling appears to have increased with the expansion of legalized gambling, that is, with this decrease in response cost necessary to bet.

Basic behavioral research suggests that once a behavioral pattern has been established, response costs can be increased and the behavior is maintained. In other words, once a rat has learned to lever press on a fixed ratio 1 schedule, the response cost can be increased markedly—even when up to hundreds of presses are needed to obtain a small piece of food, a rat will continue responding. Similarly, although people usually begin gambling on 25-cent slot machines, $100 slot machines and $500 minimum-bet black-jack tables attract some experienced gamblers. An increase in the amount bet is a criterion for pathological gambling listed in the *Diagnostic and Statistical Manual of Mental Disorders* (American Psychiatric Association, 1994); raising the stakes when gambling appears to be similar to the concept of *tolerance*. Another example of tolerance is that recreational gamblers may spend $20/night gambling, whereas pathological gamblers spend in excess of hundreds of dollars in a single evening.

Priming—providing an unearned reinforcer to reestablish a behavior pattern—is another behavioral concept with applicability to gambling (Lynch & Carroll, 2000). An example of priming is placing a food pellet in the hopper at the beginning of a session. A rat that has ceased responding because of nonreinforcement in prior sessions will respond again, and often at very high rates, after the delivery of a primer. For gamblers, an example may be a coupon for a free meal at a casino restaurant or a "welcome back" gift of $10 in free tokens offered in the mail. These promotions systems may be tempting to gamblers who are trying to abstain.

Magnitude of Reinforcement

Magnitude of reinforcement also is related to gambling. The ratio of a reinforcer to the cost of responding is an important principle in establishing a behavior (Schneider, 1973). For example, a rat would not learn to press a heavy lever to obtain a very small piece of food. Similarly, gamblers would not place $100 bets if the maximal payout were only $200. However, when a jackpot exceeds $30 million, people stand in lines for hours to purchase tickets. In this example, low response costs ($1) and high magnitude reinforcers ($30 million) interact to influence gambling. A study conducted by Garrett and Sobel (1999) revealed that even risk-averse individuals place wagers when the prize distributions are highly skewed toward large winnings.

Many forms of gambling not only offer the possibility of large payoffs but also provide lower payoffs of variable magnitude. For example, scratch tickets may have a 1 in 3 chance of winning, but the modal amount won is only $2. Small but frequent wins are also programmed into slot machines. Basic research in behavioral analysis shows that animals prefer schedules that provide varying magnitudes or probabilities of reinforcers rather than constant-reinforcer magnitude or probabilities (Caraco, 1980; Sherman & Thomas, 1968). Similarly, humans seem to prefer gambling on activities with varying levels of payoff. The unpopularity of "jackpot only" slot machines in Las Vegas (Wildman, 1997) may be a naturalistic demonstration of preference for varying and frequent payoffs. The small wins obtained in most slot machines may serve as primers, and such primers may reduce the response cost of continued gambling.

Gambling is also initiated and maintained through *modeling* and *second-order conditioning* (Rescorla, 1979). Individuals do not have to directly experience a reinforcer to have it affect behavior. A news story of a woman winning a $100 million lottery, or the sound of lights and buzzers on a slot machine, may reinforce gambling behaviors of people who witness the wins. Signals that are not associated with tangible reinforcers themselves, but that have been paired with reinforcers in the past, are considered second-order reinforcers. Such a pairing may occur directly, or it may occur indirectly, by modeling, or by observing others win. Near-wins on slot machines (e.g., two cherries in a row) or even smaller prizes for having four of the five winning lottery numbers may be considered second-order reinforcers. These reinforcers are preprogrammed into some forms of gambling (e.g., slot machines) with the intention of encouraging continued gambling.

Finally, the reinforcers of gambling are not exclusively financial in nature. Gambling is maintained by its many positive outcomes, which may consist of social reinforcement, feelings of power, or escape from negative moods. Nonmonetary reinforcers may become more important than the possibility of financial gain over time, and they may be responsible for continued gambling, regardless of the financial losses, a topic I address in chapter 13.

Immediacy of Reinforcement

Immediacy of reinforcement also is important in establishing a behavior pattern. The temporal association between a behavior and reinforcer affects the rate and strength of learning, such that reinforcers that are delayed in time are less likely to affect behavior (Roll, Reilly, & Johanson, 2000). If food is not delivered until 30 seconds after a rat presses the lever, the rat will not associate lever pressing with food. Gambling may be a popular activity because of the immediacy of the wins. Unlike spending years of hard work in college, or running a business in the hopes of earning a good living, gambling provides the hope of instant wealth. Moreover, types of gambling that provide immediate payoffs may be more attractive to gamblers. For example, slot gambling is the preferred activity in over 50% of treatment-seeking gamblers, whereas lottery gamblers constitute less than 15% of treatment-seeking individuals (Petry, 2003a).

The relationship between immediacy of reward and behavior can be studied experimentally, by allowing individuals to choose between reinforcers delivered immediately versus those delayed in time. For example, a person may be presented with a choice between receiving $1,000 right now and $1,000 one year from now. Given this choice, almost everyone would prefer to receive $1,000 now. However, when offered a choice between $800 now and $1,000 one year from now, some individuals would select the smaller amount rather than wait a year for an additional $200. By adjusting the delays and values, one can plot an *indifference curve*. An indifference curve represents how quickly a reinforcer is devalued in time, and the relationship is best described by a negatively decelerating or hyperbolic function (Mazur, 1987). A series of studies has shown that individuals with addictive disorders (Kirby, Petry, & Bickel, 1999; Madden, Petry, Badger, & Bickel, 1997), including pathological gamblers (Petry, 2001a; Petry & Casarella, 1999), have truncated time horizons and discount delayed reinforcers at extremely high rates. Furthermore, discounting functions may have a familial component, such that individuals who grow up in families affected by addictive disorders appear to have steeper discounting functions than those who do not grow up in addictive families (Petry, Kirby, & Kranzler, 2002).

A better understanding of how reinforcers are discounted over time may serve as a theoretical construct for understanding pathological gambling. Small reinforcers are discounted more rapidly than large reinforcers (Kirby et al., 1999; Myerson & Green, 1995; Rachlin, 1990). By virtue of the nature of gambling, the value of any given bet is much less than the value of a "win" and therefore may be discounted much more rapidly. In other words, a $1 bet may lose half its subjective value in a matter of minutes, whereas a $5,000 win will not lose half its subjective value for 1 year or longer. As Rachlin (1990) proposed, gamblers bet in "strings," in which subjective losses are not considered until the next win occurs. Within each string, cumulative effects of prior bets are devalued because of the gambler's rapid discounting of smaller monetary amounts. In contrast, the occasional, but larger, wins remain salient for much longer periods of time.

Understanding how reinforcers are delayed in time may also explain the commonly observed phenomenon of preference reversals in addictive disorders (Ainslie, 1975; Heyman, 1996). Before placing the first bet of the evening, for example, an individual may see the pitfalls associated with heavy gambling. One may subjectively value controlled gambling (an evening of entertainment) over heavy gambling and losing all one's paycheck. The gambler may clearly see the long-term positive effects of nonexcessive gambling, such as keeping enough money to pay the rent, and may firmly commit to spending no more than $50 gambling. However, once the gambler arrives at, say, the racetrack, the subjective value of gambling becomes much higher than the subjective value of paying one's rent, which is not due for 15 days.

Along these same lines, the practice that some casinos and racetracks allow of self-banning (Nowatzki & Williams, 2002) may be analogous to *precommitment strategies*, attempts to commit to what is in one's best interests before temptation arises. These exclusions are voluntary, and typically they are for a defined time period ranging from 3 to 12 months to a lifetime. Sanctions for being caught on the premises can include fines or charges of trespassing but, perhaps most important, winnings could be confiscated. Although the concept of these procedures is promising, limited evidence of their effectiveness exists. The only known evaluation (Ladouceur, Jacques, Giroux, Ferland, & LeBlond, 2000) found that the self-excluders rather frequently violated the ban, perhaps because the consequences of getting caught were unlikely.

These theories may help explain why people persist in engaging in behaviors that are not in their long-term best interests, including gambling. However, these theories, by their very nature of explaining learning and behavior in everyday contexts, fail to explain why some people develop problems with gambling and others do not, assuming a similar exposure history. Behavioral and biological accounts (see chap. 6), hence, may interact.

Nevertheless, because gambling appears to have a strong behavioral component, behavioral accounts may also guide treatment efforts for pathological gamblers. In the next section I focus on treatments that use these behavioral principles, and in chapter 13 I describe cognitive and behavioral principles for treating pathological gambling.

BEHAVIORAL TREATMENTS FOR PATHOLOGICAL GAMBLING

Because of the recognition of similarities between variable ratio schedules of reinforcement and gambling, initial behavioral therapies focused on reducing the positive reinforcers associated with gambling, or decreasing the conditioned place preference for gambling environments. Early behavioral therapies involved delivering aversive stimuli to patients as they gambled or were exposed to gambling stimuli. For example, Barker and Miller (1966, 1968); Goorney (1968); Koller (1972); Seager (1970); and Seager, Pokorny, and Black (1966) have described treatments in which they delivered electric shocks to individuals as they gambled or were in proximity to gambling stimuli. Salzman (1982) gave gamblers apomorphine, a drug that induces vomiting, as they wagered or thought about gambling. Across these reports, over one half the respondents ceased gambling, and substantial improvement was noted in another one third. Beneficial effects persisted for up to 2 to 3 years after treatment. The studies that have used behavioral treatments for pathological gamblers are described in Table 11.1.

Not all behavioral procedures have been found to be effective. *Systematic desensitization* refers to a technique in which the patient is taught to relax, often through hypnosis, and then gradually is exposed to the troublesome environment, without allowing the problem response (in this case, gambling) to occur. Kraft (1970) used systematic desensitization to treat a pathological gambler along with 39 other patients experiencing various nongambling problems. The gambler did not stop gambling. Greenberg and Marks (1982) characterized the results of this type of treatment with seven pathological gamblers as "unimpressive," compared with the use of this technique in 65 other patients with "unusual referrals." In both these reports, however, the therapists had little experience treating pathological gamblers. Multimodal behavioral treatments also have been described. These range from *in vivo* and stimulus control exposure along with covert sensitization (Cotler, 1971; Greenberg & Rankin, 1982) to behavioral counseling, in which the therapist gave verbal reinforcement for not gambling (Dickerson & Weeks, 1979; Rankin, 1982). Mixed results were noted across these reports.

As can be seen in Table 11.1, only a few studies of purely behavioral treatments have used random assignment procedures and compared the effects of behavioral therapy with another treatment. These studies were

TABLE 11.1
Behavioral Treatments for Pathological Gambling

Type of treatment and study	N	Type of study	Follow-up period (months)	Results
Aversive therapy (AT)				
Barker & Miller (1966)	1	Case report	2	Cessation of gambling
Barker & Miller (1968)	3	Case report	24	One stopped completely; 2 had brief lapses but otherwise ceased gambling.
Goorney (1968)	1	Case report	12	Complete cessation.
Koller (1972)	12	Descriptive	6–24	Significant improvement in 3; reductions in 8 cases.
Salzmann (1982)	4	Descriptive	n.s.	All stopped gambling.
Seager (1970)	14	Descriptive	12–36	Substantial reductions in half the cases.
Seager et al. (1966)	1	Case report	n.s.	No gambling or sports page reading during treatment.
Systematic desensitization				
Kraft (1970)	1	Case report	12	No benefit.
Greenberg & Marks (1982)	7	Descriptive	6	"Unimpressive" relative to 65 patients with other disorders.
Multimodal behavior therapy				
Cotler (1971)	1	Case report	9	Complete cessation by 16th session; relapse 4 months later, but quick recovery.
Dickerson & Weeks (1979)	1	Case report	15	Goal of a weekly small bet achieved and maintained.
Greenberg & Rankin (1982)	26	Descriptive	9–60	Five stopped or maintained control; 7 had intermittent lapses; 14 continued gambling problematically.
Rankin (1982)	1	Case report	24	Controlled gambling was the successful outcome.
Imaginal desensitization (ID)				
McConaghy et al. (1983)	20	Random assignment (AT or ID)	12	Reductions in gambling in 80% of ID vs. 60% of AT cases at 1 month (*ns*); reductions in gambling in 70% of ID vs. 30% of AT cases at 1 year ($p < .05$).
McConaghy et al. (1988)	20	Random assignment (imaginal relaxation [IR] or ID)	12	At 1 month, gambling decreased in 90% of ID and 70% of IR cases; at 1 year, reductions in 50% of ID and 70% of IR cases (*ns*).
McConaghy et al. (1991)	63 of 120	Random assignment (ID, AT, or other behavioral therapies)	24–108	79% of ID cases were "successes" vs. 33% of AT cases and 53% of other behavior therapy cases.

Note. ns = nonsignificant. n.s. = not stated.

all conducted in Australia. In the first, aversion therapy was used as a control condition. McConaghy, Armstrong, Blaszczynski, and Allcock (1983) randomly assigned 20 pathological gamblers to aversion therapy or a cognitive treatment: imaginal desensitization. In this latter treatment, patients were hospitalized for 1 week. They were taught gradual relaxation techniques and then asked to imagine responses to high-risk gambling situations. One month after treatment, no significant differences between the groups were noted with respect to gambling urges or behaviors. At a 1-year follow-up, however, 70% of the participants in the imaginal desensitization condition were still maintaining reductions in gambling, compared with only 30% of the respondents who had been in aversion therapy. The same group of researchers (McConaghy, Armstrong, Blaszczynski, & Allcock, 1988) later compared imaginal desensitization with a relaxation condition. With 10 gamblers per group, no differences were found between the two conditions, although both groups improved compared with the baseline.

McConaghy, Blaszczynski, and Frankova (1991) reported on long-term outcomes of 120 pathological gamblers who had been randomly assigned to one of four conditions: (a) aversion treatment, (b) imaginal desensitization, (c) imaginal relaxation, or (d) *in vivo* exposure to gambling situations. A total of 63 of the 120 patients (53%) were contacted 2 to 9 years after the treatment had ended. Of those contacted, 79% who received imaginal desensitization had decreased or ceased gambling, compared with 33% in the aversion treatment and about half in the other conditions. Although these differences were significant, no differences in the percentages of patients who were abstinent were noted across the groups. Furthermore, almost half of the patients were lost to follow-up. These studies nevertheless represent initial steps at conducting randomized trials in treating pathological gamblers. They demonstrate that cognitive or mixed cognitive and behavioral therapies may be useful in treating the disorder.

Today, few therapists use purely behavioral treatments with pathological gamblers; instead, behavioral therapy may be provided in the context of more traditional "talk therapy," often in conjunction with cognitive or cognitive–behavioral therapy. In the next two chapters, I describe these treatments and the rationale for their approaches.

12

COGNITIVE BIASES AND COGNITIVE THERAPY

Behavioral theories and treatments flourished in the 1960s and 1970s, and cognitive psychology began to gain popularity after that. Cognitive techniques were introduced to psychotherapy in general and, not surprisingly, also to treatment of pathological gambling. In this chapter, I first review some of the cognitive distortions associated with gambling, then I provide details on cognitive therapies and outcome studies that have evaluated the effectiveness and efficacy of these techniques.

COGNITIVE BIASES

One theory posits that the reason people gamble is because they do not accurately judge probabilistic outcomes. People seem to make inaccurate inferences when attempting to predict outcomes that are based on chance events. Failure to account for actual probabilities influences a variety of decision-making processes. Because gambling, by its very nature, involves decision making, it can be influenced by cognitive biases, distortions, and errors in judgment. A full review of cognitive psychology and decision making is beyond the scope of this book, but in this chapter I review some basic cognitive distortions and how they may influence decisions to gamble.

In the sections that follow I describe six types of cognitive distortions and their relationships to gambling.

Illusion of Control

The *illusion of control* refers to the belief that one may have a greater probability of obtaining an outcome than would be expected by chance. Stated another way, it suggests that one can control, or somehow predict, events at rates better than chance. Many years ago, Strickland, Lewicki, and Katz (1966) found that people made larger bets when they were allowed to throw the dice and choose the winning number themselves compared with when others threw the dice. Langer (1975, 1983) has demonstrated the illusion of control in several studies. She found that individuals placed a higher monetary value on lottery tickets that they had chosen themselves compared with tickets that had been randomly assigned to them. Although probabilities of winning are independent of whether one selects the ticket numbers or throws the dice, people feel they have some control over the outcome if they can be active participants in the process.

The illusion of control may be related to *attributional biases*. This concept refers to the overestimation of dispositional or situational factors in explaining outcomes of events that are influenced by chance. Skills or abilities are often used to account for positive outcomes, whereas environmental explanations may be invoked to explain adverse outcomes. For example, if one is selected for a highly sought-after job or promotion, one may attribute it to one's own intelligence, perseverance, or experience rather than to other, external explanations, such as the lack of other qualified candidates. In contrast, one may rationalize not getting a job or promotion by attributing it to external factors, such as the company not having enough resources, or the boss playing favorites, rather than considering that one may not have the appropriate skills or experience.

These same sorts of attributional biases appear to influence interpretation of gambling events. Langer and Roth (1975) found that when individuals successfully predicted the results of coin tosses, they began to express the belief that skill was involved in the guessing. Even young children exhibit this phenomenon, reporting that experience or skill will assist them in better predicting the outcome of coin tosses (Frank & Smith, 1989). Wagenaar (1988) reported that individuals who won on a series of trials at blackjack interpreted their wins as evidence of their own skill, whereas those who did not win did not make skill attributions in terms of the outcomes. Bad luck or other environmental reasons are invoked with respect to losses. If one loses a bet on a sporting event, the explanation may be situational—"The weather was too cold for my team"—rather than personal: "I didn't properly study the teams' performance across weather conditions."

In the initial studies that evaluated the illusion of control in gambling outcomes, participants were not selected for or screened for their level of gambling involvement. Instead, normal, healthy individuals participated in the studies and demonstrated these illusions of control. More recent studies have found similar effects. Dixon, Hayes, and Ebbs (1998) allowed five undergraduates to wager on roulette while either choosing their own numbers or having the experimenter select the numbers. They had to pay extra each time they selected their own numbers. Even though selection of preferred numbers did not increase the probability of winning, each participant paid extra to select his or her own numbers on about 20% to 50% of the trials. Davis, Sundahl, and Lesbo (2000) observed 351 gamblers in Reno casinos who bet on craps games. Players placed higher bets on their own dice rolls relative to when others rolled the dice. Koehler, Gibbs, and Hogarth (1994) similarly found that individuals made more risky decisions when there was an element of perceived control, relative to when the illusion of control was not present.

Outcomes of bets may influence cognitive illusions. Letarte, Ladouceur, and Mayrand (1986) assigned gamblers playing roulette to one of two conditions: (a) frequent wins or (b) infrequent wins. Gamblers in the frequent-win condition reported more illusionary control than those in the infrequent-win condition, but these results were not confirmed in a second study (Ladouceur, Gaboury, Dumont, & Rochette, 1988). Bersabe and Arias (2000) found that college students' confidence in winning dice games increased in a frequent-win condition relative to an infrequent-win condition. Ladouceur, Mayrand, and Tourigny (1987) found that the amounts bet increased over trials at roulette. In another study of roulette playing, college students bet more after experiencing a near big-loss condition than after a near big-win condition (Wohl & Enzle, 2002). These studies all suggest that some aspects of gambling may influence cognitive distortions, but most of them demonstrate these distortions in individuals who show no problem gambling behaviors.

Another approach to studying cognitive illusions is the *think-aloud paradigm*, in which participants are asked to verbalize their thoughts as they gamble. Controversy exists regarding the validity of this methodology, and a review of the literature concluded that the capacity to verbalize one's thoughts during a task is unreliable (Nisbett & Wilson, 1977). Nevertheless, studies using this paradigm may provide some insight into the role of cognitive distortions in gambling. Studies conducted in gambling situations (e.g., Coulombe, Ladouceur, Desharnais, & Jobin, 1992; Gaboury & Ladouceur, 1989; Ladouceur, Gaboury, Bujold, LaChance, & Tremblay, 1991) have found that college students and other healthy control participants make a lot of erroneous verbalizations, such as attributing causality to outcomes, predicting outcomes, and explaining losses to be out of control but attributing wins to skill. In fact, Gaboury and Ladouceur (1989) found that 70% of verbalizations were erroneous. These verbalizations were noted in all forms of gambling, including slot gambling, blackjack, and lottery ticket selections.

Some studies have compared cognitions of individuals who do and do not gamble frequently or problematically, but this methodology has resulted in mixed or inconclusive findings. Griffiths (1994) reported that irrational thinking is more prevalent in problem gamblers than in occasional gamblers, but Gaboury, Ladouceur, Beauvais, Marchand, and Martineau (1988) and Hardoon, Baboushkin, Derevensky, and Gupta (2001) noted that both occasional and regular players expressed high proportions of erroneous thoughts when gambling. Erroneous verbalizations also seem to occur whether the proportion of wins is high or low (Ladouceur et al., 1988) and whether the stakes are limited or limitless (Ladouceur & Gaboury, 1988). Thus, faulty cognitions appear to be inherent in gambling situations, but studies have yet to link directly types or frequencies of illusions to problem or pathological gambling or features of the game.

Other studies have examined personality attributes related to control among individuals with different levels of gambling involvement or problems. *Locus of control* refers to perceptions of control people feel they have over their lives. Locus of control typically can be classified as either *internal* or *external*. Individuals who score high on indexes of internal control express the belief that they have power over their own destinies, whereas those who score high on external control feel that their destinies are greatly influenced by other, uncontrollable factors. One hypothesis is that individuals with a high internal locus of control may have greater illusions of control and therefore gamble more than people scoring low on this factor. D. Carroll and Huxley (1994) administered an inventory assessing locus of control and diagnostic criteria for pathological gambling to 75 adolescents and young adult slot machine gamblers in England. The 26 youth who met criteria for pathological gambling scored significantly higher on the internal dimension than the participants who did not meet *DSM* criteria. Sprott, Brumbaugh, and Miyazaki (2001) found that, among 74 adults, frequency of lottery play was associated with increased internal locus of control and high desire for control. S. M. Moore and Ohtsuka (1999) assessed illusion of control and internal locus of control in more than 1,000 adolescents and young adults and found that both variables significantly predicted gambling frequency and problem gambling behaviors assessed with the South Oaks Gambling Screen (SOGS; Lesieur & Blume, 1987).

Conversely, one could also hypothesize that a high external locus of control may be associated with gambling, if the person feels that external events such as luck are associated with outcomes. Lester (1980) found a positive relationship in college students between an external locus of control and participation in gambling activities in which luck played a major role, but not in games for which some skill was involved. However, the reliability and validity of the questions assessing gambling were not stated, and gambling problems were not measured. In Hong Kong, Hong and Chiu (1988) assessed locus of control among 158 gamblers. As in Lester's study, no psychometric properties of the measure used to assess gambling problems were reported. Nevertheless, they found an association between gambling and scores for an external locus of control subscale labeled Powerful Others. Kweitel and Allen (1998) administered the SOGS, along with an inventory assessing locus of control, to 155 undergraduates. Although no association was noted between scores on the Internal Locus of Control subscale and gambling, a positive association between SOGS scores and the Powerful Others subscale was noted. Burger and Smith (1985) compared scores on another inventory of control between 18 Gamblers Anonymous (GA) members and control participants. Contrary to expectation, the control participants had higher scores than the GA members on this index of desired control. GA members' desire-for-control scores were correlated with frequency of betting on activities that had a relatively greater element of control or perceived control (e.g., card games, horse racing, and sports events), whereas desire for control was not correlated with frequency of gambling on activities with less perceived control (lotteries, slots, roulette). Thus, desire for control may vary depending on the type of gambling in which individuals engage.

A couple of studies have examined the relationship between desire for control and actual gambling behaviors in the laboratory or in a natural environment. Burger and Cooper (1979) divided college students into two groups on the basis of their scores on a desirability of control questionnaire. All participants placed bets on a dice game. In one condition, the participants were allowed to throw the die themselves, knowing what the winning number would be, whereas in the other, low-control condition, they also threw the die but without knowing what the winning number would be. Participants with high desire for control bet more in the high-control condition, but no differences in bets were noted between the two conditions for participants who scored low on desire for control. Another study, conducted by Atlas and Peterson (1990), evaluated explanatory style in 53 horse track patrons. They administered an attributional style questionnaire to participants and kept track of their wagering over eight consecutive races. They recorded how much the gamblers bet, whether they won or lost, major perceived cause of the outcomes, confidence about winning future bets, and rumination about past and future bets. A pessimistic explanatory style (making internal, global, and stable causal attributions) predicted rumination following a loss, and it was correlated with higher wagers on subsequent bets.

However, another laboratory study found no association between irrational verbalizations, levels of arousal, and illusion of control among 54 undergraduates while gambling on a computerized task (Coventry & Norman, 1998). In that study, the students were exposed to one of two conditions: (a) winning mainly at the start of the task or (b) winning randomly throughout the game. Although irrational verbalizations were common during both types of tasks, no differences between tasks or between individuals who chased losses and those who did not were noted.

Thus, the evidence is mixed regarding the role of locus of control or desire for control and their association with gambling. Decision-making processes, including gambling decisions, appear to be influenced by the illusion of control in both gamblers and nongamblers, but research has yet to link these cognitive biases directly to problem or pathological gambling.

Representativeness

Representativeness is another heuristic involved in decision-making processes in general and one that can also be applied to gambling decisions (Kahneman & Tversky, 1982). The *representativeness heuristic* refers to judging a sample to be likely or not on the basis of similarity and random appearances. An example of this heuristic was demonstrated by Bar-Hillel (1980), who asked people to imagine that three college men had been randomly selected from a population in which the average height was 5 ft, 9 in. She then asked people to consider which of the following outcomes was more likely:

A. John: 5 ft, 11 in.; Mike: 5 ft, 6 in.; Bob: 5 ft, 10 in.
B. John: 5 ft, 9 in.; Mike: 5 ft, 9 in.; Bob: 5 ft, 9 in.

Although Sample B is statistically about 40% more likely, over 90% of respondents stated that Sample A was more likely. Identical observations and sidedness are the most important aspects that make a sample seem unrepresentative. Identical observations are considered nonrepresentative to a greater extent than they should be. Similarly, when most or all observations are on the same side of the population mean, they are generally considered nonrepresentative.

In terms of gambling outcomes, people demonstrate the representative heuristic. If asked which lottery ticket is more likely to win, 3-4-5-6-7 versus 8-18-36-45-52, almost everyone will select the second card. However, the fact remains that any two series of numbers have an exactly equal probability of being a winning series.

The *gambler's fallacy* is a special type of bias. It describes the belief that a series of any given events will influence or be predictive of subsequent events. A typical example is that a series of losses is a signal that a win is imminent. Accordingly, individuals behave as though each segment of events must reflect the actual probabilities. To demonstrate the gambler's fallacy, consider this scenario related to a series of coin tosses: heads, heads, tails, heads, heads, heads, heads. When asked to predict what will come up in the next coin toss, the vast majority of people will state tails (Corney & Cummings, 1985). In reality, each toss of the coin is an independent event, such that regardless of the number of past heads or tails, the next toss has a 50–50 chance of being heads or tails. This fallacy is not limited to gambling; it can be illustrated in other aspects of life as well. For example, parents may feel that they have a greater chance of having a girl for their fifth child if they had four boys previously. In reality, each child has about a 50–50 chance of being a boy or a girl, regardless of how many boy or girls came before.

In a demonstration of these cognitive biases in a gambling situation, Ladouceur and Dubé (1997) asked 20 participants to produce a random sequence of outcomes from a coin toss. A screen contained a covered version of the prior sequence, and participants were told that they could remove the covering if they wanted. All participants removed the cover at least once in determining their random sequence, even though past outcomes should have no bearing on future ones. Hardoon et al. (2001) presented lottery tickets, containing different series of number sequences, to 60 undergraduates and asked them to select tickets they thought had the greatest probability of winning. Students also completed the SOGS and were classified as nonproblem, problem, or pathological gamblers. All groups demonstrated cognitive distortions and preferred tickets with seemingly random numbers relative to those with patterns, long sequences of numbers, or grouping of numbers that were all above or below the mean. Hardoon et al. (2001) asked the students to indicate why they selected the tickets they did and avoided others. Verbalizations were classified according the heuristics described above. Problem and pathological gamblers verbalized more than nongamblers, but this effect may have been related to familiarity. Furthermore, proportions of rational to irrational thoughts were similar across groups. The researchers concluded that problem and pathological gamblers were more likely to endorse some types of heuristics, but none of the group differences were significant after correcting for the large number of statistical tests conducted. Thus, this study provides further evidence for the existence of cognitive distortions in gambling situations, but it did not lend much support for the hypothesis that people with gambling problems have more distortions than those without gambling problems.

Law of Large Numbers

Related to the representative heuristic is the *law of large numbers* (Tversky & Kahneman, 1971), which states that large samples will be representative of the population from which they are selected. However, too often, small samples are considered representative. The belief that small samples may reflect a population norm is the basis of stereotypes. A person may draw unwarranted conclusions about a group of people on the basis of his or her interactions with a small number of group members. If that person met with a large number of people from the group, his or her feelings about their attributes may be very different.

In terms of gambling, people may expect that a small number of events, be they wins or losses, are representative of the probabilities of winning overall in that game. A person might believe, for example, that six consecutive wins at poker represents "good luck" or be indicative that one is "on a winning streak." A single large win on a slot machine may be taken to suggest that it is a "winning machine," whereas in reality the overall probabilities in the long run are equal across all machines.

The term *base rate* refers to the frequency with which a given event or outcome occurs within a larger population. Base rates often are not taken into account when making decisions; that is, people often fail to recognize the proportion of categories in a population when making decisions on representativeness. Consider this example, adapted from Tversky and Kahneman (1974): "Ken is a very shy and quiet man. He is helpful to others, but he prefers to be alone and has little interest in people. He has a high desire for structure and detail." People were asked to judge Ken's occupation, and the supplied possibilities included salesman, pilot, librarian, and physician. Considering base rates, people should select salesman, because that is the most common of the above professions. However, because Ken fits the stereotypical description of a librarian, far more people selected that profession, which is relatively rare.

In terms of gambling, people likewise ignore base rates in making decisions regarding whether to place a bet. The base rates, in combination with the law of large numbers, suggest that overall it would be in no one's best interest to ever wager at a casino or on the lottery, because the odds are in favor of the house. However, because people sometimes base their decisions on small but unrepresentative samples (e.g., the possibility of a big win), they gamble.

Availability Illusion

The *availability illusion* is another cognitive distortion that applies to both gambling and nongambling decisions. It refers to the tendency to estimate frequency or probabilities on the basis of how easy or difficult it is to think of examples. An example is, "Is the letter *k* more likely to appear as the first or third letter in words?" Most people think that *k* is more likely to appear as the first letter in words (Tversky & Kahneman, 1973). In reality, *k* is about twice more often to appear as the third letter in words.

Three reasons are cited as influencing the availability illusion: (a) familiarity, (b) recency, and (c) vividness. We are more easily able to think of words beginning with the letter *k* than those that have *k* in the third position. Therefore, our decisions are biased, at least in part, on familiarity. In terms of gambling, Americans may consider it silly or irrational to wager on games like Pachinko, because they are not familiar with this form of gambling. Yet, Americans may readily gamble on other activities that may have even lower probabilities of winning.

Recency refers to the phenomenon that memory for events declines with the passage of time. A real world example of the recency effect with respect to the availability heuristic is that earthquake insurance is purchased in greatest quantities after an earthquake. Purchase rates drop steadily thereafter as the quake fades in history (Slovic, Fischhoff, & Lichtenstein, 1982). In regard to gamblers, they can readily remember their most recent wins, and they may overestimate the proportion of wins on the basis of the recency of favorable outcomes.

Finally, *vividness* refers to selectively recalling events that are very unusual or dramatic. In deciding on which classes to take in college, students are much more likely to be swayed by personal interactions with former students of the courses than by large-scale course evaluations. Similarly, when gambling, individuals are likely to overestimate the probabilities of winning by selectively remembering their fourth cousin who won $1 million rather than recalling all their other first, second, third, and fourth cousins who have never won the lottery. The cousin who won big is a much more vivid event and takes precedence over less salient nonwinners.

To investigate the availability illusion in a gambling situation, Ladouceur et al. (1988) coded verbalizations while 20 individuals wagered on a computerized version of roulette. They were divided into two groups: One was scheduled to win 50% of the time, and the other was scheduled to win only 20% of the time. Verbalizations were recorded while students gambled, and the verbalizations were coded as either rational (e.g., "The odds are not better if I bet on three rows or only one") or irrational (e.g., "I won on those numbers last time, so I'm going to try them again"). Rational and irrational verbalizations were reliably coded by independent judges, and irrational verbalizations outnumbered rational ones by about 5 to 1. However, no differences between the groups with frequent and infrequent wins were noted, suggesting that winning or losing did not appear to influence the numbers or probabilities of irrational thoughts while gambling.

Illusory Correlation

Illusory correlation refers to the belief that a causal relationship exists when no objective evidence for this relationship is available. For example,

Berscheid and Walster (1974) noted that a person who is physically attractive is also perceived to have other desirable characteristics, such as intelligence, wit, and even wealth. Although some real relationship may exist between these qualities, they tend to be distorted. Similarly, people who eat spinach may be considered to be strong. These examples fail to take into account the base rates of the alternative events (e.g., the percentage of nonspinach eaters who are strong, the percentage of nonspinach eaters who are not strong, along with the percentage of spinach eaters who are not strong).

Illusory correlations are common and can result in superstitions. Toneatto (1999) described several types of superstitions in gamblers. *Behavioral superstitions* refer to actions or rituals thought to enhance outcomes of gambling events. Examples include calling out for numbers when dice are rolled, shouting for one's horse, or clapping during the play of a gambling event. Obviously, these behaviors do not influence outcomes of the event. *Cognitive superstitions* refer to the use of prayer, hope, or a strong conviction that a win is imminent (K. M. King, 1990; Toneatto, Blitz-Miller, Calderwood, Dragonetti, & Tsanos, 1997). In other words, people may feel that their mental state can influence outcomes, and if they play or pray passionately enough, their thoughts about winning will affect the outcomes. *Talismanic superstitions* refer to the belief that having certain objects or attributes will increase the chance of winning. For example, holding a lucky rabbit's foot, wearing a green shirt, or seeing a specific number or letter combination on a license plate may be thought to signify that a win is imminent (K. M. King, 1990; Wagenaar, 1988). Bersabe and Arias (2000) studied this phenomenon in college students who were exposed to a gambling situation in which they won frequently while wearing a special watch and lost frequently when not wearing the watch. They were later asked whether they wanted to wear the watch while gambling, and they chose to wear it. All these superstitions may develop via illusory correlations. When winning, one may have worn a particular shirt or carried a charm. This random pairing may reinforce subsequent desires to wear that shirt or carry the charm. This issue was also discussed in chapter 11, in terms of superstitious behaviors resulting from variable interval schedules of reinforcement.

Entrapment

Entrapment is a term used to describe the process in which individuals increase commitment to a previously chosen, albeit unsatisfactory, course of action to make good on prior investments (Brockner & Rubin, 1985). Another name for entrapment is the *sunk cost effect*. An example common to everyday life is related to car repairs. Once you spend $800 repairing the transmission, the brakes go. You fix those too, and 2 months later you have to replace the tires. The cost of the three repairs may exceed the value of the car, but once you have invested such a large amount, you want to get all the value you can from the car, and you keep putting more money into it.

Chasing is a phenomenon in gambling (Lesieur, 1977) that may be analogous to entrapment. Gamblers continue gambling in the event that a winning outcome will occur. They have already placed thousands of dollars at risk and lost it. The only way to win it back is to keep wagering. On a smaller scale, the process of not leaving a particular slot machine because one has already placed $100 in it is another example of entrapment.

Thus, several cognitive distortions have been described that appear to have face validity with respect to understanding why people gamble. Research in the field of cognitive psychology has demonstrated the effects of these cognitive distortions in everyday decision-making processes. Less research has investigated the frequency or strengths of these illusions among problem gamblers compared with nonproblem gamblers. The limited research is equivocal in terms of demonstrating whether problem gamblers have more illusions than nonproblem gamblers.

Although more research is needed to evaluate these phenomena and their association with gambling, some researchers have argued that erroneous beliefs propel individuals to gamble repeatedly (Ladouceur & Walker, 1996). Some prevention (Gaboury & Ladouceur, 1993) and intervention (Ladouceur, Sylvain, Boutin, & Doucet, 2002) efforts make use of restructuring techniques in which cognitive distortions are targeted and corrected. I describe these studies next.

COGNITIVE TREATMENTS

In the 1980s, therapists began incorporating cognitive techniques into behavioral treatments of pathological gambling. Toneatto and Sobell (1990) described beneficial effects of cognitive therapy in which the patient made imaginary bets on real life events, such as horse races, while the therapist demonstrated to him that he was unable to predict winners at an acceptable level to come out ahead in the long term. In case reports, Sharpe and Tarrier (1992, 1993) have described the theoretical basis of a multimodal cognitive approach that included a relaxation component, imaginal and *in vivo* exposure, and cognitive restructuring. Arribas and Martinez (1991) in Spain and Sylvain and Ladouceur (1992) in Quebec focused on cognitive restructuring, but they also included educational components, stimulus control, self-monitoring, and a family intervention. These approaches were used in a series of case studies, as shown in Table 12.1.

Using a multiple-baseline procedure, Bujold, Ladouceur, Sylvain, and Boisvert (1994) used cognitive restructuring, problem solving, social skills training, and relapse prevention in weekly individual sessions with three

TABLE 12.1
Cognitive Therapies for Pathological Gambling

Study	Focus of therapy	N (completers)	Months of treatment (and of follow-up)	Outcomes
Descriptive reports				
Toneatto & Sobell (1990)	Demonstrate poor odds of winning with imaginary bets on horse races.	1 (1)	4 (6)	Gambling reduced to monthly during treatment, every other month in follow-up.
Sharpe & Tarrier (1992)	Relaxation, imaginal, and *in vivo* exposure, cognitive restructuring.	1 (1)	Not stated (10)	Reduced gambling.
Bannister (1977)	Rational emotive and covert sensitization.	1 (1)	30	Reduced gambling.
Bujold et al. (1994)	Cognitive restructuring, problem solving, relapse prevention.	3 (3)	Various (9)	All gambling ceased by end of treatment, gains maintained at follow-ups.
Sylvain & Ladouceur (1992)	Cognitive restructuring, education, relapse prevention.	3 (3)	3 (6)	Reduced gambling.
Arribas & Martinez (1991)	Cognitive restructuring, stimulus control, self-monitoring.	4 (4)	3 (6)	All reduced gambling.
Ladoceur et al. (1998)	Cognitive restructuring and education.	5 (5)	Up to 4.5 (6)	80% reduced gambling substantially; gains maintained at follow-up.
Randomized trials				
Echeburúa et al. (1996)	Stimulus control, *in vivo* exposure, relapse prevention (individual; A) vs. cognitive restructuring (in group; B) vs. combined treatment (C) vs. wait list (D).	64 (50)	1.5 (12)	At 6 months, abstinence or much reduced in 75%, 63%, 38%, and 25% for Conditions A, B, C, and D, respectively. At 12 months, success in 69% in Condition A vs. 38% in Conditions B and C.
Sylvain et al. (1997)	Cognitive restructuring, problem solving/ social skills + relapse prevention vs. wait list.	22 vs. 18 (14/22 in treatment group)	Up to 30 sessions (6)	In treatment group, 36% improved by 50% on 5 dependent variables vs. 6% of control participants; gains maintained at follow-up.
Ladouceur et al. (2001)	Cognitive restructuring + relapse prevention vs. wait list.	59 vs. 29 (35/59 in treatment group)	Up to 20 sessions (12)	In treatment group, 32% improved by 50% on 4 dependent variables vs. 7% of control participants; gains maintained at follow-up.
Ladouceur et al. (2003)	Cognitive restructuring + relapse prevention in group vs. wait list	46 vs. 25 (34/46 in treatment group)	2.5 (24)	In treatment group, 43% improved by 50% on 4 dependent variables vs. 6% of control participants; gains maintained at follow-up.

gamblers. All three gamblers eventually ceased gambling, and the gains were maintained throughout a 9-month follow-up period.

In a controlled trial of this same treatment approach, Sylvain, Ladouceur, and Boisvert (1997) randomly assigned 40 pathological gamblers to cognitive therapy available immediately ($n = 22$) or to a wait-list control condition of approximately 4 months ($n = 18$). Three patients in the wait-list condition withdrew from the study, and 2 began treatment prior to the end of the wait period. Of those assigned to the immediate treatment condition, 14 (64%) attended the sessions, and treatment was delivered until they ceased gambling. The average number of sessions was approximately 17, but it ranged up to 30. The rest of the patients in the treatment condition ($n = 8$, or 36%) dropped out of therapy and were not contacted for further follow-up evaluations. The study reported significant beneficial effects in the treatment relative to the wait-list condition with respect to number of DSM–IV criteria endorsed, SOGS scores, perceived control over gambling, desire to gamble, and self-efficacy in regard to gambling. However, these results did not include data from the study withdrawals. Participants who did not complete the study may have differed in some substantial ways from those who did. A reexamination of the data using an intent-to-treat analysis and assuming no beneficial effect among individuals who withdrew prematurely again revealed a probable beneficial effect of the therapy. Clinically significant change was defined as a 50% or more reduction from baseline with respect to the five main dependent variables, and 36% of all patients assigned to the treatment condition achieved this criterion, compared with only 6% of patients assigned to the wait-list condition. Approximately 36% of individuals in the immediate treatment condition met these same success criteria at the 6-month follow-up evaluation.

Ladouceur, Sylvain, Letarte, Giroux, and Jacques (1998) applied a more purely cognitive approach when treating five pathological gamblers using a multiple-baseline across-subjects design. The therapy targeted erroneous perceptions by instructing patients on the concept of randomness and application of principles of independence among random events, increasing awareness of inaccurate perceptions while gambling, and recording and reviewing verbalizations during a session of imaginal gambling. Treatment was provided once or twice weekly for up to 20 sessions. Compared with pretreatment ratings, four of the patients showed reductions in urges to gamble and actual gambling behavior. Gains were maintained throughout a 6-month period.

In a randomized study, Ladouceur et al. (2001) applied this same treatment, or a wait-list control condition, to 88 patients. Fifty-nine of the gamblers were assigned to the immediate cognitive treatment condition, and the remaining 29 were assigned to a wait-list control condition. Of the patients assigned to the immediate condition, only 35 (59%) completed the treatment, with the remainder dropping out early. Treatment was delivered on an individual basis once weekly for a maximum of 20 sessions, or until considered successful. On average, patients received 11 hours of therapy. The therapy consisted almost exclusively of correcting inappropriate cognitions about randomness and assessing erroneous cognitions associated with high-risk situations. In evaluating posttreatment outcomes, again only data from treatment completers were included. Significant group by time effects were noted with respect to SOGS scores, desire to gamble, perception of control over gambling, and self-efficacy (all rated on a Likert scale). Frequency and dollars spent gambling also decreased in the treated group compared with the wait-list group. The wait-list group could not be included in the long-term follow-up evaluation, because they received treatment during the interim. Nevertheless, among the treatment completers who received immediate treatment, significant reductions were noted relative to the pretreatment rates of gambling and gambling urges; 71% did not meet diagnostic criteria for pathological gambling at a 12-month follow-up. If an intent-to-treat analysis were used and nontreatment completers were assumed to continue gambling at baseline rates, then the overall success rate at posttreatment would drop to 32%. This success rate appears similar to those noted in outcome studies of other therapeutic approaches (see chaps. 8 and 11).

Ladouceur, Sylvain, et al. (2003) recently evaluated the efficacy of this same cognitive therapy when applied in a group format. Seventy-one pathological gamblers were randomly assigned to a group cognitive therapy condition available immediately ($n = 46$) or to a wait-list control condition ($n = 25$). Of those assigned to the immediate-treatment condition, 24 (74%) completed the 10 weekly, 2-hour long sessions, with the remainder dropping out prior to the third session. At a posttreatment evaluation, 30 of the treatment completers (or 65% of those assigned to that condition) no longer met criteria for pathological gambling. Only 20% of the wait-list patients decreased gambling to this degree. Some relapse was noted among those in the treatment condition throughout a 24-month follow-up period. Twenty-two of the original 46 patients assigned to this condition completed the 24-month follow-up evaluation, and 68% of these (or 33% of the original sample) did not meet diagnostic criteria for pathological gambling at this follow-up. A major strength of this study is the long-term follow-up evaluation. This study also demonstrates that group therapy appears to be equally efficacious to individual treatment, and dropout rates may be lower with group therapy, although prospective randomized trials are necessary to confirm this impression.

In Spain, Echeburúa, Baez, and Fernandez-Montalvo (1996) reported on the efficacy of a cognitive therapy approach in which both the type of therapy and the format of therapy (group or individual) differed across conditions. Sixty-four pathological gamblers were randomly assigned to one of four conditions: (a) stimulus control and *in vivo* exposure delivered in an individual format, (b) cognitive restructuring delivered in a group format, (c) these two treatment conditions delivered in a combined manner (both individual and group treatment), or (d) a 6-month wait-list condition. Approximately three quarters of patients completed treatment, and an intent-to-treat analysis was conducted. Data from the posttreatment evaluation were not presented, but data from the 6-month evaluation revealed that patients assigned to the individual-treatment condition were more likely to be considered successes than those in the wait-list condition. The definition of *success* was abstinence or the occurrence of no more than one or two gambling episodes, with the total amount spent gambling being not greater than a week's worth of gambling in the pretreatment period. Patients assigned to the group therapy alone condition fared as well as those in the individual condition at the 6-month follow-up, but they did not differ significantly from the wait-list control patients, and the beneficial effects dissipated at the 12-month follow-up. It is surprising that those who received the combined treatment were less likely to respond favorably to treatment than were those who received individual treatment alone. The explanation for these unexpected findings is unclear but may be related to relatively small samples (16 per condition). Nevertheless, these results suggest that either individual therapy or the stimulus control and *in vivo* exposure condition may be more efficacious than group or cognitive therapy. Future studies will be needed to replicate and isolate the effect.

In the following case example, which was first described in chapter 4, cognitive therapy was used to help Thy, the Cambodian refugee who left his home in New York City, cease gambling.

Case example (continued from chap. 4). Thy fled to Seattle, Washington, after taking money from his family's business and losing it all in Atlantic City. He was too ashamed to contact his family and has remained in hiding for over 5 years. For the first year or so after leaving home, Thy did not gamble. He had no money and was sleeping on the streets or in shelters. Through a social services program, he eventually got a job and a small apartment.

As time went by, Thy got settled in his solitary life in Seattle. He had a night job, and he spent much of the days sleeping or watching television. He eventually saved enough money for a used car. He occasionally bought lottery and scratch tickets from convenience stores where he got his cigarettes. He would bet on lucky numbers, hoping that one day it would pay off, and he could return home, pay back the money he took, and provide for his family. He learned that there were casinos in Washington, and although he knew they would be nothing like what he was used to in Atlantic City, he decided to try it out one Sunday when he was bored. What could it hurt—he had nothing to lose anymore. He started going to a small casino on a reservation more and more regularly on Sundays, and eventually during the weekdays when he could not sleep. Within 2 years, trips to the casino had become his life again, and he was spending all his time and money there. One day, having lost all his money, he placed his last thing of value on a roulette game—he sold his car. When he lost, Thy had no way to get to work or home that evening.

Thy remembered having seen a phone number to call for help about gambling problems at the exits to the casino. He was able to find the number and, shaking inside, he called. He explained his situation to the man who answered the phone. The man told him there was a bus that ran from the casino to downtown and that he could meet Thy there, not far from the bus station, in about 2 hours. Thy said he had to go to work that evening, but the man insisted that he call in sick and start working on his gambling problem today. Feeling despondent, Thy agreed. He remembered vividly going from slot machine to slot machine, looking for enough change first to call in to work and then to get money for the bus ride. An older woman who was watching him offered him $10, if he promised not to spend it on the machines.

Thy started treatment that day. There was a part-time Cambodian social worker at the treatment center who was assigned to Thy's case. He told her his story—how he'd left his family because of gambling and was now in trouble again. The social worker picked up on what she considered Thy's primary reason for gambling: that he felt he would eventually win big by gambling and such a win, he perceived, could solve all his problems. She started educating him about the odds of gambling by reviewing probabilistic outcomes. Although Thy had only a limited formal education, he understood that the house was gaining the bulk of the money. She brought in sample scratch and lottery tickets and demonstrated how only a proportion pay off. She had Thy verbalize his thought processes as he selected which lottery tickets were winners, and recorded what he said; for example: "This one is more likely to win because it has the number 3 on it twice. I can tell that this one won't win because the numbers are too close together." They reviewed his comments in detail, with first she, then he, explaining why his thoughts were faulty.

After 6 weeks of discussing irrational cognitions with lottery tickets, the social worker asked Thy to relax and pretend he was betting on roulette. She wanted him to describe his thoughts about what numbers and colors he was betting on and how he determined the size of the bets. Relative to the lottery examples, Thy had a harder time accepting why, if he spread out his wagers on enough numbers and colors, he couldn't come out ahead. They started writing down his audio-recorded thoughts, reviewing them both in the written and the verbal forms. The social worker had Thy write an alternative explanation for each of his thoughts about winning.

During this 3-month period, Thy did not go to the casino at all. The first couple of weeks, he bought lottery tickets almost every day. Eventually, though, he started thinking about the odds as he bought the tickets. One day, he went into the convenience store and when the clerk, who recognized him, automatically handed Thy a ticket, he refused it.

At his next session, he told his therapist how he had refused the ticket. She was so pleased with him, and her concern for him reminded him of his mother and sisters, back in New York. After discussing his fears with the therapist for a few sessions, Thy finally decided to telephone his family, hoping they still were alive and living in the same area. His mother wept when she heard his voice, and she begged him to come back home, even after he confessed to taking the money from her sister's husband's store years earlier. Thy's sisters were thrilled to talk with him, and one sent him a plane ticket to return home that week.

Comment. This case is one of a happy ending, in which Thy successfully ceased gambling and his family was eager to reunite with him. In Thy's case, he was very young when he stole from his family and left home, which may in part explain his family's willingness to forgive him. With older gamblers and spouses, a 5-year disappearance would be less likely to be overlooked. As in all the case examples, the descriptions do not provide proof of efficacy of the techniques; rather, they simply give a human face to the disorder and its treatment.

SUMMARY AND CLINICAL IMPLICATIONS

Research has not yet demonstrated whether cognitive therapy that focuses on irrational cognitions actually modifies these illusions. Only one report (Breen, Kruedelbach, & Walker, 2001) has assessed cognitive aspects of gambling in response to treatment, but this study evaluated erroneous cognitions after a relatively long-term (28-day) inpatient gambling treatment that used a multimodal approach. The Gambling Attitude and Beliefs Survey (Breen & Zuckerman, 1999), a 35-item instrument that assesses a range of cognitive biases, was administered pre- and posttreatment to 66 patients. Scores decreased after treatment, and reductions were mediated by level of depression. Pretreatment severity of gambling problems, as measured by the SOGS, were not associated with changes in scores on this scale.

As noted in earlier in the chapter, erroneous cognitions are not unique to gambling; they are also noted in other aspects of life that involve making decisions that have uncertain outcomes. Although cognitive therapies have a theoretical background, and the initial results of these techniques appear promising, cognitive treatments that focus on modifying erroneous cognitions should investigate whether cognitions actually change in response to therapy. Studies should also assess whether such changes are unique to cognitive therapy, as they may be influenced by any type of therapy or even by natural reductions in gambling behaviors that may occur independently of formal treatment.

IV

A TREATMENT MODEL

13

COGNITIVE–BEHAVIORAL THERAPY

The cognitive therapies, which I described in chapter 12, focus on altering cognitions, and early behavioral treatments, which I outlined in chapter 11, center on changing gambling behaviors. Other models are more broadly based and incorporate both cognitive and behavioral features. These are called *cognitive–behavioral therapies*, a rather loose term that refers to a variety of treatments. Several review articles have described the rationale for and aspects of cognitive–behavioral therapy for treating pathological gamblers (Blaszczynski & Silove, 1995; Lopez-Viets & Miller, 1997; Petry & Armentano, 1999; Sharpe, 2002; Sharpe & Tarrier, 1993). In the first section of this chapter, I provide details on some outcome studies.

In the second section, I describe a cognitive–behavioral therapy that I have developed. This is a relatively short-term, eight-session model that was used in the largest known study of psychosocial treatments for pathological gamblers (Petry, Stinson, & Grant, manuscript submitted for publication). It was the first treatment study funded for pathological gamblers by the National Institutes of Health. More than 230 gamblers participated and were randomly assigned to receive this intervention or a control condition—referral to Gamblers Anonymous (GA) alone. The therapy was well accepted by the gamblers in the study, and acceptance rates and satisfaction were high. Outcomes from the study are described later in the chapter. Although used in an individual format in the study, gambling treatment programs have also implemented the therapy within the context of groups.

STUDIES OF COGNITIVE–BEHAVIORAL THERAPY

A few case studies have shown reductions in gambling following cognitive–behavioral therapy (Arribas & Martinez, 1991; Bannister, 1977; Sharpe & Tarrier, 1992). Some may argue that the therapies used in those reports were primarily cognitive in nature, and therefore they were discussed in chapter 12. Sylvain, Ladouceur, and Boisvert's (1997) study, which I described in chapter 12, also used cognitive–behavioral techniques, such as problem solving, social skills training, and relapse prevention, in combination with a cognitive therapy that focused on altering cognitive biases associated with gambling.

The results of a randomized trial of cognitive–behavioral therapy conducted in Spain (Echeburúa, Baez, & Fernandez-Montalvo, 1996; see chap. 12, this volume) indicate that gamblers who received individual stimulus control and *in vivo* exposure to gambling situations with response prevention had overall better results than those who received cognitive restructuring in group therapy, a combination of both treatments, or were assigned to a wait-list control condition. These investigators also reported on the effectiveness of providing cognitive–behavioral relapse prevention as a follow-up to the 6-week individual intervention (Echeburúa, Fernandez-Montalvo, & Baez, 2000, 2001). Treatment responders ($n = 69$) were randomly assigned to no further treatment or to relapse prevention therapy delivered in a group or individual format. The relapse prevention involved training gamblers to identify and cope with relapse precipitants, such as social pressure to gamble, interpersonal conflict, and negative affect. Over a 12-month period, 86% of those receiving individual therapy, and 78% of those receiving group therapy, did not relapse, compared with 52% of those who received no further treatment. These results suggest that cognitive–behavioral therapy, whether delivered individually or in a group format, may improve long-term outcomes of gamblers who have ceased gambling.

I (Petry, 1998) developed an eight-session manualized cognitive–behavioral therapy for gamblers, and 231 pathological gamblers were enrolled in a study evaluating the efficacy of this approach (Petry, Stinson, & Grant, manuscript submitted for publication). All participants were referred to and encouraged to attend GA. About two thirds of the gamblers also received cognitive–behavioral therapy, either delivered by a counselor in once-weekly individual sessions or completed alone by the patient in a workbook format.

Participants in all three conditions were equally likely to attend GA, so any beneficial effects of GA participation on outcomes were equated across the groups. The cognitive–behavioral therapy reduced gambling behaviors to a greater degree than GA referral alone. Mean days gambled in the month before entering treatment was about 14 for all three groups; at posttreatment, it decreased to about 5 days in the GA referral only condition, 4.5 in the workbook condition, and 3.5 in the individual therapy condition. Median dollars wagered in the month before treatment was about $1,200. It decreased to about $350 in the GA alone and workbook conditions compared with about $80 in the individual therapy condition. Collateral reports were highly consistent with patient reports of gambling. South Oaks Gambling Screen scores and Addiction Severity Index—Gambling scores decreased among patients receiving cognitive–behavioral therapy relative to those in the GA referral alone condition, and these effects were noted both during the treatment period and throughout a 1-year follow-up.

The individual therapy condition demonstrated improved outcomes relative to the workbook condition on some outcome measures, in both the short and long term evaluations. The effect may be related to compliance. Participants assigned to the individual therapy condition were more likely than those assigned to the workbook condition to become engaged in treatment. That is, over 60% of those in the individual therapy condition attended at least 6 sessions, whereas only 37% of those in the workbook condition completed 6 or more chapters. Satisfaction with the treatment received was high in all conditions, with mean ratings above 6 on a 9-point scale. However, satisfaction was significantly higher in the individual cognitive–behavioral therapy condition (mean of 8 points) relative to the other two conditions.

The cognitive–behavioral therapy also had some beneficial effects on other areas of psychosocial functioning. Specifically, long term benefits of the cognitive–behavioral therapy relative to GA referral alone were noted in terms of reducing employment, legal, and psychiatric difficulties.

This study demonstrates the efficacy of this cognitive–behavioral approach in one of the largest studies examining treatments for pathological gamblers. The study is highly generalized to treatment-seeking gamblers as few exclusionary criteria were employed. It utilized an intent-to-treat analysis, achieved relatively high follow-up rates (>80%), and evaluated outcomes over a reasonably long period of time. Collateral reports corroborated patient reports of gambling and GA participation, and the two were highly concordant. Furthermore, 13 different therapists provided the therapy, thereby reducing the impact of particular therapists on outcomes. Next, I describe this cognitive behavioral therapy in detail.

DESCRIPTION OF MY COGNITIVE–BEHAVIORAL TREATMENT APPROACH

Reinforcing nongambling is a central component to this treatment. The therapist works with the gambler to track his or her gambling and nongambling days on a graph throughout treatment. The gambler is encouraged to reward him- or herself for each day of nongambling. Rewards are individually selected and can include such things as a kiss from a spouse, a relaxing bath, a favorite television program, or dessert. Continuous periods of abstinence are reinforced with larger rewards, such as a meal at a favorite restaurant or a new item of clothing. If gambling occurs, the gambler is instructed to withhold such rewards, for example, by not eating dessert that night or not watching television. The larger reward planned for the end of the week is forfeited as well. The therapist promotes using this self-reward system throughout treatment.

Session 1

In addition to introducing the nongambling-reinforcer system, the first session also teaches the gambler to better understand the pattern of his or her gambling behaviors and to identify triggers of gambling. These exercises are adapted from Monti, Abrams, Kadden, and Cooney (1989). Certain events, days and times, people, and emotions have been paired with gambling in the past and may now precipitate gambling episodes or urges in a seemingly automatic manner. Common triggers include having cash available; unstructured or free time (weekends, days off); arguments with family members or coworkers; and bored, depressed, or anxious moods. Gamblers are asked to complete a worksheet in the session indicating their unique triggers associated with these various categories. They are also asked to indicate times when; people with whom; and events, moods, and other activities in response to which they do not gamble. The therapist encourages the gambler to spend more time in places where he or she does not gamble and with people with whom he or she does not gamble. A specific plan is developed for high-risk time(s) over the upcoming week, such as preparing dinner for a friend on Saturday evening, when the gambler most often goes to the casino. A homework exercise, in which the gambler is asked to monitor triggers daily over the course of the next week, is provided.

A case example is provided next to illustrate how the therapy is delivered. The handouts and homework exercises are included in Appendixes A, B, and C.

Case example (continued from chap. 2). Mary, whose case was first presented in chapter 2, had been hiding her gambling and financial problems, until she passed out one night at a casino. While in the hospital, Mary was referred to an outpatient gambling treatment program that provided cognitive–behavioral therapy.

At the first session, the therapist, Sue, showed Mary two pieces of graph paper, one with 8 weeks prior to today laid out on it, and the second with the next 2 months listed. She asked Mary to review a calendar of the past 2 months, checking which days she had gambled. Sue then transposed the days Mary had gambled on the graph and observed that more than two thirds of the days were gambling days. She then told Mary that that was her past—the next graph was her future. Sue asked Mary if she had gambled the day of their first session, and Mary said no. Sue drew a line going up on the graph. She said that every day Mary doesn't gamble, she should draw a line upward. Sue said, "If you don't gamble tomorrow, how will the line look?" to ensure that Mary understood.

Sue told Mary:

Stopping gambling can be a real struggle, but it's also something that can be done. Every day that you don't gamble is something you should be proud of. Sometimes people minimize their successes, because they think that they shouldn't have been gambling to begin with, and a day of not gambling is not a big deal. But it is a big deal, especially in the early stages of recovery. You haven't gambled in over 5 days, and that is an accomplishment. How often did you go without gambling 2 months ago?

Mary thought for a minute and said, "I haven't gone without gambling for 5 days in a row in a long time." Sue replied to Mary,

In the early stages of recovery, some people find it very useful to schedule small rewards for themselves when they don't gamble. It helps remind them, in a tangible form, of their accomplishments. Can you think of some rewards for yourself for not gambling?

Mary said, "Well, I am not embarrassed to see my daughter or my grandkids when I don't gamble."

Sue said, "That's a great idea. Why don't you agree to telephone your daughter and grandkids every evening whenever you go through the day without gambling?"

Mary said, "My daughter would like that."

Sue responded, "What about you, Mary? Would you like to talk with your family every day? Would this be something you'd look forward to?"

Mary said yes, and she agreed to draw a line upward and call her daughter every day that she didn't gamble.

Sue said, "And if you don't gamble between now and Saturday, that would be over a full week without gambling. Could you plan a get-together on Saturday as a small celebration of getting your life back on track?"

Mary said she didn't know if her daughter was busy that day, but she'd think about it.

Then Sue showed Mary a handout describing triggers of gambling. She asked Mary to describe what led to her gambling: moods, times, and days. Mary was able to indicate several moods: Boredom, guilt, and embarrassment made her want to gamble. Sue called these moods "triggers for gambling—feelings that make it more likely that you'll gamble."

Sue wanted details about other triggers—events, days, and times that Mary gambled. Mary said she gambled any day of the week, any time of the day; it just didn't matter now that she wasn't working. Sue had her think back to before she lost her job—when did she gamble then? "Mostly on the weekends," Mary said, "Although I would also go late at night if I couldn't sleep." They wrote these triggers on the handout.

Sue then said, "And what about when you don't gamble, or don't feel like gambling? What are you doing when you aren't thinking about gambling?"

Mary replied, "I was always thinking about gambling, every day. I couldn't get it off my mind."

Sue referred to the graph of the last 2 months and said "But you didn't gamble every day. On some days you weren't gambling—why didn't you gamble on those days?"

Mary said, "Because I didn't have any money, or I thought my gambling was getting out of control. I tried not to go sometimes."

Sue said, "But what differed, either within you or the circumstances, between these days when you didn't go and the days when you did?"

"That's a hard question," Mary said. She pointed to a nongambling day and said, "On that day, I remember my daughter called me in the morning because Allison was sick. She said she had been calling me for 2 days and couldn't get in touch with me. I remember I felt so worried about the baby, I rushed over to see her. I didn't even think about gambling that day."

Sue summarized, "So, when you are with other people, or helping others, you don't want to gamble. Is that right?"

"I guess so," said Mary.

"Let's think about some other people who you don't go gambling with, and some other things you do when you aren't gambling, and list them here," said Sue:

> I'm going to give you this sheet to refer to when you think you might want to gamble. Also, I'd like you to record all the triggers for gambling you encounter next week—if you feel bored or guilty, or desperate for money, write it on this sheet, and whether or not you were able to overcome the trigger without gambling.

Session 2

In the beginning of the second and each subsequent session, the therapist inquires about any gambling over the course of the week and plots each nongambling day on the chart that began in Session 1. The therapist provides praise and support for each nongambling day over the prior week. Stars can be given for days when a particularly difficult trigger was encountered but successfully managed, or for a week of continuous abstinence.

The homework exercise delineating the prior week's triggers, and the gambler's response to them, is reviewed. If the gambler did not complete or bring in the homework (which is not uncommon), then it is reviewed verbally, with the therapist asking if the patient experienced any triggers and how he or she responded to them. For each trigger the patient encountered but managed to avoid gambling in response to, the therapist inquires about skills used to overcome the trigger. The therapist then introduces the concept of *functional analysis*, a cognitive–behavioral technique commonly used in the treatment of many disorders (Monti et al., 1989).

A functional analysis consists of breaking gambling episodes into their precipitants (or triggers) and evaluating both the positive and negative consequences of gambling. By the time most gamblers come into treatment, they can readily identify negative aspects of gambling, such a loss of money or savings; guilt or poor self-esteem; troubles at work, home, or with the law; and depressed or anxious mood. Although negative aspects are often overwhelming when one presents for treatment, the positive effects are what maintain the gambling. At times, especially during desperation phases, when patients may initiate treatment, these positive effects of gambling may be difficult to identify. They may include excitement, a dream of winning big and changing one's life both financially and emotionally, and relief from boredom or anxiety. As gamblers identify the reasons for their gambling, they can begin to consider other methods for achieving these same goals, by means of more realistic and less fantastic approaches.

In conducting a functional analysis, the therapist asks the gambler to describe his or her most recent gambling experience. For example, a recent trip to the casino may have resulted subsequent to an argument with a spouse over financial concerns (the trigger). The positive or rewarding effects of gambling in response to that situation may have included the possibility of winning money and getting away from the spouse for several hours. The negative effects of gambling may have been losing another $300 and returning home to an even angrier spouse. The resentful spouse may maintain his or her anger throughout the next day. When the gambler heads home from work the following evening, he or she may suddenly change direction and head toward the casino rather than going home and facing the spouse. In this manner, the negative effects of gambling lead directly to the triggers for gambling, many of which were identified in the previous week's session. Reevaluating several gambling episodes in this manner can assist the gambler to better understand the patterning, and the automatic nature, of his or her gambling. The triggers lead to gambling, which has some transient beneficial results but, more likely than not, leads to longer term negative consequences.

These negative consequences are often congruent with the triggers that precipitate gambling. Thus occurs the vicious cycle of addiction.

Over the next week, the patient is asked to reward him- or herself for not gambling and to keep track of triggers that occur daily and his or her responses to those triggers. Homework assignments instruct the gambler to imagine what the positive and negative effects of gambling in response to each trigger would be.

Case example continued. When Mary returned the next week, she had not gambled. Sue had Mary fill in the nongambling chart, and she recorded a star for her 1-week anniversary of not gambling. She asked Mary if she had called her daughter every day as a reward for not gambling, and Mary said that she called every night but one. She also had phoned her son, with whom she had a strained relationship. Sue asked her if the conversation went OK, and Mary said that it was stressful—her son was very critical of her and angry about the gambling. Sue inquired whether the conversation made Mary feel like gambling, and Mary denied it, although she wasn't sure how she was going to reconcile her relationship with her son. Sue reminded her that the important thing now was to focus on stopping gambling:

> It seems like calling your son rather than your daughter was not really a good way to reward yourself for not gambling. Were the conversations with your daughter useful as a reward—did you look forward to them during the days? Are there other people you can also call, who will be supportive?

Mary mentioned an old friend, and Sue suggested that she call her friend that upcoming Saturday if she continued to refrain from gambling.

Sue and Mary then reviewed the triggers homework; Mary had filled it out for only 1 day. On Tuesday, she said she felt depressed and lonely and like nothing mattered. Sue asked her how she managed the feelings without gambling. Mary said she started reading a book that she had read a long time ago and really liked. It helped to distract her. Sue told her that was a great idea for managing feelings and asked Mary if she had more books at home and whether she had a card for the library. Mary confessed that she hadn't been to a library in years, but maybe she'd go next week. Sue said she was happy that Mary brought in the sheet.

She said, "So Tuesday was your hardest day last week? What about the other days—were you tempted to gamble at all on those days?"

Mary said, "No, it was only that day that I thought about it. I know I'm in so much trouble with gambling that I can't do it again."

Sue replied, "That's great that you didn't want to gamble on any other days last week. But did you encounter anything that, in the past, may have led to gambling? What about last weekend? The weekends were often hard for you." Mary said,

> This weekend, I went to my grandson's soccer game, like you suggested, and told my daughter how I had gone a week without gambling. We went out for pizza after the game, and it was fun. My grandson was happy because his team won the game.

Sue responded, "So, by keeping busy and doing things you enjoy, you were not tempted to gamble." Mary said,

> Yes, that helps, but on Monday, I had to go to the unemployment office to try to extend my benefits. I had to wait in line for hours, and I still don't even know what I'm going to do for money. I have to move to a new apartment, because my landlord is throwing me out.

Sue said, "I remember last week you also mentioned these financial concerns and how they often led to gambling in the past. What are your plans for finding a new apartment?"

Mary replied, "Well, I know that gambling isn't going to be the answer. I have an appointment with a lawyer next week. And my son thinks there's a way to restore the unemployment benefits for at least another month."

After stating that they could return to the issue of finances later that session, Sue introduced the functional analysis worksheet. She explained, "This is an exercise that can help you see why you gambled so much. Let's take the example of the day that you passed out in the casino. What was the trigger that led to your going to the casino that day?" Mary thought back:

> You mean why did I go to the casino that day? Well, I had just gotten the eviction notice. It was horrible. I started shaking. I was panicked. I thought about calling my daughter, but I was too embarrassed. I couldn't believe I had gotten into such a jam. I couldn't think of any way out. I thought that if I went to the casino, just for a couple of hours, maybe I'd win, and maybe I could get enough money to give something to my landlord.

Sue wrote this down on the sheet: Under trigger, she wrote "eviction notice." The next column said, "feelings or emotions" and she wrote, "panic, desperation." The third column, which she had filled in earlier, said "trip to casino on May 8th." The fourth column was entitled "Positive Effects of Gambling," and Sue asked Mary what she had hoped to get by gambling that day. Mary quickly said, "Money for rent," and Sue wrote that down. The fifth and last column was labeled "Long-Term Effects of Gambling."

Sue asked, "What was the overall effect of your gambling that day?"

Mary replied, "I stayed for more than a couple of hours—I stayed almost two days. I used the last cash advances on three different credit cards."

So, Sue wrote down, "Lost more money, more debt." Then she showed Mary the visual depiction of the cycle of addiction, where the trigger leads to emotions, which lead to gambling. Gambling offers brief positive effects of hope but results in greater, longer term negative effects, which lead directly to the triggers.

Mary said, "I see what you're saying—that I gamble to get money, but gambling leads to greater debt."

Sue replied, "But, it's not all just about money, Mary. You gamble for other reasons, too."

They did another exercise related to Mary's gambling on another occasion, when she went to the casino out of boredom. They realized that although gambling decreased boredom in the short term, it was also responsible for Mary's loss of friendships and alienation from her family, which resulted in more loneliness in the long-term.

Session 3

After the therapist and client review the prior week's homework and graph of nongambling days, this session is introduced as a method for increasing the client's enjoyment of life. For many gamblers, gambling is considered the only pleasurable activity that they do, or the "only thing I do for myself." People with addictive disorders often decrease time spent doing other recreational activities as the addictive behavior becomes all consuming. Establishing other hobbies or recreational activities may be central to overcoming the problem behavior.

In this session, a "leisure checklist" is presented that contains a list of more than 50 activities and hobbies. The gambler checks ones that he or she once liked to do, or ones he or she might consider trying. The represented activities include ones that are inexpensive or free and ones that can be done solo as well as social activities. The gambler is encouraged to try in the upcoming week several activities he or she has checked. Specifically, other reinforcing activities (e.g., going to the movies, gardening, or playing golf) should be planned for high-risk times (e.g., weekends, payday). Precommitment strategies, such as phoning an old friend from the therapist's office to set a date and time to meet for coffee, are used to increase the probability that a behavior will occur. By trying an array of new activities, the gambler may find some that he or she really enjoys. He or she may also meet new people, nongamblers, while participating in these activities. Development of other reinforcing activities and a social support network may reduce the probability that problem behaviors will recur.

If the patient is amenable to doing homework, he or she is asked to record the pleasurable activities in which he or she engages daily over the next week. These can include both planned events (e.g., going to a movie with a friend) as well as unexpected pleasurable activities (e.g., sitting calmly for 20 minutes, listening to the radio). The gambler may be surprised to see the diversity and number of enjoyable activities that can occur in a day, especially when gambling is not interfering.

Case example continued. When Mary returned to therapy, she had completed the homework exercise from the prior week, doing functional analyses of moods and situations that had been linked to gambling in the past. Mary had still not gambled, and she continued calling her daughter daily and even admitted to her that it was a strategy her therapist had suggested. Sue had Mary graph her nongambling days and congratulated her for her openness with her daughter.

Sue gave Mary the list of leisure activities and asked her to check all those that sounded appealing to her. Mary checked off "sewing, reading, watching sporting events (to which she added "of grandkids"), gardening, spending time with children, arts and crafts, movies, theatre, eating out, journaling, travel, and church." Sue asked Mary to pick at least one of those to do the next week, and Mary said she was going to another one of her grandson's soccer games next Saturday. Sue said that was a great idea. She then asked Mary which of those activities she could do spontaneously, without any preparation. Mary listed, "sewing, reading, gardening, and journaling."

"Do you have the materials that you need at home with you to do those things?" Sue asked.

"Not right now," Mary admitted, "but I could get a cross-stitch pattern if I had some money. I guess I could go to the library to make sure I always had a good book." Sue suggested that she do that on the way home from the session.

Sue then had Mary think about planned events she could do—alone and with others. Mary said she had called an old friend of hers for the past 2 weeks in a row. Her friend invited her for dinner the next Saturday, and Mary accepted. She expressed concern that she didn't have money to buy a nice dessert, as she normally would have done. But then she said that maybe she could bake one. She hadn't baked in years. Sue suggested she add baking to her list of activities to try. The next week, Mary was to record at least one pleasant activity that she did each day.

Session 4

After checking in with the gambler about pleasurable activities from the prior week and completing the gambling chart, the therapist teaches the gambler how to brainstorm new ways of managing triggers when they occur. Types of triggers are reviewed, including expected ones (e.g., driving by gambling locations, meeting fellow gamblers at work or social events, payday) and unexpected ones (e.g., running into a bookie, having an argument at work, seeing a gambling commercial on television). For the most problematic triggers, new methods for dealing with them are brainstormed. These could include finding new routes home to avoid convenience stores that sell lottery tickets, getting rides from others who do not gamble, not carrying cash to and from work, carrying a cell phone and promising to call a supportive friend if tempted to buy a ticket, or buying gasoline only from stations that have no lottery outlets.

Various methods for handling the trigger (in this case, driving by convenience stores that sell lottery tickets) are ranked from most to least likely to change one's mind about gambling. For example, the gambler may recognize that even if he carried no cash with him, he would be easily able to talk a coworker into giving him a couple of dollars if he wanted to buy a lottery ticket. He may also state that it would be impossible to find a route home that avoided all lottery outlets but that he could at least avoid the ones from which he most often purchased tickets.

The ideas for managing the trigger are also classified according to their feasibility. Thus, not having any cash at all and always driving with a friend may be relatively difficult, whereas the other options listed above may all be possible. By thinking of a multitude of possibilities and ranking their probable outcomes and feasibility, the gambler may come across some otherwise-unconsidered options, such as buying gas only with a credit card that does not allow cash advances. In this way, he or she would never go into the convenience store and would purchase gas only at the outside pump. Another solution may be to have the gambler's spouse always purchase the gas, so that he or she need never stop at these stores on the way home.

After analyzing several triggers in this manner, the gambler may have learned to consider a number of possibilities rather than engaging in the automatic behavior of needing gas, going into the store, and "unconsciously" buying several tickets in conjunction with the gasoline. The gambler is also encouraged to keep the session handouts with him or her to review in times of temptation. Many participants in the study (Petry, Stinson, & Grant, manuscript submitted for publication) kept their handouts in their cars or wallets, referring to them as needed. The homework exercise for this session is to analyze at least one gambling trigger each day over the next week and consider various options for handling such a trigger.

Case example continued. Mary canceled her next therapy session, calling just an hour before it was scheduled. She left a message with the receptionist that she wasn't feeling well and needed to take care of some business. Sue was concerned that something was wrong. She called Mary that afternoon, and again the next day, but Mary didn't answer the phone.

Sue finally got in touch with Mary on Monday of the following week. Mary said she wasn't sure if she wanted to continue with therapy, but Sue urged her to come in and talk about what was wrong.

Mary hesitantly came in for her regularly scheduled session that Thursday. When Sue asked her how'd she'd been, Mary started crying. She admitted to having gambled last week. When Sue responded in a nonjudgmental fashion, and thanked her for her honesty, Mary felt relief. Sue brought out the functional analysis form again and said:

> Mary, most gamblers lapse from time to time. It's no reason to be ashamed or to think treatment isn't working. Instead, we can learn from your gambling—what happened this time might tell you something so you can prevent it from happening again.

Sue continued, "What precipitated your gambling last week? Did something specific happen?"

Mary said, "No, nothing at all—not that I can think of. I was going home after a job interview, and I headed in the direction of the casino without thinking."

"You had a job interview," Sue said. "How did that go?"

"It went well," Mary replied:

> They were nice, and it was the same type of work I did before. The pay wasn't as good, but it was something. I even felt good about the interview when I left. I don't know why I went to the casino.

Sue replied, "So you felt things went well, and you hoped this might work out when you left the interview?" Mary nodded. "Is that a feeling that led to your gambling in the past?" asked Sue.

"I guess so," Mary said, "If things went well, I thought I'd do better at the slots. Or, I might want to celebrate a bit. But nothing had gone well for me for so long." Sue said,

> Well, that's interesting. You gamble when things aren't going well, and sometimes when things do go well. Let's think about that more with this week's exercise. It is about ways to handle triggers. We can start with that trigger of things going well, or your most common trigger—concern about finances. Which do you prefer to try first?

Mary said she wanted to talk about financial concerns, and Sue continued, "What are some ways you can deal with financial issues without gambling? Let's write down everything you can think of, even crazy ideas."

Mary laughed, "Well, someone could leave me a million dollars in their will."

"That's a start," said Sue. "What else?" Mary replied,

I could get a job, I could sue my ex-husband, I could ask my son for money. I could move to a cheaper apartment, which I have to do anyway. I could even move in with my daughter. I could file bankruptcy, and I'm discussing that with my lawyer now. I could work two jobs, but I think that would kill me, at my age.

Sue wrote all these ideas down. Then she said,

These are all good, concrete ideas about ways to deal with financial problems. But how about some ideas about ways of managing your feelings about financial problems, rather than solving the problem itself, which is going to take awhile.

"Oh, I see," said Mary, "You mean, whenever I get stressed about my money problems, I could write down all the things I have to be grateful for. Or I could call my daughter, or do something to distract myself?"
"Yes," said Sue,

Those kind of things are important, too. Now, let's rank these from most to least likely to be possible. For example, suing your ex or inheriting a million dollars is unlikely, but what is the likelihood of your doing these other things?

After ranking them on likelihood, Sue said, "Now, think about how well each will actually work in terms of managing your feelings about finances the next time you have concerns. Which do you think will work best, so that you don't gamble when the time comes?"

Mary thought that listing what she has to be thankful for and calling her daughter would work best. Sue then asked about how she handled her slip to gambling in terms of telling her daughter. Mary said she was too embarrassed to call her the evening she gambled, and she canceled the dinner with her friend that weekend because she was ashamed to see her. Sue asked about the remainder of the days in the past week and a half. Had she been calling her daughter and rewarding herself for not gambling? Mary said, "No. I felt bad—like I didn't deserve anything. I only left messages for my daughter last week, saying that I was OK. I called when I knew she'd be working." Sue said, "What about now? Do you think you can be honest with your daughter and tell her that you slipped, but now you're back on track?"

Mary said, "I'll have to think about it."

Session 5

This session focuses on methods of handling cravings and urges to gamble. First, gradual relaxation techniques are practiced. The gambler is asked to close his eyes, become comfortable, and concentrate on one section of his body at a time, starting with his feet and moving upward. As he becomes gradually more relaxed over 10 to 15 minutes, he then is asked to imagine that he has a very strong urge or desire to gamble. He should identify the physical sensations associated with this urge. These often range from an uneasy feeling in the stomach, to sweating hands, or tightness in the shoulders, neck, jaw, or temples. The therapist asks the gambler to verbalize all the sensations he feels when wanting to gamble. In many cases, gamblers do not even recognize such physical feelings as being related to a desire to gamble. The feelings may be associated with other stressors as well, such as interpersonal problems or work and family troubles. Thus, various forms of stress get paired with a desire to gamble and, in time, become automatic. Gambling, at least in the short term, may alleviate these negative feelings. Through this exercise, the gambler may to begin to recognize how external events and internal feelings may trigger gambling urges or cravings, because they create similar adverse sensations.

As the gambler learns to recognize the physical sensations associated with gambling urges, he is also instructed in methods to better manage these feelings. One method is the gradual relaxation technique that initiated this session. Other options are engaging in a distracting activity, such as exercise, or calling a friend and discussing something unrelated to gambling. The gambler is also encouraged to impose a timeframe (15 minutes) during which he commits to weighing the costs and benefits of not gambling before giving in to cravings or urges. Over the next week, the gambler records his urges to gamble as well as any time he experiences the physical sensations noted above. Coping responses to the sensations are also noted.

Case example continued. When Mary returned to therapy the next week, she said she had gone the entire week without gambling, and she and Sue drew a line going up on her graph. Mary did not tell her daughter about the lapse, and said she couldn't imagine telling her and worrying her more. Sue asked her if she had been calling her daughter each day that she didn't gamble, and Mary said she had. She also said she had a second interview with the company and thought she might get the job. Sue was enthusiastic and reminded her that this time she had not gone to the casino after the interview.

Sue then asked Mary if she ever experienced strong urges or cravings to gamble. Mary said, "Not really."

Sue said, "Sometimes gambling, or the anticipation of gambling, can cause physical symptoms, like butterflies in your stomach, or tenseness in your arms, neck or temples."

Mary replied, "I don't know about that. I don't think I feel anything physical from gambling."

"Well," said Sue,

Let's try this exercise. Even if you don't feel physical symptoms from gambling, you can use this when you are stressed about other things. What I want you to do is to sit comfortably in your chair, with your feet on the ground, and your arms relaxed. OK, good. Now close your eyes and first concentrate on your feet. Let your feet and ankles get really relaxed.

Sue continued talking to Mary about relaxing various parts of her body.

Once Mary said that she was very relaxed, Sue continued, "Now imagine that you are driving in the casino parking lot. You drive around and find a parking spot. Can you picture yourself doing this? How are you feeling now as you are walking into the casino?"

Mary responded, "Well, I guess I'm kind of excited. My stomach feels a little funny. I feel like something is about to happen."

"OK, good," said Sue. "Can you describe that feeling in your stomach?"

Mary replied, "It's sort of like excitement, like something good is about to happen and I'm just waiting."

"Let's think now about your choosing a slot machine. Explain your thoughts and how you're feeling in your body."

"I always pick the same machine. It's one near the corridor. If someone is using it, I get one right across from it, and I wait for them to finish. I also watch how they are doing."

"How do you feel when you are waiting for someone to get off that machine?" asked Sue.

"A little irritated. I know it's not my machine. But it's the one I always use," Mary said, and continued, "I will put a little money in another machine while I'm waiting, so the other person doesn't think I'm staring at them. But, I sometimes get anxious and, well, really annoyed, if they are taking too long."

"Describe the physical feelings when you're anxious and waiting to get that machine" Sue instructed.

"My stomach is really upset then. It's almost getting like stomach cramps. And under my nose and eyes, there's pressure there."

Sue asked Mary if she feels those kinds of symptoms other times.

Mary exclaimed, "You know—sometimes I feel like that when I'm upset about other things, too! Like when I'm worried about work, or not having enough money." Sue replied,

That's important that you recognize these physical sensations, Mary, because they are paired with gambling for you. But they are also paired with other things—anger or stress. When you feel like this, you are used to gambling in response to it. Gambling probably makes those feelings go away for you. What you can concentrate on now is finding other ways to manage those feelings rather than gambling.

Mary said, "I see what you're saying. If I feel like this while I'm driving around town, because the traffic is bad or something, it might make me feel like gambling."

"That's right," Sue said. "Now, let's talk about some other ways you can deal with these feelings."

They then discussed various strategies of relaxation and distraction.

Session 6

Because interpersonal conflicts are common triggers for gambling, skills training and role playing for handling interpersonal conflict is included during at least one session. Three interpersonal styles (aggressive, passive, and assertive) are described, especially as related to invitations to gamble, responses to disagreements, or other unique triggers to gambling. The use of "I" statements is practiced, and role-play situations are rehearsed, using personally relevant interpersonal situations that have led to gambling in the past.

For example, a gambler may respond to his wife's "nagging" about his gambling by shouting at her and reminding her that he is the breadwinner in the family. The gambler and therapist can reverse roles, with the gambler playing his wife and the therapist acting as the gambler using a confrontational style. By experiencing his reactions from his wife's perspective, the gambler may gain new insight to his actions and how they affect her. She may be concerned about finances, feel lonely because he's never at home, and be afraid that he is having an affair. The therapist and gambler can role play again, with the therapist (acting as the gambler) using assertive responses, rather than aggressive ones, this time. Thus, the gambler (acting as his wife) may begin the role play "nagging" about his always coming home late. Instead of being reactive, the therapist may state,

> I understand you get worried when I don't get home at the usual time.
> I had a big problem at work today and had to stay late. Next time, I'll
> call you to let you know when I have to stay late.

The gambler may realize that this response is less likely to result in an argument, especially if he keeps his promise to call next time when he is late. The two can then reverse roles, with the gambler practicing assertive, and nonaggressive, responses to common situations. The session concludes with a tracking form to record interpersonal difficulties and responses used to cope with such situations.

Case example continued. When Mary returned for Session 6, she had completed the prior week's homework sheet that involved recording physical sensations associated with gambling or gambling urges. She stated that it helped her better understand some of the strange times when she ended up at the casino rather unexpectedly. Sue said that she was glad it was helpful and then asked Mary to fill in her nongambling graph and inquired about whether she had planned a reward for herself for having attained another week of abstinence. Mary said she had gotten together with her old friend and that they had a good time.

Sue said that this session was going to be related to communicating with others. She remembered that Mary did not have a close relationship with her son and that she was worried about telling her daughter the truth about her gambling, including her recent lapse. She started off by explaining to Mary that there are three types of communication styles: (a) passive (letting other people get in the final word), (b) aggressive (arguing or telling other people off and doing what you need to get your way), and (c) assertive (letting both people speak what they think, but in a respectful way). She said that everybody uses all three styles from time to time, and she asked Mary to describe an instance in which she had used each style. Mary thought for a minute and said that the passive one was easy—that was how she had responded with her father growing up and with her husband throughout most of the marriage. The aggressive one was also easy—she said she sometimes, only about once a year, got in huge arguments with her ex-husband. Mary thought a moment before she could come up with an example of being assertive. Then she said, "When I'm shopping or at a store, sometimes I will be assertive if someone cuts in front of the line with me, or if I got overcharged for something."

Sue said they were good examples and asked Mary to pretend that she was in a store and noticed that she had been overcharged. Sue said that she was going to be the store manager, and Mary should address the issue with her. Mary laughed a little and said, "This is my receipt. I was charged $25, but on the sign it says this item is only $14.95." Sue, playing the manager, said, "Our computer systems are always right. I'm sure you misread the sign." Mary looked shocked momentarily and then said, "Well, maybe I did, but I'd like you to come see it with me. If I read it wrong, that is fine, but if your sign says $14.95, you have to honor the price." Sue said Mary did a good job being assertive and holding her ground. She asked her how it made her feel, when the manager initially dismissed her complaint. Mary said it made her determined.

Sue suggested that they try the same scene, but this time with Mary responding passively to the manager's remark about the computers being correct. They did, and Mary just said, "OK, I'm sorry," when the manager said the computers were always right. Sue asked her how she felt after that, and Mary said she felt disappointed in herself. Sue then suggested that they try the same things relating to triggers of gambling. Mary said she often went to the casino after having received a call from a creditor who was rude on the phone. They first role played Mary's usual reactions to the calls and how not only the calls, but also her own reactions to them, made her feel. Then Sue asked "Can you think of a way to respond assertively to these callers?" Mary said, "I can tell them that they have no right to be calling me. They should speak with my lawyer."

Sue then suggested that Mary consider her relationships with her children. Mary said she could generally be herself with her daughter, but her son brought out the worst in her. Sue reminded her that she had not been honest with her daughter about her gambling, not when she was gambling heavily or after her recent lapse. She suggested that they role play Mary telling her daughter about her trip to the casino a few weeks earlier. They took turns playing each role, and Mary finally admitted that it might make her feel better if she told her daughter about the gambling.

They then discussed her son's reactions. Mary felt he was judgmental and controlling. Sue suggested she consider writing him a letter, describing her gambling, treatment, and plans for the future. Mary said she would consider it and that she would talk with her daughter that day.

Session 7

One session is devoted to better understanding the cognitive biases associated with gambling, such as selectively remembering wins while not giving equal weight to the multitudes of losses experienced (the availability heuristic), overestimating the odds, superstitious behaviors, and the gambler's fallacy. This aspect of therapy is emphasized much more in the more purely cognitive approaches described in chapter 12; in this treatment approach it is given only modest attention. Many gamblers report subjectively that they recognize, at least intellectually, that the odds are against them, but when actually gambling or feeling strong urges to gamble, they may fall prey to these cognitive distortions.

Case example continued. Mary returned the next week, again not having gambled. She had told her daughter about her lapse, and the daughter was very understanding and relieved that Mary was confiding in her. She had started a letter to her son, but she wanted to wait on that. Mary also reported that she got a job—not the one she'd interviewed for earlier, but a new one. She was going to start in 2 weeks. Sue congratulated her, for both her honesty with her daughter and for the new job.

Sue reminded Mary that this was their second-to-last session together and asked her how she was feeling about terminating therapy. Mary said that she felt a lot better now that she had been open with her daughter and, with the new job, she thought she was going to be OK. Sue reminded her of all the progress she had made and how she had learned and practiced a lot of skills on which she could draw in the future. Sue then said that she wanted to talk with Mary about something called *cognitive illusions*, which can trick people into gambling even when they know better.

Sue showed Mary a card that said, "H,H,H,T,H,H" on it. She then took out a penny and said that she had tossed the coin six times and those were the results. She said she was going to throw it again and asked Mary what it was going to land on: heads or tails. Mary said, "I would bet on tails." Sue said, "Tell me why you choose tails." Mary said, "It's easy. You had five heads and only one tails, so you're due for tails." "That's a common cognitive illusion," Sue said. "The truth is that this penny has a 50–50 chance of landing on heads or tails on every toss. It doesn't matter what happened before this toss. Each toss is independent, and prior tosses are irrelevant." She let Mary toss it, and it came up tails. Sue said, "But you see, it could have just as easily been heads."

Sue said, "What do you think this has to do with slot machines?" Mary replied, "When I'm gambling, sometimes I think I can predict when I'm going to win, even though I know I really can't. I also know those machines are programmed to come out with the casino winning." Sue replied,

> Yes, you're right. And every time you pull the lever, you have an equal probability of winning or losing, no matter what machine you use, if the person before you won or lost, or whether your last pull landed on two sevens. Overall, the machines pay back 94 cents for every dollar that you put in.

Mary continued, "And, the more I put in, the more I lose. I know that." Sue said, "Yes, we know that intellectually, but when we're gambling, we get caught up believing that past wins or past sequences, or 'lucky' machines, can predict or signal a big win."

Session 8

The final session is designed to extend the time horizon of the gambler. Although many gamblers learn to manage their current situation and life stressors during their time in treatment, future life events, both positive and negative, may trigger gambling. For example, although retirement, the youngest child going off to college, or receipt of a large disability payment may be considered positive events, they may also result in more free and unstructured time, as well as loneliness or boredom. All of these are common triggers for gambling. Negative life events (e.g., the death of a loved one, a divorce, or being laid off from a job) may also trigger gambling in the future. The gambler is encouraged to discuss possible events over the next 1 to 10 years and to consider how these events may affect future decisions to gamble or not to gamble.

Case example continued. Mary returned for her final session. Sue congratulated her for all her successes. Mary had gained the courage to be totally honest with her daughter and established an open and supportive relationship with her. She landed a new job. She learned a lot about why she gambled, and she had gone for 2½ months gambling only one time. Sue asked Mary to describe what she had felt was most useful, and Mary replied that knowing that she didn't need to be perfect, and could still be accepted, was most important to her.

Sue said that in their final session she wanted Mary to think about the future and how changes, either good or bad, may affect her. She said that sometimes major changes, such as her divorce, can lead to stress or result in her wanting to gamble. Mary said she didn't think she'd ever want to gamble again, and Sue reminded her that it wasn't always *wanting* to gamble that led her to gamble. It's a gradual and insidious process. She had Mary list five good things that she thought may happen to her over the next couple months and up to 10 years later. Mary thought for a moment and wrote, "Start my job, retire, new grandchild, watch grandchildren growing up, and buy a small house." Sue said, "Let's discuss some of these. What if you start your new job, and it isn't what you thought it would be? What if you don't get along with your new boss? How will you handle that?" Mary said,

> Well, I need this job, so I'm going to have to get along at it. I think that if I have problems with him, or with co-workers, I will ask for help early on. I might remember that stuff about using I statements and not let people take advantage of me.

Sue said, "Those are good plans, but also remember that when things happen, they are sudden and sometimes you need to pull back and think of the big picture. What about after you retire? How will you spend your time?" Mary replied,

> I see what you're getting at. I might be tempted to gamble if I stop working, because I'll have so much time on my hands. But, I'm planning on spending it with my family, and getting involved in some volunteer work.

"These are good ideas," Sue remarked. She continued,

> Keep this paper, and you can refer back to it if ever you are tempted to gamble. Remember early on, when I had you write down all you stood to lose by gambling? Keep that with you to refer to. If you are ever tempted to gamble, pull it out, and delay your decision of whether or not to gamble for at least 10 minutes, while you weigh the pros and cons. Now, let's think about some other things that may not be good things, but things that may tempt you to gamble in the next couple of years. What kind of things are you worried about?

Mary admitted,

> I do worry a lot. I worry that I might not like this job, I worry that I won't be able to manage financially. I am still seeing that lawyer, and he recommended bankruptcy, but that means I can't buy a house for at least 7 years. That is depressing. I also worry that something bad may happen to my kids or grandkids. I don't think I could handle that.

"How would you handle that?" asked Sue, "What kind of support systems can you arrange?"

"I'm trying to spend more time with old friends, and other relatives. That helps."

As Mary finished her eighth and final session that day, Sue reminded her of all the progress she had made in the past couple of months. They said their good-byes, and although Mary felt a little sad that the therapy was ending, she also felt that it was time to move ahead with her new life—without gambling. She met a friend for dinner that night, and she started her new job 2 days later. It has now been years since her therapy, and Mary has still not returned to the casino.

Comment. This case description illustrates an example of a middle-aged female gambler and her reactions to the cognitive–behavioral therapy. As with the other case examples, the case report is not evidence of efficacy of the treatment approach; rather, it merely represents an example of how the therapy is delivered and how therapists should relate to patients within the context of the therapy guidelines.

The session handouts and weekly homework assignments are included in Appendixes A, B, and C, and they can be used with individual patients. The handouts are meant to provide some structure to the sessions, but therapists must not adhere too rigorously to the written materials, or patients may feel that they are being treated like students and the therapist as a teacher. Instead, the handouts are used as a springboard to elicit responses and to encourage patients to think about their gambling in a new manner, as illustrated in the case of Mary. Therapists should never ignore or dismiss important items that patients bring to the sessions. Skilled therapists will listen empathically to patients and use examples that patients bring in within the context of the session exercise.

In general, the handouts are filled out within the sessions. Whether the therapist writes in the patient's responses or the patient fills it out (or a mixture of both) is an individual preference of different therapists and different patients. For patients with relatively low levels of education, it may be best to discuss the exercises aloud, with less emphasis on the written materials. This will require that the therapist have extensive familiarity with the exercises. In either case, the handout should be given to the patient at the end of each session. Patients may save them and refer back to them later. The therapy handout can be also be re-created by the therapist after the session as part of the progress note or, if possible, it can be photocopied in the therapist's office at the end of the session. This way, therapists can remember specific issues that were addressed in session, many of which build on exercises in the subsequent sessions.

Financial Problems

In addition to the structured sessions, a section on managing finances and repaying debts is included. Financial concerns of pathological gamblers are often enormous. They necessitate consideration during the treatment process, as financial problems are among the most common triggers. However, most therapists are not skilled in this aspect of treatment. Gamblers can be guided toward some self-directed materials; the National Endowment for Financial Education (2000) published a workbook that can assist with reconciling debt and repayment schedules. In addition, the one used in my study (Petry, Stinson, & Grant, manuscript submitted for publication) is included in Appendix D. Gamblers with debt can also be referred to GA and their pressure-relief sessions (see chap. 8). GA typically recommends that the gambler relinquish all control of finances to a spouse or other person. Referral to GA may be particularly important in cases in which illegal debts and bookies are involved, as GA members tend to have experience with and can offer hope regarding these situations. Other options include referral to consumer credit organizations or bankruptcy lawyers. Although handling finances and gambling-related debt should not become the focal point of therapy, these issues, especially as they relate to managing triggers, cravings, and interpersonal conflict, should be addressed with gamblers who have financial concerns. If financial matters are not given appropriate consideration, the gambler may feel the therapy is not responsive to his or her needs.

Thus, this cognitive–behavioral treatment (Petry, 1998) has a theoretical basis in the behavioral analysis of gambling. It uses methods to rearrange the environment to increase the sources of reinforcement derived from not gambling, enhance the response costs associated with gambling, and alter the timeframes over which decisions are made. This treatment also contains some overlap with cognitive therapy, with one session focused on educating and modifying erroneous cognitions associated with chance events. The treatment uses some traditional cognitive–behavioral exercises adapted from treatment of substance use disorders (functional analysis) and other psychiatric conditions (tracking problem behaviors and response prevention for obsessive–compulsive disorder, examining interpersonal communication for treatment of depression). The treatment is time limited. Although an order for the eight sessions is suggested, sessions can be rearranged to occur earlier or later in the sequence, depending on specific needs of individual patients.

For patients with clear issues with communication, for example, the assertiveness training could come earlier, such as in Session 3, and then reviewed briefly in each subsequent session. If other issues are apparent, the treatment could be extended and adapted to include other aspects of cognitive–behavioral therapy, such as conjoint sessions, anger management, and awareness and management of negative thinking and seemingly irrelevant decisions. Sections of the cognitive–behavioral treatment for substance abusers described by Monti et al. (1989) can readily be adapted for gamblers.

FUTURE RESEARCH

Analyses of data from my study evaluating the efficacy of this cognitive–behavioral therapy in the eight-session format indicate efficacy compared with a real world control condition consisting of referral to GA. A logical next step will be to evaluate whether changes in coping patterns in response to internal and external triggers actually change with treatment. Although cognitive–behavioral therapies are efficacious in treating a number of psychiatric conditions, few studies have assessed how they affect coping strategies. Youth with unstructured free time gamble more often (S. M. Moore & Ohtsuka, 2000), and one study of adult pathological gamblers suggests they have coping skills deficits (McCormick, 1994). However, prospective studies demonstrating treatment-specific changes in coping styles are needed.

Along these lines, few gamblers in the study (less than 30%; Petry, Stinson, & Grant, manuscript submitted for publication) completed the homework assignments. This is a common problem in cognitive–behavioral therapy. Failure to practice the skills is likely to limit adaptations of these techniques in everyday situations. A follow-up study has been evaluating the efficacy of an intervention that reinforces homework completion with small gift certificates (see Petry, 2000a). Although only 40 gamblers have thus far been assigned to this condition, weekly homework compliance has increased markedly, to over 75%. Such a procedure may result in greater compliance, which in turn may be associated with increased understanding of techniques and ultimately reduce gambling in both the short and long term.

A recent randomized study of 40 gamblers (Milton, Crino, Hunt, & Prosser, 2002) suggests that another compliance improvement intervention, consisting of motivational interviewing techniques (see chap. 14), frequent therapist praise for reductions in gambling, and regular letter reminders of sessions can improve outcomes when combined with cognitive–behavioral therapy. Although only 35% of those who received cognitive–behavioral therapy alone completed treatment, 65% of patients in the cognitive–behavioral therapy plus compliance enhancement intervention finished therapy. They also had improved outcomes with respect to a number of gambling variables (decreased money spent and lower scores on the South Oaks Gambling Screen [Lesieur & Blume, 1987]), at least in the short term.

Other issues that need to be addressed include optimal length of treatment and duration of effects. The study described in this chapter allowed for only eight sessions and included evaluations for a 1-year period. Because of natural variations in gambling intensity and problems over time, follow-up evaluations of even longer durations may be informative. As Echeburúa et al. (2000, 2001) have shown, relapse prevention treatment or booster sessions provided on a less than weekly basis may extend beneficial effects of treatments, especially in certain subgroups of patients. However, short-term treatments may be sufficient to reduce gambling in a subset of gamblers. Hand (1998) reported that, of 110 gamblers who attended an initial evaluation and who were followed up at a later time (68% of the original sample), 42 never returned after the intake interview. Of the 42 nontreatment engagers, 64% reported reductions in gambling at the follow-up. Similarly, of the 68 gamblers who came to 5 to 25 sessions of multimodal therapy, 68% reported decreasing gambling. Thus, short durations of treatment, or simply following through on attending an evaluation of one's gambling, may be associated with reduced gambling (see chap. 14).

Group-based treatments may have some benefits over individual therapy (Coman, Evans, & Burrows, 2002), including less expense, enhancement of social skills, opportunities to learn from and practice new behaviors with others, and feedback and support from other group members. Although in my study (Petry, Stinson, & Grant, manuscript submitted for publication) the cognitive–behavioral therapy described above was delivered individually, it is readily adaptable for use in a group format. The relatively poor results of group cognitive therapy in Echeburúa et al.'s (1996) study suggest that perhaps group therapy may not be as beneficial in this population, although in that study the format of delivery was confounded by type of treatment. In Echeburúa et al.'s second study (Echeburúa et al., 2001), group and individual therapy engendered roughly equivalent outcomes. In Ladouceur, Sylvain, et al.'s (2003) recent study, group cognitive therapy was efficacious relative to a wait-list condition, similarly to a study in which they compared individual cognitive therapy with a wait-list condition (Ladouceur et al., 2001).

The goal of therapy is also debated. Typically, abstinence from all forms of gambling is recommended. The rationale for total abstinence is that another form of gambling may become problematic or act as a precipitant to relapse to the primary form of wagering. However, some therapies allow the patient to set a personal goal of reduced, or "controlled" gambling (Dickerson & Weeks, 1979). Some argue that strict abstinence goals may discourage gamblers from seeking treatment and that flexibility may encourage more gamblers to seek and remain in treatment. Alcoholics who begin treatment with a goal of controlled drinking often move toward a goal of abstinence (Hodgins, Leigh, Milne, & Gerrish, 1997). A similar effect may or may not occur with gamblers. Nevertheless, a controlled-gambling option is supported by some data on a small group of gamblers interviewed 2 to 9 years after treatment (McConaghy, Blaszczynski, & Frankova, 1991). At the follow-up, 18 were abstinent, 25 gambled in a manner that did not create problems for them, and 21 gambled problematically. Another report (Blaszczynski, McConaghy, & Frankova, 1991) compared 9 of these abstinent gamblers with 9 intermittently relapsed gamblers, who again achieved abstinence. The two groups did not differ in terms of any indicators of psychosocial stability, but clinical trials comparing treatments with varying treatment goals are necessary.

Pathological gambling co-occurs with a number of psychiatric disorders, as I discussed in chapter 5, but the impact that other conditions have on outcomes of gambling treatment requires further study. The therapy may need to address other symptoms in these cases. One possibility with cognitive–behavioral therapy is to expand the focus, such as examining triggers to substance abuse (or depression) in addition to triggers for gambling. Pharmacological treatments also can be provided for some comorbid disorders, such as depression, anxiety, or obsessive–compulsive disorder. If symptoms of the other disorder abate, gambling may also decrease. Similarly, if gambling stops, symptoms associated with another disorder may also dissipate. Large studies with patients who have comorbid disorders will be necessary to tease out these possibilities.

SUMMARY AND CLINICAL IMPLICATIONS

In this chapter I reviewed studies evaluating cognitive–behavioral therapy for treating pathological gamblers. Studies from Spain, Canada, and Australia were reviewed, as was a recently completed study conducted in the United States. All the data seem to suggest the efficacy of cognitive–behavioral techniques in treating pathological gamblers. In addition, areas for future research were suggested.

The chapter also provided a detailed description of how to deliver cognitive–behavioral therapy as used in my recent treatment study (Petry, Stinson, & Grant, manuscript submitted for publication). A case example illustrated the implementation of the technique. Although the exercises are fairly standardized, they allow for a wide variation in responses, such that the therapy can be individualized for many types of patients. A primary advantage of the technique is that it is time limited; eight sessions are recommended. Although some exercises could be repeated or stretched into two sessions, most patients found the length to be appropriate. In the next chapter I describe an even briefer therapy, one that appears to engender beneficial effects in gamblers with less severe problems and who are less motivated for treatment.

14

BRIEF AND MOTIVATIONAL
INTERVENTIONS

Data reviewed in chapter 8 indicate that only gamblers with the most severe gambling-related problems seek treatment. Some data from the field of alcohol abuse suggest that brief interventions may hold promise for individuals with less severe alcohol problems. In this chapter I describe the rationale for brief interventions as well as some outcome studies that used these techniques with gamblers.

RESEARCH SUPPORT FOR BRIEF AND
MOTIVATIONAL TREATMENT

An extensive cross-cultural literature review suggests that brief interventions, ranging from 5 minutes of simple advice to one to four complete therapy sessions, are more effective than no treatment, and often as effective as more extended treatment, in reducing alcohol problems (Babor, 1994; Bien, Miller, & Tonigan, 1993; Chick, Ritson, Connaughton, & Stewart, 1988). These interventions are especially efficacious and cost-effective for patients with less severe forms of a disorder, such as for problem alcohol users compared with dependent patients (Babor, 1994; Heather, 1989). The nature and content of brief interventions vary across studies, but they can range from advice about the consequences of harmful behavior patterns

257

(e.g., Bien et al., 1993; Chick et al., 1988), to motivational interviewing or enhancement therapy (e.g., W. R. Miller & Rollnick, 2002), to workbooks containing educational materials and skills training (e.g., Apodaca & Miller, 2003).

The small but growing literature on gambling treatment suggests that brief interventions may be useful in reducing gambling. Dickerson, Hinchy, and England (1990) randomly assigned 29 gamblers to a workbook-alone condition or a workbook in conjunction with a single in-depth motivationally based interview. The workbook included cognitive–behavioral and motivational enhancement techniques to reduce ambivalence regarding change. Both groups reported significant reductions in gambling at a 3-month follow-up, but no significant between-groups effects were noted.

Freidenberg, Blanchard, Wulfert, and Malta (2002) provided motivational enhancement plus cognitive–behavioral therapy to nine pathological gamblers who also participated in a study assessing physiological arousal in response to personally relevant gambling situations. The treatment duration ranged from 14 to 20 sessions, with the first several sessions being motivational in nature, followed by an assessment of gambling triggers, corrections of cognitive errors, and finally relapse prevention. All patients decreased gambling, and they showed reductions in physiological arousal in posttreatment relative to pretreatment responses to gambling vignettes. These declines in arousal were correlated with changes in scores on the South Oaks Gambling Screen (Lesieur & Blume, 1987). However, physiological reactivity also decreased from pre- to posttreatment in a control condition, so the specificity of the physiological effect to gambling scenarios is unclear. Furthermore, because this was not a randomized controlled trial, the efficacy of the intervention is unknown.

Robson, Edwards, Smith, and Colman (2002) described 1-year outcomes of problem gamblers participating in an early intervention program. Participants selected their preferred form of treatment: two 1-hour individual sessions plus a workbook, or the workbook plus six weekly 90-minute group sessions. The workbook contained an assessment of gambling, examples of coping strategies, and guidelines for handling relapse. Forty percent chose the individual format, and 60% selected the group format. Of 117 eligible individuals, 38 (32%) never attended or dropped out after one session. Of 79 individuals who participated fully, 60 (or approximately 50% of those eligible) completed the follow-up evaluations 6 and 12 months later. Days gambled decreased from about 9 at pretreatment to 4.4 at posttreatment and remained at about this level throughout a 12-month follow-up period. The amount of money wagered was about $600 (Canadian) per month pretreatment, and this decreased to about $100 per month at the follow-up evaluations. No differences were noted between participants who received therapy in an individual or a group format. Although this study demonstrates the potential effectiveness of the intervention, the lack of a control group and random assignment procedures, as well as failure to use an intent-to-treat analysis, render the results speculative.

Hodgins, Currie, and el-Guebaly (2001) randomly assigned 102 problem gamblers to receive a workbook only, a workbook plus a telephone motivational enhancement intervention, or a wait-list control condition. One month after the intake evaluation, all groups had decreased gambling relative to pretreatment rates, but a significant beneficial effect of the motivational intervention was noted. Days gambled per month decreased from about 10 days at pretreatment to 4 in the workbook-only and workbook-plus-motivational-interview groups, whereas the reduction in the wait-list control group was less impressive (about 6 days per month). The average amount gambled was about $1,500 (Canadian) in the 2 months prior to the intake evaluation. These amounts decreased to about $800 in the wait-list and workbook-only conditions, whereas the workbook-plus-motivational-interview group had a more precipitous reduction, to about $400. A statistically significant beneficial effect of the workbook-plus-motivational-interview condition was noted relative to the wait-list group, but none of the other groups differed from one another. Using Clinical Global Impression (Guy, 1976) scores, 74% of individuals in the combined intervention were judged "improved" versus 61% of those in the workbook condition and 44% of those in the wait-list control condition. Abstinence rates at the 1-month posttreatment interview were 32%, 21%, and 18%, respectively.

These beneficial effects were maintained throughout a 1-year follow-up period, although few between-group differences were statistically significant (Hodgins et al., 2001). Three months after treatment, numbers of days gambled were about 5.5 in the workbook condition and 3.2 in the workbook-plus-motivational-interview condition. This level of gambling did not change greatly over the next 9 months. At the 12-month follow-up, about one third of participants in the combined condition were abstinent, and another 60% were rated as improved. In the workbook-only condition, the rates were 21% and 57%, respectively. Participants were generally satisfied with the treatment, with 45% indicating they were mostly or completely satisfied, 78% reporting they would recommend the program to a friend, and only 7% reporting they were quite dissatisfied. Only 6% indicated that they had not read the workbook at all, and 80% stated that they had read it completely. Note that the natural course of gambling over this interval could not be assessed, because the wait-list control participants received treatment and were excluded from further evaluation.

I am currently also evaluating brief treatments for problem gamblers. More than 170 problem gamblers have been randomly assigned to receive one of four conditions: (a) no treatment (control condition); (b) 5 min of brief advice about reducing gambling (see Exhibit 14.1); (c) a one-session

EXHIBIT 14.1
Brief Advice on Reducing Gambling

HOW DO PEOPLE GAMBLE?

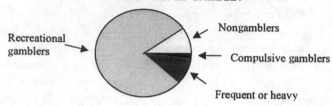

Nongamblers. About 10% of the population does not gamble at all.

Recreational or occasional gamblers. The majority of adults are recreational or occasional gamblers. They usually gamble between 1 and 20 times per year. They never spend more than they intend to spend on gambling and usually gamble as a form of entertainment.

Frequent or heavy gamblers. About 10% of the population gambles frequently or heavily. They usually gamble 2 to 10 times per month and typically spend $50 per month or more on gambling. They do not have severe problems related to their gambling, but sometimes they may gamble more money than they intend, lose track of time while they are gambling, or hide the amount they gamble from others. Other people may tease or criticize them about their gambling. Some of these gamblers will develop compulsive gambling.

Compulsive gamblers. About 1% to 2% of the adult population suffers from compulsive gambling. Compulsive gamblers usually gamble 4 to 30 days per month and spend $500 or more each month on gambling. Compulsive gamblers develop severe financial problems and also frequently experience employment, legal, and family problems related to their gambling. Gambling becomes the focus of their lives. Compulsive gambling can lead to bankruptcy, depression, and even suicide.

What are risk factors for compulsive gambling?

1. People with a history of alcohol or drug abuse are at greater risk of developing gambling problems.
2. People with some psychiatric conditions (obsessive–compulsive disorder, bipolar disorder, attention deficit disorder) may be at greater risk of developing problems with gambling.
3. People who gamble frequently or heavily may be at risk for developing gambling problems.
4. People who report strong superstitious behaviors, such as a preferred slot machine(s), lucky numbers, or a feeling of "knowing" when they are "due" a win may be at greater risk for developing gambling problems.
5. Major life changes (divorce, death in the family, retirement, children leaving home) may be associated with development of gambling problems.

What can you do to reduce the risk of developing gambling problems?

1. Limit the amount of money you spend gambling. If you go to the casino, bring a set amount of cash. Leave your ATM cards, your credit cards, and your checks at home. Never buy more than an allotted number of scratch or lottery tickets. When the money runs out, stop gambling.
2. Limit the amount of time and the days you gamble. If you buy scratch or lottery tickets, don't buy them everyday. If you bet on sports, watch some games without betting on them. If you go to the casino, make a commitment to your partner or a friend to meet them later that day so that you must leave at a reasonable time. When the time runs out, leave whether you are winning or losing.
3. Don't look to gambling as a way of making money. Remember that the house is guaranteed to win in the long run. The more you gamble, the more likely you are to come out behind.
4. Spend time doing other recreational activities. Most problem gamblers gamble as a way of relieving boredom, anxiety, or depression. Find other activities that you enjoy and that fill these needs for you. Join a sports team, take a continuing education class, or volunteer somewhere. Go to a movie, out to dinner, or take a walk. Plan these activities during times you are most likely to gamble.

motivational intervention based on Miller and Rollnick (2002); or (d) a four-session intervention that combines motivational interviewing and cognitive–behavioral therapy, to identify triggers of gambling and teach coping methods for addressing gambling precipitants that are internal (e.g., emotional cues) and external (e.g., interpersonal relationships, avoiding gambling-related people, places, and things). The mean number of days per month gambled at the pretreatment interview was about 15, and this decreased to approximately 12 days a month 1 month after initializing the study. The reduction in days appeared similar across all four conditions, none of which were abstinence oriented. The average amount gambled was approximately $500 per month at pretreatment, and this decreased to about $350 per month in the no-treatment and one-session intervention groups. Participants assigned to the brief-advice and four-session interventions reduced their gambling to about $150 per month. At the 9-month follow-up, gains were maintained in all groups, but participants in the brief-advice and four-session intervention groups further decreased the days they gambled. This study is ongoing, and final results will demonstrate whether the effects are maintained as more participants are enrolled.

An example of how the brief advice is administered is detailed next, using the case of Betty from chapter 2. Betty is a 78-year-old widow, who spent much of her inheritance from her husband at the casinos, yet she did not consider herself to have a gambling problem.

Case example. A health fair was held in Betty's hometown that summer. One booth at the fair paired a behavioral health assessment and brief intervention program in conjunction with blood pressure screening. Betty came to the fair because she was afraid she was having heart problems. As part of the screening, she was also asked about any alcohol use, smoking, and gambling. Although Betty doesn't smoke or drink, she indicated that she goes to the casino about weekly. Her response triggered a more thorough evaluation of Betty's gambling using the South Oaks Gambling Screen, and she scored a 4. The nurse took Betty's blood pressure, which was normal, and she then told her she wanted to talk with her a bit about gambling.

The nurse showed Betty a pie chart (see Exhibit 14.1) of how people gamble and said,

> Betty, you see this chart here? Most people gamble from time to time, and they comprise this group, the bulk of this chart. A small percentage doesn't gamble at all—they are shown here. Then, there is the group of compulsive or severe gamblers—people who lose everything because of gambling. Do you know anyone like that?

Betty acknowledged that she knew of one of her son's friends, who gambled so much that he lost his house, and his wife and children left him. The nurse continued,

That's right. There are people like that, whose gambling is really out of control and they get in serious problems. You are not like those people, but you gamble like this group here [she points to the heavy gambler group on the graph]. You gamble often, and you gamble more than 9 of 10 people. Although you haven't had any major problems from gambling and usually you like it, you have experienced some effects that you don't like. What we *don't* want is for you to move from this group to this group [she points from the heavy to the compulsive gambling section].

Betty replied, "I won't become like that. I only gamble what I can afford." The nurse continued,

You're right. You are not gambling what you don't have, and it's important that your gambling stays that way, right? There are some risk factors that may make it more likely that certain people develop problems with gambling. Let's see if you have any of those. One risk factor is gender— men have more problems with gambling than women, but in older adults, like you, women are just as likely as men to have problems. Another issue is related to how often people gamble. Those who gamble often, weekly or more, are more likely to develop problems with gambling. How often did you say you go to the casino?

Betty, again underestimating her gambling, replied, "I go just about once a week. Sometimes less."
"I see," said the nurse:

Once a week puts you on the brink here. Let's look at some of these other risk factors. People who have a problem with drugs or alcohol themselves are also more likely to have a gambling problem. I know you don't drink and haven't smoked in 30 years, and that's great. But the thing is that you don't even have to have the drinking or smoking problem yourself to be at risk, because gambling, alcohol abuse, and smoking all run in families. Did any of your relatives have problems with gambling or alcohol?"

Betty started getting a little worried. She acknowledged the following:

My father was a drinker. He was drunk most of the time. That's why I got married and left home as soon as I could. I also remember him gambling on cards. My mother was often crying that there never was any money—not even enough to feed us.

The nurse replied,

You have some bad memories from your childhood, and you have done a really good job creating a better life for yourself and your children. But you do seem to have some risk factors for gambling problems, and you don't want your gambling to get out of control. Let's talk about some things you can do to make sure that gambling doesn't progress to that level, like your friend's son and maybe even your father.

At the bottom of this sheet are four things you can do to make sure your gambling doesn't get out of control now or in the future. One thing you can do is that when you do decide to gamble, you bring only as much money with you as you would feel comfortable losing. So, think about it this way. If you're willing to spend $30 on a nice dinner, take that amount of money with you to the casino, and no more. Don't bring your ATM or credit cards, or even checks. Just the amount of cash that you think it's OK to lose.

Betty replied that she had never owned a credit card but that she used an ATM card because of its convenience and didn't like carrying cash anymore. The nurse responded that if she insisted on bringing the ATM card, she could arrange with the bank to limit daily cash withdrawals to $50. That way, she couldn't gamble more than $50 a day. Betty agreed that this would be helpful.

The nurse then said that another thing that she could do was limit the number of days and amount of time she spent at the casino. She inquired as to how often Betty went and how long she stayed. It was at this point that Betty admitted to going to the casino with her neighbor, Kate, and staying throughout her work shift. The nurse asked her if she thought that was a good idea—to stay at the casino for 8 hours at a time. Betty replied that she sometimes was ready to leave but couldn't because she had to wait for Kate's shift to end. The nurse suggested that she not go to the casino with Kate anymore and find alternative transportation. Another idea she suggested was that Betty begin doing some other things rather than just going to the casino.

> You can go to the senior center in town—they have coffee every morning and afternoon, and they will even arrange transportation to and from the senior center and your home. There is also the local library—they have sewing groups and a reading group you could attend from time to time. It's important that gambling isn't the only fun thing that you do—that you also find other hobbies.

Finally, the nurse asked Betty if she ever thought gambling would be a solution to financial problems. Betty looked ashamed momentarily. Then she said, "I am having some problems. And, I do think that if I can win, even just a couple thousand dollars, that I wouldn't ever be a burden to my children." The nurse told Betty,

> That is the trap that gambling brings people into. As you gamble more, you start to feel that you are due a win, or really need a win. Gambling should never be considered a way of making money—I think you already know that in your heart, but once you're at the casino, you can fall

into the trap. I think that if you follow these suggestions, and start limiting the amount of time and money spent gambling, and also start to do some other positive things with your time, you'll find that your life will be even more fulfilling. What do you think? Will you give it a try?

Betty nodded and thanked her.

A year later, Betty's gambling had decreased markedly. She became active at the senior center and started volunteering at a local nursing home. Although she could not regain the money she had lost gambling the previous years, she was able to maintain her independent living. She was going to the casino only about once a month, and never for more than a few hours at a time.

Comment. This example describes how brief advice can be delivered. It was directive, yet interactive; that is, the nurse asked Betty some questions, and she used Betty's responses to individualize the advice. Specific useful knowledge about problem gambling, along with practical advice, was provided in a nonjudgmental and nonthreatening manner. Through the use of these techniques, problem gamblers who do not consider themselves to have a problem, or who are ambivalent about their feelings, may be willing to listen and engage in the discussion, which in turn may result in their reducing their gambling behaviors (see also chap. 8).

SUMMARY AND CLINICAL IMPLICATIONS

Motivational interventions in combination with cognitive–behavioral therapy appear to have some beneficial effects in case reports and descriptive studies. One randomized study showed potential advantages of these techniques relative to a wait-list control condition and workbook-only condition. An ongoing study has found that very brief direct advice may be more beneficial than a no-treatment condition and as efficacious as a more intensive four-session intervention. However, all these reports also suggest that even individuals assigned to wait-list and nontreatment control conditions reduce gambling over the time periods studied. These results appear consistent with those reported in other chapters (e.g., chaps. 7 and 13) and may suggest that gambling is a highly variable phenomenon (Slutske, Jackson, & Sher, 2003). The data may also be interpreted to mean that simply seeking assistance (or participating in an assessment evaluation) may lead to reductions in gambling; that is, individuals may recognize the extent of their gambling during the evaluations and find ways to further decrease their gambling on their own. Future studies evaluating the natural progression of gambling over time and in response to brief interventions are needed. Finally, because few problem and pathological gamblers seek treatment on their own (see chap. 8), efforts are needed to identify problem gamblers in the community and to assess the effects of these interventions in non-help-seeking gamblers. This is especially true for one high-risk group—youth and young adults—as I describe in the next chapter.

V

CONCLUSIONS

15

PREVENTION: FOCUS ON GAMBLING IN YOUTH AND YOUNG ADULTS

Treating gambling in youth may prevent pathological gambling in adulthood, when the problem can manifest with more significant and widespread adverse consequences. Adolescents may deplete their spending money and steal from parents or others to gamble; however, when they become adults, they have even greater access to a variety of sources of money, and they can more easily accumulate large debts via credit card, second mortgages, and so on. Furthermore, adults are more likely to be financially and emotionally supportive of others, such as spouses, children, and older parents. Gambling problems in adolescents typically affect the adolescent, his or her parents, and possibly members of his or her social circle.

As mentioned in earlier chapters, gambling often begins in adolescence, and age is inversely associated with rates of disordered gambling. In this chapter I outline some of the instruments that are used to assess disordered gambling in youth. I review prevalence rates and risk factors for problem and pathological gambling in adolescents and young adults, and I describe the few reports of treating gambling problems in this population. I conclude the chapter with a section on prevention and early intervention strategies that are applicable to both adolescents and adults.

269

SCREENING AND DIAGNOSIS

Several instruments are available to identify youth with gambling problems. One is the South Oaks Gambling Screen—Revised for Adolescents (SOGS–RA; Winters, Stinchfield, & Fulkerson, 1993). This 16-item scale assesses gambling behaviors and problems over the past year. Compared with the adult version, the youth version places less emphasis on sources of borrowing money, as youth presumably have less access to various sources of income and borrowing. Winters et al. (1993) reported satisfactory reliability (.80) as well as construct and concurrent validity of the SOGS–RA, but they noted that it was not adequately tested in girls (see also Poulin, 2002). Wiebe, Cox, and Mehmel (2000) observed that some items had high positive response rates, whereas others were rarely endorsed. Ladouceur, Bouchard, et al. (2000) found that youth, like adults, misinterpret some items.

The Massachusetts Adolescent Gambling Screen (MAGS; Shaffer, LaBrie, Scanlan, & Cummings, 1994) was developed to assess gambling problems among adolescents in the general population. The scale consists of two subscales: (a) the *DSM–IV* subscale, containing 12 questions based on *Diagnostic and Statistical Manual of Mental Disorders* (*DSM–IV*; American Psychiatric Association, 1994) criteria, and (b) the MAGS subscale, consisting of 14 questions about gambling behavior. Of the 14 questions on the MAGS subscale, 7 items correctly classified adolescents in the original sample as either pathological gamblers or nonpathological gamblers. The internal consistencies of the *DSM–IV* subscale and the 7-item MAGS subscale were .87 and .83, respectively.

The *DSM–IV* Adapted for Juveniles (DSM–IV–J; Fisher, 1992) consists of 12 questions that assess nine dimensions of pathological gambling: (a) progression and preoccupation, (b) tolerance, (c) withdrawal and loss of control, (d) escape, (e) chasing, (f) lies and deception, (g) illegal acts, (h) family and academic disruptions, and (i) financial bailouts. It also contains age-appropriate questions about money acquisition and crime involvement, querying about using money from school lunch or bus transportation for gambling and crime involvement such as theft from home and shoplifting, rather than the adult examples of forgery and fraud. The questionnaire was modified for use in nonclinical populations in the Multiple Response—Juvenile version (Fisher, 2000a). This 9-item version uses response options such as "never," "once or twice," "sometimes," or "often" rather than simple "no" or "yes" responses as the original questionnaire does. The internal consistencies of the original and multiple-response versions are .78 and .75, respectively. The scale is represented by one factor that explains approximately one third of the variance in responses, and construct validity is established with respect to differences between regular and nonregular gamblers.

Derevensky and Gupta (2000) compared responses on the SOGS–RA, DSM–IV–J, and the 20 questions of Gamblers Anonymous (GA–20; see chap. 8) in 980 Canadian youth. The questionnaires identified somewhat similar prevalence rates: The DSM–IV–J classified 3.4% of the sample as problem/pathological gamblers, the SOGS–RA classified 5.3% of the sample as problem/pathological gamblers, and the GA–20 classified 6.0% of the sample as problem/pathological gamblers. Thus, the three measures had an adequate agreement identifying gambling problems, but differences were found, especially with regard to estimating gambling problems in girls. The DSM–IV–J identified the lowest percentage of girls (<1%), whereas the GA–20 identified the highest percentage (3.5%).

These instruments assess somewhat different domains of behavior. The SOGS–RA contains questions related to the parental/family and peer contexts, the GA–20 focuses on monetary expenditures, and the DSM–IV–J inventories clinical and behavioral correlates. As with adult instruments, inventories such as the SOGS–RA identify "probable" problem or pathological gambling, whereas the MAGS and the DSM–IV–J are more likely to be used for diagnosis. Controversy exists regarding diagnosing disordered gambling in youth (National Research Council, 1999). DSM symptom counts, for example, may need to be more lenient than among adults (Poulin, 2002; Stinchfield, 2002b), because some criteria that are appropriate for adults may not be applicable to adolescents. As yet, no gold standard exists for identifying disordered gambling in youth.

GAMBLING PARTICIPATION AND PREVALENCE RATES IN YOUTH

Gambling begins at a very early age. Dell, Ruzicka, and Palisi (1981) found that 33% of adult pathological gamblers began betting before 10 years of age, and 47% began betting between ages 11 and 18. Only 14% began gambling after the age of 19. Studies of youth (Griffiths, 1990a, 1990b; Ide-Smith & Lea, 1988; Ladouceur, Boisvert, & Dumont, 1994; Ladouceur, Dubé, & Bujold, 1994) similarly have found that adolescents with gambling problems usually started gambling between the ages of 9 and 11. Although most youth do not gamble problematically, the vast majority gamble on occasion. Studies generally report that between 50% and 90% of adolescents gamble in any given year (e.g., National Research Council, 1999). Problem gamblers often report having parents or other family members who gamble (B. A. Browne & Brown, 1994), and siblings and friends influence youth gambling behavior by providing early gambling opportunities (e.g., Gupta & Derevensky, 1997; Kearny & Drabman, 1992).

Informal games of chance, games of skill, and sports betting are the most popular forms of gambling among U.S. youth (Lesieur & Klein, 1987; Stinchfield, 2000, 2002b). With respect to lottery and scratch tickets, some studies have found high participation rates (Lesieur & Klein, 1987; Gerstein et al., 1999; Westphal, Rush, Stevens, & Johnson, 2000), whereas others have found that less than 20% of youth ever gamble in this manner (Stinchfield, 2000, 2002b). Casino gambling is relatively rare, so long as the legal age is 21 years and the policy is enforced (Stinchfield, 2002b; Westphal et al., 2000).

Although youth and adults gamble on different games (cf. chap. 2), estimates are fairly consistent that gambling problems are more prevalent in youth than in adults (Shaffer & Hall, 1996). In a meta-analysis of 22 studies that included more than 27,700 youth, Shaffer, Hall, and Vander Bilt (1999) estimated that past-year prevalence rates were 5.77% (95% confidence interval: 3.17% to 8.37%) for Level 3 gambling and 14.82% (95% confidence interval: 8.99% to 20.66%) for Level 2 gambling.

Results from studies conducted since Shaffer, Hall, and Vander Bilt's (1999) review are shown in Table 15.1. Level 2 gambling occurred in 3% to 12% of youth sampled, and Level 3 gambling occurred in 2% to 8%. Only 1 of the 18 studies found rates of disordered gambling to be lower in youth than adults. Gerstein et al. (1999) conducted phone interviews of five hundred thirty-four 16- to 17-year-olds. They found only about two thirds had ever gambled, and the rate of combined Level 2–3 gambling was only 1.5%. The low rates in that survey may be related to the use of an instrument that was not geared toward this age group (the National Opinion Research Center DSM Screen for Gambling Problems [National Gambling Impact Study Commission, 1999]; see chap. 3); although similar to some other youth-specific instruments, the instrument was based on DSM criteria.

Studies from other countries generally have found high rates of gambling participation and problems in youth as well. In Australia, S. M. Moore and Ohtsuka (1999) noted that approximately 14% of youth between the ages of 14 and 25 were problem or pathological gamblers. Clarke and Rossen (2000) surveyed 68 first-year college students in New Zealand and asked them to retrospectively recall their gambling prior to 20 years of age. All reported gambling; 18% gambled regularly, 13% gambled problematically, and 5% gambled pathologically. Becoña (1997) and Becoña, Miguez, and Vazquez (2001) have found that fewer Spanish youth than North American youth gamble, but rates of pathological gambling ranged from 2% to 6%, rates comparable to or higher than those of adults in Spain (see chap. 2). A study from Romania revealed clinically significant rates of problem gambling in youth there as well (Lupu et al., 2001). The United Kingdom is

TABLE 15.1
Prevalence Rates of Gambling and Gambling Disorders in Youth

Study	N	Sample	State/province	Instrument	Interval	Any gambling (%)	Level 2 (%)	Level 3 (%)
United States and Canada								
Shaffer et al. (1997)	27,741	22 studies before 1997	Meta-analysis	Primarily SOGS	PY LT	82.3 89.6	14.8 9.5	5.8 3.9
Adalf & Ialomiteanu (2000)	2,371	12–19 years	Ontario	SOGS–RA	PY		7.5	5.8
Carlson & Moore (1998)	997	13–17 years	Oregon	SOGS	PY	66	11.7	4.1
Gerstein et al. (1999)	534	16–17 years	National	NODS	PY	67	1.5-	3.0[a]
Gupta & Derevensky (1998)	817	12–17 years	Montreal	DSM–IV–J	PY	80.2	3.3	4.7
Ladouceur, Boudreault, et al. (1999)	3,426	12–18 years	Quebec	SOGS–RA	PY	87 LT; 77 PY	4.8	2.6
Poulin (2000)	13,549	Grades 7–12	Atlantic provinces	SOGS–RA	PY	53	6.4	2.2
Proimos et al. (1998)	16,948	12–18 years	Vermont	One item	PY		7%[a,b]	
Stinchfield (2000)	78,582	Grades 9–12	Minnesota	Two items	PY	70	2.5-	7.5[b]
Westphal et al. (2000)	12,066	Grades 6–12	Louisiana	SOGS–RA	PY	86 (LT)	10.1	5.8
Australia								
Delfabbro & Thrupp (2003)	505	15–17 years	Adelaide	DSM–IV–J	PY	60	15.3	3.5
S. M. Moore & Ohtsuka (1999)	1,017	14–25 years	Melbourne area	SOGS–R	LT	90	10.8	3.8
New Zealand								
Clarke & Rossen (2000)	68	15–24 years	Massey University	SOGS	LT	100	13.3	4.5
Romania								
Lupu et al. (2001)	500	14–19 years						6.8
Spain								
Becoña (1997)	1,200 2,185	11–16 years 11–16 years	Galicia Gijon	DSM–IV–J DSM–IV–J	PY PY	14.1 6.3	4.9 4.7	2.2 1.6
Becoña et al. (2001)	2,790	14–21 years	Galicia	SOGS–RA	PY	13.9 (LT)	8.2	5.6
United Kingdom								
Fisher (1993)	467	11–16 years	Costal town	DSM–IV–J	PY	99		5.7
Fisher (1999)	9,774	12–15 years	National	DSM–IV–J	PY	50.7		5.6
Wood & Griffiths (1998)	1,195	11–16 years		DSM–IV–J	PY			6.0

Note. PY = past year; SOGS = South Oaks Gambling Screen; LT = lifetime; SOGS– R = South Oaks Gambling Screen Revised; SOGS–RA = South Oaks Gambling Screen Revised for Adolescents; NODS = National Opinion Research Center *DSM* Screen for Gambling Problems; DSM–IV–J = *DSM–IV* Adapted for Juveniles. - = a value between 1.5 and 3.0%.
[a]Combined rates of Level 2–3 gambling. [b]Problem gambling was defined as an affirmative response to a direct question.

the only known country that allows youth to wager legally on fruit machines, which are similar to slot machines, and active research programs related to youth gambling exist in that country (e.g., Fisher, 1993, 1999; Griffiths, 1995). Large proportions of youth gamble on fruit machines as well as on the national lottery, which allows purchases to individuals 16 years of age and older.

Surveys conducted specifically with college students also have demonstrated high rates of gambling problems. Shaffer, Hall, and Vander Bilt's (1999) meta-analysis of 16 studies conducted in 8,918 college students indicated that lifetime rates of Level 3 and Level 2 gambling were 4.67% and 9.28%, respectively. Winters, Bengston, Dorr, and Stinchfield (1998) found that 87% of 1,361 college students in Minnesota had gambled at least once in the prior year. According to South Oaks Gambling Screen (Lesieur & Blume, 1987) criteria, 2.9% were Level 3 gamblers, and 4.4% scored in the Level 2 range. Lesieur et al. (1991) surveyed 1,771 college students in New York, New Jersey, Nevada, Oklahoma, and Texas: Eighty-five percent reported some gambling, with 23% gambling weekly. Fifteen percent were classified as Level 2 gamblers, and an additional 5.5% were Level 3 gamblers. Oster and Knapp (2001) surveyed 894 college students in a setting close to casinos and found that approximately 9% were Level 3 gamblers. Neighbors, Lostutter, Larimer, and Takushi (2002) found that 6.3% of 560 students in Washington state were Level 3 gamblers, and another 9.8% were Level 2 gamblers. International surveys outlined in chapter 4 similarly have found that younger age is associated with increased gambling problems. The evidence is fairly conclusive that gambling behaviors and problems are relatively common among youth and young adults throughout the world.

RISK FACTORS

Risk factors for disordered gambling in adolescents appear to be similar to those reported for adults (see chap. 4). First, gender differences in gambling participation and problems are consistently reported in North American as well as international studies. Carlson and Moore (1998) found that 74% of boys versus 57% of girls had wagered in the past year. Similarly, Proimos, DuRant, Pierce, and Goodman (1998) found rates of gambling participation to be 67% for boys and 39% for girls. Volberg (1998) noted that 80% of boys and 70% of girls had gambled at least once in the past year, but 23% of boys and only 7% of the girls wagered weekly or more often. Stinchfield (2000) found that 15% of 12th-grade boys, compared with 5.2% of 12th-grade girls, felt bad about how much they gamble or what happens when they bet. Becoña (1997) found that male gender was associated with increased rates of pathological gambling in Spain. Wood and Griffiths (1998) found a much higher rate of pathological gambling in boys than girls, but Pugh and Webley (2000) did not find any association between gender and participation in national lottery games in the United Kingdom. In a laboratory study, Derevensky, Gupta, and Della-Cioppa (1996) found that boys wagered larger amounts than girls on blackjack, and they were more likely to view gambling as involving large amounts luck and skill.

A few studies also have noted increased rates of gambling problems among youth who are members of racial and ethnic minority groups. Stinchfield (2000) found that American Indian youth were most likely (29.8%) to report gambling weekly or more often, followed by Mexican American and African American youth (about 22% each). Only about 4% to 5% of Asian American and Caucasian youth reported this frequency of gambling. In Texas, Wallisch (1993) reported that Hispanic youth were more likely than Caucasian youth to gamble weekly or more often. Zitzow (1996) compared gambling patterns in 116 American Indian youth and 115 non-American Indian youth; the American Indians initiated gambling at a younger age, gambled more frequently, and evidenced more gambling problems.

Adolescents who gamble often have co-occurring alcohol and drug use behaviors (e.g., Griffiths & Sutherland, 1998; Ladouceur, Boudreault, Jacques, & Vitaro, 1999b). Jacobs (2000) found that adolescents with gambling problems had twice the rate of tobacco use, and more than twice the rate of alcohol and marijuana use, than their non-problem-gambling peers. Alcohol use was the strongest predictor of problem gambling in adolescents in two studies (Stinchfield, Cassuto, Winters, & Latimer, 1997; Vitaro, Ferland, Jacques, & Ladouceur, 1998). In Westphal et al.'s (2000) sample of 11,736 Louisiana youth, those with a gambling problem were more likely to use illicit drugs, drink alcohol to intoxication, smoke cigarettes, and use marijuana than adolescents without a gambling disorder. In the United Kingdom, Fisher (1993) found that pathological fruit machine gambling correlated with cigarette and alcohol use as well as videogame playing. In a study of adolescents seeking treatment for marijuana abuse, Petry and Tawfik (2001) found that problem gamblers identified in that sample used alcohol and marijuana more often, and participated in more risky sexual behaviors, than their non-problem-gambling counterparts. A prospective study of gambling in 305 adolescents in Minnesota found that substance abuse was associated with both Level 2 and Level 3 gambling (Winters, Stinchfield, Botzet, & Anderson, 2002). Another longitudinal study of 669 adolescents, conducted in Buffalo, New York, similarly found that gambling and alcohol use were linked to other problem behaviors, including illicit drug use, cigarette smoking, and delinquency (Barnes, Welte, Hoffman, & Dintcheff, 1999).

Psychological characteristics such as impulsivity are also risk factors for adolescent gambling disorders. Impulsivity is higher among male problem-gambling adolescents than among male non-problem-gambling adolescents (Vitaro, Arseneault, & Tremblay, 1997). Furthermore, Vitaro, Arseneault, and Tremblay (1999) found that impulsivity among 12- to 14-year-old boys of low socioeconomic status predicted problem gambling in late adolescence, even after controlling for sociodemographic variables, early gambling behavior, aggressiveness, and anxiety. These relationships may be related to the developmental theory that adolescence, especially among boys, is characterized by risk-taking behaviors (Jessor & Jessor, 1977). Given that gambling is a form of risk taking, it is not surprising that this constellation of behaviors co-occurs and that it is more common in boys. Some adolescents may outgrow these behavior patterns on their own, requiring no formal interventions (Slutske, Jackson, & Sher, 2003). Others, however, may benefit from interventions directed toward problem behaviors in general and gambling behaviors in particular.

TREATMENTS

Even fewer adolescents than adults present for gambling treatment (Hardoon, Derevensky, & Gupta, 2003; Stinchfield, 2002b), and little research is available to guide therapy for young problem gamblers. No controlled studies have been conducted of youth, but a couple of reports describe treatments. Ladouceur, Boisvert, and Dumont (1994) used a cognitive–behavioral approach, similar to the one described in chapter 12, with four 17- to 19-year-old male pathological gamblers. The therapy provided education about gambling, addressed irrational cognitions, and included problem-solving training, social skills training, and relapse prevention. After 3 months (M = 17 sessions), reductions in gambling occurred. One month after treatment ended, one of the adolescents relapsed, but all four were abstinent 3 to 6 months later.

Gupta and Derevensky (2000) used an eclectic therapy to treat 36 male adolescent problem gamblers ranging in age from 14 to 21 years who sought treatment in their clinic over a 5-year period. Individual therapy was conducted on a weekly basis and consisted of the following: detailed assessment, acceptance of the problem, identification of key personal problems, development of effective coping skills, modification of free time, involvement of family and social supports, cognitive restructuring, establishment of debt repayment plans, and relapse prevention. Treatment duration varied across the sample from 20 to 50 sessions, and 35 of the gamblers were abstinent at a 1-year follow-up evaluation. They also improved on measures of depression, drug and alcohol use, and peer and family relationships. The high success rate observed in this study may be because all gamblers were actively seeking gambling treatment and possibly were pressured by external sources. However, because no control group was used, the efficacy of the intervention cannot be determined.

PREVENTION AND EARLY INTERVENTION

Because gamblers, regardless of their age, present with a multiplicity of problems, early intervention and prevention may be useful in alleviating problems before they become severe and adversely affect other areas of life. Unfortunately, little empirical research is available to guide prevention strategies for gamblers. Dickson, Derevensky, and Gupta (2002) described a model for youth gambling prevention based on tobacco, alcohol, and illicit drug abuse prevention programs, but no outcome data are available. Similarly, public-awareness campaigns that educate about risks of gambling and teach odds of winning are available on certain Web sites. Some are directed at youth, and others are targeted toward adults.

Only one known study is available that evaluated outcomes following a prevention intervention, but it did not include a control condition. Gaboury and Ladouceur (1993) implemented a three-session gambling prevention program that was based on an alcohol prevention model for youth. It included an overview of gambling, discussion of legal issues, education about odds of winning and myths and beliefs about gambling, and a description of pathological gambling and its consequences. It also included strategies for reducing or controlling gambling. About 300 high school juniors and seniors received the intervention. Although the majority learned about gambling risks and coping skills, the program did not significantly reduce gambling behavior or alter attitudes about gambling 6 months later.

For adults, data regarding the efficacy of prevention strategies are not available. However, in recent years many states in the United States and provinces in Canada have been making increasing efforts toward outreach, prevention, and treatment. Communities that invest in public-awareness campaigns appear to attract fairly large numbers of gamblers into treatment programs (e.g., Stinchfield & Winters, 2001), but still youth are rarely represented in these programs. Staff of gambling help lines indicate that few calls are received from individuals under the age of 18 years (Cuadrado, 1999; Griffiths, Scarfe, & Bellringer, 1999; Potenza et al., 2001; Sullivan, Abbott, McEvoy, & Arroll, 1994). To the extent that outreach efforts can be directed at high-risk populations, more at-risk, problem, and pathological gamblers may benefit from these services. In particular, screening for gambling problems should be the norm, not the exception, among both youth and adults seeking treatment for substance use disorders. Children of adults with substance use disorders should also be targeted for enhanced screening and early intervention and prevention efforts. Among adolescents, such efforts should be directed toward youth experiencing externalizing disorders. Given the high rates of gambling problems in adolescents and young adults, schools and universities should begin to consider including at least some education about problem gambling in health or related curricula. As I noted in chapter 14, even very brief, personalized advice may be useful in alleviating gambling problems in some individuals.

16

CONCLUSIONS

In this book I have provided an up-to-date summary of the etiology, consequences, treatment, and prevention of problem and pathological gambling. Prevalence rates in North American and other countries throughout the world have been described. In general, pathological gambling appears to affect up to 1% to 2% of the general population, and the subthreshold condition, termed *problem* or *Level 2 gambling*, affects another 3% to 4%. In certain high-risk populations, such as substance abusers, youth, minorities, and lower socioeconomic class groups, the percentages are even higher. Different screening and diagnostic instruments for assessing problem and pathological gambling were reviewed, along with their advantages and disadvantages.

Problem and pathological gambling appears to share comorbidity with other psychiatric conditions, most notably substance use disorders, antisocial personality disorder, and affective disorders. Rates of suicidal ideation and attempts are high in pathological gamblers, and therefore these conditions should be evaluated and addressed as necessary during the course of treatment for gambling problems.

Some data suggest that biological abnormalities may predispose individuals to pathological gambling or that repeated, heavy gambling may lead to some physiological changes. However, biology does not entirely explain the condition. Behavioral accounts of pathological gambling also have been reviewed, including the similarities of gambling to other behaviors maintained by intermittent schedules of reinforcement. Cognitive accounts, such as overestimating odds and other heuristics, were described as well, although none of these theories can entirely or adequately explain why some individuals develop problems with gambling whereas others do not.

In addition to data and theory regarding etiology, I have reviewed different treatment strategies. These ranged from pharmacological to psychodynamic, family, behavioral, cognitive, and cognitive–behavioral. Brief and motivational interventions were also described. Case examples depicted individual gamblers, the development and manifestation of their disorder and, in some cases, how they ceased gambling. Although the case examples were not meant to be definitive, or to support the efficacy of any particular technique, they provide personal accounts of gambling of the type typically encountered by treatment providers.

FUTURE DIRECTIONS

As more and more clinicians and researchers become interested in problem and pathological gambling, a better understanding of this disorder will emerge. A number of high-priority issues require attention.

One issue that is imperative to tackle is the development of a reliable and valid instrument for assessing problem and pathological gambling. Although many instruments exist, none have adequately been tested in general populations. In particular, a relatively brief screening instrument would be useful in general population surveys. Such an instrument would also be invaluable for identifying individuals who present for treatment for other psychiatric or medical conditions and who may be at high risk for having a concurrent problem with gambling.

The criteria and presenting problems, especially for the subthreshold condition of Level 2 or problem gambling, need to be clearly articulated. Researchers also need to develop reliable and valid instruments that can gauge changes in gambling behaviors, and other gambling-related problems, over time. These issues become quite complicated because of the many types of gambling that exist and the socioeconomic standing of the individuals engaging in them—that is, frequency of gambling tends to vary by type, such that lottery and scratch ticket gamblers may wager daily, whereas casino gamblers may be more likely to bet less frequently, albeit with the same or even increased intensity. In terms of intensity or amounts spent gambling, wealthy individuals may bet hundreds of dollars a month without experiencing gambling problems, whereas people with lower incomes may suffer difficulties with substantially lower overall rates of wagering. No assessment instruments available at present adequately take such differences into account in assessing gambling and gambling problems. Because no biological indicator of gambling exists, the objective confirmation of the frequency and intensity of gambling behaviors is difficult, if not impossible, to assess.

In addition to developing better instruments for determining diagnoses and severity of gambling problems, identification of unique risk factors and their relation to disordered gambling is needed. Although gender, lower socioeconomic status, age, and minority race are all linked to gambling problems, the manner by which these variables influence gambling is not well delineated. The interactions of these variables with access to gambling opportunities, initiation of gambling, and progression to regular and problematic gambling is of interest. A greater knowledge of biological factors that affect gambling, ranging from genetic to physiological, is also important. More detailed assessment of the comorbidity of disordered gambling with other psychiatric conditions, especially from general population surveys, is needed. Effort also needs to be directed toward evaluating the longitudinal progression of disordered gambling, both when it occurs alone and when it occurs in conjunction with other psychiatric conditions. Subtypes of disordered gamblers may exist, each with specific risk factors and constellations of symptoms, but these subgroups need to be ascertained empirically using large samples derived across many geographical settings.

Consequences of disordered gambling range from financial to psychological, familial, social, legal, employment, and health. Future studies should delineate these issues in specific groups of problem and pathological gamblers, such as substance-abusing, female, young, and older adult gamblers. How these problems relate to gambling cessation and treatment seeking requires investigation. Methods for expanding services and attracting such patients into prevention, early intervention, and treatment services should be explored. Understanding the natural progression of the disorder is of great importance, as a substantial proportion of gamblers stop or reduce gambling on their own without formal intervention. How other psychosocial problems may abate with reductions in gambling is also of interest.

Debate exists regarding the goal of gambling treatment. Whether controlled gambling is feasible and possible to maintain is of import. Some former pathological gamblers report the ability to wager in a nonproblematic manner, at least with some forms of gambling, whereas others maintain that such controlled gambling is impossible to achieve. Variables that distinguish controlled from noncontrolled gamblers need to be identified.

As services for gamblers expand, and more clinicians gain interest and experience treating this disorder, detailed therapy manuals describing efficacious interventions are needed. Comparisons of different types of interventions should be conducted to ascertain whether simple support, or specific techniques, improves outcomes in both the short and long term. If specific interventions, such as cognitive, cognitive–behavioral, or motivational enhancement techniques, decrease gambling, then understanding the mechanisms of their efficacy is also important. Cognitions, coping strategies, or motivation should be measured before, during, and after treatment.

In addition, pharmacological and psychosocial treatments may be integrated. Although the initial testing of pharmacotherapies may require minimal psychosocial interventions to isolate the medication effect, in practice, pharmacotherapy will be provided in conjunction with psychotherapy. How the two treatment approaches interact, and the best combinations of them, should be investigated empirically. Biological techniques such as neuroimaging may also be useful in evaluating how medications and psychotherapy affect information and attention processes in the brain. These techniques may also be useful in understanding the etiology of gambling and problem gambling; that is, some individuals may demonstrate differential activation of brain regions in response to gambling or a gambling win, which in turn may be associated with propensity to develop gambling problems. Successful treatments may reverse these deficits.

Because compliance with mental health treatments is generally poor even among people who seek treatment, methods for improving treatment initiation and engagement are needed. These may vary across different subgroups such that youth and older adults may benefit from tailored interventions, as may ethnic or racial minorities. Finally, an examination of predictors of response to therapies is needed. Gamblers with some characteristics may respond very well to brief interventions, whereas others may need more extensive or specific support that modifies erroneous cognitions, decreases concomitant psychiatric symptoms, or enhances coping mechanisms. Understanding not just the efficacy but also the mechanisms of action of these various techniques may generate further hypotheses regarding the etiology of the condition and may lead to further improvement of therapies, with the ultimate goal of enhancing long-term outcomes.

It is clear that research in pathological gambling is expanding. As the field grows, these and other issues will be addressed. Psychological, sociological, historical, economic, and legal fields ultimately may converge to provide guidelines and assistance to improve the quality of life for those who gamble heavily as well as for their loved ones.

APPENDIX A
Tracking Your Progress

WEEKS 1–8:

TRACKING YOUR PROGRESS

AND REWARDING YOURSELF

Track your progress!
Weeks 1–8

On the last page of this appendix, you will find a graph. We will teach you how to use this graph to track your progress and to reward yourself for not gambling.

1. Tracking progress:

Starting on the far left of the graph, draw a diagonal line going upward like this ⁄ for each day that you don't gamble. If you ever have a lapse and gamble, you draw a horizontal line for each gambling day, like this — . Once you stop gambling, you continue drawing diagonal lines again, going upward toward the top of the page. An example is shown below.

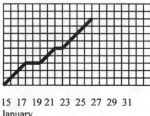

This sample shows 3 days of nongambling between Jan. 15–17, then, a 2-day lapse (Jan 18 and 19). This lapse is followed by 2 days of abstinence, a 1-day lapse, and then 4 days of nongambling.

15 17 19 21 23 25 27 29 31
January

⟵ Date

The point of this exercise is for you to get as far up to the top of the page as you can. Each small step toward the top of the page indicates days of nongambling.

By putting all your nongambling days together onto one sheet, you will see how much progress you have made. As you are doing this, the bottom of the graph reminds you of the exercises and skills you are learning and practicing each week. Go to the last page of this appendix to see your chart. Fill in the dates and the exercises you complete each week.

2. Rewarding yourself!

When learning to stop gambling, it can be helpful to reward yourself for your progress. For example, some people decide that for each day they don't gamble, they will allow themselves something special — like dessert, a relaxing bath, or an hour of television. Other people make a contract with a loved one; for each day they don't gamble, their spouse gives them a kiss before going to bed.

It doesn't matter what the reward is, just as long as it is something that you like and something that you will NOT give yourself (or allow yourself to do) if you do gamble. So, don't reward yourself with dinner or breakfast for not gambling, because eating is something you need to do. But special foods or a meal at a favorite restaurant are good ideas for rewards.

Make a contract with yourself below.

For my first day of abstinence, I will give myself:_____

Remember to reward yourself tonight if you don't gamble today!

You may want to choose the same reward for each day you don't gamble, or you may want to vary the rewards over time.

Other small rewards I can give myself for not gambling each day:
_____
_____
_____
_____

Special rewards should be made for longer periods of abstinence. For example, have a big reward planned each time you successfully refrain from gambling for an entire week. This big reward could be a special dinner out, a long walk in the woods, an evening at the movies, or a new CD. For 1 month of abstinence, you may plan to reward yourself with a very special reward, like a weekend ski trip.

For my first full week
of abstinence, I will
give myself:

_____
_____

Date first week of
abstinence achieved:

_____

Remember, you can easily see your first full week of nongambling by counting seven consecutive lines going up on your nongambling chart.

After you have achieved your first week of nongambling, decide upon the rewards you will give yourself for other full weeks of nongambling. You may want to decide on these rewards early on, or you may want to find new rewards as you go along.

For my 2nd week of nongambling, I will give myself:_____

For my 3rd week of nongambling, I will give myself:_____

For my 4th week of nongambling, I will give myself:_____

For my 5th week of nongambling, I will give myself:_____

For my 6th week of nongambling, I will give myself:_____

For my 7th week of nongambling, I will give myself:_____

For my 8th week of nongambling, I will give myself:_____

Days of Abstinence

Week

Week

Week

Week

Week

Week

Week

Week

Week

Week

APPENDIX B
Session Handouts[1]

[1] Many of these handouts were adapted from *Treating Alcohol Dependence: A Coping Skills Guide*, by P. M. Monti, D. B. Abrams, R. K. Kadden, and N. L. Cooney, 1989, New York: Guilford Press. Copyright 1989 by Guilford Press. Adapted with permission.

WEEK 1: WELCOME!

You have just taken your first steps toward regaining control of your life!

Compulsive gambling affects up to 4 million Americans.

Approximately 80% of the population gambles at least occasionally, and up to 5% of the adult population are probable or potential compulsive gamblers.

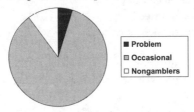

Compulsive gambling is related to a number of serious problems.

List the worst things that have happened to you as a result of your gambling.

1. _____
2. _____
3. _____
4. _____
5. _____

Problem gambling can make you feel overwhelmed. But by learning to take control of your problem, you will feel much better about yourself. List 5 positive things that can happen if you learn to stop gambling.

1. _____
2. _____
3. _____
4. _____
5. _____

Discovering Triggers of Your Gambling

Compulsive gamblers have situations in which they are more likely to gamble. These are called "triggers." Gambling is often triggered by places, people, events, times, and emotions.

List <u>places</u> where you are likely to gamble:

List <u>people</u> with whom you are likely to gamble:

List <u>times or days</u> when you are likely to gamble:

List <u>activities</u> that make it likely that you will gamble:

Feelings and emotions can also trigger gambling. Are you likely to gamble when (check all that apply):

_____ You've had a tense or bad day?
_____ You are anxious or worried?
_____ You feel you've been taken advantage of?
_____ You are bored?
_____ You are in a social situation?
_____ You feel bad about yourself or guilty?
_____ You are depressed?
_____ You want to feel energized or "high?"

Other feelings that trigger gambling for you:

_____
_____
_____
_____

Not all situations, feelings, and people trigger gambling. It is important that you recognize when you are unlikely to gamble.

List the places where you are <u>unlikely</u> to gamble:

List the people with whom you are <u>unlikely</u> to gamble:

List the times or days when you are <u>unlikely</u> to gamble:

List the activities that you engage in when you are <u>unlikely</u> to gamble:

Throughout the next week, you should try to spend time in places where, and with people whom, you are least likely to gamble. You should avoid those people and places where you are most likely to gamble.

For example, you're probably not likely to gamble if you go fishing.

WEEK 2: FUNCTIONAL ANALYSIS: UNDERSTANDING AND TAKING CONTROL OF YOUR BEHAVIOR

Functional Analysis

Gambling is a learned habit. However, learned habits can be unlearned. Identifying the immediate causes and long-term consequences of your gambling may help you stop gambling.

The situations around us can have powerful control over our behavior. Some situations that can influence gambling were discussed last week. These triggers may include:

- *people you are with*
- *places you happen to be*
- *the time and the day*
- *how much money you have*
- *how much alcohol you've consumed*
- *how you are feeling*

List your top triggers for gambling:

1. _____
2. _____
3. _____
4. _____
5. _____

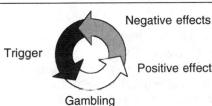

Trigger — Negative effects — Positive effects — Gambling

Gambling is one behavior that can occur following a trigger. If a person responds to a recurrent trigger by gambling, then a habit will develop. Each time that trigger occurs, the person will be more likely to gamble. A common example of this is a family argument. If you respond to arguments by going to the casino, then eventually you may find yourself at the casino after every argument (or even in anticipation of an argument) without even stopping to think. Once gambling becomes "automatic," you lose confidence in your ability to handle the situation without gambling.

The reason you gamble is that it has some positive consequences. Gambling may take your mind off the argument and help you relax. You may also think that the argument may be avoided if you win big this time. Gambling may help you feel energized or less depressed.

List <u>positive</u> effects you experience from gambling.

1. _____
2. _____
3. _____
4. _____
5. _____

The positive effects usually are experienced soon after you start gambling and last only while you are gambling. Once you've finished, you probably experience negative effects from gambling. You may have lost a lot of money, you may feel guilty for having gambled, and your argument may be even worse than before!

List the <u>negative</u> effects of gambling—those that brought you into treatment.

1. _____
2. _____
3. _____
4. _____
5. _____

Note that these negative effects from gambling do not necessarily occur right after or while you are gambling. Many of them take months or years to develop. That is why it is easy to fall into the trap of gambling—the short-term effects are mostly positive, and the negative effects are delayed. It is hard to trace these delayed negative effects to a single instance of gambling.

Putting it all together . . .

- Think back to the last time you gambled. List that gambling episode under the "Behavior" column.
- Immediately prior to that gambling episode, what were you thinking and feeling? Were you tense, irritable, or feeling lucky? List your feelings under the "Thoughts and Feelings" column.
- Now, think about the events that led to your feelings. Were you feeling lucky because you just found a $10 bill on the ground? Were you irritable because you just got a call from a creditor?
- List the positive effects you experienced from gambling during your last gambling experience. Did it make you feel in control for a while; did it help you forget about your troubles for a time?
- Finally, list the negative consequences of that gambling episode. Did you lose a lot of money; did you feel guilty?

<u>Trigger</u> → <u>Thoughts and Feelings</u> → <u>Behavior</u> → <u>Positive Consequences</u> <u>Negative Consequences</u>

Now, try this exercise for a trigger **you expect to encounter** in the upcoming week, imagining the positive and negative consequences of gambling in response to that trigger.

<u>Trigger</u> → <u>Thoughts and Feelings</u> → <u>Behavior</u> → <u>Positive Consequences</u> <u>Negative Consequences</u>

IMPORTANT: If you have a lapse, you should do a functional analysis to try to understand your behavior.

WEEK 3: INCREASING PLEASANT ACTIVITIES

The Need for Pleasant Activities

The number of pleasant activities in a person's life is related to how often they experience positive feelings. The fewer pleasant activities, the greater the chance of loneliness and depression. Many people find there is a void in their lives after they quit gambling. In fact, simple boredom is a common reason people gamble.

Many people spend most of their time doing things that are not rewarding in and of themselves, but things that simply must be done. Grocery shopping, filling the car with gas, and many job activities fall into the category of "shoulds".

 We do most things because we should. We need to do something every day simply because we want to.

Complete the pleasant events form, checking off items that seem like they might be fun.

- ❏ Being in the country.
- ❏ Talking about sports.
- ❏ Meeting new people.
- ❏ Going to a rock concert.
- ❏ Playing baseball or softball.
- ❏ Planning trips or vacations.
- ❏ Being at the beach.
- ❏ Doing art work or crafts.
- ❏ Rock climbing or mountaineering.
- ❏ Reading the Scriptures or other sacred works.
- ❏ Playing golf.
- ❏ Rearranging/redecorating a room.
- ❏ Going to a sports event.
- ❏ Reading "How To Do It" books.
- ❏ Reading stories, novels, poems.
- ❏ Going to lectures, hearing speakers.
- ❏ Playing musical instruments.
- ❏ Boating (canoeing, sailing, motorboats).
- ❏ Camping.
- ❏ Working in politics.
- ❏ Working on machines (cars, bikes, etc.).
- ❏ Solving problems, puzzles, crosswords.
- ❏ Having lunch with friends or colleagues.
- ❏ Playing tennis.
- ❏ Taking a relaxing, hot shower.
- ❏ Woodworking, carpentry.
- ❏ Writing short stories, novels, plays.

- ❏ Exploring (hiking, cave exploring).
- ❏ Having a frank and open conversation.
- ❏ Singing in a group.
- ❏ Going to church functions.
- ❏ Going to service or social club meetings.
- ❏ Going to business meetings/ conventions.
- ❏ Snow skiing.
- ❏ Acting.
- ❏ Being with friends.
- ❏ Being in a big city.
- ❏ Playing pool or billiards.
- ❏ Being with children.
- ❏ Playing chess or checkers.
- ❏ Designing or crafting.
- ❏ Visiting people who are sick or shut in.
- ❏ Bowling.
- ❏ Gardening.
- ❏ Dancing.
- ❏ Sitting in the sun.
- ❏ Riding a motorcycle.
- ❏ Just sitting and thinking.
- ❏ Going to fairs, carnivals, amusement parks.
- ❏ Talking about philosophy, religion, politics.

- ❏ Having friends come visit.
- ❏ Playing in a sports competition.
- ❏ Getting massages, backrubs.
- ❏ Going on outings (park, picnic, barbeque).
- ❏ Photography.
- ❏ Gathering objects (shells, leaves, flowers).
- ❏ Helping someone.
- ❏ Being in the mountains.
- ❏ Meeting new people.
- ❏ Eating good meals.
- ❏ Wrestling or boxing.
- ❏ Hunting or target shooting.
- ❏ Going to a museum or exhibit.
- ❏ Going to a health club.
- ❏ Being with my family.
- ❏ Horseback riding.
- ❏ Talking on the phone.
- ❏ Going to movies.
- ❏ Cooking.
- ❏ Coaching someone.
- ❏ Writing in a diary.
- ❏ Playing football.
- ❏ Meditating, doing yoga.
- ❏ Playing board games (Monopoly, Scrabble).
- ❏ Reading the newspaper or magazines.
- ❏ Swimming.
- ❏ Running, jogging.
- ❏ Listening to music.
- ❏ Knitting, crocheting, needlework.
- ❏ Going to the library.
- ❏ Watching people.
- ❏ Repairing things.
- ❏ Bicycling.
- ❏ Writing letters, cards, notes.
- ❏ Caring for houseplants.
- ❏ Taking a walk.

My Top-Ten Favorite Activities

1. _____
2. _____
3. _____
4. _____
5. _____
6. _____
7. _____
8. _____
9. _____
10. _____

Some of these activities can be done on the spur of the moment, while others are better as planned activities. List some for each category.

Spontaneous	Planned
1. _____	1. _____
2. _____	2. _____
3. _____	3. _____
4. _____	4. _____

Some of these things you've chosen can be done alone, some with friends or family, some maybe even with your dog. Identify people who may enjoy doing some of these activities with you.

_____

_____

_____

Substitute Pleasant Activities for High-Risk Situations

Having fun will also help you get through high-risk situations. Here are some specific high-risk times and pleasant alternatives that can be done instead of gambling.

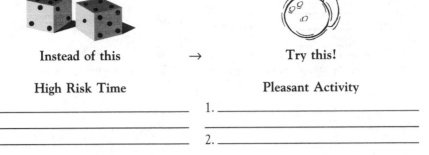

Instead of this → **Try this!**

High Risk Time	Pleasant Activity
1. _____	1. _____
2. _____	2. _____
3. _____	3. _____
4. _____	4. _____
5. _____	5. _____

Whenever you encounter a high-risk situation in the upcoming weeks, **plan to do a pleasant activity instead!**

WEEK 4: SELF-MANAGEMENT PLANNING

Now that you've learned to identify the antecedents (triggers) and consequences of your gambling, you can effectively learn to deal with these triggers.

There are four basic ways of handling triggers so that they will not lead to gambling.

1. You can <u>avoid</u> your triggers.

   - *You can take a different route home so that you don't pass the store where you used to buy lottery tickets.*
   - *You can choose not to go to bars where you used to bet.*
   - *You can choose not to go to places where your gambling friends hang out.*

What are some other ways you can avoid your triggers?

_____

_____

_____

_____

_____

_____

2. You can <u>actively rearrange your environment</u> so that you will be less likely to encounter your triggers.

   - *You can throw away all your old gambling paraphernalia (ticket stubs, bookie numbers, lucky rabbit's foot).*
   - *You can not carry money with you when you know you'll be passing risky places.*

List some other ways you can rearrange your environment so that you will be less likely to gamble.

_____

_____

_____

_____

3. You can be prepared! By developing <u>new coping methods</u>, you will be less likely to gamble when you do encounter a trigger.

   - *If you find extra cash in your pocket, plan to give it to your partner, rather than spend it on a bet.*
   - *If you get into an argument, go to the gym, rather than a casino.*
   - *If you get a call from a creditor, have a realistic plan to pay him back and make your first payment (even if a small one).*

List some other plans you can have for when you encounter a trigger.

_____

_____

_____

_____

Hint: Some of these plans may include substituting pleasant activities.

4. You can <u>keep completing these exercises</u>!

  ▪ By *learning* more about your problems, you can learn to <u>deal</u> with them.

Small steps, if taken consistently,

can lead to big changes!

<h2 align="center">Self-Management Planning</h2>

▪ Select a trigger that has led to gambling recently or a trigger that you expect to encounter in the near future.

▪ List possible ways of handling that trigger. All possibilities, no matter how simple, complex, or crazy should be included.

▪ Now, write down <u>all</u> the positive and negative consequences of each proposed strategy. Include all you can think of.

▪ Write down how difficult it would be to carry out that strategy on a scale of 1 (very easy) to 10 (impossible).

▪ After considering all the potential strategies, consequences, and perceived difficulty, select the best strategy.

Trigger: _____

Strategies (brainstorm)	Positive Consequences	Negative Consequences	Difficulty (1–10)
1.			
2.			
3.			
4.			

Best strategy: _____

Trigger: _____

Strategies (brainstorm)	Positive Consequences	Negative Consequences	Difficulty (1–10)
1.			
2.			
3.			
4.			

Best strategy: _____

WEEK 5: COPING WITH CRAVINGS AND URGES TO GAMBLE

Urges or cravings to gamble are normal among people giving up gambling. The craving may be uncomfortable, but it is a very common experience.

Urges to gamble can be triggered by things in your environment (hearing the sports on the news), your emotions and feelings (feeling lucky or stressed), or physical sensations (anxiety, tightness in your stomach, sweaty palms).

However, cravings and urges are time limited. They usually peak in a few minutes, and then die down, like a wave.

Urges become less frequent and less intense as you learn how to cope with them. The easiest ways to deal with cravings and urges are to try to <u>avoid them</u>.

When urges do occur, however, you must find a way to cope with them. List some ways you have handled your cravings so far:

1. _____
2. _____
3. _____
4. _____
5. _____

Other ways to cope with cravings are to do as follows:

(1) Get involved in some distracting activity. Reading, going to a movie, and exercising are some good examples of distracting activities. Once you get interested in something else, you'll find the urges drift away.

(2) Talk it through! Talk to friends or family about craving when it does occur. Talking can help relieve the feeling, and can restore honesty in your relationship.

(3) Learn to Urge Surf!

Relax! Sit down in a chair, take deep breaths, and focus your attention inward. Notice where in your body you feel the urges. Focus on that area. Notice the exact sensations. Do you feel hot, cold, tingly or numb? How large an area is involved?

Where do you feel your cravings?_____

_____

Focus, one at a time, on each area of your body that feels the urge. Pay attention to changes that occur. Experience the craving in a new way. If you practice urge surfing, you will become familiar with your cravings and learn how to ride them out naturally.

(4) Challenge and change your thoughts! When experiencing a craving, most people only remember the positive effects of gambling. Each time you experience an urge, remind yourself of all the <u>negative</u> consequences of gambling. Remember why it really WON'T make you feel better if you "make just one bet."

Talk constructively!

- What's the evidence that if you don't gamble in 10 minutes you will die?
- What's so awful about experiencing an urge? They are normal, and they pass.

Make a list of your craving triggers:

_____

_____

_____

Circle those that you can avoid, or those that you can reduce your exposure to.

For those that are not circled (e.g., those that are "uncontrollable,"), develop a <u>craving plan</u>. Using the strategies described, pick two or three ways you can cope with each of those cravings when they occur.

Craving-trigger #1: _____

Coping strategies:

1. _____
2. _____
3. _____

Craving-trigger #2: _____

Coping strategies:

1. _____
2. _____
3. _____

Craving-trigger #3: _____

Coping strategies:

1. _____
2. _____
3. _____

Craving-trigger #4: _____

Coping strategies:

1. _____
2. _____
3. _____

WEEK 6: ASSERTIVENESS TRAINING AND GAMBLING REFUSAL SKILLS

Last week, you learned new ways to cope with triggers. These included avoiding them, rearranging your environment, and planning new strategies. This week, we will focus on a new method of coping with situations that may lead to gambling—being assertive.

Assertiveness skills are important for developing positive communication with others. Assertive responses can help you gain and stay in control of situations that previously produced anger, frustration, or anxiety. These adverse responses often lead to gambling.

People typically use three styles:

1. <u>Passive responses</u> involve giving in when conflicts arise. Passive people tend not to express their thoughts or feelings, and this response style can lead to anxiety, anger, and depression.

2. <u>Aggressive responses</u> involve doing what one wants, regardless of needs or wants of others. Aggressive people may often get what they want, but in the long run, they are often left out and may feel isolated.

3. <u>Assertive responses</u> involve expressing opinions, feelings, and wants. Assertive people avoid threats or negative statements, and ask for input and suggestions from others. Assertive people are able to say NO when necessary (e.g., when someone asks them to make a bet), but they do so in a way that makes them feel good about their decisions.

Below are a number of suggestions for acting assertively.

1. Clearly express your needs and wants.
2. Tell the other person why you want it.
3. Balance the negative with the positive. If you have to say something critical, say something positive first.
4. Use "I" statements. Say, "<u>I</u> am angry because <u>I</u> feel no one cares about my needs," not "<u>You</u> make me feel awful."
5. Try not to use "you" statements. These can make the other person act defensively.
6. Acknowledge the other person's rights and feelings in the matter.
7. Be strong and specific in describing your needs and feelings. Instead of saying, "I don't feel much like gambling today," say, "No, I don't want to gamble."
8. Speak firmly. Say it with authority, but not hostility.
9. Respond promptly to others' requests. This will demonstrate your certainty.
10. Make good eye contact; look at the person while you speak and while you listen. This shows that you are certain.
11. Body gestures and facial expressions should be consistent with your message. For example, don't smile if you're angry.

Now, think about situations that may arise in the next week in which you may benefit by acting assertively.

1. _____
2. _____
3. _____

What ways can you respond assertively in these situations? Use the guidelines from the previous page.

Practice assertive responding in these situations with your therapist, partner, a friend, or even in front of the mirror. Note how you feel by responding assertively.

Most gamblers who are trying to quit continue to have some contact, either planned or unexpected, with friends or acquaintances who are active gamblers.

Turning down opportunities to gamble, or social invitations that are likely to lead to gambling, is much more difficult than most people think. The ability to refuse to gamble is a special case of assertiveness.

Effective Refusal Skills

1. NO should be the FIRST thing you say.
   - No, thank you.
   - No, I'm not gambling anymore; it's causing me too many problems.
   - No, I have a gambling problem, so I'm not gambling anymore.

2. Tell the person offering you an opportunity to gamble <u>not to ask you now or in the future</u>. Don't say things like "maybe later," "I have to get home," or "I don't have any money." These responses just make it more likely that he or she will ask you again.

3. Body language is important. Your eye contact, expression, and tone should indicate that you are serious.

4. Change the conversation to a new topic.

5. Offer an alternative if you want to do something else with that person. Be sure the alternative is something incompatible with gambling (go to the movies, play basketball, or go out to dinner—but NOT at the casino).

Pick three <u>specific</u> situations in which you have had or may have difficulty refusing a gambling opportunity:

1. _____
2. _____
3. _____

Practice gambling refusal skills in these situations with your therapist.

Reverse roles, and now you offer the gambling opportunity.

What strategies seem most effective:

1. _____
2. _____
3. _____

The more you practice, the easier and more natural assertive responding will become!

WEEK 7: CHANGING IRRATIONAL THINKING

What are the odds of winning $1 million (or more) in the lottery?

Your response: 1 in _____

This week, we will explore reasons why people gamble despite the odds of winning.
One reason people gamble is they **overestimate the odds of winning.** Did you?
The odds of

Winning a $1 million lottery are 1 in 13,000,000
Being killed in a car accident are 1 in 53,000
Choking to death are 1 in 68,000
Being struck by lightning are 1 in 2,000,000

*Your chances of being struck by lightning are greater than
your chances of winning big in the lottery!*

Another reason people gamble is that they encountered a big win at some point.
The big win led to feelings of excitement, control, and empowerment. These positive
feelings keep the gambler coming back. The anticipation of another win is alluring.
Gamblers often think as follows:

- This is my lucky ticket.
- This is going to be THE lucky deck.
- This is MY machine.

Sports bettors and lottery players also often develop intricate strategies for predicting
winning teams or numbers.

List <u>self-deceptions</u> you had when gambling:

1. _____
2. _____
3. _____
4. _____
5. _____

6. _____

7. _____

Once you stop gambling, you may realize many of these strategies are simply that—strategies. But why did you have these self-deceptions?

Let's try another example:

Kim is the mother of 7 girls, and she is again pregnant. She is hoping desperately for a son, and the odds are in her favor! While Kim is in labor, she can just feel that this one will finally be the boy. However, the baby turns out to be a girl. Although she is pleased that they baby is healthy, Kim thinks to herself, "How can this be? Even the doctors told me that the chances of this baby being a girl are less than 1 in 200."

What is wrong with Kim's and her doctors' predictions about the gender of the new baby? _____

_____

What is wrong with Kim's doctor's prediction is that her chances of having a girl or a boy are always 1 in 2 for each child she has. Prior to her having had a first child, the odds of having 8 girls are 1 in 256 ($1/2 \times 1/2 \times 1/2 \times 1/2 \times 1/2 \times 1/2 \times 1/2 \times 1/2$). But the gender of her previous children has no bearing on the gender of future babies. This example is called the "**gambler's fallacy.**" It means that past performance (past girls) do not affect the probability of wins (or boys) now or in the future.

Gamblers often think that past performances predict future events. When you were on a "lucky streak," did you feel more wins were virtually guaranteed? If so, place "good luck" on your deception chart.

Gamblers also think that if they've experienced a string of losses, they must be "due" a win. Did you also feel this way? If so, place "bad luck" on your chart.

But stop and think about this. How can both wins and losses signal winning? How can either losses or wins signal winning? Chances of winning have nothing to do with past wins or past losses. The house sets the odds, and they ensure they are the winner!

Have you ever heard of a casino going out of business because it's losing money?

Here's another example:

Guess whether the letter "k" is more likely to appear as the first or third letter in words.

Most people guess "k" is more likely to appear as the first letter in words. However, "k" is 2 times more likely to be the third letter in words. This is an example of the **availability illusion**. It is easier to recall words starting with "k," like *kitty*, *kind* and *Kim*, than words that have "k" as the third letter.

Similarly, it is easy to recall the few times when you pulled the lever and hundreds of quarters rolled out. It is also easy to recall your fourth cousin who won $1 million in the lottery.

But don't forget the millions of times you pulled the lever and no quarters rolled out. Don't forget your first, second, and third cousins, your siblings, and your friends who, among them, bought thousands of lottery tickets and never won big.

Review your self-deception chart. List causes of each self-deception. Are any related to overestimating odds, gambler's fallacy, or the availability illusion?

1. _____
2. _____
3. _____
4. _____
5. _____

There are both outside and inside causes to self-deceptions. <u>Outside</u> causes can include the following:

- Financial problems.
- People criticizing your gambling.

List your outside causes for self-deceptions:

_____
_____
_____

The major <u>inside</u> causes are related to feelings of desperation and a need to raise self-esteem. Gamblers may think as follows:

- I can't handle life without gambling.
- People won't respect me unless I win.
- Gambling is the one thing I'm good at.

What are your own <u>inside</u> causes?

_____
_____
_____

These kinds of thoughts can lead to bad feelings about yourself. You may have tried to compensate for these by thinking as follows:

- I'm luckier than most people.
- I'm smarter than other gamblers.
- I can change my luck.

**The more desperate a gambler becomes, the more
convinced the gambler is that these self-deceptions are correct!**

WEEK 8: PLANNING FOR EMERGENCIES AND COPING WITH LAPSES

Over the last 8 weeks, you have learned a number of skills to stop gambling.

No matter how confident you feel right now about avoiding gambling, you will always need to be aware that gambling may again cause you problems at times in the future. Major life events happen to everyone, and these changes can be disruptive, often leading to gambling. Some life events include the following:

- Social separations (divorce, death, child leaves home, friend moves)
- Health problems
- New responsibilities
- Work-related events
- Financial changes

Life events do not have to be negative to lead to a relapse. Positive life changes can also pose a risk. Moving, promotion, graduation, or a large inheritance can leave you feeling "on the top of the world," and perhaps a little too confident.

Life events happening to those close to you can also affect you. Family members or close friends may become upset or preoccupied with their own concerns, and may begin acting differently toward you.

Any of these life changes may lead to gambling. Lapses or slips back to gambling can be accompanied by feelings of guilt and shame. These must be dealt with immediately, before they lead to further gambling. After a slip, one should learn from the events that preceded it (do a functional analysis). Learn to reduce the likelihood of a repetition of that slip.

Below list some major life events that may happen to you in the next 10 years.

_____
_____
_____
_____
_____

What are some strategies you can use for coping with these or similar situations?

Personal Emergency Reminder Sheet

If I encounter a high-risk situation,

1. I will leave or change the situation.
2. I will put off the decision to gamble for 15 minutes. I will remember that cravings are time-limited. I **can** wait it out.

3. I will challenge my thoughts about gambling. Do I really need to gamble? I will remind myself that my only true needs are for air, water, food, and shelter.
4. I will think of and do something not related to gambling. I will review my pleasant activities.
5. I will remind myself of my successes.
6. I will remind myself of all the things I have to lose by gambling.
7. I will remind myself that my thinking becomes irrational when I gamble.
8. I will call my emergency numbers:

Name	Phone

RIDING OUT A CRISIS WILL STRENGTHEN MY RECOVERY!

Even among people who haven't gambled in years, slips can occur. A slip is a major crisis in recovery. Returning to abstinence after a slip requires an all-out effort, but it can be done!

If I experience a lapse,

1. I will get rid of the gambling paraphernalia and get away from the setting where I lapsed.
2. I will realize that one slip or even one day of gambling does not have to result in a full-blown relapse. I will not give in to feelings of guilt or blame because I know these feelings will pass in time, especially if I stop gambling NOW.
3. I will call someone for help.
4. I will examine this lapse, discuss the events prior to it, and identify triggers and my reaction to them. I will explore what I expected gambling to change or provide by doing a functional analysis.
5. I will set up a self-management plan so that I will be able to cope with a similar situation in the future.
6. I will write down my illogical thinking and the causes of these self-deceptions.

A LAPSE IS ONLY A TEMPORARY DETOUR ON THE ROAD TO ABSTINENCE.

Congratulations! You've successfully completed this treatment program!

It is important to keep in mind why you came into treatment in the first place. Remind yourself of what you hoped to accomplish by coming to this program:

_____
_____
_____
_____

List the progress that you've made below:

_____
_____
_____
_____
_____

Finally, indicate what you hope to accomplish in the future:

_____
_____
_____
_____
_____

Use the skills you've learned throughout treatment to accomplish your goals.

APPENDIX C
Homework Exercises

Triggers Monitoring

Date	List all triggers you experienced. Include people, places, things, events, and times that were associated with gambling today, or that have led to gambling in the past.	List people you were with, places you went, and things you did that were not triggers for gambling. In other words, list things that kept you from gambling that day.	Did you gamble in response to each trigger?
Sample 12/12	1. Met Tom unexpectedly in town. 2. Drove by off track betting. 3. Saw a scratch ticket on ground. 4. Received paycheck.	1. Told Tom I wasn't playing poker anymore. 2. Made sure I had an appointment so I couldn't stop at off track betting. 3. Bought 10 scratch tickets, left—felt guilty. 4. Gave Mary my paycheck.	1. No 2. No 3. Yes 4. No

FUNCTIONAL ANALYSIS

	Trigger →	Thoughts and Feelings →	Behavior →	Consequences Positive	Negative
1.					
2.					
3.					
4.					
5.					

Functional Analysis

Date	Trigger(s)	Thoughts and feelings about the trigger.	Behavior (did you gamble?)	Positive consequences (if you were to gamble.)	Negative consequences (if you were to gamble.)
12/28	Received paycheck.	Felt I deserved a chance to gamble.	No.	Would feel excited.	Would lose money and self-respect

Pleasant Activities

Date	Pleasant activity I <u>plan</u> to do on this day. Be specific! Include times and places, and make plans with others.	Other possible activities for today.	List pleasant activities you actually did today.	Did you gamble today?
Example 1/18/98	Go to the gym at 5 p.m. Read a book. Go to dinner with John.	Watch television.	Went to gym. Dinner with John. Watched television.	No.

Self-Management Planning Sheet

Trigger:_____

	Plans	+ Consequences	– Consequences	Difficulty (1–10)
a				
b				
c				
d				
e				
f				
g				
h				

Best plan:_____

Date:_____	Trigger:_____		
Strategies (brainstorm)	Positive consequences	Negative consequences	Difficulty (1–10)
1.			
2.			
3.			
4.			
5.			
Best choice:_____		Did you gamble?_____	

Date:_____	Trigger:_____		
Strategies (brainstorm)	Positive consequences	Negative consequences	Difficulty (1–10)
1.			
2.			
3.			
4.			
5.			
Best choice:_____		Did you gamble?_____	

Date:_____	Trigger:_____		
Strategies (brainstorm)	Positive consequences	Negative consequences	Difficulty (1–10)
1.			
2.			
3.			
4.			
5.			
Best choice:_____		Did you gamble?_____	

DAILY RECORD OF URGES TO GAMBLE

Reminders:
- Urges are common when one stops gambling. They do not signify a failure. Instead, try to learn from urges and what leads to them.
- Urges are like ocean waves. They get stronger to a point, then they start to go away.
- You win every time you defeat an urge by not gambling.

Date	Trigger(s)	Craving(s) how / where do you feel it?	Craving intensity (1-100)	Coping behaviors used	Did you gamble?

Assertiveness Skills Monitoring

Date	Situation(s)/trigger(s)	Your response(s) to the situation(s)	Feelings	Did you gamble?
12/12	1. Got in an argument with wife about car. 2. John asked me to go to the races on Friday.	1. Passive—let her have her way. 2. Assertive—told him I wasn't gambling. Asked him NOT to ask me again.	1. Felt angry, reviewed assertive responses. 2. Felt good, determined not to gamble.	No No

Personal Emergency Plan
High-Risk Situation

Reminder Sheet

1. I will alter or leave the situation.

2. I will put off the decision to gamble for 15 minutes. I will remember that cravings do stop, and that I can wait for them to stop. I **can** not gamble.

3. I will challenge my thoughts about gambling. Do I really need to gamble? I will remind myself that my only real needs are air to breathe, water to drink, food to eat, and shelter.

4. I will think of something unrelated to gambling. I will do something unrelated to gambling. I will review my pleasant activities.

5. I will remind myself of my successes.

6. I will remind myself of all the things I have to lose by gambling. I will do a functional analysis and a self-management plan.

7. I will remind myself that my thinking becomes irrational when I gamble.

8. I will call my list of emergency numbers:

Name	Phone
_____	_____
_____	_____
_____	_____
_____	_____
_____	_____

RIDING OUT A CRISIS WILL STRENGTHEN MY RECOVERY!

Personal Emergency Plan
Coping With a Lapse

Reminder Sheet

Even among people who haven't gambled in years, slips can occur.
A slip can be a major event in recovery.
Returning to abstinence after a slip requires an all-out effort, but it can be done!

If I have a lapse to gambling:

1. I will get rid of the gambling paraphernalia and leave the environment where I lapsed.

2. I will remember that one slip or one day of gambling does not have to result in a full-blown relapse. I will not be overwhelmed by feelings of guilt. I know these feelings will pass in time, especially if I stop gambling NOW.

3. I will call someone for help.

4. I will explore this lapse, review the events leading to the lapse, and identify triggers and my reactions to them. I will examine what I expected gambling to change or provide for me, by doing a functional analysis of my gambling.

5. I will set up a self-management plan so that I will be able to cope with such a situation in the future.

6. I will write down my illogical thinking and the causes of these self-deceptions.

I WILL REMEMBER A LAPSE IS ONLY A TEMPORARY DETOUR ON THE ROAD TO ABSTINENCE.

APPENDIX D
Financial Planning and Handling Creditors

Financial Planning and Handling Creditors

Managing financial pressures is a very important part of regaining control of your life. Large debts are common among problem gamblers, and money concerns are a common reason for relapse.

This section will help you reduce financial pressures, no matter how overwhelming they may appear. Included are worksheets and strategies that have been effective for many gamblers. By using them, you can take control of your financial problems.

This section has four major parts:
- a debt analysis,
- an income inventory,
- an expense record, and
- a debt management plan.

For each part, instructions and a worksheet are included. We recommend that you do these sections slowly and over several weeks' time. Doing one section each week for 4 weeks is the best strategy. In this way, you will have time to decide whether all the information you provided is correct, or whether there is additional information to add before you move to the next section.

It is important to remember that financial problems, no matter how severe, are not the end of the world. Thousands of gamblers have faced similar circumstances. The steps provided in this section will help you resolve your financial problems and learn to handle your finances _without gambling_. We recommend that you attend Gamblers Anonymous and a "pressure relief" session if your financial problems are severe or if you need additional support.

Section 1: Debt Analysis

The first task is an analysis of debts. Start by making a list of all the money you owe. Include car payments, mortgage payments, electric and phone bills, as well as gambling-related debts such as credit card debts, personal loans, and so forth. Here is an example of a debt inventory.

Leave this column
blank for now

Debt	Amount owed ($)	Monthly payment ($)	Months behind	Pressure index* (0,1,2,3,4,5)	G, g (amount), N
Fleet mortgage	87,000	630	0	1	
Back taxes on house	2,300	Not determined	12	5	
Visa card #1	4,600	156	4	4	
Visa card #2	3,208	98	1	2	
Frank	6,000	Not determined	12	5	
Tony	80	Not determined	6	2	

*The pressure index rates each debt according to how much pressure you feel as a result of this debt. 0 = *no pressure*, 3 = *moderate pressure*, 5 = *extreme pressure*. G = totally related to gambling; g = partially related to gambling; N = not related to gambling.

Create your own debt inventory below. Use pencil so you can erase if you make mistakes.

DEBT INVENTORY

Debt	Amount owed	Monthly payment	Months behind	Pressure index* (0,1,2,3,4,5)	G, g (amount), N

As you examine the debts that cause the most pressure, you will probably notice some similarities and differences between your debts and your feelings about them. Debts that cause pressure usually fall into one of four categories:

- debts owed to friends and relatives;
- debts that are collected aggressively through calls from bill collectors, letters from attorneys, or threats from loan sharks and bookies;
- debts with mounting interest, fees, and late charges; and
- debts that may result in the loss of a car, home, or other important item.

Each source of pressure can be dealt with effectively. We show you how later on in this section.

Remember that most problem gamblers are tempted to try to solve financial problems in the familiar way—by gambling. To remain in control of your life, it is essential that you develop new ways of coping with bills, creditors, and pressure.

Often, one major source of pressure is the "hidden debt." This is the debt that you have been afraid to tell anyone about. It is the debt that you want to hide to avoid conflict and criticism. If you have a secret debt, you have probably said to yourself, "I'll handle this one all by myself. It is better for everyone that I keep this one hidden."

Usually, keeping your debts hidden is a bad idea. The best solution is usually full disclosure of all your debts to the person(s) most affected by your financial decisions. Most of the time this person is your spouse.

The short-term consequences of being honest about your debts may be painful, but they are usually not as bad as feared. The long-term benefits of being honest are usually many. They include emotional relief, increased self-respect, and an honest relationship with your partner.

It is important that you take full responsibility for your gambling-related debts. There are several positive rewards for you to do so.

- The first is the feeling of accomplishment by tackling a large problem.
- The second is the self-respect and respect from family and friends you will receive for shouldering your own burden.
- The third is the good feelings you will experience monthly as you pay your bills. These monthly payments to creditors, even in small amounts, will serve as a reminder of the importance of abstaining from gambling.

Taking responsibility means that you alone will manage your gambling-related debt, without financial help from your spouse, parent, other relative, or friend. There may be instances in which accepting money from others is necessary to solve a financial crisis. In general, however, it is best to pay your debts, and especially your gambling debts, with your own money.

The next step in taking responsibility is to review your debt inventory and separate out the debt that is gambling related. You may want to put a "G" next to the debts that are clearly and entirely gambling related, and a "g" next to those that may be partially gambling-related and partially normal expenditures. You can put an "N" next to those that are entirely not related to gambling.

For example, if you are up to date on your mortgage payments, you would place an "N" next to mortgage, as this is a normal expenditure that has not been affected by your gambling. The $2,300 back taxes owed on your home, however, may be directly related to gambling, so you would put a "G" by it. Your credit card debts may be partially gambling-related (direct withdrawals from the casino) and partially normal expenditures (e.g., the new clothes and groceries you bought). If this is the case, you would place a "g" by the credit card debts.

Next, you should decide on exactly how much of the "g" debts are gambling-related and how much are not gambling related. You may decide, for example, that $2,300 of the VISA card is from gambling, and the remainder is normal expenditures. In this example, you would put $2,300 in the shaded gray column next to that VISA debt.

Go through your list of debts that are partially ("g") or totally ("G") gambling-related, and place a dollar amount in the shaded column to indicate your total gambling-related debt.

Gambling-related debt, unless you are not the only problem gambler in your home, is yours alone. These debts may be large, but they can be managed. In the next sections, we show you how.

Section 2: Income Inventory

First, make a list of your current income, using the chart below. Include only income that you regularly receive and expect to continue receiving for at least the next 6 months. In other words, do not include income that you *may* receive. If your job provides overtime or commission, state an average—not the highest (or the lowest) possible total. Do not include a disability settlement that is not yet certain or a raise that you *hope* to get. The goal is to create a reasonable estimate of the income you will receive.

If you are married:

*If you are married and your spouse contributes income to the household, you will need to decide whether to complete the worksheets combining both your incomes and expenses, or whether only your income and expenses will be included. This decision may depend on whether your debts are joint or in your name only.

For example, if most of the debts are listed in both your names (e.g., your spouse was a cosigner on your credit cards and mortgage), then you will have to complete the forms using total household income and expenses (use both yours and your spouse's).

If most of your debts are in your name only and your spouse's income pays for the majority of the household expenses, then you may want to complete the remaining worksheets using only your income and including only your portion of the household expenses. If this is the case, then on the next page (budget), write in only expenses for which you are responsible (e.g., food, entertainment, your car expenses).

Similarly, if you pay the majority of the household expenses but your spouse pays for the food, his or her car, and entertainment, then indicate your income only and on the Budget sheet, leave blank or write $0 for those items that your spouse buys.

Indicate *monthly amounts*. If you are paid weekly, multiply that amount by 4.

Source	$ per month
Primary job	
Secondary job	
Pensions	
Unemployment	
Disability	
Child support	
Alimony	
Property income	
*Spouse's income available	
Others (list)	

Total funds available per month   _____

Section 3: Expense Record

Now, estimate your monthly expenses. If you are expecting major changes in your lifestyle as a result of your gambling-related debt or a change in jobs, indicate the *lowest* reasonable amounts that you will need to pay. For example, if you know you must move apartments, list the lowest reasonable rent you can expect to pay.

Again, calculate all expenses as per month expenses. For items you buy weekly, multiply by 4. For items you pay yearly, divide by 12. For variable expenses (e.g., doctor bills), use your *best estimate* of monthly expenditures. For example, last year you may have spent $1400 on medical bills, and you expect no changes this year, so write $120/month under Doctor.

	Average $/month
Alimony	
Auto insurance	
Auto payments	
Auto registration, license	
Auto repairs	
Auto taxes	
Baby-sitter	
Child support	
Children's allowance	
Cigarettes	
Clothing (include children's if appropriate)	
Dentist	
Doctor	
Donations (church, etc.)	
Dry cleaning and laundry	
Electricity	
Emergencies (home repairs, upkeep)	
Entertainment	
Food	
Gas (home)	
Gasoline (car)	
Gifts (birthday, Christmas, etc.)	
Haircuts	
Home or renter's insurance	
Life insurance	
Lunches (work)	
Medical/dental/disability insurance	
Mortgage: First	
Second	
Music lessons	
Newspapers, magazines	
Oil Heat	

Pet care	
Prescriptions	
Rent	
School tuition	
Taxes (income)	
Taxes (property)	
Telephone	
Therapy	
Toiletries	
Union dues	
Vacation	
Water	
Other items (list)	

Total monthly expenses: _____

Now subtract your total monthly expenses from your total monthly income.

Total monthly income from previous page: _____

Total monthly expenses from this page: - _____

Available monthly income for repayment = _____

If your expenses are higher than your income (you get a negative number when you subtract), you will need to reassess your expenses. Check your math. Try to eliminate or reduce those items that you can. Decide whether you can bring your lunch to work and reduce your lunch expenditures or decrease your entertainment costs. Also, check that you are not including expenses that your spouse may be paying.

If your expenses are still higher than your income after checking your worksheets, then you will need to think about other ways to reduce your expenses. Can you move to a less expensive apartment, can you get a roommate, can you sell your car and get a cheaper one? Can you get a part-time job for the evenings or weekends? The goal is to end up with a monthly budget that you can stick to that allows at least some money left over to repay gambling loans.

Once your available monthly income exceeds your monthly expenses,
you can continue on to the next section.

Section 4: Debt Management Plan

A. Determining Gambling-Related Debt

    The next step in solving your financial problems is to make a detailed list of all the debts that you owe because of gambling. Be sure to write down bad checks, court-ordered judgments, credit union loans, personal loans, bank or finance company loans, back payments due on mortgage and car loans (but do not include these if you are up-to-date on payment), credit card debt, back taxes, family and friends, bookmarkers and loan sharks, and any others. Continue on another page if necessary.

Creditor's name	Original amount of loan	Present balance	Monthly payment (leave blank if not explicitly stated)	Months in default	Is this loan gambling related? Yes or No	Is this loan secured? Yes or No

B. Creating a Debt Management Plan

The final steps in Financial Management are settling on a debt payment plan and sticking to it. Listed below are two basic options followed by some sample cases, providing examples of how these strategies work. In the last several pages, you will find worksheets for determining a repayment schedule and tracking monthly payments.

Option 1 (for people with relatively small debts that can be paid off in the next 1–10 years): Pay a set amount to each creditor every month. Pay it consistently over the short-term or long-term, depending on what is comfortable for you. You may want to pay some creditors larger amounts to reduce debts that are causing the most pressure. But never commit to paying more than you can afford. The steps on the next page provide general guidelines for determining repayment schedules.

Option 2 (for people with relatively large debts that cannot be reasonably paid off in the next 5–10 years): Prioritize and postpone. If your income does not allow you to pay off something to each creditor every month, you may have to use alternative methods to reduce your financial pressures.

- Negotiate with creditors for reduced payments, reduced liability, or suspension of interest and late charges. This strategy is possible with some creditors, ranging from bookies, to banks to credit card companies.

- Negotiate with creditors to pay at a later date. This strategy may be useful when the creditor is someone who can afford to be patient. Sometimes, family and friends fall into this category.

- Remember that the most important thing is that you *not gamble*. Financial problems will take time to resolve. But by not gambling, you *can* resolve financial problems, no matter how large. Skip the next page, and go to the section for those with larger debts.

Option 1 (for those with relatively small debts):
If you can manage paying your debt back within a few years, then we recommend that you develop a payment plan for each creditor you listed on your Debt Inventory.

➢ For some debts, you have a monthly payment amount that has already been determined. For example, your mortgage amount may be $613 per month. A credit card loan may have a minimum payment of $52 per month.

➢ If you have additional loans with no predetermined monthly payment rates, decide on a monthly payment rate for _each_ loan. The amount you pay back on each loan depends on the "Pressure Index" for each loan and how much you can afford.

> Designate a greater proportion of your available income toward paying off the debts high on the "Pressure Index" first.

> Even if you can afford very little, you can still pay down most debts by extending the period for repayment. For example, a $3,000 debt can be paid off in one year at $250/month or in 10 years at $25/month. Extending the period of repayment may require you to negotiate with creditors for smaller monthly payments. Tips for doing this are included in the final parts of this section.

➢ Although you may want to pay off some loans more quickly, it is _strongly recommended that you pay something each month toward each and every one of your loans_. Even if you can afford only $10 a month per loan, pay this small amount toward each loan rather than nothing on a given loan. Paying back something will show your creditors that you are _responsible_ and _serious_ about paying them back.

➢ Using the LONG-TERM REPAYMENT PLAN worksheet, set up your repayment schedule for each loan you listed earlier.

➢ Write a letter to each creditor (even family and friends) detailing your repayment schedule, if this has not already been done. Get the creditor to sign and date the agreement, and make a copy of it. This way, you both have a record of the agreement.

➢ Then, use the ONE-YEAR REPAYMENT SCHEDULE to to keep track of all your payments for the upcoming year and to track yourself as you pay them off.

➢ As you are paying back your loans, be sure to stick within your monthly budget that you created for yourself on the Expense Worksheet. As you get paid each month, first pay your rent or mortgage, and then pay out all your debts. Keep track of where all your money goes throughout the month, and do not exceed your budget. By not gambling, you will find you have a lot more money available!

LONG-TERM REPAYMENT PLAN

Use this form to record your long-term repayment schedule.

Creditor	Contact person's name	Original amount of loan	Present balance (including penalties)	Monthly payment agreed on	Interest rate	Date of first and last payments
Sample VISA	Joe Smith 1-800-555-4261	$8,320	$8,270	$22.97	0%	2/16/05 1/16/2035

ONE-YEAR REPAYMENT SCHEDULE

Creditor	Amount of monthly payment	Date due	Check each month as paid
Sample — VISA	$22.97	2/24	√
	$22.97	3/24	√
	$22.97	4/24	√
	$22.97	5/24	√
	$22.97	6/24	√
Sample — Tom	$25	2/1	√
	$25	3/1	√
	$25	4/1	√last payment!

ONE-YEAR REPAYMENT SCHEDULE

Creditor	Amount of monthly payment	Date due	Check each month as paid

Option 2 (for those with relatively large debts):

Establish a 60-Day Grace Period

If your debts are relatively large, the first step is to contact all your creditors and explain your situation. You will need to tell them that you are a compulsive gambler, you are in a lot of debt, and you wish to pay back your debt to the best of your ability. Tell them that you are in the process of developing a repayment schedule, but that you will need 60 days to work it out. Tell them that you want interest and late charges to stop accruing during this 60-day grace period. During this time, focus on *not gambling*.

You will need to negotiate this plan with each of your creditors individually. They may require you to send detailed descriptions of your financial situation (like what you have completed in this section) before they agree to a repayment plan or before they agree to stopping interest or late fees. You also will need to separate out your gambling debt from your nongambling debt. It will be more difficult to ask for this "special treatment" for nongambling debt (such as mortgages, credit card purchases for household items or clothes, etc.), than for debt that is clearly associated with gambling (e.g., cash advances from a casino).

You may need to speak to several people before you will find one that agrees to give you 60 days interest free and to stop or reverse late charges. The key is to keep asking for the individual's supervisor, until you get to someone who has experience working with people in bad financial circumstances. This will be a tiresome process, and you will need to remain calm and determined. See the TIPS section that follows.

If your debts are large, you have one of two options—long-term repayment or bankruptcy. Typically, gamblers who are heavily in debt will develop 30-year repayment plans for each of their debts. Your creditors will realize that if you declare bankruptcy and if you do not have a cosigner on your loan, they will never recover any money from you. Therefore, small payments over 30 years is in both *your best interest* and *their best interest*. Negotiating this process, however, will take a lot of patience and a strong will.

During this 60-day period, you want to *focus on not gambling*. Before you begin paying back your gambling debts, give yourself enough time to do the work outlined. It can be discouraging to make payments at a rate you cannot maintain. Being discouraged will increase the chances of returning to gambling.

The following examples and guidelines show you how long-term repayment schedules work. Each one deals with different circumstances. But they all have four steps in common:

1. Subtract expenses from income to determine how much money is available for debt repayment.

2. Negotiate with creditors as needed.

3. Establish a manageable payment schedule.

4. Make regular monthly payments.

EXAMPLES:

Joe A. and his spouse have enough income for normal living expenses. What they lack is the money to keep up the monthly payments on eight different "maxed-out" credit cards. These were the source of Joe's gambling money. Monthly payments totaled $1,100 or about $700 more than Joe determined he had left over for debt reduction. To make up the difference, he took a part-time job that brought in an extra $100 per week, but this still left him about $300 short each month. So, he contacted each credit card company and asked to talk with someone who could help him. Several of the companies stopped interest charges after they reviewed the budget information he supplied. This brought the total payments to a manageable $400 per month, or about $50 per card.

Rita K. had a similar problem, but she had less income and owed her employer money as well. Once she determined what money was left over for debt reduction, she found she fell short by about $600 per month.

One problem was that she had committed to paying her boss $100 each week. This amount was being taken directly taken out of her paycheck. At that rate, she would have paid back her boss in about 18 months. Unfortunately, this plan left her too little money to develop a pressure-free debt reduction plan for her other debts.

With the help assertiveness training and a GamblersAnonymous member who coached her on how to approach her boss, she was able to renegotiate the payment to a manageable $50 per month. Her boss remembered that at one time she had been a terrific employee. He was hopeful that without gambling, she would be able to return to form. After she explained the importance of manageable finances to reducing the likelihood of relapse, he readily agreed to the lower payment.

How 30-Year Repayment Schedules Can Make Virtually Any Debt Manageable

Because businesses do not want you to file bankruptcy and do not want to go to court, many creditors allow people with gambling problems to negotiate long-term (and sometimes even interest-free) repayment schedules. For example, a $10,000 debt to be repaid over 30 years with no interest would entail the following:

$$\$10,000 \,/\, 30 \text{ years} = \$333.33 \text{ /year}$$

$$(\$333.33/\text{year}) \,/\, (12 \text{ months/year}) = \$27.78/\text{month to be paid}$$

A credit card company is not likely to agree to this repayment schedule if you have an annual income of $30,000 per year and the $10,000 you owe them is the only outstanding loan you have. However, if your gambling-related debt is $126,000 (e.g., you owe on two home mortgages plus $10,000 to their company and $10,000 to another credit card company), you may be able to get credit card companies to agree to accepting $27.78 per month for 30 years, rather than your filing bankruptcy.

Banks may also agree to long-term, interest-free payments rather than bankruptcy. If you owe $106,000 on two mortgages on a house with a market value of only $70,000, banks may agree to allow you to repay the $106,000 at just $500 per month for 30 years.

In the situation described above, the gambler with a $126,000 gambling debt would only be paying $556 per month. This payment would clear his debt ($27.78 to each of two credit card companies) and pay his mortgage ($500 per month to the bank). Even on a relatively low income, this payment schedule is possible!

Be sure that you get the name, address, and phone number of each person you talk with at each lending institution. You should hold on to all records and correspondence. Be sure to get someone at each institution to sign an agreement with you. You want to be sure that you have something in writing specifying the terms in case your contact person changes jobs or retires over the next 30 years!

If you are heavily in debt, we recommend that you contact a professional or Gamblers Anonymous for a "pressure relief" session.
They will assist you with this process.
You should contact a lawyer if you are considering bankruptcy.

Additional Tips

Talking With Family Members

♦ Your family can be an ally in managing your gambling debt. Tell your family about your gambling. Tell them about where all the money went. Tell them about your treatment and what you are doing and learning. Invite them to Gamblers Anonymous or Gam-Anon.

♦ We have repeatedly seen families express relief when gamblers tell the truth about money. Sometimes family members are initially angry, but this anger usually is short-lived. If you are honest and continue making a sincere effort to stop gambling and manage your debts, your family will regain their respect for you.

♦ Strong expressions of anger or fear do not mean that your family members do not want to help you. Expect strong emotional reactions. Accept them and continue to address money issues.

♦ Make sure your family understands that when you are developing a payment plan, the family welfare will always come first. Debt payments do not start until after household expenses are met.

♦ Hold this thought…

If I stop gambling, continue earning money, and address my debt payment, my situation has to improve.

♦ Many casinos have their own collections department. In each collections department is a person who has the task of negotiating payments with recovering gamblers. To contact him or her, call the casino's main number and ask for the collections or credit department.

♦ Contact the casinos immediately to let them know your intention to pay them. Generally, the casino's collections department is much more reasonable than the private agencies they could retain to collect your debt.

♦ It may help to tell them that you are receiving help for your gambling problem.

♦ It may also help to offer to exclude yourself from the casino by signing a self-banning agreement. Signing this agreement will show that you are serious about your commitment to stop gambling.

♦ Do not forget... *all the casinos want you to do is to pay them what you owe. Most of the time, they are pleased you called.*

Talking With Bookies and Loan Sharks

♦ Bookies and loan sharks are creditors too. All they want is what you owe them. They usually can wait and accept long-term payment plans, like everyone else.

♦ Long-term GamblersAnonymous members, called "Trusted Servants," have a great deal of experience addressing bookies and loan sharks. Ask for advice.

♦ Before negotiating with a bookie or loan shark, plan what you are going to say. Tell them:

   - You *fully intend to pay*, but you cannot pay *in full at this time*.

   - You have a gambling problem, and you have sought help.

   - You are working on a payment plan in accordance with treatment or G.A.

♦ Bookies may try to intimidate you. These threats are intended to increase your resolve to address your debt responsibly. Do not ignore, avoid, or insult your bookies or loan sharks. Be humble but dignified when speaking with them.

♦ Remember... bookies are businessmen who know you cannot pay if a broken leg prevents you from working. Also, if they get arrested, they will be out of business for awhile. Hurting you or your family puts them at risk of arrest.

♦ If threats continue, or if actual harm is done, contact the police immediately. Often Gamblers Anonymous members have a lot of experience handling threats. Call them for advice.

♦ Be cautious... *meetings with bookies and loan sharks may trigger urges to gamble. Before meeting with a bookie or loan shark, make a definite plan to meet a trusted, nongambling friend immediately after.*

Dealing With the IRS

- If you owe delinquent federal taxes, the large penalties and late fees make this debt one of the most expensive and troubling. Address it as soon as possible.

- Tax law is a specialized area. If you are concerned about the risk of criminal prosecution, speak to a certified public accountant. He or she can refer you to a tax attorney, if needed. You can address most of your nonpayment problems with the help of an IRS representative.

- The IRS is like any other creditor. Their primary goal is to get paid.

- The IRS usually tries to work out 36-month payment plans, if your financial circumstances allow your debt to be paid over that time period. If not, the IRS will develop an alternative payment plan based on your income and debt circumstances.

- The IRS has a special program for people whose medical problems prevent them from working and paying. Pathological gambling IS a psychiatric condition. You may qualify for this special repayment program.

- Remember, unattended financial problems, especially with the IRS, only worsen with age. The sooner they are contacted, the better.

- Keep these three important thoughts in mind:

    - Do not panic.

    - Face the problem.

    - The IRS is more likely to be helpful if you are honest with them.

Negotiating With Creditors

- Your creditors want only one thing—for you to pay them what you owe. Although they may speak to you in an intimidating way about collections and prosecution, they do not want to do that. All they want is a financial agreement. If you are feeling intimidated, tell them so. Ask to speak with their supervisor and negotiate with that person.

- Do your homework before you call to negotiate. Have an accurate and realistic income and payment plan prepared. The goal is to have them agree with your payment schedule.

- Remember ... If your creditors know you have prepared an accurate income and payment plan and that if the case goes to court, a judge will not order unreasonably large payments. In fact, they know that a judge may order even lower payments.

- Some lending institutions have trained staff who negotiate with recovering gamblers. They usually are more reasonable than untrained personnel and will have an understanding about the style of payment being discussed. Ask to speak with that person. If you go to Gamblers Anonymous, ask if anyone has tips on determining who these employees may be at specific businesses.

- Lending institutions are well aware of the possibility that you may declare bankruptcy. Most will settle for your terms of some money over the long-term rather than the option of no money because of bankruptcy.

- Do not forget ... <u>you</u> have the edge in negotiating payment.

- Hold on to this thought—

This is my debt. I am going to pay my debt. I am going to pay my debt in a reasonable way. I have a lot to say about what is reasonable for my financial status.

Handling Harassing Calls From Creditors and Bill Collectors

Calls from creditors can be very disturbing, and they can sometimes trigger a return to gambling. Below are guidelines that should help reduce pressures from bill collectors.

♦ By law, creditors have certain restrictions on collection activity:

-Creditors may call only between 8:00 a.m. and 9:00 p.m.
-Creditors cannot call you at work if you have sent them written notification that your employer prohibits such calls. (Most employers prohibit calls that interfere with doing your job).
-Creditors are not allowed to communicate with or through a third party about you.

♦ It is recommended that you notify creditors in writing if you want them to stop any of the activities mentioned above. If they continue, contact the state's banking department or retain an attorney.

♦ Creditors are not permitted to "harass" you. However, there are no specific guidelines about what constitutes harassment. If you feel you are being treated unfairly or too aggressively, you should notify the creditor in writing. It is important to include specifics, like dates, times, and details of conversations. This information should also be passed on to your attorney or the state banking department if you are working with either one.

♦ Calls from creditors can be stopped by hiring an attorney. Once you notify your creditors that you have legal representation, they must correspond only with the attorney. However, they may call you in the event your attorney fails to respond in a reasonable period of time.

♦ If you need help locating an attorney, call your local lawyer referral service.

♦ In some states, there are no specific guidelines to determine harassment. However, if you think you are being harassed, you have legal options.

-If, like most problem gamblers, you cannot afford an attorney, call your statewide legal services.
-A state banking department may also be able to help you. Ask to speak with an examiner.

REFERENCES

Abbott, M. W., & Volberg, R. A. (1991). *Gambling and problem gambling in New Zealand: A report on Phase One of the national survey.* Wellington, New Zealand: Department of Internal Affairs.

Abbott, M. W., & Volberg, R. A. (2000). *Taking the pulse on gambling and problem gambling in New Zealand: A report on Phase One of the 1999 National Prevalence Survey: Selections from Report No. 3 of the New Zealand Gaming Survey.* Wellington, New Zealand: Department of Internal Affairs.

Adalf, E. M., & Ialomiteanu, A. (2000). Prevalence of problem gambling in adolescents: Findings from the 1999 Ontario Student Drug Use Survey. *Canadian Journal of Psychiatry, 45,* 752–755.

Ainslie, G. (1975). Specious reinforcement: A behavioral theory of impulsiveness and impulse control. *Psychological Bulletin, 82,* 463–496.

Alterman, A. I., McLellan, A. T., O'Brien, C. P., August, D. S., Snider, E. C., Cornish, C., et al. (1994). Effectiveness and costs of inpatient versus day hospital cocaine rehabilitation. *Journal of Nervous and Mental Disease, 182,* 157–163.

American Psychiatric Association. (1980). *Diagnostic and statistical manual of mental disorders* (3rd ed.). Washington, DC: Author.

American Psychiatric Association. (1987). *Diagnostic and statistical manual of mental disorders* (3rd ed., rev.). Washington, DC: Author.

American Psychiatric Association. (1994). *Diagnostic and statistical manual of mental disorders* (4th ed.). Washington, DC: Author.

American Psychiatric Association. (2000). *Diagnostic and statistical manual of mental disorders* (4th ed., text rev.). Washington, DC: Author.

Anderson, G., & Brown, R. I. F. (1984). Real and laboratory gambling, sensation-seeking and arousal. *British Journal of Psychology, 75,* 401–410.

Apodaca, T. R., & Miller, W. R. (2003). A meta-analysis of the effectiveness of bibliotherapy for alcohol problems. *Journal of Clinical Psychology, 59,* 289–304.

Arribas, M. P., & Martinez, J. J. (1991). Tratamiento individual de jugadores patologicos: Descripcion de casos [Individual treatment of pathological gamblers: Case descriptions]. *Analisis y Modificacion de Conducta, 17,* 255–269.

Atlas, G. D., & Peterson, C. (1990). Explanatory style and gambling: How pessimists respond to losing wagers. *Behaviour Research & Therapy, 28,* 523–529.

Babor, T. F. (1994). Avoiding the horrid and beastly sin of drunkenness: Does dissuasion make a difference? *Journal of Consulting and Clinical Psychology, 62,* 1127–1140.

Bannister, G. (1977). Cognitive behaviour therapy in a case of a compulsive gambler. *Cognitive Therapy and Research, 1,* 223–227.

Bar-Hillel, M. (1980). What features make samples seem representative? *Journal of Experimental Psychology: Human Perception and Performance, 6,* 578–589.

Barker, J. C., & Miller, M. (1966). Aversion therapy for compulsive gambling. *The Lancet, 1,* 491–492.

Barker, J. C., & Miller, M. (1968). Aversion therapy for compulsive gambling. *Journal of Nervous and Mental Disease, 146,* 285–302.

Barnes, G. M., Welte, J. W., Hoffman, J. H., & Dintcheff, B. A. (1999). Gambling and alcohol use among youth: Influences of demographic, socialization, and individual factors. *Addictive Behavior, 24,* 749–767.

Baron, E., & Dickerson, M. (1999). Alcohol consumption and self-control of gambling behavior. *Journal of Gambling Studies, 15,* 3–16.

Bazargan, M., Bazargan, S., & Akanda, M. (2001). Gambling habits among aged African Americans. *Clinical Gerontologist, 22,* 51–62.

Bechara, A., Damasio, H., Tranel, D., & Damasio, A. R. (1997, February). Deciding advantageously before knowing the advantageous strategy. *Science, 275,* 1293–1295.

Becoña, E. (1993). The prevalence of pathological gambling in Galicia (Spain). *Journal of Gambling Studies, 9,* 353–369.

Becoña, E. (1997). Pathological gambling in Spanish children and adolescents: An emerging problem. *Psychological Reports, 81,* 275–287.

Becoña, E., Miguez, M., & Vazquez, F. L. (2001). Problem gambling in secondary school students. *Psicothema, 13,* 551–556.

Bellaire, W., & Caspari, D. (1992). Diagnosis and therapy of male gamblers in a university psychiatric hospital. *Journal of Gambling Studies, 8,* 143–150.

Bergh, C., Eklund, T., Sodersten, P., & Nordin, C. (1997). Altered dopamine function in pathological gambling. *Psychological Medicine, 27,* 473–475.

Bergh, C., & Kuehlhorn, E. (1994). Social, psychological and physical consequences of pathological gambling in Sweden. *Journal of Gambling Studies, 10,* 275–285.

Bergler, E. (1958). *The psychology of gambling.* New York: International University Press.

Berrettini, W., & Post, R. M. (1984). GABA in affective illness. In R. M. Post & J. Ballenger (Eds.), *Neurobiology of mood disorders* (pp. 673–685). Baltimore: Williams & Wilkins.

Bersabe, R., & Arias, R. M. (2000). Superstition in gambling. *Psychology in Spain, 4,* 28–34.

Berscheid, E., & Walster, E. (1974). Physical attractiveness. In L. Berkowitz (Ed.), *Advances in experimental social psychology* (pp. 158–215). New York: Academic Press.

Bien, T. H., Miller, W. R., & Tonigan, J. S. (1993). Brief interventions for alcohol problems: A review. *Addiction, 88,* 315–336.

Bienvenu, O. J., Samuels, J. F., Riddle, M. A., Hoehn-Saric, R., Liang, K., Cullen, B. A., et al. (2000). The relationship of obsessive–compulsive disorder to possible spectrum disorders: Results from a family study. *Biological Psychiatry, 48,* 287–293.

Black, D. W., Goldstein, R. B., Noyes, R., & Blum, N. (1994). Compulsive behaviors and obsessive–compulsive disorder (OCD): Lack of a relationship between OCD, eating disorders, and gambling. *Comprehensive Psychiatry, 35,* 145–148.

Black, D. W., & Moyer, T. (1998). Clinical features and psychiatric comorbidity of subjects with pathological gambling behavior. *Psychiatric Services, 49,* 1434–1439.

Black, D. W., Moyer, T., & Schlosser, S. (2003). Quality of life and family history in pathological gambling. *Journal of Nervous and Mental Disease, 191,* 124–126.

Blanchard, E. B., Wulfert, E., Freidenberg, B. M., & Malta, L. S. (2000). Psychophysiological assessment of compulsive gamblers' arousal to gambling cues: A pilot study. *Applied Psychophysiology and Biofeedback, 25,* 155–165.

Blanco, C., Moreyra, P., Nunes, E. V., Sáiz-Ruiz, J., & Ibàñez, A. (2001). Pathological gambling: Addiction or compulsion? *Seminars in Clinical Neuropsychiatry, 6,* 167–176.

Blanco, C., Orensanz-Muñoz, L., Blanco-Jerez, C., & Sáiz-Ruiz, J. (1996). Pathological gambling and platelet MAO activity: A psychobiological study. *American Journal of Psychiatry, 153,* 119–121.

Blanco, C., Petkova, E., Ibàñez, A., & Sáiz-Ruiz, J. (2002). A pilot placebo-controlled study of fluvoxamine for pathological gambling. *Annals of Clinical Psychiatry, 14,* 9–15.

Bland, R. C., Newman, S. C., Orn, H., & Stebelsky, G. (1993). Epidemiology of pathological gambling in Edmonton. *Canadian Journal of Psychiatry, 38,* 108–112.

Blaszczynski, A. P. (1999). Pathological gambling and obsessive–compulsive spectrum disorders. *Psychological Reports, 84,* 107–113.

Blaszczynski, A. P., Huynh, S., Dumlao, V. J., & Farrell, E. (1998). Problem gambling within a Chinese speaking community. *Journal of Gambling Studies, 14,* 359–380.

Blaszczynski, A. P., & McConaghy, N. (1988). SCL–90 assessed psychopathology in pathological gamblers. *Psychological Reports, 62,* 547–552.

Blaszczynski, A. P., & McConaghy, N. (1989). Anxiety and/or depression in the pathogenesis of addictive gambling. *International Journal of the Addictions, 24,* 337–350.

Blaszczynski, A. P., & McConaghy, N. (1994a). Antisocial personality disorder and pathological gambling. *Journal of Gambling Studies, 10,* 129–145.

Blaszczynski, A. P., & McConaghy, N. (1994b). Criminal offenses in Gamblers Anonymous and hospital treated pathological gamblers. *Journal of Gambling Studies, 10,* 99–127.

Blaszczynski, A. P., McConaghy, N., & Frankova, A. (1989). Crime, antisocial personality and pathological gambling. *Journal of Gambling Behavior, 5,* 137–152.

Blaszczynski, A. P., McConaghy, N., & Frankova, A. (1990). Boredom proneness in pathological gambling. *Psychological Reports, 67*, 35–42.

Blaszczynski, A. P., McConaghy, N., & Frankova, A. (1991). A comparison of relapsed and non-relapsed abstinent pathological gamblers following behavioural treatment. *British Journal of Addiction, 86*, 1485–1489.

Blaszczynski, A. P., & Nower, L. (2003). A pathways model of problem and pathological gambling. *Addiction, 97*, 487–499.

Blaszczynski, A. P., & Silove, D. (1995). Cognitive and behavioral therapies for pathological gambling. *Journal of Gambling Studies, 11*, 195–220.

Blaszczynski, A. P., Wintor, S. W., & McConaghy, N. (1986). Plasma endorphin levels in pathological gambling. *Journal of Gambling Behavior, 2*, 3–14.

Blum, K., Sheridan, P. J., Wood, R. C., Braverman, E. R., Chen, T., & Comings, D. E. (1995). Dopamine D2 receptor gene variants: Association and linkage studies in impulsive–addictive–compulsive behavior. *Pharmacogenetics, 5*, 121–141.

Blumberg, H. P., Leung, H.-C., Skudlarski, P., Lacadie, C. M., Fredericks, C. A., Harris, B. C., et al. (2003). A functional magnetic resonance imaging study of bipolar disorder: State- and trait-related dysfunction in ventral prefrontal cortices. *Archives of General Psychiatry, 60*, 601–609.

Bondolfi, G., Osiek, C., & Ferrero, F. (2000). Prevalence estimates of pathological gambling in Switzerland. *Acta Psychiatrica Scandinavica, 101*, 473–475.

Boutin, C., Dumont, M., Ladouceur, R., & Montecalvo, P. (2003). Excessive gambling and cognitive therapy: How to address ambivalence. *Clinical Case Studies, 2*, 259–269.

Boyd, W. H., & Bolen, D. W. (1970). The compulsive gambler and spouse in group psychotherapy. *International Journal of Group Psychotherapy, 20*, 77–90.

Boyer, M., & Dickerson, M. (2003). Attentional bias and addictive behaviour: Automaticity in a gambling-specific modified Stroop task. *Addiction, 98*, 61–70.

Breen, R. B., Kruedelbach, N. G., & Walker, H. I. (2001). Cognitive changes in pathological gamblers following a 28-day inpatient program. *Psychology of Addictive Behavior, 15*, 246–248.

Breen, R. B., & Zuckerman, M. (1999). Chasing in gambling behavior: Personality and cognitive determinants. *Personality and Individual Differences, 27*, 1097–1111.

Breiter, H. C., Aharon, I., Kahneman, D., Dale, A., & Shizgal, P. (2001). Functional imaging of neural responses to expectancy and experience of monetary gains and losses. *Neuron, 30*, 619–639.

Brockner, J., & Rubin, J. Z. (1985). *Entrapment in escalating conflicts: A social psychological analysis.* New York: Springer Verlag.

Brown, R. I. F. (1986). Dropouts and continuers in Gamblers Anonymous: Life-context and other factors. *Journal of Gambling Behavior, 2*, 130–140.

Brown, R. I. F. (1987a). Dropouts and continuers in Gamblers Anonymous: Part Two. Analysis of free-style accounts of experiences with GA. *Journal of Gambling Behavior, 3,* 68–79.

Brown, R. I. F. (1987b). Dropouts and continuers in Gamblers Anonymous: Part Three. Some possible specific reasons for dropout. *Journal of Gambling Behavior, 3,* 137–151.

Brown, R. I. F. (1987c). Dropouts and continuers in Gamblers Anonymous: Part Four. Evaluation and summary. *Journal of Gambling Behavior, 3,* 202–210.

Browne, B. A., & Brown, D. J. (1994). Predictors of lottery gambling among American college students. *Journal of Social Psychology, 134,* 339–347.

Browne, B. R. (1991). The selective adaptation of the Alcoholics Anonymous program by Gamblers Anonymous. *Journal of Gambling Studies, 7,* 187–206.

Browne, B. R. (1994). Really not God: Secularization and pragmatism in Gamblers Anonymous. *Journal of Gambling Studies, 10,* 247–260.

Brunelle, C., Assaad, J. M., Phil, R. O., Tremblay, R. E., & Vitaro, F. (2003). Exaggerated ethanol-induced cardiac reactivity as an indicator of increased risk for gambling. *Psychology of Addictive Behaviors, 17,* 83–86.

Brunner, H. G., Nelen, M. R., van Zandvoort, P., Abeling, N. G., van Genniip, A. H., Wolters, E. C., et al. (1993). X linked borderline mental retardation with prominent behavioral disturbance: Phenotype, genetic localization and evidence for disturbed monoamine metabolism. *American Journal of Human Genetics, 52,* 1032–1039.

Bujold, A., Ladouceur, R., Sylvain, C., & Boisvert, J. M. (1994). Treatment of pathological gamblers: An experimental study. *Journal of Behavior Therapy and Experimental Psychiatry, 25,* 275–282.

Burger, J. M., & Cooper, H. M. (1979). The desirability of control. *Motivation and Emotion, 3,* 381–393.

Burger, J. M., & Smith, N. G. (1985). Desire for control and gambling behavior among problem gamblers. *Personality and Social Psychology Bulletin, 11,* 145–152.

Cahlan, J. (1964). It was always with us. *Nevada Centennial Magazine, 1864–1964,* 151–155.

Campbell, F., Simmons, C., & Lester, D. (1999). The impact of gambling on suicidal behavior in Louisiana. *Omega: Journal of Death and Dying, 38,* 235–239.

Caraco, T. (1980). On foraging time allocations in a stochastic environment. *Ecology, 61,* 119–128.

Carlson, M. J., & Moore, T. L. (1998). *Adolescent gambling in Oregon: A report to the Oregon Gambling Addiction Treatment Foundation.* Wilsonville, OR: Herbert & Louis.

Carlton, P. L., & Manowitz, P. (1992). Behavioral restraint and symptoms of attention deficit disorder in alcoholics and pathological gamblers. *Biological Psychiatry, 25,* 44–48.

Carrasco, J. L., Sáiz-Ruiz, J., Hollander, E., Cesar, J., & Lopez-Ibor, J. J. (1994). Low platelet monoamine oxidase activity in pathological gambling. *Acta Psychiatrica Scandinavica, 90*, 427–431.

Carroll, D., & Huxley, J. A. (1994). Cognitive, dispositional, and psychophysiological correlates of dependent slot machine gambling in young people. *Journal of Applied Social Psychology, 24*, 1070–1083.

Carroll, K. M. (1997). Integrating psychotherapy and pharmacotherapy to improve drug abuse outcomes. *Addictive Behaviors, 22*, 233–245.

Castellani, B., Wootton, E., Rugle, L., Wedgeworth, R., Prabucki, K., & Olson, R. (1996). Homelessness, negative affect, and coping among veterans with gambling problems who misused substances. *Psychiatric Services, 47*, 298–299.

Cavedini, P., Riboldi, G., Keller, R., D'Annucci, A., & Bellodi, L. (2002). Frontal lobe dysfunction in pathological gambling patients. *Biological Psychiatry, 51*, 334–341.

Chen, C.-N., Wong, J., Lee, N., Chan-Ho, M.-W., & Lau, J. T.-F. (1993). The Shatin Community Mental Health Survey in Hong Kong. *Archives of General Psychiatry, 50*, 125–133.

Chick, J., Ritson, B., Connaughton, J., & Stewart, A. (1988). Advice versus extended treatment for alcoholism: A controlled study. *British Journal of Addiction, 83*, 159–170.

Childress, A. R., Mozley, P. D., McElgin, W., Fitzgerald, J., Reivich, M., & O'Brien, C. P. (1999). Limbic activation during cue-induced cocaine craving. *American Journal of Psychiatry, 156*, 11–18.

Cho, M. J., Hahm, B.-J., Suh, T., Suh, G.-H, Cho, S.-J., & Lee, C. K. (2002). Comorbid mental disorders among the patients with alcohol abuse and dependence in Korea. *Journal of Korean Medical Science, 17*, 236–241.

Ciarrocchi, J. W. (1993). Rates of pathological gambling in publicly funded outpatient substance abuse treatment. *Journal of Gambling Studies, 9*, 289–293.

Ciarrocchi, J. W., & Reinert, D. F. (1993). Family environment and length of recovery for married male members of Gamblers Anonymous and female members of GamAnon. *Journal of Gambling Studies, 9*, 341–352.

Ciarrocchi, J. W., & Richardson, R. (1989). Profile of compulsive gamblers in treatment: Update and comparisons. *Journal of Gambling Behavior, 5*, 53–65.

Clarke, D., & Rossen, F. (2000). Adolescent gambling and problem gambling: A New Zealand study. *New Zealand Journal of Psychology, 29*, 10–16.

Coman, G. J., Evans, B. J., & Burrows, G. D. (2002). Group counseling for problem gambling. *British Journal of Guidance & Counseling, 30*, 145–158.

Comings, D. E., Gade, R., Muhleman, D., Chiu, C., Wu, S., To, M., et al. (1996). Exon and intron mutations in the human tryptophan 2.3-dioxygenase gene and their potential association with Tourette's syndrome, substance abuse and other psychiatric disorders. *Pharmacogenetics, 6*, 307–318.

Comings, D. E., Gade, R., Wu, S., Chiu, C., Dietz, G., Muhleman, D., et al. (1997). Studies of the potential role of the dopamine D1 receptor gene in addictive behaviors. *Molecular Psychiatry, 2,* 44–56.

Comings, D. E., Gade-Andavolu, R., Gonzalez, N., Wu, S., Muhleman, D., Blake, H., et al. (2000). Comparison of the role of dopamine, serotonin, and noradrenergic genes in ADHD, OCD and conduct disorder: Multivariate regression analysis of 20 genes. *Clinical Genetics, 57,* 178–196.

Comings, D. E., Gade-Andavolu, R., Gonzalez, N., Wu, S., Muhleman, D., Chen, C., et al. (2001). The additive effect of neurotransmitter genes in pathological gambling. *Clinical Genetics, 60,* 107–116.

Comings, D. E., Gonzalez, N., Wu, S., Gade, R., Muhleman, D., Saucier, G., et al. (1999). Studies of the 48 bp repeat polymorphism of the DRD4 gene in impulsive, compulsive, addictive behaviors: Tourette syndrome, ADHD, pathological gambling, and substance abuse. *American Journal of Medical Genetics, 88,* 358–368.

Comings, D. E., Rosenthal, R. J., Lesieur, H. R., Rugle, L. J., Muhleman, D., Chiu, C., et al. (1996). A study of the dopamine D2 receptor gene in pathological gambling. *Pharmacogenetics, 6,* 223–234.

Commission on the Review of the National Policy Toward Gambling. (1976). *Gambling in America: Final report of the Commission on the Review of the National Policy Toward Gambling.* Washington, DC: Author.

Cooper, B. (1961). Social class and prognosis in schizophrenia—Part 1. *British Journal of Preventive and Social Medicine, 15,* 17–30.

Corney, W. J., & Cummings, W. T. (1985). Gambling behavior and information processing biases. *Journal of Gambling Studies, 1,* 111–118.

Cornish, D. B. (1978). *Gambling: A review of the literature and its implications for policy and research.* London: Her Majesty's Stationery Office.

Costello, E. J., Compton, S. N., Keeler, G., & Angold, A. (2003). Relationships between poverty and psychopathology. *Journal of the American Medical Association, 290,* 2023–2029.

Cotler, S. B. (1971). The use of different behavioral techniques in treating a case of compulsive gambling. *Behavior Therapy, 2,* 579–584.

Coulombe, A., Ladouceur, R., Desharnais, R., & Jobin, J. (1992). Erroneous perceptions and arousal among regular and occasional video poker players. *Journal of Gambling Studies, 8,* 235–244.

Coventry, K. R., & Norman, A. C. (1997). Arousal, sensation seeking and frequency of gambling in off-course horse racing bettors. *British Journal of Psychology, 88,* 671–681.

Coventry, K. R., & Norman, A. C. (1998). Arousal, erroneous verbalizations and the illusion of control during a computer-generated gambling task. *British Journal of Psychology, 89,* 629–645.

Crisp, B. R., Thomas, S. A., Jackson, A. C., & Thomason, N. (2001). Partners of problem gamblers who present for counseling: Demographic profile and presenting problems. *Journal of Family Studies, 7,* 208–216.

Crisp, B. R., Thomas, S. A., Jackson, A. C., Thomason, N., Smith, S., Borrell, J., et al. (2000). Sex differences in the treatment needs and outcomes of problem gamblers. *Research on Social Work Practice, 10*, 229–242.

Crockford, D. N., & el-Guebaly, N. (1998a). Naltrexone in the treatment of pathological gambling and alcohol dependence. *Canadian Journal of Psychiatry, 43*, 86.

Crockford, D. N., & el-Guebaly, N. (1998b). Psychiatric comorbidity in pathological gambling: A critical review. *Canadian Journal of Psychiatry, 43*, 43–50.

Cuadrado, M. (1999). A comparison of Hispanic and Anglo calls to a gambling help line. *Journal of Gambling Studies, 15*, 83–90.

Culleton, R. P. (1989). The prevalence rates of pathological gambling: A look at methods. *Journal of Gambling Studies, 5*, 22–41.

Cunningham-Williams, R. M., Cottler, L. B., & Books, S. J. (2002, December). *Development of a diagnostic gambling assessment.* Paper presented at the National Center for Responsible Gaming Conference, Las Vegas, NV.

Cunningham-Williams, R. M., Cottler, L. B., Compton, W. M., & Spitznagel, E. L. (1998). Taking changes: Problem gamblers and mental health disorders: Results from the St. Louis Epidemiological Catchment Area (ECA) Study. *American Journal of Public Health, 88*, 1093–1096.

Cunningham-Williams, R. M., Cottler, L. B., Compton, W. M., Spitznagel, E. L., & Ben-Abdallah, A. (2000). Problem gambling and comorbid psychiatric and substance use disorders among drug users recruited from drug treatment and community settings. *Journal of Gambling Studies, 16*, 347–376.

Curry, S., Wagner, E. H., & Grothaus, L. C. (1990). Intrinsic and extrinsic motivation for smoking cessation. *Journal of Consulting and Clinical Psychology, 58*, 310–316.

Custer, R. L. (1982). Gambling and addiction. In R. Craig & S. Baker (Eds.), *Drug dependent patients: Treatment and research* (pp. 367–381). Springfield, IL: Charles C Thomas.

Custer, R. L., & Milt, H. (1985). *When luck runs out.* New York: Warner Books.

Daghestani, A. N. (1987). Impotence associated with compulsive gambling. *Journal of Clinical Psychiatry, 48*, 115–116.

Daghestani, A. N., Elenz, E., & Crayton, J. W. (1996). Pathological gambling in hospitalized substance abusing veterans. *Journal of Clinical Psychiatry, 57*, 360–363.

Davis, D., Sundahl, I., & Lesbo, M. (2000). Illusory personal control as a determinant of bet size and type in casino craps games. *Journal of Applied Social Psychology, 30*, 1224–1242.

DeArment, R. F. (1982). *Knights of the green cloth: The saga of the frontier gamblers.* Norman: University of Oklahoma Press.

DeCaria, C. M., Hollander, E., Begaz, T., Schmeidler, J., Wong, C. M., Cartwright, C., & Mosovich, S. (1998, July). *Reliability and validity of a pathological gambling modification of the Yale–Brown Obsessive–Compulsive Scale (PG–YBOCS): Preliminary findings*. Presented at the 12th National Conference on Problem Gambling, Las Vegas, NV.

DeCaria, C. M., Hollander, E., Nora, R., Stein, D., Simeon, D., & Cohen, I. (1997, May). *Gambling: Biological/genetic, treatment, government, and gambling concerns: Neurobiology of pathological gambling*. Presented at the 150th annual meeting of the American Psychiatric Association, San Diego, CA.

de la Gandera, J. J. (1999, May). *Fluoxetine: Open-trial in pathological gambling*. Presented at the 152nd annual meeting of the American Psychiatric Association, Washington, DC.

Del Boca, F. K., & Noll, J. A. (2000). Truth or consequences: The validity of self-report data in health services research on addictions. *Addiction, 95*(Suppl. 3), 347–360.

Delfabbro, P., & Thrupp, L. (2003). The social determinants of youth gambling in South Australian adolescents. *Journal of Adolescence, 26*, 313–330.

Dell, L., Ruzicka, M. F., & Palisi, A. T. (1981). Personality and other factors associated with the gambling addiction. *International Journal of Addictions, 16*, 149–156.

Derby, K. (1992). Some difficulties in the treatment of character-disordered addicts. In B. C. Wallace (Ed.), *The chemically dependent: Phases of treatment and recovery* (pp. 115–124). New York: Brunner/Mazel.

Derevensky, J. L., & Gupta, R. (2000). Prevalence estimates of adolescent gambling: A comparison of the SOGS–RA, DSM–IV–J, and the GA 20 questions. *Journal of Gambling Studies, 16*, 227–251.

Derevensky, J. L., Gupta, R., & Della-Cioppa, G. (1996). A developmental perspective on gambling behavior in children and adolescents. *Journal of Gambling Studies, 12*, 49–66.

Dickerson, M. G., Baron, E., Hong, S. M., & Cottrell, D. (1996). Estimating the extent and degree of gambling related problems in the Australian population: A national survey. *Journal of Gambling Studies, 12*, 161–178.

Dickerson, M. G., Hinchy, J., & England, S. (1990). Minimal treatments and problem gamblers: A preliminary investigation. *Journal of Gambling Studies, 6*, 87–102.

Dickerson, M. G., Hinchy, J., England, S., Fabre, J., & Cunningham, R. (1992). On the determinants of persistent gambling behaviour: I. High-frequency poker machine players. *British Journal of Psychology, 83*, 237–248.

Dickerson, M. G., & Weeks, D. (1979). Controlled gambling as a therapeutic technique for compulsive gamblers. *Journal of Behavior Therapy and Experimental Psychiatry, 10*, 139–141.

Dickson, L. M., Derevensky, J. L., & Gupta, R. (2002). The prevention of gambling problems in youth: A conceptual framework. *Journal of Gambling Studies, 18*, 97–159.

DiClemente, C. C., & Prochaska, J. O. (1982). Self-change and therapy change of smoking behaviour: A comparison of processes of change in cessation and maintenance. *Addictive Behaviors, 7*, 133–142.

DiClemente, C. C., Prochaska, J. O., Fairhurst, S. K., Velicer, W. F., Velasquez, M. M., & Rossi, J. S. (1991). The process of smoking cessation: An analysis of precontemplation, contemplation, and preparation stages of change. *Journal of Consulting and Clinical Psychology, 59,* 295–304.

Dixon, M. R., Hayes, L. J., & Ebbs, R. E. (1998). Engaging in "illusory control" during repeated risk-taking. *Psychological Reports, 83,* 959–962.

Dohrenwend, B. P. (1990). Socioeconomic status (SES) and psychiatric disorders: Are the issues still compelling? *Social Psychiatry and Psychiatric Epidemiology, 25,* 41–47.

Driver-Dunckley, E., Samanta, J., & Stacy, M. (2003). Pathological gambling associated with dopamine agonist therapy in Parkinson's disease. *Neurology, 61,* 422–423.

Duvarci, I., & Varan, A. (2001). Reliability and validity study of the Turkish form of the South Oaks Gambling Screen. *Turkish Psikiyatri Dergisi, 12,* 34–45.

Echeburúa, E., Baez, C., Fernandez, J., & Paez, D. (1994). The South Oaks Gambling Screen Questionnaire: The Spanish validation. *Analisis y Modificación de Conducta, 74,* 769–791.

Echeburúa, E., Baez, C., & Fernandez-Montalvo, J. (1996). Comparative effectiveness of three therapeutic modalities in the psychological treatment of pathological gambling: Long-term outcome. *Behavioural and Cognitive Psychotherapy, 24,* 51–72.

Echeburúa, E., Fernandez-Montalvo, J., & Baez, C. (2000). Relapse prevention in the treatment of slot-machine pathological gambling: Long-term outcome. *Behavior Therapy, 31,* 351–364.

Echeburúa, E., Fernandez-Montalvo, J., & Baez, C. (2001). Predictors of therapeutic failure in slot-machine pathological gamblers following behavioural treatment. *Behavioural and Cognitive Psychotherapy, 29,* 379–383.

Edwards, J. E. (1995). Gambling and politics in Nevada. In R. Lowitt (Ed.), *Politics in the postwar American West* (pp. 147–161). Norman: University of Oklahoma Press.

Eisen, S. A., Lin, N., Lyons, M. J., Scherer, J. F., Griffith, K., True, W. R., et al. (1998). Familial influences on gambling behavior: An analysis of 3359 twin pairs. *Addiction, 93,* 1375–1384.

Elia, C., & Jacobs, D. F. (1993). The incidence of pathological gambling among Native Americans treated for alcohol dependence. *International Journal of the Addictions, 28,* 659–666.

Elkin, I., Pilkonis, P. A., Docherty, J. P., & Sotsky, S. M. (1988). Conceptual and methodological issues in comparative studies of psychotherapy and pharmacotherapy: II. Nature and timing of treatment effects. *American Journal of Psychiatry, 145,* 1070–1076.

Emerson, M. O., & Laundergan, J. C. (1996). Gambling and problem gambling among adult Minnesotans: Changes 1990 to 1994. *Journal of Gambling Studies, 12,* 291–304.

Fals-Stewart, W., O'Farrell, T. J., Freitas, T. T., McFarlin, S. K., & Rutigliano, P. (2000). The timeline followback reports of psychoactive substance use by drug-abusing patients: Psychometric properties. *Journal of Consulting and Clinical Psychology, 68*, 134–144.

Feigelman, W., Kleinman, P. H., Lesieur, H. R., Millman, R. B., & Lesser, M. L. (1995). Pathological gambling among methadone patients. *Drug and Alcohol Dependence, 39*, 75–81.

Feigelman, W., Wallisch, L. S., & Lesieur, H. R. (1998). Problem gamblers, problem substance users, and dual problem individuals: An epidemiological study. *American Journal of Public Health, 88*, 467–470.

Ferster, C. B., & Skinner, B. F. (1957). *Schedules of reinforcement.* New York: Appleton-Century-Crofts.

Fisher, S. (1992). Measuring pathological gambling in children: The case of fruit machines in the UK. *Journal of Gambling Studies, 8*, 263–285.

Fisher, S. (2000a). Developing the *DSM–IV* criteria to identify adolescent problem gambling in non-clinical populations. *Journal of Gambling Studies, 16*, 253–273.

Fisher, S. (2000b). Measuring the prevalence of sector-specific problem gambling: A study of casino patrons. *Journal of Gambling Studies, 16*, 25–51.

Fisher, S. E. (1993). Gambling and pathological gambling in adolescents. *Journal of Gambling Studies, 9*, 277–287.

Fisher, S. E. (1999). A prevalence study of gambling and problem gambling in British adolescents. *Addiction Research, 7*, 509–538.

Fleming, A. M. (1978). *Something for nothing: A history of gambling.* New York: Delacorte Press.

Forman, R. F., Bovasso, G., & Woody, G. E. (2001). Staff beliefs about addiction treatment. *Journal of Substance Abuse Treatment, 21*, 1–9.

France, C. J. (1902). The gambling impulse. *American Journal of Psychology, 13*, 364–407.

Frank, M. L., Lester, D., & Wexler, A. (1991). Suicidal behavior among members of Gamblers Anonymous. *Journal of Gambling Studies, 7*, 249–255.

Frank, M. L., & Smith, C. (1989). Illusion of control and gambling in children. *Journal of Gambling Behavior, 5*, 127–136.

Franklin, J., & Thoms, D. R. (1989). Clinical observations of family members of compulsive gamblers. In H. J. Shaffer, S. A. Stein, B. Gambino, & T. N. Cummings (Eds.), *Compulsive gambling: Theory, research, and practice* (pp. 135–146). Lexington, MA: Lexington Books.

Freidenberg, B. M., Blanchard, E. B., Wulfert, E., & Malta, L. S. (2002). Changes in physiological arousal to gambling cues among participants in motivationally enhanced cognitive–behavior therapy for pathological gambling: A preliminary study. *Applied Psychophysiology and Biofeedback, 27*, 251–260.

Friedman, M., & Savage, L. J. (1948). The utility analysis of choices involving risk. *Journal of Political Economy, 56*, 279–304.

Freud, S. (1953). Recommendations to physicians practicing psychoanalysis. In J. Strachey (Ed. and Trans.), *Standard edition of the complete psychological works of Sigmund Freud* (Vol. 12). London: Hogarth Press. (Original work published 1912)

Freud, S. (1961). Dostoevsky and parricide. In J. Strachey (Ed. and Trans.), *Standard edition of the complete psychological works of Sigmund Freud* (Vol. 21, pp. 222–242). London: Hogarth Press. (Original work published 1928)

Fuller, R. K., Branchey, L., Brightwell, D. R., Derman, R. M., Emrick, C. D., Iber, F. L., et al. (1986). Disulfiram treatment for alcoholism: A Veterans Administration cooperative study. *Journal of the American Medical Association, 256*, 1449–1455.

Gaboury, A., & Ladouceur, R. (1989). Erroneous perceptions and gambling. *Journal of Social Behavior and Personality, 4*, 411–420.

Gaboury, A., & Ladouceur, R. (1993). Evaluation of a prevention program for pathological gambling among adolescents. *Journal of Primary Prevention, 14*, 21–28.

Gaboury, A., Ladouceur, R., Beauvais, G., Marchand, L., & Martineau, Y. (1988). Dimensions cognitives et comportementales chez les joueurs reguliers et occasionnels au Blackjack [Cognitive and behavioral dimensions in regular players and occasional Blackjack players]. *International Journal of Psychology, 23*, 283–291.

Galdston, J. (1960). The gambler and his love. *American Journal of Psychiatry, 117*, 553–555.

Gallup, G. H. (1976). *Gambling in Britain*. London: Social Surveys (Gallup Poll) Ltd.

Gambino, B., Fitzgerald, R., Shaffer, H., Benner, J., & Courtnage, P. (1993). Perceived family history of problem gambling and scores on SOGS. *Journal of Gambling Studies, 9*, 169–184.

Garrett, T. A., & Sobel, R. S. (1999). Gamblers favor skewness, not risk: Further evidence from the United States' lottery games. *Economics Letters, 63*, 85–90.

Gehring, W. J., & Willoughby, A. R. (2002, March 22). The medial frontal cortex and the rapid processing of monetary gains and losses. *Science, 295*, 2279–2282.

Gerstein, D. R., Volberg, R. A., Toce, M. T., Harwood, H., Johnson, R. A., Buie, T., et al. (1999). *Gambling Impact and Behavior Study: Report to the National Gambling Impact Study Commission*. Chicago: National Opinion Research Center.

Getty, H. A., Watson, J., & Frisch, G. R. (2000). A comparison of depression and styles of coping in male and female GA members and controls. *Journal of Gambling Studies, 16*, 377–391.

Glare, P. G. W. (1982). *Oxford Latin dictionary*. Oxford, England: Clarendon Press.

Goldstein, J. M., & Simpson, J. C. (1995). Validity: Definitions and applications to psychiatric research. In M. T. Tsuang, M. Tohen, & G. E. Zahner (Eds.), *Textbook in psychiatric epidemiology* (pp. 229–242). New York: Wiley-Liss.

Goldstein, L., Manowitz, P., Nora, R., Swartzburg, M., & Carlton, P. L. (1985). Differential EEG activation and pathological gambling. *Biological Psychiatry, 20,* 1232–1234.

Goorney, A. B. (1968). Treatment of a compulsive horse race gambler by aversive therapy. *British Journal of Psychiatry, 114,* 329–333.

Gotestam, K. G., & Johansson, A. (2003). Characteristics of gambling and problem gambling in the Norwegian context: A *DSM–IV*-based telephone interview study. *Addictive Behaviors, 28,* 189–197.

Govoni, R., Frisch, R. G., Rupcich, N., & Getty, H. (1998). First year impacts of casino gambling in a community. *Journal of Gambling Studies, 14,* 347–358.

Grant, J. E., & Kim, S. W. (2002a). Gender differences in pathological gamblers seeking medication treatment. *Comprehensive Psychiatry, 43,* 56–62.

Grant, J. E., & Kim, S. W. (2002b). Parental bonding in pathological gambling disorder. *Psychiatric Quarterly, 73,* 239–247.

Grant, J. E., Kim, S. W., & Brown, E. (2001). Characteristics of geriatric patients seeking medication treatment for pathological gambling disorder. *Journal of Geriatric Psychiatry and Neurology, 14,* 125–129.

Grant, J. E., Kim, S. W., Potenza, M. N., Blanco, C., Ibàñez, A., Stevens, L., et al. (2003). Paroxetine treatment of pathological gambling: A multi-centre randomized controlled trial. *International Clinical Psychopharmacology, 18,* 243–249.

Greenberg, D., & Marks, I. (1982). Behavioral psychotherapy of uncommon referrals. *British Journal of Psychiatry, 141,* 148–153.

Greenberg, D., & Rankin, H. (1982). Compulsive gamblers in treatment. *British Journal of Psychiatry, 140,* 364–366.

Griffiths, M. D. (1990a). Addiction to fruit machines: A preliminary study among young males. *Journal of Gambling Studies, 6,* 113–126.

Griffiths, M. D. (1990b). The acquisition, development, and maintenance of fruit machine gambling in adolescents. *Journal of Gambling Studies, 6,* 193–204.

Griffiths, M. D. (1993). Tolerance in gambling: An outcome measure using the psychophysiological analysis of male fruit machine gamblers. *Addictive Behaviors, 18,* 365–372.

Griffiths, M. D. (1994). The role of cognitive bias and skill in fruit machine playing. *British Journal of Psychology, 85,* 351–369.

Griffiths, M. D. (1995). *Adolescent gambling.* London: Routledge.

Griffiths, M. D., Scarfe, A., & Bellringer, P. (1999). The UK national telephone gambling help line: Results on the first year of operation. *Journal of Gambling Studies, 15,* 83–90.

Griffiths, M. D., & Sutherland, I. (1998). Adolescent gambling and drug use. *Journal of Community and Applied Social Psychology, 8,* 423–427.

Grun, L., & McKeigue, P. (2000). Prevalence of excessive gambling before and after introduction of a national lottery in the United Kingdom: Another example of the single distribution theory. *Addiction, 95,* 959–966.

Gschwandtner, U., Aston, J., Renaud, S., & Fuhr, P. (2001). Pathologic gambling in patients with Parkinson's disease. *Clinical Neuropharmacology, 24*, 170–172.

Gupta, R., & Derevensky, J. L. (1997). Familial and social influences on juvenile gambling behavior. *Journal of Gambling Studies, 13*, 179–192.

Gupta, R., & Derevensky, J. L. (1998). Adolescent gambling behavior: A prevalence study and examination of the correlates associated with excessive gambling. *Journal of Gambling Studies, 14*, 319–345.

Gupta, R., & Derevensky, J. L. (2000). Adolescents with gambling problems: From research to treatment. *Journal of Gambling Studies, 16*, 315–342.

Guy, W. (1976). *ECDEU assessment manual for psychopharmacology.* (U.S. Department of Health, Education, and Welfare publication No. ADM 76-338, pp. 218–222). Rockville, MD. National Institute of Mental Health.

Hall, G. W., Carriero, N. J., Takushi, R. Y., Montoya, I. D., Preston, K. L., & Gorelick, D. A. (2000). Pathological gambling among cocaine-dependent outpatients. *American Journal of Psychiatry, 157*, 1127–1133.

Haller, R., & Hinterhuber, H. (1994). Treatment of pathological gambling with carbamazepine. *Pharmacopsychiatry, 27*, 129.

Hand, I. (1998). Pathological gambling: A negative state model and its implications for behavioral treatments. *CNS Spectrums, 3*, 58–69.

Hardoon, K. K., Baboushkin, H. R., Derevensky, J. L., & Gupta, R. (2001). Underlying cognitions in the selection of lottery tickets. *Journal of Clinical Psychology, 57*, 749–763.

Hardoon, K. K., Derevensky, J. L., & Gupta, R. (2003). Empirical measures vs. perceived gambling severity: Why adolescents don't present themselves for treatment. *Addictive Behaviors, 28*, 933–946.

Harris, H. I. (1964). Gambling addiction in an adolescent male. *Psychoanalytic Quarterly, 33*, 513–525.

Heather, N. (1989). Psychology and brief interventions. *British Journal of Addiction, 84*, 357–370.

Heineman, M. (1987). A comparison: The treatment of wives of alcoholics with the treatment of wives of pathological gamblers. *Journal of Gambling Behavior, 3*, 27–40.

Heineman, M. (1994). Compulsive gambling: Structured family intervention. *Journal of Gambling Studies, 10*, 67–76.

Heineman, M. (2001). *Losing your shirt: Recovery for compulsive gamblers and their families* (2nd ed.). Center City, MN: Hazelden.

Heyman, G. (1996). Resolving the contradictions of addiction. *Behavior and Brain Science, 19*, 561–610.

Hodgins, D. C. (2001). Processes of changing gambling behavior. *Addictive Behaviors, 26*, 121–128.

Hodgins, D. C. (2002). Using the NORC *DSM* Screen for Gambling Problems (NODS) as an outcome measure for pathological gambling: Reliability and validity. *National Association for Gambling Studies Journal, 14*, 9–17.

Hodgins, D. C., Currie, S. R., & el-Guebaly, N. (2001). Motivational enhancement and self-help treatments for problem gambling. *Journal of Consulting and Clinical Psychology, 69,* 50–57.

Hodgins, D. C., & el-Guebaly, N. (2000). Natural and treatment-assisted recovery from gambling problems: A comparison of resolved and active gamblers. *Addiction, 95,* 777–789.

Hodgins, D. C., Leigh, G., Milne, R., & Gerrish, R. (1997). Drinking goal selection in behavioral self-management treatment of chronic alcoholics. *Addictive Behaviors, 22,* 247–255.

Hodgins, D. C., & Makarchuk, K. (2003). Trusting problem gamblers: Reliability and validity of self-reported gambling behavior. *Psychology of Addictive Behaviors, 17,* 244–248.

Hodgins, D. C., Makarchuk, K., el-Guebaly, N., & Peden, N. (2002). Why problem gamblers quit gambling: A comparison of methods and samples. *Addiction Research and Theory, 10,* 203–218.

Hodgins, D. C., Ungar, J., el-Guebaly, N., & Armstrong, S. (1997). Getting back on the wagon: Reasons and strategies for terminating alcoholic relapses. *Psychology of Addictive Behaviors, 11,* 174–181.

Hodgins, D. C., Wynne, H., & Makarchuk, K. (1999). Pathways to recovery from gambling problems: Follow-up from a general population survey. *Journal of Gambling Studies, 15,* 93–104.

Hollander, E., DeCaria, C. M., Finkell, J. N., Begaz, T., Wong, C. M., & Cartwright, C. (2000). A randomized double-blind fluvoxamine/placebo crossover trial in pathologic gambling. *Biological Psychiatry, 47,* 813–817.

Hollander, E., DeCaria, C., Mari, E., Wong, C. M., Mosovich, S., Grossman, R., & Begaz, T. (1998). Short-term single-blind fluvoxamine treatment of pathological gambling. *American Journal of Psychiatry, 155,* 1781–1783.

Hollander, E., Frenkel, M., DeCaria, C., Trungold, S., & Stein, D. (1992). Treatment of pathological gambling with clomipramine. *American Journal of Psychiatry, 149,* 710–711.

Hollander, E., Stein, D. J., Kwon, J. H., Rowland, C., Wong, C. M., Broatch, J., & Himelein, C. (1997). Psychosocial function and economic costs of obsessive–compulsive disorder. *CNS Spectrums, 2,* 16–25.

Hollander, E., & Wong, C. M. (1995). Body dysmorphic disorder, pathological gambling, and sexual compulsions. *Journal of Clinical Psychiatry, 56,* 7–12.

Hong, Y. Y., & Chiu, C. Y. (1988). Sex, locus of control and illusion of control in Hong Kong as correlates of gambling involvement. *Journal of Social Psychology, 128,* 667–673.

Hope, J., & Havir, L. (2002). You bet they're having fun! Older Americans and casino gambling. *Journal of Aging Studies, 16,* 177–197.

Horodecki, I. (1992). The treatment model of the Guidance Center for Gamblers and Their Relatives in Vienna, Austria. *Journal of Gambling Studies, 8,* 115–129.

Hraba, J., & Lee, G. (1995). Problem gambling and policy advice: The mutability and relative effects of structural, associational and attitudinal variables. *Journal of Gambling Studies, 11*, 105–121.

Hwu, H.-G., Yeh, E.-K., & Chang, L.-Y. (1989). Prevalence of psychiatric disorders in Taiwan defined by the Chinese Diagnostic Interview Schedule. *Acta Psychiatrica Scandinavica, 79*, 136–147.

Ibàñez, A., Blanco, C., Donahue, E., Lesieur, H. R., Pérez de Castro, I., Fernández-Piqueras, J., & Sáiz-Ruiz, J. (2001). Psychiatric comorbidity in pathological gamblers seeking treatment. *American Journal of Psychiatry, 158*, 1733–1735.

Ibàñez, A. G., Mercade, P. V., Sanroma, M. N. A., & Cordero, C. P. (1992). Clinical and behavioral evaluation of pathological gambling in Barcelona, Spain. *Journal of Gambling Studies, 8*, 299–310.

Ibàñez, A., Pérez de Castro, I., Fernández-Piqueras, J., Blanco, C., & Sáiz-Ruiz, J. (2000). Genetic association study between pathological gambling and DNA polymorphic markers at MAO-A and MAO-B genes. *Molecular Psychiatry, 5*, 105–109.

Ide-Smith, S. G., & Lea, S. E. G. (1988). Gambling in young adolescents. *Journal of Gambling Behavior, 4*, 110–118.

Imhoff, J. E. (1991). Countertransference issues in the treatment of drug and alcohol addiction. In N. S. Miller (Ed.), *Drug and alcohol addiction* (pp. 931–946). New York: Marcel Dekker.

Institute of Medicine. (1990). *Broadening the base of treatment for alcohol problems.* Washington, DC: National Academy of Sciences.

Isaranurug, S., Nitirat, P., Chauytong, P., & Wongarsa, C. (2001). Factors relating to the aggressive behavior of primary caregivers toward a child. *Journal of the Medical Association of Thailand, 84*, 1481–1489.

Jackson, A. C., Thomas, S. A., Ross, L., & Kearney, E. (2000). *Analysis of clients presenting to problem gambling counselling services, July 1999 to June 2000* (Client and Services Analysis Report No. 6). Melbourne, Australia: Victorian Department of Human Services.

Jacobs, D. F. (1989a). A general theory of addictions: Rationale for and evidence supporting a new approach for understanding and treating addictive behaviors. In H. J. Shaffer, S. A. Stein, B. Gambino, & T. N. Cummings (Eds.), *Compulsive gambling: Theory, research, and practice* (pp. 35–64). Lexington, MA: Lexington Books.

Jacobs, D. F. (1989b). Illegal and undocumented: A review of teenage gambling and the plight of children of problem gamblers in America. In H. Shaffer (Ed.), *Compulsive gambling: Theory, research and practice* (pp. 249–292). Toronto, Ontario, Canada: Lexington Books.

Jacobs, D. F. (2000). Juvenile gambling in North America: An analysis of long term trends and future prospects. *Journal of Gambling Studies, 16*, 119–152.

Jacobs, D. F., Marston, A. R., Singer, R. D., Widaman, K., Little, T., & Veizades, J. (1989). Children of problem gamblers. *Journal of Gambling Behavior, 5*, 261–268.

Jaisoorya, T. S., Reddy, Y. C. J., & Srinath, S. (2003). The relationship of obsessive–compulsive disorder to putative spectrum disorders: Results from an Indian study. *Comprehensive Psychiatry, 44,* 317–323.

Jessor, R., & Jessor, S. (1977). *Problem behavior and psychosocial development: A longitudinal study of youth.* New York: Academic Press.

Johnson, E. E., Hamer, R. M., & Nora, R. M. (1998). The Lie/Bet Questionnaire for screening pathological gamblers: A follow-up study. *Psychological Reports, 83,* 1219–1224.

Johnson, E. E., Hamer, R., Nora, R. M., Tan, B., Eisenstein, N., & Engelhart, C. (1997). The Lie/Bet Questionnaire for screening pathological gamblers. *Psychological Reports, 80,* 83–88.

Johnson, E. E., & Nora, R. M. (1992). Does spousal participation in Gamblers Anonymous benefit compulsive gamblers? *Psychological Reports, 71,* 914.

Johnson, J. G., Cohen, P., Dohrenwend, B. P., Link, B. G., & Brook, J. S. (1999). A longitudinal investigation of social causation and social selection processes involved in the association between socioeconomic status and psychiatric disorders. *Journal of Abnormal Psychology, 108,* 490–499.

Kahneman, D., & Tversky, A. (1982). The psychology of preferences. *Scientific American, 246,* 160–173.

Kallick, M., Suits, D., Dielman, T., & Hybels, J. (1976). *Survey of American gambling attitudes and behaviors.* Washington, DC: U.S. Government Printing Office.

Kallick, M., Suits, D., Dielman, T., & Hybels, J. (1979). *A survey of American gambling attitudes and behavior.* Ann Arbor: University of Michigan Press.

Kaufman, E. (1989). The psychotherapy of dually diagnosed patients. *Journal of Substance Abuse Treatment, 6,* 9–18.

Kaufman, E. (1992). Countertransference and other mutually interactive aspects of psychotherapy with substance abusers. *American Journal on Addictions, 1,* 185–202.

Kearny, C. A., & Drabman, R. S. (1992). Risk taking/gambling-like behavior in preschool children. *Journal of Gambling Studies, 8,* 287–297.

Kennedy, P. F., Phanjoo, A. L., & Shekim, W. O. (1971). Risk-taking in the lives of parasuicides (attempted suicides). *British Journal of Psychiatry, 119,* 281–286.

Khantzian, E. J. (1975). Self-selection and progression in drug dependence. *Psychiatry Digest, 10,* 19–22.

Kim, S. W. (1998). Opioid antagonists in the treatment of impulse-control disorders. *Journal of Clinical Psychiatry, 59,* 159–164.

Kim, S. W., & Grant, J. E. (2001). An open naltrexone treatment study in pathological gambling disorder. *International Clinical Psychopharmacology, 16,* 285–289.

Kim, S. W., Grant, J. E., Adson, D. E., & Shin, Y. C. (2001). Double-blind naltrexone and placebo comparison study in the treatment of pathological gambling. *Biological Psychiatry, 49,* 914–921.

Kim, S. W., Grant, J. E., Adson, D. E., Shin, Y. C., & Zaninelli, R. (2002). A double-blind placebo-controlled study of the efficacy and safety of paroxetine in the treatment of pathological gambling. *Journal of Clinical Psychiatry, 63,* 501–507.

King, A. C., Volpicelli, J. R., Gunduz, M., O'Brien, C. P., & Kreek, M. J. (1997). Naltrexone biotransformation and incidence of subjective side effects: A preliminary study. *Alcoholism: Clinical and Experimental Research, 21,* 906–909.

King, K. M. (1990). Neutralizing marginally deviant behavior: Bingo players and superstition. *Journal of Gambling Studies, 6,* 43–62.

Kirby, K. N., Petry, N. M., & Bickel, W. K. (1999). Heroin addicts have higher discount rates for delayed rewards than non-drug using controls. *Journal of Experimental Psychology: General, 128,* 78–87.

Kleber, H. D., Weissman, M. M., Rounsaville, B. J., Prusoff, B. A., & Wilber, C. H. (1983). Imipramine as treatment for depression in opiate addicts. *Archives of General Psychiatry, 40,* 649–653.

Koehler, J. J., Gibbs, B. J., & Hogarth, R. M. (1994). Shattering the illusion of control: Multi-shot versus single-shot gambles. *Journal of Behavioral Decision Making, 7,* 183–191.

Koller, K. N. (1972). Treatment of poker machine addicts by aversion therapy. *Medical Journal of Australia, 1,* 742–745.

Koob, G. F. (1992). Drugs of abuse: Anatomy, pharmacology and function of reward pathways. *Trends in Pharmacological Science, 13,* 177–184.

Kosten, T. R., Rounsaville, B. J., & Kleber, H. D. (1983). Concurrent validity of the Addiction Severity Index. *Journal of Nervous and Mental Disease, 171,* 606–610.

Kraft, T. (1970). A short note on forty patients treated by systematic desensitization. *Behavior Research and Therapy, 8,* 219–220.

Kranzler, H. R., Amin, H., Modesto-Lowe, V., & Oncken, C. (1999). Pharmacologic treatments for drug and alcohol dependence. *Psychiatric Clinics of North America, 22,* 401–423.

Kranzler, H. R., Burleson, J. A., Korner, P., Del Boca, F. K., Bohn, M. J., Brown, J., & Liebowitz, N. (1995). Placebo-controlled trial of fluoxetine as an adjunct to relapse prevention in alcoholics. *American Journal of Psychiatry, 152,* 391–397.

Kranzler, H. R., Escobar, R., Lee, D. K., & Meza, E. (1986). Elevated rates of early discontinuation from pharmacotherapy trials in alcoholics and drug users. *Alcoholism: Clinical and Experimental Research, 20,* 16–20.

Kroeber, H. L. (1992). Roulette gamblers and gamblers at electronic game machines: What are the differences? *Journal of Gambling Studies, 8,* 79–92.

Krystal, H. (1978). Self-representation and the capacity for self-care. *Annual Psychoanalysis, 6,* 209–246.

Kweitel, R., & Allen, F. C. L. (1998). Cognitive processes associated with gambling behaviour. *Psychological Reports, 82,* 147–153.

Kyngdon, A., & Dickerson, M. (1999). An experimental study of the effect of prior alcohol consumption on a simulated gambling activity. *Addiction, 94,* 697–707.

Ladd, G. T., Molina, C. A., Kerins, G. J., & Petry, N. M. (2003). Gambling participation and problems among older adults. *Journal of Geriatric Psychiatry & Neurology, 16,* 172–177.

Ladd, G. T., & Petry, N. M. (2002a). Disordered gambling among university-based medical and dental patients: A focus on Internet gambling. *Psychology of Addictive Behaviors, 16,* 76–79.

Ladd, G. T., & Petry, N. M. (2002b). Gender differences among pathological gamblers seeking treatment. *Experimental and Clinical Psychopharmacology, 10,* 302–309.

Ladd, G. T., & Petry, N. M. (2003). A comparison of pathological gamblers with and without substance abuse treatment histories. *Experimental and Clinical Psychopharmacology, 11,* 202–209.

Ladouceur, R. (1991). Prevalence estimates of pathological gambling in Quebec. *Canadian Journal of Psychiatry, 36,* 732–734.

Ladouceur, R. (1996). The prevalence of pathological gambling in Canada. *Journal of Gambling Studies, 12,* 129–142.

Ladouceur, R., Boisvert, J. M., & Dumont, J. (1994). Cognitive–behavioral treatment for adolescent pathological gamblers. *Behavior Modification, 18,* 230–242.

Ladouceur R., Boisvert, J. M., Pepin, M., Loranger, M., & Sylvain, C. (1994). Social cost of pathological gambling. *Journal of Gambling Studies, 10,* 399–409.

Ladouceur, R., Bouchard, C., Rheaume, N., Jacques, C., Ferland, F., Leblond, J., & Walker, M. (2000). Is the SOGS an accurate measure of pathological gambling among children, adolescents and adults? *Journal of Gambling Studies, 16,* 1–24.

Ladouceur, R., Boudreault, N., Jacques, C., & Vitaro, F. (1999). Pathological gambling and related problems among adolescents. *Journal of Child and Adolescent Substance Abuse, 8,* 55–68.

Ladouceur, R., & Dubé, D. (1997). Erroneous perceptions in generating random sequences: Identification and strength of a basic misconception in gambling behavior. *Swiss Journal of Psychology, 56,* 256–259.

Ladouceur, R., Dubé, D., & Bujold, A. (1994). Prevalence of pathological gambling and related problems among college students in the Quebec metropolitan area. *Canadian Journal of Psychiatry, 39,* 289–293.

Ladouceur, R., & Gaboury, A. (1988). Effects of limited and unlimited stakes on gambling behavior. *Journal of Gambling Behavior, 4,* 119–126.

Ladouceur, R., Gaboury, A., Bujold, A., LaChance, N., & Tremblay, S. (1991). Ecological validity of laboratory studies of videopoker gambling. *Journal of Gambling Studies, 7,* 109–116.

Ladouceur, R., Gaboury, A., Dumont, M., & Rochette, P. (1988). Gambling: Relationship between the frequency of wins and irrational thinking. *Journal of Psychology, 122,* 409–414.

Ladouceur, R., Jacques, C., Ferland, F., & Giroux, I. (1999). Prevalence of problem gambling: A replication study 7 years later. *Canadian Journal of Psychiatry, 44*, 802–804.

Ladouceur, R., Jacques, C., Giroux, I., Ferland, F., & LeBlond, J. (2000). Analysis of a casino's self-exclusion program. *Journal of Gambling Studies, 16*, 453–460.

Ladouceur, R., Mayrand, M., & Tourigny, Y. (1987). Risk-taking behavior in gamblers and non-gamblers during prolonged exposure. *Journal of Gambling Behavior, 3*, 115–122.

Ladouceur, R., Sevigny, S., Blaszczynski, A. P., O'Connor, K., & Lavoie, M. E. (2003). Video lottery: Winning expectancies and arousal. *Addiction, 98*, 733–738.

Ladouceur, R., Sylvain, S., Boutin, C., & Doucet, C. (2002). *Understanding and treating pathological gambling.* New York: Wiley.

Ladouceur, R., Sylvain, C., Boutin, C., Lachance, S., Doucet, C., & Leblond, J. (2003). Group therapy for pathological gamblers: A cognitive approach. *Behaviour Research and Therapy, 41*, 587–596.

Ladouceur, R., Sylvain, S., Boutin, C., Lachance, S., Doucet, C., Leblond, J., & Jacques, C. (2001). Cognitive treatment of pathological gambling. *Journal of Nervous and Mental Disease, 189*, 774–780.

Ladouceur, R., Sylvain, C., Letarte, H., Giroux, I., & Jacques, C. (1998). Cognitive treatment of pathological gamblers. *Behaviour Research and Therapy, 36*, 1111–1119.

Ladouceur, R., & Walker, M. (1996). A cognitive perspective on gambling. In P. M. Salkovskis (Ed.), *Trends in cognitive and behavioral therapies* (pp. 89–119). New York: Wiley.

Langenbucher, J., Bavly, L., Labouvie, E., Sanjuan, P. M., & Martin, C. S. (2001). Clinical features of pathological gambling in an addictions treatment cohort. *Psychology of Addictive Behaviors, 15*, 77–79.

Langer, E. J. (1975). The illusion of control. *Journal of Personality and Social Psychology, 32*, 311–328.

Langer, E. J. (1983). *The psychology of control.* Beverly Hills, CA: Sage.

Langer, E. J., & Roth, J. (1975). Heads I win, tails it's chance: The illusion of control as a function of the sequence of outcomes in a purely chance task. *Journal of Personality and Social Psychology, 32*, 951–953.

Leary, K., & Dickerson, M. (1985). Levels of arousal in high- and low-frequency gamblers. *Behaviour Research and Therapy, 23*, 635–640.

Ledgerwood, D. M., & Downey, K. K. (2002). Relationship between problem gambling and substance use in a methadone maintenance population. *Addictive Behaviors, 27*, 483–491.

Lee, C. K., Kwak, Y. S., Yamamoto, J., Rhee, H., Kim, Y. S., Han, J. H., et al. (1990). Psychiatric epidemiology in Korea: Part I. Gender and age differences in Seoul. *Journal of Nervous and Mental Disease, 178*, 242–246.

Legarda, J. J., Babio, R., & Abreu, J. M. (1992). Prevalence estimates of pathological gambling in Seville (Spain). *British Journal of Addiction, 87*, 767–770.

Lejoyeux, M., Arbaretaz, M., McLoughlin, M., & Ades, J. (2002). Impulse control disorders and depression. *Journal of Nervous and Mental Disease, 190,* 310–314.

Lejoyeux, M., Loi, S., Solomon, J., & Ades, J. (1999). Study of impulse-control disorders among alcohol-dependent patients. *Journal of Clinical Psychiatry, 60,* 302–305.

Lepage, C., Ladouceur, R., & Jacques, C. (2000). Prevalence of problem gambling among community service users. *Community Mental Health Journal, 36,* 597–601.

Lesieur, H. R. (1977). *The chase: Career of the compulsive gambler.* Oxford, England: Anchor.

Lesieur, H. R. (1989). Experience of employee assistance programs with pathological gamblers. *Journal of Drug Issues, 19,* 425–436.

Lesieur, H. R., & Anderson, C. W. (1995). *Results of a 1995 survey of Gamblers Anonymous members in Illinois.* Evanston: Illinois Council on Problem and Compulsive Gambling.

Lesieur, H. R., & Blume, S. B. (1987). The South Oaks Gambling Screen (The SOGS): A new instrument for the identification of pathological gamblers. *American Journal of Psychiatry, 144,* 1184–1188.

Lesieur, H. R., & Blume, S. B. (1990). Characteristics of pathological gamblers identified among patients on a psychiatric admissions service. *Hospital and Community Psychiatry, 41,* 1009–1012.

Lesieur, H. R., & Blume, S. B. (1991a). Evaluation of patients treated for pathological gambling in a combined alcohol, substance abuse and pathological gambling treatment unit using the Addiction Severity Index. *British Journal of Addiction, 86,* 1017–1028.

Lesieur, H. R., & Blume, S. B. (1991b). When Lady Luck loses: The female pathological gambler. In N. van den Bergh (Ed.), *Feminist perspectives on addictions* (pp. 181–197). New York: Springer.

Lesieur, H. R., & Blume, S. B. (1992). Modifying the Addiction Severity Index for use with pathological gamblers. *American Journal on Addictions, 1,* 240–247.

Lesieur, H. R., & Blume, S. B. (1993). Pathological gambling, eating disorders and the psychoactive substance use disorders. *Journal of Addictive Diseases, 12,* 89–102.

Lesieur, H. R., Blume, S. B., & Zoppa, R. M. (1986). Alcoholism, drug abuse and gambling. *Alcoholism: Clinical and Experimental Research, 10,* 33–38.

Lesieur, H. R., Cross, J., Frank, M., Welch, M., White, C., Rubenstein, G., et al. (1991). Gambling and pathological gambling among college students. *Addictive Behaviors, 16,* 517–527.

Lesieur, H. R., & Heineman, M. (1988). Pathological gambling among youthful multiple substance abusers in a therapeutic community. *British Journal of Addiction, 83,* 765–771.

Lesieur, H. R., & Klein, R. (1987). Pathological gambling among high school students. *Addictive Behaviors, 12,* 129–135.

Lesieur, H. R., & Rothschild, J. (1989). Children of Gamblers Anonymous members. *Journal of Gambling Behavior*, 5, 269–281.

Lester, D. (1980). Choice of gambling activity and belief in locus of control. *Psychological Reports*, 47, 22.

Letarte, H., Ladouceur, R., & Mayrand, M. (1986). Primary and secondary illusory control and risk-taking in gambling (roulette). *Psychological Reports*, 58, 299–302.

Linden, R. D., Pope, H. G., & Jonas, J. M. (1986). Pathological gambling and major affective disorder: Preliminary findings. *Journal of Clinical Psychiatry*, 47, 201–203.

Lindner, R. M. (1950). The psychodynamics of gambling. *Annals of the American Academy of Political and Social Science*, 269, 93–107.

Lobsinger, C., & Beckett, L. (1996). *Odds on the break even: A practical approach to gambling awareness*. Canberra: Relationships Australia, Inc.

Lopez-Viets, V. C., & Miller, W. R. (1997). Treatment approaches for pathological gamblers. *Clinical Psychology Review*, 17, 689–702.

Lorenz, V. C., & Shuttlesworth, D. E. (1983). The impact of pathologic gambling on the spouse of the gambler. *Journal of Community Psychiatry*, 11, 67–75.

Lorenz, V. C., & Yaffee, R. A. (1988). Pathological gambling and psychosomatic, emotional and mental difficulties as reported by the spouse. *Journal of Gambling Behavior*, 4, 13–26.

Lorenz, V. C., & Yaffee, R. A. (1989). Pathological gamblers and their spouses: Problems in interaction. *Journal of Gambling Behavior*, 5, 113–126.

Lumley, M. A., & Roby, K. J. (1995). Alexithymia and pathological gambling. *Psychotherapy and Psychosomatics*, 63, 201–206.

Lupu, V., Lupu, D., Onaca, E., Balta, L., Sauca, A., & David, A. (2001). Pathological gambling in Romanian teenagers. *Cognitie Creier Comportament*, 5, 19–28.

Lynch, W. J., & Carroll, M. E. (2000). Reinstatement of cocaine self-administration in rats: Sex differences. *Psychopharmacology*, 148, 196–200.

Maccallum, F., & Blaszczynski, A. P. (2002). Pathological gambling and comorbid substance abuse. *Australia and New Zealand Journal of Psychiatry*, 36, 411–415.

Madden, G. J., Petry, N. M., Badger, G., & Bickel, W. K. (1997). Impulsive and self-control choices in opioid-dependent and non-drug-using controls. *Experimental and Clinical Psychopharmacology*, 5, 256–263.

Makarchuk, K., Hodgins, D. C., & Peden, N. (2002). Development of a brief intervention for concerned significant others of problem gamblers. *Addictive Disorders and Their Treatment*, 1, 126–134.

Mark, M. E., & Lesieur, H. R. (1992). A feminist critique of problem gambling research. *British Journal of Addiction*, 87, 549–565.

Martin, C. S., Earleywine, M., Musty, R. E., Perrine, M. W., & Swift, R. (1993). Development and validation of the Biphasic Alcohol Effects Scale. *Alcoholism: Clinical and Experimental Research*, 17, 140–146.

Mazur, J. E. (1987). An adjusting procedure for studying delayed reinforcement. In M. L. Commons, J. E. Mazur, J. A. Nevin, & H. Rachlin (Eds.), *Quantitative analysis of behavior: Vol. 5. The effect of delay and of intervening events on reinforcement value* (pp. 55–73). Hillsdale, NJ: Erlbaum.

McCartney, J. (1996). A community study of natural change across the addictions. *Addiction Research, 4,* 65–83.

McCleary, R., Chew, K. S. Y., Merrill, V., & Napolitano, C. (2002). Does legalized gambling elevate the risk of suicide? An analysis of U.S. countries and metropolitan areas. *Suicide and Life-Threatening Behavior, 32,* 209–221.

McConaghy, N., Armstrong, M. S., Blaszczynski, A. P., & Allcock, C. (1983). Controlled comparison of aversive therapy and imaginal desensitization in compulsive gambling. *British Journal of Psychiatry, 142,* 366–372.

McConaghy, N., Armstrong, M. S., Blaszczynski, A. P., & Allcock, C. (1988). Behavior completion versus stimulus control in compulsive gambling: Implications for behavioral assessment. *Behavior Modification, 12,* 371–384.

McConaghy, N., Blaszczynski, A. P., & Frankova, A. (1991). Comparisons of imaginal desensitization with other behavioral treatments of pathological gambling: A two- to nine-year follow-up. *British Journal of Psychiatry, 159,* 390–393.

McCormick, R. A. (1988). Pathological gambling: A parsimonious need state model. *Journal of Gambling Behavior, 3,* 257–263.

McCormick, R. A. (1993). Disinhibition and negative affectivity in substance abusers with and without a gambling problem. *Addictive Behaviors, 18,* 331–336.

McCormick, R. A. (1994). The importance of coping skill enhancement in the treatment of the pathological gambler. *Journal of Gambling Studies, 10,* 77–86.

McCormick, R. A. (1996). Pathological gambling. In *The Hatherleigh guide to psychiatric disorders* (pp. 153–169). New York: Hatherleigh Press.

McCormick, R. A., Russo, A. M., Ramirez, L. F., & Taber, J. I. (1984). Affective disorders among pathological gamblers seeking treatment. *American Journal of Psychiatry, 141,* 215–218.

McCormick, R. A., Taber, J. I., & Kruedelbach, N. (1989). The relationship between attributional style and post-traumatic stress disorder in addicted patients. *Journal of Traumatic Stress, 4,* 477–487.

McGue, M., Pickens, R. W., & Svikis, D. S. (1992). Sex and age effects on the inheritance of alcohol problems: A twin study. *Journal of Abnormal Psychology, 101,* 3–17.

McLellan, A. T., Arndt, I. O., Woody, G. E., & Metzger, D. (1993). Psychosocial services in substance abuse treatment. *Journal of the American Medical Association, 269,* 1953–1959.

McLellan, A. T., Luborsky, L., Cacciola, J., Griffith, J., Evans, F., Barr, H. L., & O'Brien, C. P. (1985). New data from the Addiction Severity Index: Reliability and validity in three centers. *Journal of Nervous and Mental Disease, 173,* 412–423.

McLellan, A. T., Woody, G. E., Metzger, D., McKay, J., Alterman, A., & O'Brien, C. P. (1996). Evaluating effectiveness of treatments for substance abuse disorders: Reasonable expectations, appropriate comparisons. *Milbank Quarterly, 74*, 51–85.

McNeilly, D. P., & Burke, W. J. (2000). Late life gambling: The attitudes and behaviors of older adults. *Journal of Gambling Studies, 16*, 393–415.

Meyer, G., Hauffa, B. P., Schedlowski, M., Pawlak, C., Stadler, M. A., & Exton, M. S. (2000). Casino gambling increases heart rate and salivary cortisol in regular gamblers. *Biological Psychiatry, 48*, 948–953.

Meyers, R. J., & Smith, J. E. (1997). Getting off the fence: Procedures to engage treatment-resistant drinkers. *Journal of Substance Abuse Treatment, 14*, 467–472.

Miller, L. K. (1970). Some punishing effects of response-force. *Journal of the Experimental Analysis of Behavior, 13*, 215–220.

Miller, W. (1986). Individual outpatient treatment of pathological gambling. *Journal of Gambling Behavior, 2*, 95–107.

Miller, W. R., Meyers, R. J., & Tonigan, J. S. (1999). Engaging the unmotivated in treatment for alcohol problems: A comparison of three strategies for intervention through family members. *Journal of Consulting and Clinical Psychology, 67*, 688–697.

Miller, W. R., & Rollnick, S. (1992). *Motivational interviewing: Preparing people to change addictive behavior*. New York: Guilford Press.

Miller, W. R., & Rollnick, S. (2002). Motivational interviewing: Preparing people for change (2nd ed.). New York: Guilford Press.

Milton, S., Crino, R., Hunt, C., & Prosser, E. (2002). The effect of compliance-improving interventions on the cognitive–behavioral treatment of pathological gambling. *Journal of Gambling Studies, 18*, 207–229.

Modesto-Lowe, V., & van Kirk, J. (2002). Clinical uses of naltrexone: A review of the evidence. *Experimental and Clinical Psychopharmacology, 10*, 213–227.

Mok, W. P., & Hraba, J. (1991). Age and shifting gambling behavior: A decline and shifting pattern of participation. *Journal of Gambling Studies, 7*, 313–335.

Molina, J. A., Sainz-Artiga, M. J., Fraile, A., Jimenez-Jimenez, F. J., Villanueva, C., Orti-Pareja, M., & Bermejo, F. (2000). Pathologic gambling in Parkinson's disease: A behavioral manifestation of pharmacologic treatment? *Movement Disorders, 15*, 869–872.

Monti, P. M., Abrams, D. B., Kadden, R. K., & Cooney, N. L. (1989). *Treating alcohol dependence: A coping skills training guide*. New York: Guilford Press.

Moore, S. M., & Ohtsuka, K. (1999). Beliefs about control over gambling among young people, and their relation to problem gambling. *Psychology of Addictive Behaviors, 13*, 339–347.

Moore, S. M., & Ohtsuka, K. (2000). The structure of young people's leisure and their gambling behaviour. *Behaviour Change, 17*, 167–177.

Moore, T. (2001). *Older adult gambling in Oregon: An epidemiological survey*. Salem: Oregon Gambling Addiction Treatment Foundation.

Moravec, J. D., & Munley, P. H. (1983). Psychological test findings on pathological gamblers and treatment. *International Journal of Addictions, 18,* 1003–1009.

Moreno, I., Sáiz-Ruiz, J., & López-Ibor, J. J. (1991). Serotonin and gambling dependence. *Human Psychopharmacology, 6,* S9–S12.

Moreyra, P., Ibàñez, A., Liebowitz, M. R., Sáiz-Ruiz, J., & Blanco, C. (2002). Pathological gambling: Addiction or obsession. *Psychiatric Annals, 32,* 161–166.

Moskowitz, J. A. (1980). Lithium and Lady Luck: Use of lithium carbonate in compulsive gambling. *New York State Journal of Medicine, 80,* 785–788.

Moss, H. B., Yao, J. K., & Panzak, G. L. (1990). Serotonergic responsivity and behavioral dimensions in antisocial personality disorder with substance abuse. *Biological Psychiatry, 28,* 325–338.

Muelleman, R. L., DenOtter, T., Wadman, M. C., Tran, T. P., & Anderson, J. (2002). Violence: Recognition, management and prevention. *Journal of Emergency Medicine, 23,* 307–312.

Myerson, J., & Green, L. (1995). Discounting of delayed reinforcers: Models of individual choice. *Journal of the Experimental Analysis of Behavior, 64,* 263–276.

National Endowment for Financial Education. (2000). *Personal financial strategies for the loved ones of problem gamblers.* Retrieved November 1, 2003, from http://www.nefe.org

National Gambling Impact Study Commission. (1999). *National Gambling Impact Study Commission final report.* Retrieved November 1, 2003, from http://govinfo.library.unt.edu/ngisc/reports/fullrpt.html

National Research Council. (1999). *Pathological gambling: A critical review.* Washington, DC: National Academy Press.

Neighbors, C., Lostutter, T. W., Larimer, M. E., & Takushi, R. Y. (2002). Measuring gambling outcomes among college students. *Journal of Gambling Studies, 18,* 339–360.

Niederland, W. G. (1967). A contribution to the psychology of gambling. *Psychoanalytic Forum, 2,* 175–185.

Niederland, W. G. (1968). Clinical observations on the survivor syndrome. *International Journal of Psychoanalysis, 49,* 313–315.

Nielsen, D. A., Virkkunen, M., Lappalainen, J., Eggert, M., Brown, G. L., Long, J. C., et al. (1998). A tryptophan hydroxylase gene marker for suicidality and alcoholism. *Archives of General Psychiatry, 55,* 593–602.

Nisbett, R., & Wilson, T. D. (1977). Telling more than we can know: Verbal reports on mental processes. *Psychological Review, 84,* 231–259.

Nordin, C., & Eklundh, T. (1999). Altered CSF 5-HIAA disposition in pathological male gamblers. *CNS Spectrums, 4,* 25–33.

Nowatzki, N. R., & Williams, R. J. (2002). Casino self-exclusion programmes: A review of the issues. *International Journal of Gambling Studies, 2,* 3–25.

Nowinski, J., Baker, S., & Carroll, K. M. (1995). *Twelve-step facilitation therapy manual: A clinical research guide for therapists treating individuals with alcohol abuse and dependence.* (Project MATCH Monograph Series, Vol. 1, NIH Publication No. 94-3722). Rockvillle, MD: U.S. Department of Health and Human Services.

Nunes, E. V., Quitkin, F. M., Brady, R., & Stewart, J. W. (1991). Imipramine treatment of methadone maintenance patients with affective disorder and illicit drug use. *American Journal of Psychiatry, 148,* 667–669.

Oliveria, M. P. M. T., & Silva, M. T. A. (2000). Pathological and nonpathological gamblers: A survey in gambling settings. *Substance Use and Misuse, 35,* 1573–1583.

O'Malley, S. S., Jaffe, A. J., Chang, G., Schottenfeld, R. S., Meyer, R. E., & Rounsaville, B. J. (1992). Naltrexone and coping skills therapy for alcohol dependence: A controlled study. *Archives of General Psychiatry, 49,* 881–887.

Oreland, L., Ekblom, J., Garpenstrand, H., & Hallman, J. (1998). Biological markers, with special regard to platelet monoamine oxidase (trbc-MAO), for personality and personality disorders. *Advances in Pharmacology, 42,* 301–304.

Oster, S. L., & Knapp, T. J. (2001). Underage and pathological gambling by college students: Emerging problem on campus? *Psychology and Education: An Interdisciplinary Journal, 38(2),* 15–19.

Pallanti, S., Quercioli, L., Sood, E., & Hollander, E. (2002). Lithium and valproate treatment of pathological gambling: A randomized single-blind study. *Journal of Clinical Psychiatry, 63,* 559–564.

Paton-Simpson, G. R., Gruys, M. A., & Hannifin, J. B. (2002). *Problem gambling counselling in New Zealand: 2001 national statistics.* Palmerston North, New Zealand: Problem Gambling Purchasing Agency.

Pérez de Castro, I., Ibàñez, A., Sáiz-Ruiz, J., & Fernández-Piqueras, J. (1999). Genetic contribution to pathological gambling: Association between a functional DNA polymorphism at the serotonin transporter gene (5-HTT) and affected males. *Pharmacogenetics, 9,* 397–400.

Pérez de Castro, I., Ibàñez, A., Sáiz-Ruiz, J., & Fernández-Piqueras, J. (2002). Concurrent positive association between pathological gambling and functional DNA polymorphisms at the MAO-A and the 5-HT transporter genes. *Molecular Psychiatry, 7,* 927–932.

Pérez de Castro, I., Ibàñez, A., Torres, P., Sáiz-Ruiz, J., & Fernández-Piqueras, J. (1997). Genetic association study between pathological gambling and a functional DNA polymorphism at the D4 receptor. *Pharmacogenetics, 7,* 345–348.

Petry, N. M. (1998). *Cognitive–behavioral therapy for treatment of pathological gambling: A therapist's manual.* Unpublished manual.

Petry, N. M. (2000a). A comprehensive guide for the application of contingency management procedures in standard clinic settings. *Drug and Alcohol Dependence, 58,* 9–25.

Petry, N. M. (2000b). Gambling problems in substance abusers are associated with increased sexual risk behaviors. *Addiction, 95,* 1089–1100.

Petry N. M. (2000c). Psychiatric symptoms in problem gambling and non-problem gambling substance abusers. *American Journal on Addictions, 9,* 163–171.

Petry, N. M. (2001a). Pathological gamblers, with and without substance use disorders, discount delayed rewards at high rates. *Journal of Abnormal Psychology*, *110*, 482–487.

Petry, N. M. (2001b). Substance abuse, pathological gambling, and impulsivity. *Drug and Alcohol Dependence*, *63*, 29–38.

Petry, N. M. (2002a). A comparison of young, middle age, and older adult treatment-seeking pathological gamblers. *The Gerontologist*, *42*, 92–99.

Petry, N. M. (2002b). Psychotherapies and pharmacotherapies from substance abuse treatment may inform development of treatments for pathological gambling. *Experimental and Clinical Psychopharmacology*, *10*, 184–192.

Petry, N. M. (2003a). A comparison of treatment-seeking pathological gamblers based on preferred gambling activity. *Addiction*, *98*, 645–655.

Petry, N. M. (2003b). Patterns and correlates of Gamblers Anonymous attendance in pathological gamblers seeking professional treatment. *Addictive Behaviors*, *27*, 1–14.

Petry, N. M. (2003c). Validity of the Addiction Severity Index in assessing gambling problems. *Journal of Nervous and Mental Disease*, *191*, 399–407.

Petry, N. M. (in press). Stages of change in treatment-seeking pathological gamblers. *Journal of Consulting and Clinical Psychology*.

Petry, N. M., Ammerman, Y., Bohl, J., Doersch, A., Gay, H., Kadden, R., et al. (2004). *Cognitive–behavioral therapy for pathological gamblers*. Manuscript submitted for publication.

Petry, N. M., & Armentano, C. (1999). Prevalence, assessment, and treatment of pathological gambling: A review. *Psychiatric Services*, *50*, 1021–1027.

Petry, N. M., Armentano, C., Kuoch, T., Norinth, T., & Smith, L. (2003). Gambling participation and problems among South East Asian refugees to the United States. *Psychiatric Services*, *54*, 1142–1148.

Petry, N. M., & Casarella, T. (1999). Excessive discounting of delayed reinforcers in substance abusers with gambling problems. *Drug and Alcohol Dependence*, *56*, 25–32.

Petry, N. M., & Kiluk, B. D. (2002). Suicidal ideation and suicide attempts in treatment-seeking pathological gamblers. *Journal of Nervous and Mental Disease*, *190*, 462–469.

Petry, N. M., Kirby, K. N., & Kranzler, H. R. (2002). Effects of gender and family history of alcohol dependence on a behavioral task of impulsivity in healthy subjects. *Journal of Studies on Alcohol*, *63*, 83–90.

Petry, N. M., & Mallya, S. (2004). Gambling participation and problems among employees at a university health center. *Journal of Gambling Studies*, *20*, 155–170.

Petry, N. M., & Oncken, C. (2002). Cigarette smoking is associated with increased severity of gambling problems in treatment-seeking gamblers. *Addiction*, *97*, 745–753.

Petry, N. M., & Pietrzak, R. H. (2004). Comorbidity of substance use and gambling disorders. In H. R. Kranzler & J. A. Tinsley (Eds.), *Dual diagnosis and psychiatric treatment: Substance abuse and comorbid disorders* (2nd ed., pp. 437–459). New York: Marcel Dekker.

Petry, N. M., & Roll, J. M. (2001). A behavioral approach to understanding and treating pathological gambling. *Seminars in Clinical Neuropsychiatry, 6*, 177–183.

Petry, N. M., Steinberg, K. L., & The Women's Problem Gambling Research Group. (in press). Childhood maltreatment in men and women pathological gamblers. *Psychology of Addictive Behaviors*.

Petry, N. M., Stinson, F. S., & Grant, B. F. (2004). *Comorbidity of DSM–IV pathological gambling and psychiatric disorders: Results from the National Epidemiologic Survey on Alcohol and Related Conditions*. Manuscript submitted for publication.

Petry, N. M., & Tawfik, Z. (2001). Comparison of problem-gambling and non-problem-gambling youths seeking treatment for marijuana abuse. *Journal of the American Academy of Child and Adolescent Psychiatry, 40*, 1324–1331.

Phillips, D. P., Welty, W. R., & Smith, M. M. (1997). Elevated suicide levels associated with legalized gambling. *Suicide and Life-Threatening Behavior, 27*, 373–378.

Potenza, M. N., Leung, H. C., Blumberg, H. P., Peterson, B. S., Fulbright, R. K., Lacadie, C. M., et al. (2003). An fMRI Stroop task study of ventromedial prefrontal cortical function in pathological gamblers. *American Journal of Psychiatry, 160*, 1990–1994.

Potenza, M. N., Steinberg, M. A., McLaughlin, S. D., Wu, R., Rounsaville, B. J., & O'Malley, S. S. (2001). Gender-related differences in the characteristics of problem gamblers using a gambling help line. *American Journal of Psychiatry, 158*, 1500–1505.

Potenza, M. N., Steinberg, M. A., Skudlarski, P., Fulbright, R. K., Lacadie, C. M., Wilber, M. K., et al. (2003). Gambling urges in pathological gamblers. *Archives of General Psychiatry, 60*, 828–836.

Poulin, C. (2000). Problem gambling among adolescent students in the Atlantic provinces of Canada. *Journal of Gambling Studies, 16*, 53–78.

Poulin, C. (2002). An assessment of the validity and reliability of the SOGS–RA. *Journal of Gambling Studies, 18*, 67–91.

Preston, F. W., & Smith, R. W. (1985). Delabeling and relabeling in Gamblers Anonymous: Problems with transferring the Alcoholics Anonymous paradigm. *Journal of Gambling Behavior, 1*, 97–105.

Prochaska, J. O., Velicer, W. F., DiClemente, C. C., & Fava, J. S. (1988). Measuring the processes of change: Applications to the cessation of smoking. *Journal of Consulting and Clinical Psychology, 56*, 520–528.

Productivity Commission. (1999). *Australia's gambling industries: Report No. 10* (Vol. 1). Canberra, Australia: Author.

Proimos, J., DuRant, R. H., Pierce, J. D., & Goodman, E. (1998). Gambling and other risk behaviors among 8th- to 12th-grade students. *Pediatrics, 102*, 1–6.

Pugh, P., & Webley, P. (2000). Adolescent participation in the U.K. national lottery games. *Journal of Adolescence, 23*, 1–11.

Rabow, J., Comess, L., Donovan, N., & Hollos, C. (1984). Compulsive gambling: Psychodynamic and sociological perspectives. *Israel Journal of Psychiatry and Related Sciences, 21*, 189–207.

Rachlin, H. (1990). Why do people gamble and keep gambling despite heavy losses? *Psychological Science, 1*, 294–297.

Ramirez, L. F., McCormick, R. A., Russo, A. M., & Taber, J. I. (1983). Patterns of substance abuse in pathological gamblers undergoing treatment. *Addictive Behaviors, 8*, 425–428.

Rankin, H. (1982). Case histories and shorter communications. *Behavior Research and Therapy, 20*, 185–187.

Regard, M., Knoch, D., Gütling, E., & Landis, T. (2003). Brain damage and addictive behavior: A neuropsychological and electroencephalogram investigation with pathologic gamblers. *Cognitive and Behavioral Neurology, 16*, 47–53.

Regier, D. A., Farmer, M. E., Rae, D. S., Locke, B. Z., Keith, S. J., Judd, L. L., & Goodwin, F. K. (1990). Comorbidity of mental disorders with alcohol and other drug abuse. *Journal of the American Medical Association, 264*, 2511–2518.

Rescorla, R. A. (1979). Aspects of the reinforcer learned in second-order Pavlovian conditioning. *Journal of Experimental Psychology: Animal Behavior Processes, 5*, 79–95.

Robins, L., Cottler, L. B., Bucholz, K., & Compton, W. M. (1996). *Diagnostic Interview Schedule, fourth version (DISIV)*. Saint Louis, MO: Washington University Press.

Robson, E., Edwards, J., Smith, G., & Colman, I. (2002). Gambling decisions: An early intervention program for problem gamblers. *Journal of Gambling Studies, 18*, 235–255.

Roll, J. M., Reilly, M. P., & Johanson, C. E. (2000). The influence of exchange delays on cigarette vs. money choice: A laboratory analog of voucher-based reinforcement therapy. *Experimental and Clinical Psychology, 8*, 366–370.

Room, R., Turner, N. E., & Ialomiteanu, A. (1999). Community effects of the opening of the Niagara casino. *Addiction, 94*, 1449–1466.

Rose, I. N. (1980). The legalization and control of casino gambling. *Fordham Urban Law Review, 8*, 245–300.

Rosecrance, J. (1988). Active gamblers as peer counselors. *International Journal of the Addictions, 23*, 751–766.

Rosenthal, R. J. (1986). The pathological gambler's system of self-deception. *Journal of Gambling Behavior, 2*, 108–120.

Rosenthal, R. J. (1987). The psychodynamics of pathological gambling: A review of the literature. In T. Galski (Ed.), *The handbook of pathological gambling* (pp. 41–70). Springfield, IL: Charles C Thomas.

Rosenthal, R. J., & Lesieur, H. R. (1992). Self-reported withdrawal symptoms and pathological gambling. *American Journal on Addictions, 1*, 150–154.

Rosenthal, R. J., & Rugle, L. J. (1994). A psychodynamic approach to the treatment of pathological gambling: Part I. Achieving abstinence. *Journal of Gambling Studies, 10*, 21–42.

Roy, A., Adinoff, B., Roehrich, L., Lamparski, D., Custer, R., Lorenz, V., et al. (1988). Pathological gambling: A psychobiological study. *Archives of General Psychiatry, 45*, 369–373.

Roy, A., Berrettini, W., Adinoff, B., & Linnoila, M. (1990). CSF galanin in alcoholics, pathological gamblers and normal controls: A negative report. *Biological Psychiatry, 27*, 923–926.

Roy, A., Custer, R., Lorenz, V. C., & Linnoila, M. (1988). Depressed pathological gamblers. *Acta Psychiatrica Scandinavica, 77*, 163–165.

Roy, A., DeJong, J., Ferraro, T., Adinoff, B., Gold, P., Rubinow, D., & Linnoila, M. (1989). CSF GABA and neuropeptides in pathological gamblers and normal controls. *Psychiatry Research, 30*, 137–144.

Roy, A., DeJong, J., & Linnoila, M. (1989). Extraversion in pathological gamblers: Correlates with indexes of noradrenergic function. *Archives of General Psychiatry, 46*, 679–681.

Roy, A., & Linnoila, M. (1989). CSF studies on alcoholism and related behaviours. *Progress in Neuropsychopharmacology and Biological Psychiatry, 13*, 505–511.

Rugle, L. J. (1993). Initial thoughts on viewing pathological gambling from a physiological and intrapsychic perspective. *Journal of Gambling Studies, 9*, 3–16.

Rugle, L. J., & Melamed, L. (1993). Neuropsychological assessment of attention problems in pathological gamblers. *Journal of Nervous and Mental Disease, 181*, 107–112.

Rugle, L. J., & Rosenthal, R. J. (1994). Transference and countertransference reactions in the psychotherapy of pathological gamblers. *Journal of Gambling Studies, 10*, 43–65.

Rupcich, N., Frisch, G. R., & Govoni, R. (1997). Comorbidity of pathological gambling in addiction treatment facilities. *Journal of Substance Abuse Treatment, 6*, 573–574.

Russo, A. M., Taber, J. I., McCormick, R. A., & Ramirez, L. F. (1984). An outcome study of an inpatient treatment program for pathological gamblers. *Hospital and Community Psychiatry, 35*, 823–827.

Salzmann, M. M. (1982). Treatment of compulsive gambling. *British Journal of Psychiatry, 141*, 318–319.

Schlosser, S., Black, D. W., Repertinger, S., & Freet, D. (1994). Compulsive buying: Demography, phenomenology, and comorbidity in 46 subjects. *General Hospital Psychiatry, 16*, 205–212.

Schneider, J. W. (1973). Reinforcer effectiveness as a function of reinforcer rate and magnitude: A comparison of concurrent performances. *Journal of the Experimental Analysis of Behavior, 20*, 461–471.

Schwarz, J., & Lindner, A. (1992). Inpatient treatment of male pathological gamblers in Germany. *Journal of Gambling Studies, 8*, 93–109.

Seager, C. P. (1970). Treatment of compulsive gamblers by electrical aversion. *British Journal of Psychiatry, 117,* 545–553.

Seager, C. P., Pokorny, M. R., & Black, D. (1966, March 5). Aversion therapy for compulsive gamblers. *The Lancet, 1,* 546.

Seedat, S., Kesler, S., Niehaus, D. J. H., & Stein, D. J. (2000). Pathological gambling behaviour: Emergence secondary to treatment of Parkinson's disease with dopaminergic agents. *Depression and Anxiety, 11,* 185–186.

Sellman, J. D., Adamson, S., Robertson, P., Sullivan, S., & Coverdale, J. (2002). Gambling in mild–moderate alcohol-dependent outpatients. *Substance Use and Misuse, 37,* 199–213.

Shaffer, H. J. (1994). Denial, ambivalence, and countertransferential hate. In J. D. Levin, & R. H. Weiss (Eds.), *The dynamics and treatment of alcoholism: Essential papers* (pp. 421–437). Northvale, NJ: Jason Aronson.

Shaffer, H. J., Freed, C. R., & Healea, D. (2002). Gambling disorders among homeless persons with substance use disorders seeking treatment at a community center. *Psychiatric Services, 53,* 1112–1117.

Shaffer, H. J., & Hall, M. N. (1996). Estimating the prevalence of adolescent gambling disorders: A quantitative synthesis and guide toward standard gambling nomenclature. *Journal of Gambling Studies, 12,* 193–214.

Shaffer, H. J., Hall, M. N., & Vander Bilt, J. (1997). *Estimating the prevalence of disordered gambling behavior in the United States and Canada: A meta-analysis.* Boston: Harvard Medical School, Division on Addictions.

Shaffer, H. J., Hall, M. N., & Vander Bilt, J. (1999). Estimating the prevalence of disordered gambling behavior in the United States and Canada: A research synthesis. *American Journal of Public Health, 89,* 1369–1376.

Shaffer, H. J., LaBrie, R., Scanlan, K. M., & Cummings, T. N. (1994). Pathological gambling among adolescents: Massachusetts Gambling Screen (MAGS). *Journal of Gambling Studies, 10,* 339–362.

Shaffer, H. J., Vander Bilt, J., & Hall, M. N. (1999). Gambling, drinking, smoking and other health risk activities among casino employees. *American Journal of Industrial Medicine, 36,* 365–378.

Sharpe, L. (2002). A reformulated cognitive–behavioral model of problem gambling: A biopsychosocial perspective. *Clinical Psychology Review, 22,* 1–25.

Sharpe, L., & Tarrier, N. (1992). A cognitive–behavioral treatment approach for problem gambling. *Journal of Cognitive Psychotherapy, 6,* 193–203.

Sharpe, L., & Tarrier, N. (1993). Towards a cognitive–behavioural theory of problem gambling. *British Journal of Psychiatry, 162,* 407–412.

Sharpe, L., Tarrier, N., Schotte, D., & Spence, S. H. (1995). The role of autonomic arousal in problem gambling. *Addiction, 90,* 1529–1540.

Sherman, J. A., & Thomas, J. R. (1968). Some factors controlling preference between fixed-ratio and variable-ratio schedules of reinforcement. *Journal of the Experimental Analysis of Behavior, 11,* 689–702.

Shinohara, K., Yanagisawa, A., Kagota, Y., Gomi, A., Nemoto, K., Moriya, E., et al. (1999). Physiological changes in Pachinko players: Beta-endorphin, catecholamines, immune system substances and heart rate. *Applied Human Science, 18,* 37–42.

Siever, L. J. (1987). Role of noradrenergic mechanisms in the etiology of the affective disorders. In H. Y. Meltzer (Ed.), *Psychopharmacology: Third generation of progress* (pp. 493–504). New York: Raven Press.

Simmel, E. (1920). Psychoanalysis of the gambler. *International Journal of Psychoanalysis, 1,* 352–353.

Skinner, B. F. (1948). "Superstition" in the pigeon. *Journal of Experimental Psychology, 38,* 168–172.

Slovic, P., Fischhoff, B., & Lichtenstein, S. (1982). Facts versus fears: Understanding perceived risk. In D. Kahneman, P. Slovic, & A. Tversky (Eds.), *Judgment under uncertainty: Heuristics and biases* (pp. 463–489). New York: Cambridge University Press.

Slutske, W. S., Eisen, S., True, W. R., Lyons, M. J., Goldberg, J., & Tsuang, M. (2000). Common genetic vulnerability for pathological gambling and alcohol dependence in men. *Archives of General Psychiatry, 57,* 666–673.

Slutske, W. S., Eisen, S., Xian, H., True, W. R., Lyons, M. J., Goldberg, J., & Tsuang, M. (2001). A twin study of the association between pathological gambling and antisocial personality disorder. *Journal of Abnormal Psychology, 110,* 297–308.

Slutske, W. S., Jackson, K. M., & Sher, K. J. (2003). The natural history of problem gambling from age 18 to 29. *Journal of Abnormal Psychology, 112,* 263–274.

Smart, R. G., & Ferris, J. (1996). Alcohol, drugs and gambling in the Ontario adult population, 1994. *Canadian Journal of Psychiatry, 41,* 36–45.

Smith, S. S. (1948). Lotteries. *Journal of Criminal Law and Criminology, 38,* 547–556, 559–569.

Snow, M., Prochaska, J. O., & Rossi, J. (1994). Processes of change in Alcoholics Anonymous: Maintenance factors in long-term sobriety. *Journal of Studies on Alcohol, 55,* 362–371.

Sobell, L. C., Agrawal, S., & Sobell, M. B. (1997). Factors affecting agreement between alcohol abusers' and their collaterals' reports. *Journal of Studies on Alcohol, 58,* 405–413.

Sobell, L. C., Cunningham, J. A., & Sobell, M. B. (1996). Recovery from alcohol problems with and without treatment: Prevalence in two population surveys. *American Journal of Public Health, 86,* 966–972.

Sobell, M. B., Maisto, S. A., Sobell, L. C., Cooper, A. M., Cooper, T., & Saunders, B. (1980). Developing a prototype for evaluating alcohol treatment effectiveness. In L. C. Sobell, M. B. Sobell, & E. Ward (Eds.), *Evaluating alcohol and drug abuse treatment effectiveness: Recent advances* (pp. 129–150). New York: Pergamon Press.

Soubrie, P. (1986). Reconciling the role of central serotonin neurons in human and animal behavior. *Behavior and Brain Science, 9,* 319–364.

Specker, S. M., Carlson, G. A., Christenson, G. A., & Marcotte, M. (1995). Impulse control disorders and attention deficit disorder in pathological gamblers. *Annals of Clinical Psychiatry, 7,* 175–179.

Specker, S. M., Carlson, G. A., Edmonson, K. M., Johnson, P. E., & Marcotte, M. (1996). Psychopathology in pathological gamblers seeking treatment. *Journal of Gambling Studies, 12,* 67–81.

Sproston, K., Ernst, B., & Orford, J. (2000). *Gambling behaviour in Britain: Results from the British Gambling Prevalence Survey.* London: National Centre for Social Research.

Sprott, D. E., Brumbaugh, A. M., & Miyazaki, A. D. (2001). Motivation and ability as predictors of play behavior in state-sponsored lotteries: An empirical assessment of psychological control. *Psychology and Marketing, 18,* 973–983.

Spunt, B., Lesieur, H., Hunt, D., & Cahill, L. (1995). Gambling among methadone patients. *International Journal of the Addictions, 30,* 929–962.

Stahl, S. M. (2000). *Essential psychopharmacology: Neuroscientific basis and practical applications* (2nd ed.). New York: Cambridge University Press.

Steel, Z., & Blaszczynski, A. (1998). Impulsivity, personality disorders and pathological gambling severity. *Addiction, 93,* 895–905.

Steinberg, M. A. (1993). Couples treatment issues for recovering male compulsive gamblers and their partners. *Journal of Gambling Studies, 9,* 153–167.

Steinberg, M. A., Kosten, T. R., & Rounsaville, B. J. (1992). Cocaine abuse and pathological gambling. *American Journal on Addictions, 1,* 121–132.

Stewart, R. M., & Brown, R. I. F. (1988). An outcome study of Gamblers Anonymous. *British Journal of Psychiatry, 152,* 284–288.

Stinchfield, R. D. (2000). Gambling and correlates of gambling among Minnesota public school students. *Journal of Gambling Studies, 16,* 153–173.

Stinchfield, R. D. (2002a). Reliability, validity, and classification accuracy of the South Oaks Gambling Screen (SOGS). *Addictive Behaviors, 27,* 1–19.

Stinchfield, R. D. (2002b). Youth gambling: How big a problem? *Psychiatric Annals, 32,* 197–202.

Stinchfield, R. D. (2003). Reliability, validity, and classification accuracy of a measure of DSM–IV diagnostic criteria for pathological gambling. *American Journal of Psychiatry, 160,* 180–182.

Stinchfield, R. D., Cassuto, N., Winters, K. C., & Latimer, W. (1997). Prevalence of gambling among Minnesota public school students in 1992 and 1995. *Journal of Gambling Studies, 13,* 25–48.

Stinchfield, R. D., & Winters, K. C. (1996). *Effectiveness of six state-supported compulsive gambling treatment programs in Minnesota.* St. Paul: Minnesota Department of Human Services.

Stinchfield, R. D., & Winters, K. C. (2001). Outcome of Minnesota's gambling treatment programs. *Journal of Gambling Studies, 17,* 217–245.

Stojanov, W., Karayanidis, F., Johnston, P., Bailey, A., Carr, V., & Schall, U. (2003). Disrupted sensory gating in pathological gambling. *Biological Psychiatry, 54*, 474–484.

Strickland, L. H., Lewicki, R. J., & Katz, A. M. (1966). Temporal orientation and perceived control as determinants of risk-taking. *Journal of Experimental Social Psychology, 2*, 143–151.

Sullivan, S. (1994). Why compulsive gamblers are a high suicide risk. *Community Mental Health in New Zealand, 8*, 40–47.

Sullivan, S., Abbott, M., McAvoy, B., & Arroll, B. (1994). Pathological gamblers: Will they use a new telephone help line? *New Zealand Medical Journal, 107*, 313–315.

Sylvain, C., & Ladouceur, R. (1992). Correction cognitive et habitudes de jeu chez les joueurs de poker video [Cognitive correction and practices of play in players of video poker]. *Revue Canadienne des Sciences du Comportement, 24*, 479–489.

Sylvain, C., Ladouceur, R., & Boisvert, J.-M. (1997). Cognitive and behavioral treatment of pathological gambling: A controlled study. *Journal of Consulting and Clinical Psychology, 65*, 727–732.

Taber, J. I., & Chaplin, M. P. (1988). Group psychotherapy with pathological gamblers. *Journal of Gambling Behavior, 4*, 183–196.

Taber, J. I., McCormick, R. A., & Ramirez, L. F. (1987). The prevalence and impact of major life stressors among pathological gamblers. *International Journal of the Addictions, 22*, 71–79.

Taber, J. I., McCormick, R. A., Russo, A. M., Adkins, B. J., & Ramirez, L. F. (1987). Follow-up of pathological gamblers after treatment. *American Journal of Psychiatry, 144*, 757–761.

Tavares, H., Zilberman, M. L., Beites, F. J., & Gentil, V. (2001). Gender differences in gambling progression. *Journal of Gambling Studies, 17*, 151–159.

Taylor, J. S. (1838). *The victims of gambling: Being extracts from the diary of an American physician*. New York: Boston, Weeks, Jordon.

Tepperman, J. H. (1985). The effectiveness of short-term group therapy upon the pathological gambler and wife. *Journal of Gambling Behavior, 1*, 119–130.

Thompson, W., Gazel, R., & Rickman, D. (1996). The social costs of gambling in Wisconsin. *Wisconsin Policy Research Institute Report, 9*, 1–44.

Toce-Gerstein, M., Gerstein, D. R., & Volberg, R. A. (2003). A hierarchy of gambling disorders in the community. *Addiction, 98*, 1661–1672.

Toneatto, T. (1999). Cognitive psychopathology of problem gambling. *Substance Use and Misuse, 34*, 1593–1604.

Toneatto, T., Blitz-Miller, T., Calderwood, K., Dragonetti, R., & Tsanos, A. (1997). Cognitive distortions in heavy gambling. *Journal of Gambling Studies, 13*, 253–261.

Toneatto, T., & Brennan, J. (2002). Pathological gambling in treatment-seeking substance abusers. *Addictive Behavior, 27*, 465–469.

Toneatto, T., Skinner, W., & Dragonetti, R. (2002). Patterns of substance use in treatment-seeking problem gamblers: Impact on treatment outcomes. *Journal of Clinical Psychology, 58,* 853–859.

Toneatto, T., & Sobell, L. C. (1990). Pathological gambling treated with cognitive theory: A case report. *Addictive Behaviors, 15,* 497–501.

Trevorrow, K., & Moore, S. (1998). The association between loneliness, social isolation, and women's electronic gaming machine gambling. *Journal of Gambling Studies, 14,* 263–284.

Turner, D. N., & Saunders, D. (1990). Medical relabeling in Gamblers Anonymous: The construction of an ideal member. *Small Group Research, 21,* 59–78.

Tversky, A., & Kahneman, D. (1971). The belief in the law of small numbers. *Psychological Bulletin, 76,* 105–110.

Tversky, A., & Kahneman, D. (1973). Availability: A heuristic for judging frequency and probability. *Cognitive Psychology, 5,* 207–232.

Tversky, A., & Kahneman, D. (1974, September). Judgement under uncertainty: Heuristics and biases. *Science, 185,* 1124–1131.

Victor, R. G., & Krug, C. M. (1967). "Paradoxical intention" in the treatment of compulsive gambling. *American Journal of Psychotherapy, 21,* 808–814.

Vitaro, F., Arseneault, L., & Tremblay, R. E. (1997). Dispositional predictors of problem gambling in male adolescents. *American Journal of Psychiatry, 154,* 1769–1770.

Vitaro, F., Arseneault, L., & Tremblay, R. E. (1999). Impulsivity predicts problem gambling in low SES adolescent males. *Addiction, 94,* 565–575.

Vitaro, F., Ferland, F., Jacques, C., & Ladouceur, R. (1998). Gambling, substance use, and impulsivity during adolescence. *Psychology of Addictive Behavior, 12,* 185–194.

Volberg, R. A. (1988). *Compulsive gambling treatment program evaluation: Final report.* Albany: New York State Office of Mental Health.

Volberg, R. A. (1994). The prevalence and demographics of pathological gamblers: Implications for public health. *American Journal of Public Health, 84,* 237–241.

Volberg, R. A. (1995). *Gambling and problem gambling in Iowa: A replication study. Report to the Iowa Department of Human Services.* Roaring Spring, PA: Gemini Research.

Volberg, R. A. (1998). *Gambling and problem gambling among adolescents in New York.* Albany: New York Council on Problem Gambling.

Volberg, R. A., & Abbott, M. W. (1994). Lifetime prevalence estimates of pathological gambling in New Zealand. *International Journal of Epidemiology, 23,* 976–983.

Volberg, R. A., & Abbott, M. W. (1997). Ethnicity and gambling: Gambling and problem gambling among indigenous peoples. *Substance Use and Misuse, 32,* 1525–1538.

Volberg, R. A., Abbott, M. W., Ronnberg, S., & Munck, I. M. E. (2001). Prevalence and risks of pathological gambling in Sweden. *Acta Psychiatrica Scandinavica, 104,* 250–256.

Volberg, R. A., & Steadman, H. J. (1988). Refining prevalence estimates of patho-logical gambling. *American Journal of Psychiatry, 145,* 502–505.

Volberg, R. A., & Steadman, H. J. (1989a). Prevalence estimates of pathological gambling in New Jersey and Maryland. *American Journal of Psychiatry, 166,* 1618–1619.

Volberg, R. A., & Steadman, H. J. (1989b). *Problem gambling in Iowa.* Delmar, NY: Policy Research Associates, Inc.

Volpicelli, J. R., O'Brien, C., Alterman, A. I., & Hayashida, M. (1992). Naltrexone in the treatment of alcohol dependence. *Archives of General Psychiatry, 49,* 867–880.

Wagenaar, W. (1988). *Paradoxes of gambling behaviour.* London: Erlbaum.

Wallisch, L. S. (1993). *Gambling in Texas: 1992 Texas survey of adolescent gambling behavior.* Austin: Texas Commission on Alcohol and Drug Abuse.

Walters, G. D. (2002). Behavior genetic research on gambling and problem gam-bling: A preliminary meta-analysis of available data. *Journal of Gambling Studies, 17,* 255–271.

Wanda, G., & Foxman, J. (1971). *Games compulsive gamblers, wives and families play.* New York: Gam-Anon National Services Office.

Wardman, D., el Guebaly, N., & Hodgins, D. (2001). Problem and pathological gambling in North American aboriginal populations: A review of the empirical literature. *Journal of Gambling Studies, 17,* 81–100.

WEFA Group, ICR Survey Research Group, Lesieur, H. R., & Thompson, W. (1997). *A study concerning the effects of legalized gambling on the citizens of the state of Connecticut.* Newington: State of Connecticut Department of Reve-nue Services.

Weiner, H. (1962). Some effects of response cost upon human operant behavior. *Journal of the Experimental Analysis of Behavior, 5,* 201–208.

Weisner, C., McLellan, A. T., & Hunkeler, E. N. (2000). Addiction Severity Index data from general membership and treatment samples of HMO members: One case of norming the ASI. *Journal of Substance Abuse Treatment, 19,* 103–109.

Weiss, R. D., Griffin, M. L., Gallop, R., Onken, L. S., Gastfriend, D. R., Daley, D., et al. (2000). Self-help group attendance and participation among cocaine dependent patients. *Drug and Alcohol Dependence, 60,* 169–177.

Wells, J. E., Bushnell, J. A., Hornblow, A. R., Joyce, P. R., & Oakley-Brown, M. A. (1989). Christchurch Psychiatric Epidemiology Study: I. Methodology and lifetime prevalence for specific psychiatric disorders. *Australian and New Zealand Journal of Psychiatry, 23,* 315–326.

Welte, J., Barnes, G. M., Wieczorek, W., Tidwell, M. C., & Parker, J. (2001). Alcohol and gambling pathology among U.S. adults: Prevalence, demographic patterns and comorbidity. *Journal of Studies on Alcohol, 62,* 706–712.

Westphal, J. R., Rush, J. A., Stevens, L., & Johnson, L. J. (2000). Gambling behavior of Louisiana students in Grades 6 through 12. *Psychiatric Services, 51,* 96–99.

Wexler, B. E., Gottschalk, C. H., Fulbright, R. K., Prohovnik, I., Lacadie, C. M., Rounsaville, B. J., & Gore, J. C. (2001). Functional magnetic resonance imaging of cocaine craving. *American Journal of Psychiatry, 158,* 86–95.

Whitman-Raymond, R. G. (1988). Pathological gambling as a defense against loss. *Journal of Gambling Behavior, 4,* 99–109.

Wiebe, J., & Cox, B. J. (2001). A profile of Canadian adults seeking treatment for gambling problems and comparisons with adults entering an alcohol treatment program. *Canadian Journal of Psychiatry, 46,* 418–421.

Wiebe, J. M. D., Cox, B. J., & Mehmel, B. G. (2000). The South Oaks Gambling Screen revised for adolescents (SOGS–RA): Further psychometric findings from a community sample. *Journal of Gambling Studies, 16,* 275–288.

Wildman, R. W. (1997). *Gambling: An attempt at an integration.* Edmonton, Alberta, Canada: Wynne Resources.

Wilson, J. R., & Nagoshi, C. T. (1988). Adult children of alcoholics: Cognitive and psychomotor characteristics. *British Journal of Addiction, 83,* 809–820.

Winters, K. C., Bengston, P., Dorr, D., & Stinchfield, R. D. (1998). Prevalence and risk factors of problem gambling among college students. *Psychology of Addictive Behaviors, 12,* 127–135.

Winters, K. C., & Rich, T. (1998). A twin study of adult gambling behavior. *Journal of Gambling Studies, 14,* 213–225.

Winters, K. C., Specker, S. M., & Stinchfield, R. D. (2002). Measuring pathological gambling with The Diagnostic Interview for Gambling Severity (DIGS). In J. J. Marotta, J. A. Cornelius, & W. R. Eadington (Eds.), *The downside: Problem and pathological gambling* (pp. 143–148). Reno: Institute for the Study of Gambling and Commercial Gaming, University of Nevada.

Winters, K. C., Stinchfield, R. D., Botzet, A., & Anderson, N. (2002). A prospective study of youth gambling behaviors. *Psychology of Addictive Behaviors, 16,* 3–9.

Winters, K. C., Stinchfield, R. D., & Fulkerson, J. (1993). Toward the development of an adolescent gambling problem severity scale. *Journal of Gambling Studies, 9,* 371–386.

Wohl, M. J. A., & Enzle, M. E. (2002). The effects of near wins and near losses on self-perceived personal luck and subsequent gambling behavior. *Journal of Experimental Social Psychology, 39,* 184–191.

Wong, I. L., & So, E. M. (2003). Prevalence estimates of problem and pathological gambling in Hong Kong. *American Journal of Psychiatry, 160,* 1353–1354.

Wood, R. T. A., & Griffiths, M. D. (1998). Adolescent machine gambling and crime. *Journal of Adolescence, 19,* 99–104.

Ziedonis, D. M., & Kosten, T. R. (1991). Depression as a prognostic factor for pharmacological treatment of cocaine dependency. *Psychopharmacology Bulletin, 27,* 337–343.

Zimmerman, M., Breen, R. B., & Posternak, M. A. (2002). An open-label study of citalopram in the treatment of pathological gambling. *Journal of Clinical Psychiatry, 63,* 44–48.

Zion, M. M., Tracy, E., & Abell, N. (1991). Examining the relationship between spousal involvement in Gam-Anon and relapse behaviors in pathological gamblers. *Journal of Gambling Studies, 7,* 117–131.

Zitzow, D. (1996). Comparative study of problematic gambling behaviors between American Indian and non-Indian adolescents within and near a Northern Plains reservation. *American Indian and Alaska Native Mental Health Research, 7,* 14–26.

AUTHOR INDEX

SUBJECT INDEX

ASI–G (Addiction Severity Index—
Gambling Severity Index), 35,
48–50, 53, 54
ASPD. *See* Antisocial personality
disorder
Assertiveness skills monitoring (home-
work exercise), 322
Assertiveness training (handout),
304–305
Assessment, 35, 54
diagnosis and screening instruments
case example on, 45–46, 52–54
Diagnostic Interview for Gam-
bling Severity (DIGS), 35,
39–41, 54
Diagnostic Interview Schedule
(DIS), 35, 43 (*see also* Diag-
nostic Interview Schedule)
Gambling Assessment Module for
DSM–IV (GAM–IV), 35,
43–44
Lie/Bet Questionnaire, 35, 44–
45, 46, 53
National Opinion Research
Center DSM Screen for
Gambling Problems (NODS),
35, 41–43, 46, 53, 54, 58, 272
South Oaks Gambling Screen
(SOGS), 35, 36–39 (see also
South Oaks Gambling
Screen)
improvement in needed, 280–281
and other (nongambling) disorders
or conditions, 54
severity assessment instruments, 47
Addiction Severity Index—
Gambling Severity Index
(ASI–G), 35, 48–50, 53, 54
Clinical Global Impression
(CGI) scales, 51, 52, 54
Gambling Symptom Assessment
Scale (G-SAS), 35, 51–52, 54
Gambling Treatment Outcome
Monitoring System
(GAMTOMS), 35, 47–48, 54
Pathological Gambling Modifica-
tion, Yale–Brown Obsessive–
Compulsive Scale (PG–
YBOCS), 35, 51, 54
timeline followback (TLFB), 35,
50–51, 54

Atlantic City, suicide rate in, 98
At-risk gambling, 10–11
Attention-deficit disorder, among cocaine
abusers with gambling problems,
92
Attention-deficit/hyperactivity disorder
(ADHD), comorbidity with, 104,
106
Attorney, for harassment by creditors,
350
Attributional biases, 210
Australia
characteristics of treatment-seeking
gamblers in, 74
prevalence rates in, 16, 18, 20
by age, 58, 59, 60
by ethnicity, 62, 63, 73
by gender, 71, 78
by marital status, 69
by socioeconomic status, 67
for youth, 272, 273
Austria, characteristics of treatment-
seeking gamblers in, 74
Availability illusion, 216–217, 307
Aversive therapy, 205, 206

Base rate, 216
Behavioral accounts of gambling, 199,
279
and cognitive–behavioral treatment,
251
immediacy of reinforcement in,
203–205
magnitude of reinforcement in,
202–203
response costs in, 200–202
in treatment for pathological
gambling, 205–207
variable ratio schedules of reinforcement in, 199–200
Behavioral processes, 159
abstinence maintained by, 160
Behavioral superstitions, 218
Behavioral theories and treatments, 209
Benzodiazepines, 148
Biases, cognitive. See Cognitive biases
Bill collectors, harassing calls from, 350
Biological abnormalities in gamblers, 124,
133
arousal, 121–122, 124

Lapses
    coping with, 309–310, 324
    and functional analysis, 296
Las Vegas, suicide rate in, 98
Law of large numbers, 215–216
Legalized gambling
    prevalence of, 5
    and prevalence rates of disordered
        gambling, 9
    increase in, 30–33
    programs for communities in
        proximity to, 33
    See also Casinos
Level 0 gambling or gamblers, 10
Level 1 gambling or gamblers, 10, 13
    prevalence rates of (North
        America), 15
Level 2 gambling or gamblers, 10–11, 13,
        14, 119, 279
    and consecutive vs. simultaneous
        symptoms, 154
    in DIS, 43
    prevalence rates of, 14–25, 27–28
        (see also Prevalence rates)
Level 3 gambling or gamblers, 11–14,
        119
    case examples on, 12–13
    in DIS, 43
    prevalence rates of, 14–25, 27–28
        (see also Prevalence rates)
Lie/Bet Questionnaire, 35, 44–45
    in case example, 46, 53
Lithium, 139, 145, 151
Loan sharks, negotiating with, 347
Locus of control, 212–213
Louisiana, increasing opportunities to
    gamble in, 98

Magnitude of reinforcement, 202–203
Maintenance drugs, 148
Male gender, as risk factor. See Gender,
    as risk factor
Manuals on therapy, need for, 281
Marijuana use disorders
    comorbidity with, 22, 23, 93
    and medications, 148, 150
    See also Cannabis problems,
        comorbidity with
Marital status, as risk factor, 68–69, 74–
    75, 77

Massachusetts Adolescent Gambling
    Screen (MAGS), 270
Medicalization of psychiatric disorders,
    6–7
Methadone, 148
Methadone patients, as pathological
    gamblers, 93
    in case study, 95
Modeling gambling behaviors, 202
Mohegan Sun Casino, 31
Molecular genetics, of pathological
    gambling, 131–132
    and dopamine, 131
    and norepinephrine, 129
    and serotinin, 126–127
Mood disorders, comorbidity with
    in general population, 95, 96, 98
    and medications, 149–150
Mood stabilizers, 139, 145
Motivational interventions, 258, 264
Motivational interviewing techniques,
    252
Multimodal behavior therapy, 206
Multiple-problem families, 186

Naltrexone, 132, 139, 146–147, 148, 149,
    151
Narcissism, and therapeutic relationship,
    196
Narcissistic entitlement, and chasing,
    193
Narcissistic fantasies of gamblers, 191
Narcissistic personality disorder, 109, 113
National Endowment for Financial
    Education, 251
National Epidemiologic Survey on
    Alcohol and Related Conditions
    (NESARAC), 98
National Gambling Impact Study, 43
National Gambling Impact Study
    Commission, 15, 41, 153, 201
National Institutes of Health, 229
National Opinion Research Center,
    University of Chicago, 15
    DSM–IV Screen for Gambling
        Problems (NODS), 35, 41–43, 54
    age-related prevalence data from,
        58
    in case example, 46, 53
    and youth, 272

National Research Council (NRC)
on age as risk factor, 58
assessment instruments identified
by, 35
and classification of gamblers, 10
on gamblers seeking treatment,
153
Native Americans
casinos on reservations of, 5
gambling restrictions of, 6
gambling among youth of, 275
prevalence rates among, 61–62
Natural recovery, 161
and abstinence-maintaining
methods, 158–160, 161
case example on, 157–158, 160
and reasons for ceasing, 155–157
and reasons for not seeking
treatment, 160–161
and resolution rates, 153–155
Natural selection, and risky decisions, 6
Nefazodone (Serzone), 138, 140
Negative transference, 196
NESARC, 100, 103, 114
Neurobiological mechanism, and arousal,
122
Neurobiology of pathological gambling,
124–125
dopamine, 129–132
noradrenergic function, 127–129
opiods, 132
serotonin, 125–127
Neuroimaging, need for development of,
282
New Zealand
characteristics of treatment-seeking
gamblers in, 74
prevalence rates in, 16, 18
by age, 59
by ethnicity, 62, 63, 73
by gender, 71, 74
by marital status, 69
by socioeconomic status, 67
for youth, 272, 273
Niagara Falls area, casino in, 31–32
Nicotine use and dependence
comorbidity with
in general population, 87, 88
in treatment-seeking pathological
gamblers, 90, 92
and medications, 150

See also Smoking; Substance use
disorders
NODS (National Opinion Research
Center *DSM–IV* Screen for
Gambling Problems), 35,
41–43, 46, 53, 54, 58, 272
Nongambling and nongamblers, 260
reinforcing of, 231–232, 287–288
See also Abstinence from gambling
Noradrenergic function (norepinephrine),
in neurobiology of pathological
gambling, 127–129
North America, prevalence rates in,
14–16, 17. *See also* Canada;
United States
Norway, prevalence rates in, 18, 20
by age, 59
by gender, 70, 71
by marital status, 69
by socioeconomic status, 67

Obsessive–compulsive disorder
comorbidity with, 114
in dually diagnosed substance
abusers, 92
in general population, 101,
111
in treatment seekers with disorders other than substance
abuse, 107
in treatment-seeking gamblers,
100, 102, 103, 113
and gambling medications, 140
Older adults
case example of, 25–27
gambling prevalence rates among,
23–27
screening for, 33
Omnipotent provocation, 192
Opioid antagonists, 132, 139, 146–147,
149
Opioid use or dependence
comorbidity with 93
and prevalence rates, 22, 23
and medications, 150
in neurobiology of pathological
gambling, 132
See also Drug abuse or dependence,
illicit; Substance use disorders
Options, resistance to, 194

Panic disorder, comorbidity with
    in general population, 101
    in treatment-seeking gamblers, 102
Parenting factors, 190
Parkinson's disease, 130
Paroxetine, 138, 141
Participants at gaming establishments,
        prevalence rates among, 27–28
Partners of gamblers. *See* Spouses of
        gamblers
Past-year Level 0 gamblers, 10
Past-year prevalence rates, 15
Pathological gambling. *See* Gambling,
        pathological
Pathological Gambling Modification,
        Yale–Brown Obsessive–
        Compulsive Scale (PG–YBOCS),
        35, 51, 54, 140
    and CGI scores, 52
Patient–therapist relationships, 195–197
Personal emergency plan
    coping with lapse, 324
    high-risk situation, 323
Personality disorders, comorbidity of,
        108–109, 111–113, 114
    case example on, 109–110
PG–YBOCS (Pathological Gambling
        Modification, Yale–Brown
        Obsessive–Compulsive Scale
        (PG–YBOCS), 35, 51, 54, 140
Pharmacotherapies for gambling, 137,
        148, 151
    case examples on, 143–144,
        147–148
    in comparison with substance-use
        medications, 148–151
    lack of compliance with, 150
    mood stabilizers, 139, 145
    opioid antagonists, 139, 146–147, 149
    and psychosocial interventions, 282
    serotonin reuptake inhibitors, 138,
        140–143, 151
Phobia, comorbidity with
    in general population, 101
    in treatment-seeking gamblers, 102
Physical feelings, and desire to gamble,
        243, 244
Placebo effect, in treatment of pathologi-
        cal gambling, 142–13, 146, 150
Pleasant activities
    as homework exercise, 318

in session handout, 297–299
Posttraumatic stress disorder, comorbidity
        with, 103
    in treatment-seeking gamblers, 102
Powerful Others subscale, 213
Precommitment strategies, 204, 238
Preference reversals, in addictive
        disorders, 204
Presenting problem, 280
Pressure-relief meetings (GA), 164, 251,
        344
Prevalence rates, 20, 33, 279
    and legalized gambling, 30–33
    by nation
        Australia, 16, 18, 20
        Canada, 16, 17
        Hong Kong, 18, 20
        Korea, 18, 20
        New Zealand, 16, 18
        Norway, 18, 20
        Spain, 19, 20
        Sweden, 19, 20
        Switzerland, 19, 20
        Taiwan, 19, 20
        United Kingdom, 19, 20
        United States, 14–16, 17
    past-year vs. lifetime, 15, 153–154
    in special populations
        employees in special fields, 27
        gaming-establishment
            participants, 27–28
        older adults, 23–27
        substance abusers, 21–23
    by type of gambling activity, 28–
        30
    in youth, 271–274
Prevention and early intervention
    for low-income employees, 76
    for young problem gamblers,
        277–278
Priming, 201–202
Probabilistic outcomes, 209, 306–308
Probable pathological gambling, 38
Problem gambling and gamblers, 10, 11
    brief treatments for, 259, 261,
        264
    need to identify, 265
Problems, gambling. *See* Gambling
        problems
Processes of Change Questionnaire,
        158–159

ABOUT THE AUTHOR

Nancy M. Petry earned a BA in 1990 from Randolph–Macon Woman's College and a PhD from Harvard University in 1994. In 1996, she joined the faculty of the University of Connecticut Health Center, where she is a professor of psychiatry. She conducts research on the treatment of addictive disorders, ranging from substance use disorders to pathological gambling, and has published more than 80 peer-reviewed articles. Her work is funded by the National Institute on Drug Abuse, the National Institute of Mental Health, and the National Institute on Alcohol Abuse and Alcoholism. Dr. Petry serves as a consultant and advisor for the National Institute of Health, and she is on the editorial boards of six academic journals. She received the American Psychological Association Distinguished Scientific Award for Early Career Contribution to Psychology in 2003.